T0299010

Healthcare IT Transformation

Bridging Innovation, Integration, Interoperability, and Analytics

Healthcare IT Transformation

Bridging Innovation, Integration, Interoperability, and Analytics

John C. Dodd

CRC Press

Taylor & Francis Group

Boca Raton London New York

CRC Press is an imprint of the
Taylor & Francis Group, an **informa** business

A PRODUCTIVITY PRESS BOOK

CRC Press
Taylor & Francis Group
6000 Broken Sound Parkway NW, Suite 300
Boca Raton, FL 33487-2742

First issued in paperback 2021

© 2017 by Taylor & Francis Group, LLC
CRC Press is an imprint of Taylor & Francis Group, an Informa business

ISBN-13: 978-1-4987-7844-2 (hbk)
ISBN-13: 978-1-03-217941-4 (pbk)
DOI: 10.1201/9781315366876

**Visit the Taylor & Francis Web site at
http://www.taylorandfrancis.com**

**and the CRC Press Web site at
http://www.crcpress.com**

Contents

Preface: Shift to Patient–Consumer-Centric Health IT with Innovation at All Levels

What is the motivation for this book, and why is it necessary? Although healthcare information technology (IT) transformation is contentious and has some unusual safety and coordination of care features, it is fragmented and has not had the foundation necessary to leverage the IT capabilities that other industries have used so successfully. The transformation also has to shift the focus to the patient–consumer, and to the complete needs of that patient–consumer, especially the high risk, highly vulnerable populations who are the major users of care in a fragmented and non-coordinated way.

This book focuses on the shift to the patient–consumer and to those with high cost conditions, both chronic and cancer; it considers those who have disabilities, and those who live in poverty and who are suffering from more than healthcare issues, but also nutritional, housing, and literacy issues, and who are confused by both the healthcare and the human services available. The appropriate information is available. The services that the patients–consumers need do exist, especially in those states that have expanded Medicaid. In addition, there are disease foundations, caring neighbors, and professional doctors, nurses, pharmacists, and many other professionals who want to provide better care. However, these providers are frustrated by the current state of health IT that blocks their desire to be innovative. They have seen progress in other industries, and are waiting for similar changes in healthcare.

The subject of this book is that pivot toward the patient–consumer, and establishing the foundation for integration, interoperability, and analytics that can be the springboard to innovation.

This work represents the integration of the knowledge and experience of the author, with a vision for improvement in healthcare IT transformation:

- As an integrator with years of experience in organization transformation, the author discusses the ways that complex systems, including air traffic control systems, space systems and networks, weather systems, and defense and intelligence systems, went through growing pains similar to those in healthcare, and illustrates ways the experiences of those other systems could be utilized while leveraging both the healthcare research and the standards efforts that have been working in healthcare for years.
- The author has shared these ideas with others, and is grateful to the many colleagues and customers who have commented and provided insights (see Acknowledgement section). The author believes that the vision for future healthcare IT needs a more detailed roadmap,

and provides more of an implementation guide. This document will require updating and refinement because its vision is a phased incremental approach to transformation. This book should provide implementation guidance that complements and extends the recently released Federal Health IT Strategy, the Health Interoperability Roadmap, and 2015 Health IT Standards Advisory and recent efforts in the Federal Health Architecture. Although these documents provide excellent information, more implementation guidance is needed. The perspective is that of a joint and aligned Government and Health Community with the patient as the central focus. The government must lead and advocate, but the diverse communities of healthcare stakeholders must be engaged. Achieving this engagement may require slight pivots, such as renaming the Federal Health Architecture to be "the Government and Health Communities Health Architecture," and also providing clear responsibility and tracking of the commitments of the many organizations that are the advocates for health, the patients, and the standards groups. Many of these surrogates for the stakeholders have been engaged and are engaged with congressional dialogs, such as the twenty-first century cures. Transparent, open, idea-driven, pragmatic dialogs are needed, and this book hopes to foster those dialogs by gathering more specific draft ideas that can be discussed and debated.

■ The author has stepped back and taken a patient–consumer perspective, focusing on those populations that are at risk and vulnerable, and on areas where more effective and efficient care can improve their lives, but also can both improve quality and outcomes, and lower cost.

■ This is what has happened in other industries as they looked at the issues from a consumer point of view and determined how the industry can both cooperate and compete to provide innovative solutions.

■ Health IT with innovation can be the driver for change, but the process has to be visible with a definitive roadmap from which to work, a roadmap that can be built upon and adapted.

John C. Dodd
Lead Consultant, President and Founder of BDC HealthIT

Acknowledgments

I first have to begin by thanking my wife, Chris, who has put up with me, my reading, studying, and general visioning for 45 years. She reviewed the ideas and slides, and kept saying, "no new ideas; just get this done." She put up with my chatting with everyone about it, sometimes boring folks about their healthcare problems, and many times hearing their problems and frustrations. She heard too much discussion about this idea and that. She also helped improve many of my graphics. LOVE YOU!

On this journey, I have enjoyed the input of colleagues like Phil Cooke with his diverse industry and company transformation experience, and his strategic vision of what transformation should look like, while acting as a sounding board on the often incomplete ideas I presented. I have talked at conferences and with many folks within the Stewards of Change, Delaware Health Innovation Center, especially the patient–consumer committee and the many colleagues with whom I have worked over the years at CMS, NIH, CDC, state Medicaid programs, and other human services agencies, like the Administration of Children and Families and SAMSHA. But most importantly, I appreciate the stories that I have heard for years about the struggles and confusions with how to handle the health systems and their fragmentation and need for a shift in perspective.

To my daughters: Maureen, Anna, and Monica. Anna has provided some great insights by just asking "what do you mean"; Monica has given me the big hospital point of view; and Maureen has assisted me with the e-learning plan. I am grateful to Byron Brooks for the website and Ron Brooks for partnering with me on Brooks and Dodd Consulting (BDC)—HealthIT.

Thanks to special needs and rare disease exposure from the disabled Frannie, Steve, Bella, and to all the folks with cancer—Arthur Dodd, Lawrence Dodd, Rosemary Dodd Simmons, Linda Gabriel, Ken Todd, Charlie Clark, and those who have been exposed to adverse and preventable healthcare accidents: Such as that of Dr. Al Bishop, kidney donor with adverse reactions, and many case studies reviewed, including personal stories from the ground about patient–consumers and their improved access to care and the patient consume work group for the Delaware Center for Health Innovation (DCHI) lead by Secretary of Health from Delaware Rita Landgraf and the support of Jill Fredell—Communications Director for her fostering of Infographics diagrams.

Thanks to all the colleagues over the years at CSC and at CMS, NIH, CDC, and the many Medicaid contacts. There are too many to name, but many will receive an invitation to give me feedback.

Thanks to my extended family—the Simchocks, Fehlners, Curleys, Roberts, and my wife's many cousins who seem to be everywhere. I have bored all with the idea of this book.

To my grandkids, who I hope get better health services: Avery, Carson, Brennan, Dawson, and Zach!

All have been extremely valuable. I have also shared my ideas with Professor Roy Rada and received a more academic perspective and been forced to gather and create a detailed appendix.

I am especially grateful to Linda Howard for editing and having a good sense of humor about my lack of grammar and my run-on sentences. This effort would not move forward without her. Thanks to all, and to those that get this (as Linda hopes) "ready for prime time" version.

Yes, I know some of you were looking for a book that you can read at the beach. I hope to keep refining the ideas and posting blogs and developing applications that will fill in the gaps, especially to the disabled and underserved, and to reduce the confusion level that everyone seems to experience.

Beach readers—This book does have waves! (Don't wait for the movie!)

Please provide feedback.

Author

John C. Dodd earned a BS in manufacturing engineering from the University of Maryland in 1970. He earned an MS in computer systems and management information systems from American University in 1974.

Dodd taught for 10 years in the Technology Commercialization Program, a joint University of Baltimore, JHU, UMBC program from 1994 to 2004.

He completed numerous courses at the University of Maryland and Johns Hopkins University in computer science and medical informatics.

Health Services Enterprise Architect and Patient–Consumer Population Solution Leader 9/2014—present

Dodd has a broad knowledge of government and industry practices involving e-government and enterprise architecture with a focus on health IT. He has over 40 years of development, integration, and consulting experience with large complex system from the Apollo Systems, to Air Traffic Control, to Intelligence, and to the many Health Information Systems that are involved in healthcare transformation.

His company, Brooks and Dodd Consulting (BDC) Health IT, is a disabled veteran owned small business focused on the integration, interoperability, and analytics of the next wave of healthcare transformation. The approach and filling of gaps are being in prepared and a companion book, *Healthcare Transformation Wave 3: Integrating System Medicine with Personalized Medicine* is under development. Dodd is actively involved in standards committees, industry advisory associations, and is working with the Delaware Center for Health Innovation.

Dodd has defined a new patient–consumer-population reference architecture and is working with an alliance of technology partners to develop the initial demonstration and phased product release. The initial focus is on a series of bridging innovations for patient–consumer and population health. The focus is the underserved and high-risk populations including patients on Medicaid, patients with behavioral health and substance abuse, the disabled, and those with rare and complex care management.

Summary of Previous Experience

Dodd defined the architecture for the Center for Medicare and Medicaid Services (CMS) HealthCare Quality Information System as the chief architect. He was also the lead partner for the Computer Sciences Corporation (CSC) Healthcare Service Transformation Practice that supported not only CMS, but also other Health and Human Services (HHS) and state health agencies along with the Military Health Agency and Veterans Administration (VA) integration. For state healthcare agencies, Dodd created an overall design approach that began with the Medicaid IT Architecture (MITA) that defined a service oriented enterprise using business architecture with new business process, human task flows, rules management, new data integration, and interoperability technology along with an ensemble of shared services. The approach is now used by all state Medicaid programs, with Dodd having worked closely with the North Carolina, New York, and Maryland programs. He has defined a series of platform-as-a-service offerings to address the common needs of the healthcare focused enterprise. Dodd worked on all the major system integration systems from the Apollo Project, the Air Traffic Control System, the Space Network, Weather Network, Weather Systems, and Intelligence Information Sharing including the design of the security and data alignment for the Terrorist Watch-list systems. They all were complex, needed information sharing and were distributed and had complex data and analytics needs. Throughout the years there were many steps into the healthcare market such as the first intensive care monitoring software that came out of the Apollo project and systems for CDC and NIH Clinical Center. Since 2004, his primary focus has shifted to Healthcare Transformation and leverage the experience from other large-scale transformation efforts.

Chapter 1

Wave 2: Integration–Interoperability and Analytics Overview

Abstract

A patient–consumer focused health learning system with active engaged patients will take new forms of integration, channels of interoperability, and fact-based analytics that both providers, health systems, and most importantly, the patients can use. Some of the key building blocks for this type of transformation are described. The book provides a framework that many can fill in the missing pieces. The current use of health IT has not shown true benefits and improved usability, better focus on integration, and use of new underlying technology that reduces the confusion, the complexity, and the burden on both the patient–consumer and the providers-community case-workers. This can improve a new enabler of practice transformation for providers of the providers, commute foster engagement by patient–consumers, and link them to their neighborhoods and the communities of health interest. These new simplified interfaces and aligned systems can be real enablers for many with rare diseases, those suffering from cancer, and the most vulnerable populations.

1.1 Introduction

New approaches to health and human services (HHSs) IT can evoke fear and reluctance to change. Most organizations are now on some path toward transformation with a roadmap that is either ad hoc or planned. Those organizations taking the ad hoc path are not sure where that path is leading. The ad hoc path may have started by installing an electronic health record (EHR) system. In some cases, the transitions have not gone smoothly. Are the pieces integrated? Will they interoperate? Will they really contribute to better decision making and analytics? Will this IT transition simplify the provider's life or make it more complicated? The first ad hoc steps are a key to making change happen.

However, the numerous changes have left many people frustrated, and a more systematic planning approach would be welcome, especially an approach based on lessons learned from the first wave of this transformation, and from other industries. As illustrated in Figure 1.1, we believe that

- Wave 1 provides the initial building blocks for the transition
- Wave 2 provides the integration, interoperability, and analytics steps
- Wave 3 fully achieves systems medicine

There are some early models of Wave 2, such as the State Innovation Models and the Pilot Innovation Projects. However, they need to be integrated together and all turn toward the patient–consumer with each of the major population needs being addressed. Because all of these projects are physician driven, they listen to their colleagues about the payment system, the usability problems of EHRs, the blocking of interoperability by some of the vendors, and the pressure they face to transform their practices. Those issues all have to be addressed, but the key is to understand the needs of the high risk patient–consumer populations and to integrate those needs together into services, information, and actions that include their support teams. While functionality and process in hospitals have improved, and will continue to improve, the key is to keep the patient–consumer healthy and at home, but with the right level of care coordination. This transformation journey is focused on integration, interoperability, analytics, and security from the patient–consumer's perspective.

A planned Roadmap is needed to move the healthcare and related human services toward better delivery of care to the patient–consumer. Currently, there is a lot of concern about physicians and other professionals. However, if integrated–interoperable IT systems only focus on hospital-to-hospital-to-doctor's office, we will not make the necessary transformation. Those many fragmented system of systems (SOS) need interoperability as a foundation, but the current systems do not provide an integrated view for the patient–consumers. The focus must

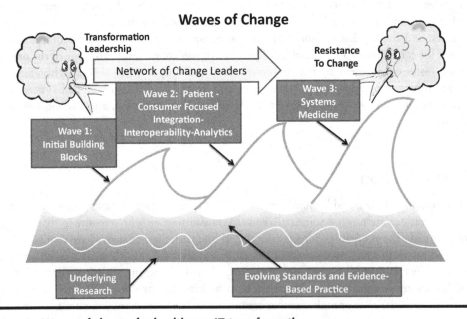

Figure 1.1 Waves of change for healthcare IT transformation.

shift to the patient–consumer with special attention to high risk, high cost, and vulnerable populations. This book provides the foundational steps for this Patient–Consumer Focused Roadmap, and defines the choices that associations of family advocates, disease foundations, and professional groups along with State Innovation Programs and all healthcare organizations can use in creating their own individual Roadmaps. Establishing this patient–consumer centric foundation will require leadership from government organizations and standards groups. Patient consumer centric solutions and recommendations are defined in each chapter, but ultimately each organization will have to define its own Roadmap. This does not mean throwing away the existing systems and the many EHRs systems or the websites or tools. It does mean integrating the many topics, services, and sources of information together without introducing any more confusion and complexity. Actually, we want to reduce the confusion by providing new frameworks for both the patient–consumer and a flexible care team with the right support tools (team scaffolding). All of the elements exist today. They just do not exist in the field of HHSs. Ideas are liberally brought from many other fields but adapted to the patient–consumer focus.

This book provides advice that can be tailored and adapted to the needs of the individual organization, but there are some foundational elements that are recommended for all. This tailoring and adaptation begins with a focus in Chapter 2 on population patient–consumer needs analysis, the key focal point for the transformation. Many of the elements of confusion are common across all populations. All patient–consumers seem to suffer from some of the same issues with fragmented healthcare, confusing directions from physicians, unclear diagnostics, and a care plan that seems very challenging to follow and understand.

Throughout 2015, there were new messages given by leaders like Dr. Karen DeSalvo of the Office of the National Coordinator for Health Information Technology (ONC) in her many public meetings. Patient–consumer approaches were called for, along with encouraging patient engagement, such as in the October 12, 2015—Strategies for Improving Engagement through Health IT, and also in blogs, such as the December 11, 2015 post noting the meeting at the Bipartisan Policy Center (BPC) on December 8, 2015.

- Dr. DeSalvo addressed a few key issues, including "the key in my transformation planning—Consumer Access. *Consumer Access*: Help consumers easily and securely access their electronic health information, direct it to any desired location, learn how their information can be shared and used, and be assured that this information will be effectively and safely used to benefit their health and that of their community."
- At the same time, the Secretary of Health for the State of Delaware delivered the same message—Rita Landgraf and the Delaware Center for Health Innovation: Patient and Consumer Messages.
- As I shared my approaches with many, I heard about the confusion and the need to take the perspective of the patient and consumer rather than always using the physician's point of view. *Nurses and other front line family caregivers stated that they were not being heard.*
- I would even hear confusion at home as my wife dealt with potential health issues with her disabled sister who moved among the family caregivers.
- The process of understanding the needs of the high risk, vulnerable population is the essence of this Roadmap, with the related solutions that are described, and with the related gap filling solutions that are being developed.
- But the key is the shift in focus to the patient–consumer, and not to the functions performed in the clinician's offices and hospitals. I resist the call from the many doctors who state that

"those people" could not understand what is needed! In that case, the necessary changes must be presented in a better way. The Roadmaps also must be packaged in a way that is less confusing and that is engaging and interesting.

Those patient–consumer centric interoperable foundational steps are based on the integration and interoperability actions that other industries and other ultra-large systems of systems have undergone. However, these steps are tailored to healthcare IT and to some of the unique patient–provider–policy maker and payer ecosystems that exist in the current fragmented system. They are also tailored to ways the steps can be used as "bridges" connecting with a common set of keystone elements. Those integration and interoperable keystone elements can then create a platform that will allow many paths to transformation with healthcare IT, and will also allow innovation and the individual organization's own strategic approach.

Today, change is occurring throughout the healthcare IT community, but there is a gap in the guidance. It only now has shifted to patient–consumer engagement. The types of solutions and recommendations in this book fill that void. It will take a number of years to shift the direction from the functional collection tools that are the focus of healthcare IT to those that are user friendly and interoperable, and that provide integrated information, unified content, and services that make sense to patient–consumers and their family caregivers. While this Roadmap aligns with the Federal Health IT Strategy and the ONC Interoperabilities, its focus is in the homes, with the families, and on the neighbors and other supports of those patients most in need of integrated services and information. This patient–consumer centric Roadmap must work at all levels: federal, state, community and, most importantly, with each population group. It will take some time, but most of the building blocks already exist; they just need to be integrated and be interoperable. Yes, easier said than done. But we got a "man on the moon" and we can solve this.

Change is difficult, especially without a Roadmap. Change has its challenges, controversies, and issues, including the overall challenge of political recognition of, and desire for, change. The architecture must be constructed so that it can adapt to

- Different federal changes (new laws in 2015)
- New policies and payment reforms
- New Medicare networks of networks
- Wider adoption of accountable care organizations (ACOs)

Each healthcare organization needs a flexible underlying integration–interoperability–analytics approach. But this approach does not have to start from scratch.

IT transformations affecting other industries have taken 10 or more years, but these transformations have not been intertwined with the government as is healthcare transformation. The need for IT transformation in many industries, as well as in healthcare, has begun with many small-scale innovations (Wave 1) with limited integration and interoperability. In other industries, Wave 2 would usually address integration and interoperability issues before Wave 3 introduced new innovations and radical new processes, like smart phones or, in the case of medicine, genomics and other new areas of medicine that will arrive.

But first, where are we today and what can we do over the next few years? Wave 3 will have to address not only cost effectiveness and payment reform, but also systems medicine. Wave 3 may break into two more waves, but first address the integration and interoperability that should have been included in Wave 2.

1.1.1 Do We Really Have to Change to Get Patient–Consumer Engagement?

There is currently a critical mass of IT changes being made now. All changes in healthcare IT are local and personal. The United States watched on the sideline while other countries began transformation efforts. The United States has finally moved onto the field, but without a political consensus, and with some rough implementation "incidents." Incidents, like Healthcare.gov, and like hospitals and doctors' offices installation of EHR and other systems that contain the basic building blocks but still lack full integration, have often resulted in poor interoperability and inadequate support for analytics. The year 2014 saw improvement in Healthcare.gov, and new standards are starting to address some of the key interoperability gaps. However, many organizations have still not focused on their healthcare IT transformation activities, and have demanded improvement from the vendors, the standards organizations, and the government. More community push is needed.

Engaging the patient–consumers will take more than pointing the folks to the portal. It will require a tailored, focused population-based approach as shown in Figure 1.2.

Some of the ideas have been borrowed from the field of education where those students who are poor (Title 1) or have other special needs are addressed with their own individual instructional education plan. Nursing clinical care plan and the education of nurses use many of those ideas, and also use concept mapping and a phased approach to presenting the complex health information in a more gradual manner. While doctors take pride in their ability to absorb the most complex information and make it through medical schools, they are survivors who recognize that the process they used in graduate school and residency cannot work in a life time of learning.

The Institute of Medicine (IOM) has worked to provide the conceptual basis for a Learning Health System. In the IOM 2011 Workshop Summary report Patients Charting the Course: Citizens Engagement and Learning Health System, there is a great summary and vision statement

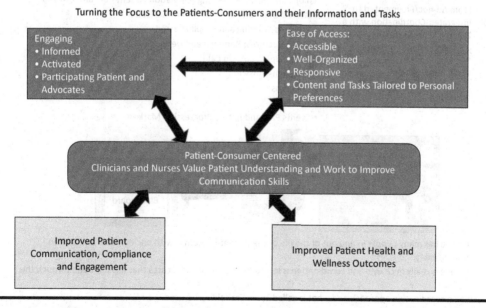

Figure 1.2 Making engagement fit the information need, providing the patient–consumer ease, and integrating clinicians and peers together with bi-directional communication.

that begins the report. "The prosperity of a nation is tied fundamentally to the health and well-being of its citizens. It follows, then, that citizens—each one a past, current, or future patient—should represent both the healthcare system's unwavering focus, and it's fully engaged agents of change." But that engagement is missing and not encouraged. The health system is confusing, fragmented, and does not actively engage and learn from the most important part of the system the patient–consumers. This book providers design elements and building blocks to move toward the Health Learning System.

Healthcare IT activities have been intense, and these fast and furious activities have left very little time to create the vision and the Roadmap(s) for

1. Ways that the systems connect
2. Ways that new operations can save money and improve patient care

In this book, we define a vision for the next Wave, and show how a linked set of SOS can define clear ecosystems that are open for change. Integration and interoperability must be addressed so that healthcare can evolve to new payment reforms and provide the backbone to evolve into the vision of systems medicine.

Complex patients or those with long-term disabilities or substance abuse, mental health issues, rare diseases, or the many forms of cancer, need an integrated plan of care that must be flexible but structured. Melissa Valentine and Donna Edmondson, Professors at Stanford and Harvard, have researched organizations that are effective for emergency departments (EDs). A type of flexible teams and scaffolding are described in Figure 1.3. The underserved, who are difficult to support, have a flexible team of family, volunteers, and nurse clinicians who need to coordinate information and patient status as shown here in a Coordination Blackboard as one of many techniques.

Need More then a Medical Home; Need a Flexible Support Team with the Right Tools

From Ad-hoc/Fragmented to Integrated-Coordination with a Tailored Team Scaffolding

Tailor Team Scaffold Meeting Population Patient-Consumer Needs
• Shared Goals and Shared Agenda/Care Plan
• Progress-Tracking and Results Posted
• Role Structures; Bounded and Defined
• Who's Up! Who's On Call!
• Questions/Answers
• Concerns
• Hand-offs
• Events Past and Future Progression Markers

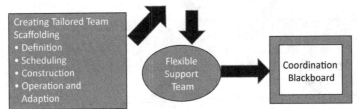

Creating Tailored Team Scaffolding
• Definition
• Scheduling
• Construction
• Operation and Adaption

Flexible Support Team

Coordination Blackboard

Ad-hoc has many people in and out of the life of the patient-consumer with unclear roles and limited responsibility.
No one is really in charge and coordination is left to the sick or the advocates that has not been through this before.
Can a coordination approach and what is called Team Scaffolding be used?

Figure 1.3 Many patients need a family and flexible professional to coordinate their care.

This chapter summarizes the key foundation process steps and architectural components for the integration–interoperability keystone platform, and considers the challenges–controversies–issues each organization faces. It summarizes the way to create a Roadmap, and move to a vision with a common integration–interoperability foundation and a set of strategic-situational specific choices.

This chapter also summarizes the common challenges, controversies, and issues faced in making changes with healthcare IT. The pressure to improve healthcare has opened the door to automation and use of new decision support tools that have been introduced in other industries. The initial steps that have been taken have often been directed by a healthcare IT vendor or systems consultant. These steps were frequently accomplished with little or no planning with one or more vendors, a small health IT organization, and a newly appointed Chief Medical Information Office. This ad hoc approach is defined as Wave 1, the building block approach, and the result has been driven by: (1) the force of change and (2) the resistance from those who have fought the change.

The largest change drivers have come from the Affordable Care Act (ACA). This legislation has eliminated "rejection" for pre-existing conditions and created health insurance "marketplaces" for new states. It has also created incentive programs for EHR under the American Recovery and Reinvestment Act (ARRA), especially the Health Information Technology for Economic and Clinical Health Act (HITECH) section that has provided incentive payments to purchase EHR systems with payments from the Centers for Medicare & Medicaid Services (CMS). The Act also required that the EHRs meet initial standards and be certified. In addition, many states expanded the population they serve and have improved their eligibility and enrollment programs, while throughout the country Medicaid has expanded.

Resistance has come from those trying to overturn the ACA with numerous votes or actions by the courts, and by many states not actively marketing the new insurance exchanges and not expanding Medicaid. This inaction has left the working poor uncovered, and the threat has been voiced that, for the population who has healthcare coverage, their high quality care will be ruined. One problem created by resistance and the confusion over the law is that those states with large working poor populations are not addressing their citizen's needs, and healthcare disparities based on incomes may actually increase in some parts of the country. The healthcare you receive should not depend on your zip code. The working poor in New York and Alabama may be receiving different types of care. But, through planning and an incremental approach, those disparities can be overcome. The politicians, state health administrators, and, most importantly, citizen advocates need to demand better health in their communities. Health means not only having health insurance, but also having a doctor who coordinates your care (often called a medical home), or coordinates your complex needs, and provides help working through the fragmented system; your doctor works to make the system better.

Currently, there are small beacons of hope like Dr. Karen Smith in a rural county of North Carolina, and like the new Medicaid-focused accountable care and medical homes in New York and in Philadelphia using GSI Health; these instances and examples need to be spread. A community-based approach is necessary for planning and architecting a government-community health architecture, and for creating a series of Roadmaps that leverage and build upon the investment at the federal level and share the funding at the state level. We can create Strategic Transformation with Reusable Technology (START) with federal, state, and community leadership. Such a program was attempted in 2010 and almost launched, but the partisanship was too heavy; are we at the tipping point again? There is now more of a foundation in place, and, with this benefit, we can create an open "starting point" that everyone can use as a draft for change. The book provides a draft future vision and the scaffolding for pathways forward that will require engagement with the federal government, states, and health advocates, and with patients who want more, and expect more, from their healthcare. To get aboard the next wave, discussion and action are both necessary (Figure 1.4).

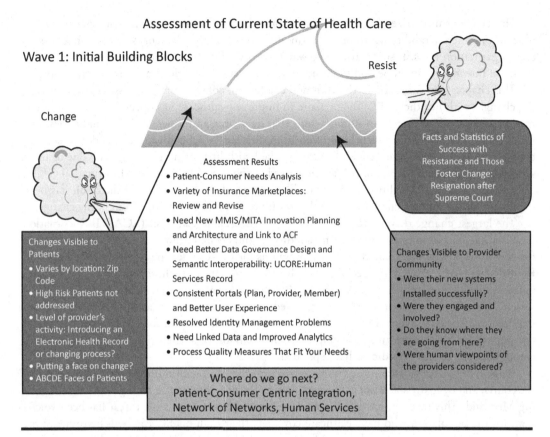

Figure 1.4 Wave 1 started with change drivers and strong political resistance to healthcare reform led by the government.

1.2 Must Change! Current Progress: Shift to Patient–Consumer Focus

Healthcare must change because of mounting high cost, recognition of poor quality, and unintended risks. Many leaders are pushing for improvements, and the public is pulling for better healthcare and improved interactions on personal health issues.

An individual's view of healthcare can be very different depending on where that individual lives and his or her access to care, in addition to his or her health literacy, personal assertiveness, and employment status. Healthcare currently has broken and fragmented systems, and, although some improvements have been made, many issues exist because of the "let's get started ad hoc approach." Software engineering describes these resulting problems as building up technical debts that have to be repaid. Those debts must be "repaid" or fixed so that the foundation is stable and can be built upon and extended. Those debts may have established a skepticism of and frustration with healthcare reform. This frustration is typical in any industry transformation; however, now is the time for leaders to create the plan and architecture to overcome those debts. Version 1 of almost anything needs to mature and be refined. Wave 1 was such an immature version and, although many are moving on, better implementation guidance is necessary. The problems with the immature versions may have an effect on patients, providers, and policy makers.

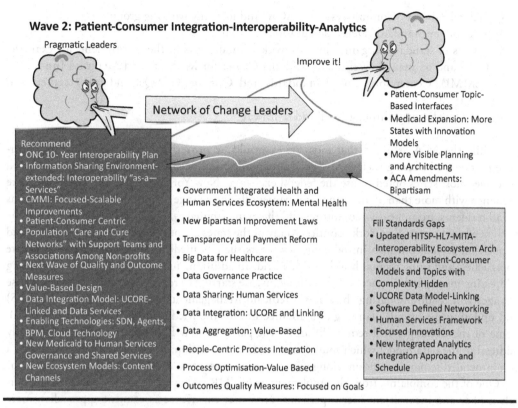

Figure 1.5 Because Wave 1 is coming to completion, it is time to assess where we are and to provide visibility into areas of success and areas needing improvement.

The first cell phones were clunky, there were all kinds of roaming charges, connecting to banks was difficult. But those initial stages in other industries were overcome, and can be overcome in healthcare with our new Roadmaps.

So, where are we currently? The building blocks are being installed, but there are problems.

It is recommended that all healthcare organizations, states, and regions pause and assess the state of their current systems. Some of the findings we have gathered from the press and from our own exposure are shown in the middle of the diagram (Figure 1.5).

1.3 Government: Medical Providers—Health Information Industry Partnerships

The government plays a key role in healthcare. However, integration, interoperability, and analytics must have a partnership that includes the government, providers, and the health IT industry. There must be a balance achieved with standards, collaboration, competition, and especially around interoperability. All the key players must learn to find a balanced approach—what has been called "coopetition." There are several government players, such as

■ The Department of HHSs
■ The 10-year-old Office of National Coordinator of Health IT (ONC)

- Federal Advisory Committees Act (FACA) and its many working groups
- A set of key Standards Development Organizations
- Efforts of standards organizations to work with all parts of the government, for example, CMS and its many key elements (like the Center for Medicare and Medicaid Innovation (CMMI), Center for Clinical Standards and Quality (CCSQ), and other centers and divisions)
- State involvement through Medicaid is critical

While the ACA assumed that most states would be proactive and create their own insurance markets, addressing their own special urban and rural needs, and ensuring there was good coverage, most states opted to use the federal exchange. New York created a very successful state exchange with more than 30 insurance companies offering a range of options and special programs for all residents, from the diverse cultures and the many languages spoken in New York City to the rural needs of upstate New York counties. Many of the states are not only expanding the Medicaid population served, but also introducing new costs such as medical homes, new managed care approaches, and tying mental health to Medicaid. In addition, a range of innovations, including addressing interoperability across HHSs domains, are starting to reflect significant changes. Those changes will require updating the states' Medicaid Management Information Systems (MMIS) and updating the overall planning and architecture for the Medicaid IT Architecture (MITA). Some of these changes will require filling in the gaps of the MITA reference model, especially addressing the data model which must focus on data integration; in later sections, we describe a recommended semantic solution, along with a needed cross-state and cross-HHSs data approach.

One of the complaints from the implementers of EHR systems and patient and provider portals is poor and inconsistent user experience. New user experience assessment approaches, more focus on the level of health literacy, and the maturing of the EHR software products will help to resolve the complaints on usability, interoperability, and other foundational issues. But change must be demanded. EHR's there are systems that need to be connected together. Also, leveraging some of the research and best practices in this area from Strategic Health IT Advanced Research Program collaboration (SHARPC) and usability defined in the projects will also help. These grants can be valuable to improve EHR systems and to resolve the problems with ease of use. The tipping point of pressure to move to the next level may be created by the interoperability grants of $28 million, the demands of the defense department and the Veterans Health Administration for interoperability, and the congressional mandate to track the health IT vendors that are not creating interoperable products. The Precision Medicine Initiative recently announced for one million patients to provide DNA with a strong focus on cancer genomics can lead to Wave 3.

One of the key vulnerabilities in the healthcare system has been the identity issue and the exploitation of identity theft for Medicare and Medicaid fraud. Each system (Medicare and Medicaid) has reported on these problems for years, but neither has entered the world of analytics and population health. Each system creates its own reports, but the data have not been linked together to provide clear answers to the questions that policy makers and researchers ask, and to provide facts and statistics that can be used in political debates on cost and improvements.

Over the last 10 years, there have been quality improvement efforts, and organizations like the Institute for Health Improvement and a series workshops and reports from the IOM have highlighted the need for improvement in healthcare safety. Again there are many isolated examples of improvement in healthcare safety. These focus areas have documented that health safety and improved outcome can occur. But the results of these dramatic improvements have not been widely adopted and deployed. This is consistent with what has been reported by the Dartmouth Health Atlas on the great practice variations by region, and even within regions. This trend may be growing as the ceiling is raised, but many are not performing the basic safety elements. Citizens should demand safe healthcare. Some organizations are getting better; but others are not making progress. Wave 2 should begin by providing facts and comparisons that are visible to local, state, and regional organizations on how the provider community is doing. Results are transparent, and everyone can locate the best and worst hospitals by using Hospital Compare.gov and looking at the results from the Dartmouth Health Atlas. It is important to the state of healthcare within your community, within your hospital, and within your zip code. This information has not been available in the past. However, now the local planning and architecture collaborative group can gather information to achieve the following:

1. List the problems as "technical debt" in the hospitals
2. Compare your region with others and leverage their improvements
3. Create a plan to correct the problems that need to be addressed
4. Make the changes visible
5. Provide facts and statistics about what went right and ways the organization succeeded

Chapter 2 discusses in more depth the assessment process and how a healthcare organization determines what collaborative activities to support, when to compete, and how to form agreements and create value-driven networks.

1.4 Years, Not Months

This second wave of change is driven NOT only by incentives, but also by a strategic vision and demand for better healthcare IT systems. These new systems must address more than merely adding more features or providing incentives or, as one person called it, "the government bribing doctors." It must also address the demands of the doctors and disruptive patients demanding more interoperable and more user friendly products that provide information for both the patients and providers. The products must also make their lives easier and not waste time. This higher level of expectation will, like any change, create vendor winners and losers. The healthcare community needs to be a demanding shopper that requires interoperable and more user-centric design features from the vendor products. EPIC, Cerner, Allscripts, and other vendors must have more of a community and patient focus, rather than just supporting the department within the healthcare organization. Some vendors are now working together as part of the CommonWell Health Alliance, and others are working on their Semantic Health and Clinical Modeling initiatives or new simplified approaches to Fast Healthcare Interoperability Resources (FHIR). ONC is developing an interoperability and shared services model, and the HL7 Argonaut has an open application program interface (API) project. These approaches must be integrated into a pragmatic blend of existing standards that can: (1) move forward without requiring replacement of current systems and (2) provide an evolving incremental modernization pathway that does not destroy the work that has so painfully been achieved over the last few years. Modernization must be accomplished in an incremental fashion that reduces risk and builds on the current return on investment. Standards, technologies, and approaches have been established, but they have to integrate into linked viewpoints to achieve true success.

All healthcare stakeholders need a skeleton Roadmap with which they can align their system goals. A coordinated approach can be achieved that builds upon the efforts of many other industries and other ultra-large scale industry transformations.

Key events need to occur over the next year. However, the plan has to address the next 5–10 years. The Roadmap must factor in legislation, the funding of innovations and grants, and the investments in EHRs, early health interoperability solutions, and emerging trends.

There are many policy analysts looking at the effects of the IT transformation in EHRs, health information exchanges (HIEs), and health insurance exchanges to date. (Additional information is provided in an extensive appendix of notes and pointers to key reference information.) But most importantly, healthcare organizations, states, regions, and individual organizations need to pause and assess their current situations. Then, these organizations must accomplish the planning and architecture that takes their individual systems to a more integrated and interoperable healthcare IT set of SOS. A proposal illustrating the value of this assessment must explain why this often unglamorous step is essential, and not jump too quickly into coordination of care, safety, new telehealth or mobile services, or any other new trend. Some foundational investment should be made, but integrated with some of the organization's business/clinical-focused improvements.

Version 1 of the organization's health IT environment has issues. Consumers have not seen the promised improvements, and the road looks long and uncertain. Chief Medical Information Officers have been appointed and teams created, but the result is prompting questions from healthcare providers like:

■ We installed our EHRs in our hospital, but there are so many issues. What is our next step?
■ Why do these systems not work together?
■ This is causing more work and not helping me make better decisions! What can I do to improve analytics?

Or issues from patients, such as

■ I'm moving; can I get my health records in an electronic form?
■ Why do I have to repeat all this information from one doctor to the next? Why don't they talk to each other? Why do I have to coordinate my care when I don't understand what I need? Can anyone help me?
■ How can I get health insurance?
■ How can I find a doctor for my multiple conditions?
■ It seems like I am taking all kinds of medicine, and having all kinds of side effects. But I am not getting any better.

1.5 Mixed World: Fitting the Pieces Together from the Middle

At least in the United States, healthcare is a mix of for-profit businesses and non-profit organizations working through an array of policies and disconnected processes. Processes at the detail and macrolevel are being improved, and new quality and outcome measures are being collected. However, the state of the best practices is still an unconnected, non-integrated set of poorly interoperable systems.

This book goes beyond the discussion of the problems, to provide solution pieces and a skeleton Roadmap that can be used by a range of organizations. These reference models and process steps are the building blocks of change that can fit into many strategic Roadmaps. The key is to define a set of keystone integration and interoperability platforms, ontology-based smart APIs, and the process steps that allow the keystone interoperability platforms to support a migration path to define a clear and practical set of Meaningful Use 2 and 3 measures and incentives. The ARRA and the HITECH portion called not only for paying for EHRs, but also for ensuring that they were meaningfully used by Medicare and Medicaid providers and hospitals. There are controversies that it excluded other key players and did not address other healthcare IT needs. CMS administered the payment program and the collection of information that proved that the provider or hospital actually used the data based on claims data or the proof of data that had to be supplied to make a good decision. There were healthcare IT extension centers in states to help especially the small providers. Proof of use included use of electronic prescribing and sharing of post-visit directives, but as the measures level increases more advanced and interoperable exchanges need to occur. In some states that had been working on HIEs like New York, or the New England states or Maryland, Delaware, and DC that are working together, those health exchanges have defined a natural path of Meaningful Use 2 and 3, and most actually support the measures and what is called attestation. However, many other states are concerned. ONC has worked to create an open source capability to address that in DIRECT and CONNECT, but there are still concerns about whether they are ready and about whether ONC will be funded. The early February 2015 federal budget and annual conference show that the elements needed will be provided: (1) a foundation by 2017 and (2) a complete national integration and interoperability model based on a Medicare and Medicaid foundation by 2020, and the move to accountable care organizations will be in place.

However, although the interoperability push has been underway for more than 10 years, there is no certainty that a consistent roll-out across the country can occur.

The skeleton Roadmaps can be the building elements into any clear pathways of change that are aligned on a bi-annual basis. This change process will require strong government-industry partnership with a balance of collaboration and competition—recently defined as coopetition. This type of leadership has been found to be key in fostering both standards and innovation. Coopetitive integration and interoperability leadership from the ONC, CMS, Medicaid groups, and industry leaders will be discussed in more detail in Chapter 2. A coopetition strategy has been derived from many companies like Amazon and Google, and from industries like telecom and cellular phones. It matured when there was a blend of collaboration and competition, and when there were underlying platforms and common standards that could be built upon. Coopetition is achieved at a tipping point when industry and, in this case, government all agree on some basic elements needed for change.

This coopetitive leadership and collaboration environment can share and leverage the best practices that exist, fill the standards, and create an "open public library" of integration and interoperability shared services. Healthcare can learn from other industries based on a series of coopetitive case studies. The success of Homeland Security, the Justice Department, and Intelligence with the Information Sharing Environment (ISE) are discussed in Chapter 3. This Roadmap can define what needs to be done, why, and by whom, and can research both the work that has been done by others, and the aspects that are unique for healthcare and for integrating with human services. One of the key goals will be to define an interoperability scorecard and to note the progress and report successes like the ISE does with its Annual Report to Congress.

This pragmatic approach realizes that all states and regions will not be able to move at the same rate, but, by providing shared services in a cloud with tailoring and extensibility, everyone can leverage the combined experience of the leaders.

The government can support the creation of an Information Sharing Platform and set of Public APIs in an open service environment with strong reuse policies that require all government contracts for Medicare, Medicaid, Health Research, Defense, and Veterans medicine to contribute to, and use, the reusable and open integration and interoperable elements. This open service governance can use a "carrot and stick" approach to award contracts only when a "reuse shared service plan" is defined, including, for example, the 18 states that have applied for interoperability funding within Medicaid, and the many CMS contracts for innovation grants and other contracts. A shared services repository and interoperability agreements can be established and used for more than the DIRECT and CONNECT products currently open source and to acknowledge healthcare organizations and contractors with annual recognition by the Secretary of HHSs.

ONC has existed for 10 years, and there have been many successful HIEs in individual states, standards have made slow progress, and other building blocks exist. But neither top–down central direction nor ad hoc bottom–up innovation can move the mixture of components into an integrated–interoperable healthcare IT world without a solid stable middle. IT transformation has happened in other industries, and that set of keystone processes and architecture is defined along with the gaps and barriers that need to be overcome by standards groups and the combined federal–state–industry leadership to create open integration–interoperability platforms. Integration and interoperability elements must be put in each organization's Roadmap along with its strategic choices and the situation in its local, state, or regional environment.

Creating that Roadmap will take time and effort, and it must be planned and architected. The Roadmap must be open to changes, open for patients and providers, foster innovation, and encourage change. This book offers opinions and ideas to provide a coherent story and approach, looking at the issues and challenges providing a path of change forward from a policy-solution point of view, while illustrating its effects on patients and the many provider types.

Currently, ONC is in the process of building a 10-year Roadmap and creating planning sessions open to the public that will recommend the next steps and, at the same time, the CMMI is focusing on the lessons learned from the first round of grants. Other initiatives, like improving quality and outcome measures, and making interim progress reports easier for hospitals and doctors, are occurring.

However, there are issues that are not being addressed and that need a pragmatic approach. For example, in the other ultra-large scale projects, like the integration of the military and the intelligence systems, one of the key efforts required the creation of data integration models and the use of new agent and semantic technologies. There has been a strong embrace of smart phones and strong interest in cloud technology. However, who provides these keystone platforms and common shared services on a sustainable basis? Some states have good efforts like NY SHINE and Maryland CRISP that address message exchanges. However, those organizations with patient and provider portals may fear that the effort will not be sustained. Massachusetts has recently turned to the Medicaid program to fund the bridging between Medicaid and mental health and the human services areas. It is expected that more states will turn to Medicaid. Chapter 4 describes an approach to using Medicaid as one of the keystones to improve integration and interoperability.

The healthcare IT standards organizations are now in the process of simplifying and accelerating the many complex standards that have been trying to address "all needs." Other industries have experienced this same simplification and incremental modernization approach, and this approach should be key practice going forward.

Resistance will still exist. However, visible planning and the progress of others, and allowing local variations, will weaken that resistance. Also, it is expected that Congress will address the

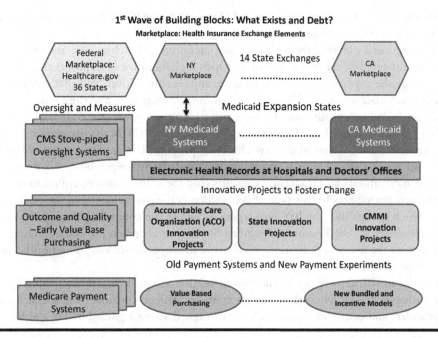

Figure 1.6 Wave 2 is about to start—plan needed accepting the ACA, improving and not replacing it.

known and newly discovered weaknesses of the ACA in legislation during 2016 as a "between-election" effort to deal with the issues that occur with Version 1 of any law.

The key, however, is to create a set of reference models and a skeleton Roadmap that will represent Wave 2 and that is the heart of this book (Figure 1.6).

A series of new initiatives must be planned not just by government, but with industry and healthcare organizations, and these initiatives must have a very transparent approach. While many healthcare organizations are focused only on installing their upgraded or new systems:

1. ONC has been creating task forces
2. Medicaid directors have been planning
3. Standards organizations have been conducting meetings
4. ONC industry volunteers have supported the workgroups and have been pulling the pieces together into a draft Interoperability Roadmap (opening the comment period)
5. There have been a series of Public Open APIs, defining the integration and interoperability platform and defining the need for other new initiatives that have 2015–2017 biannual milestones, with others in the 2018, 2019, and 2020 time frames

Keeping the many volunteers engaged and getting other standards organizations to work together and to leverage the seed funding will require the continued leadership of professionals like Dr. Karen DeSalvo and the dedicated work of a group of civil servants and contractors. Each year, there are new bright individuals who enter the field, the progress continues, and more volunteers continue to work toward improving healthcare. Now with the new plans and the mandate to report the progress, and a congressional committee working on making progress (Twenty-First

Century Cures—Rep. Don Upton (Chair) and Donna DeGette (Co-Chair)), there are many positive signs that progress can be sustained.

Success requires a different approach, not just planning and architecture and the use of new enabling technology, but the formation of an Open Collaborative (non-profit) that can coordinate and bridge the gaps among the federal, state, and local initiatives, and that can also provide shared services. Other industries, like telecom, banking, bookselling, and the computer hardware industry, have found non-profits, standards organizations to encourage the right balance of coopetition. The Health Information Management Systems Society (HIMSS) Innovation Center and the International Health Enterprises New Direction program (along with CommonWell Health Alliance, and many ONC FACA working groups), and the Interoperability Roadmap may be defining the motivational and leadership elements that are needed for coopetition to be fostered. One of the new ingredients in this type of coopetition is the government and the political atmosphere in which groups like the BPC are trying to define the common policy ground that can be a strategic driver for the Roadmap described in the next chapters. For those interested in the alphabet soup of the many organizations involved in interoperability and using healthcare IT for transformation, please see the Appendix (Figure 1.7).

One of the initial steps to get to the transformation vision is to create an infograph of the vision of the happier world where the currently confused patient–consumer and stressful and overloaded providers and community caseworkers are aligned across a guided dialog and fit with the

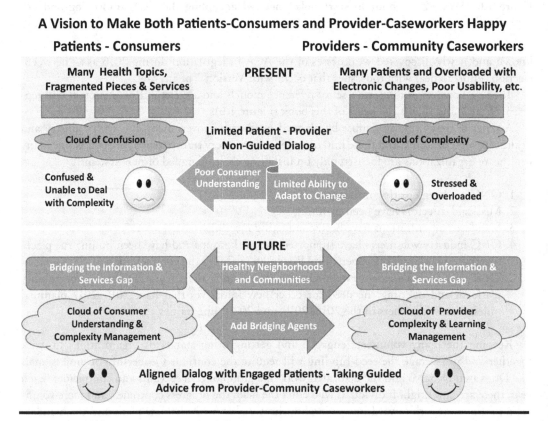

Figure 1.7 Developing an executive infograph of the progress from today to the happier aligned and automated future.

neighborhood and disease related communities and where new birding agents hide the confusion, the complexity, the health literacy differences and help manage the overload. More detail on how this will be done is shown in many chapters with specific detail in Chapter 10.

1.6 Background: Build upon the Accomplishments

Many installations of EHR systems are driven by Meaningful Use incentive payments. While some of the largest organizations may have had strategic plans and some level of architecture, most organizations "just did it," and are now assessing their situations and relating to their positive and negative experiences to learn how to move forward. Presentations at the HIMSS Conference in February 2014, including conference handouts and documents, along with many discussions, made clear that, as the building blocks were put in place, some organizations had success in creating the right foundation and others would need to resolve some technical debt. However, most would need to stop and assess their current status.

1.7 Where is Healthcare Transformation Now? At the Federal Level, within State Innovation Models, Medicaid Reforms, and CMMI Grants

A number of healthcare IT projects are concluding, and some projects are just beginning, or will begin determining their next steps. Any efforts must involve conducting an assessment of the project's current situation, resolving the technical debt, and determining whether it has a foundation that can be built upon as the organization enters into Wave 2. Some of the associated papers in this section are case studies performed by others.

Roles, responsibilities, and accountable actions must be clarified. The new health interoperability draft Roadmap defines many of the players; however, at this point, there are no contracts or governance agreements. Clarifying roles is problematic, but crucial; just trying to summarize the roles below is difficult.

It is clear that the government (ONC, etc.), the many standards organizations, and the vendor market must define those standards that are ready for use, and must have an accelerated program to fill in the gaps. Buyers must demand interoperability. EHR vendors must be required to improve usability. The requirements for security and privacy must support mobile applications that are context sensitive. Mobility must be built into all applications, must know the user's location, and must understand the type of information that can be delivered as one is seated in Starbucks. But to move forward, the master plan and the governance structure must be in place, and an integration master schedule must be created. Some proposals are made on accomplishing those goals.

Vendors or their support groups, like the EHR Association, need to have their own plans with a clear understanding of those new common attributes for interoperability, while having their own company plan to create more competitive EHRs. Creating a common concept of operations (often used in complex military system developments) with stories and use cases should be supported by industries' interoperability demonstrations and what are often called hackathons. Clearly defining those health information environments that we are entering, and actually giving them a name, could be important. Each Apollo mission had a clear mission; there were badges and celebrations of success. Annual or even quarterly "Thematic Deliveries" with graphical focus could be reported.

There could be ways to Tweet the results or Skype the experience for those who like to be a part of something. The ONC annual Conference is big on Tweeting! But sometimes the old school approach of giving out recognition patches and giving contractors positive recognition (and not congressional hearings) can be very beneficial. Just as we learned from our parents, saying "thank you" can really be a motivator!

This process of change will need to be transparent and have methods to share ideas and to share complaints. It is important to recognize those who have volunteered and shared their time and effort. Complaints and limitations must be addressed with a plan for new versions. Vendors and provider organizations must keep up with the organization's competition, and determine whether each organization is an innovative leader, a rapid follower of other innovations, or "waiting for things to mature." Any individual organization is probably in each of these categories in some of the critical elements of the transformation. It is doubtful that any organization can have too much leadership or too little, but each must find a comfortable, happy medium to handle the amount of change that can work and still keep the business running. Each organization's situation and its fits in the "ecosystems" will drive its focus areas and selections, and help to create its own Roadmap for future planning (Figure 1.8).

Change has required a large push forward with legislation and a long-term ground swell of improvement initiatives often driven by reports from groups and from the IOM and many local hospital or state efforts. The funding of EHRs increased patient access to healthcare, and the

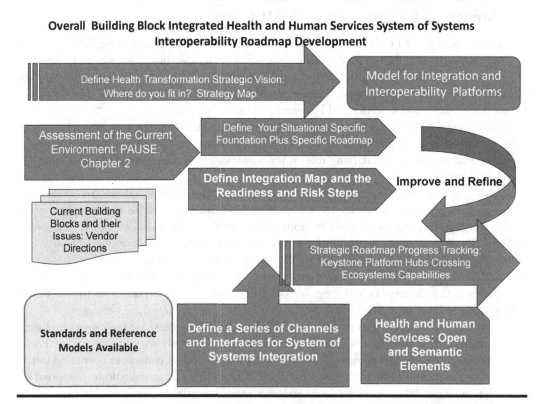

Overall Building Block Integrated Health and Human Services System of Systems Interoperability Roadmap Development

Define Health Transformation Strategic Vision: Where do you fit in? Strategy Map

Model for Integration and Interoperability Platforms

Assessment of the Current Environment: PAUSE: Chapter 2

Define Your Situational Specific Foundation Plus Specific Roadmap

Define Integration Map and the Readiness and Risk Steps

Improve and Refine

Current Building Blocks and their Issues: Vendor Directions

Strategic Roadmap Progress Tracking: Keystone Platform Hubs Crossing Ecosystems Capabilities

Standards and Reference Models Available

Define a Series of Channels and Interfaces for System of Systems Integration

Health and Human Services: Open and Semantic Elements

Figure 1.8 Change drivers and underlying standards efforts: resulting in visible changes such as the insurance markets places, Medicaid innovations, etc., but many still fighting resistance to change.

creation of standardized health insurance markets has resulted in great variations in changes, but that is often the normal first wave seen in other industries. The underlying currents of political movement toward patient safety, efficiency through electronic support, and efficient care coordination have been difficult to install, train, and show immediate benefit. There are problems that have to be solved—similar to Version 1 of most products. The push forward by leaders shows great benefit, while others find more work that has to be done. The following chapters show both the early results and those areas that need to be improved upon by product vendors and standards providers, and also illustrate the need for better information and improved procedures and training.

1.8 Integration: Start from the Patient–Consumer Perspective and Use Information-Centric Content Management Approaches

Currently, the integration of key government systems, like Healthcare.gov and the many insurance exchanges, along with other elements to create what is defined as "meaningful use," has been left to the "leaders" to determine and then to share their experiences at conferences and open forums. This process has proven to be problematic and demonstrates that a new SOS approach with a set of cross-enterprise integration patterns and an integration Roadmap is needed. The activities of the Software Engineering Institute (SEI), and the intelligence and defense initiatives that have been addressed for nearly a dozen years, now need to be brought forward into healthcare. Chapter 6 addresses some initial ideas and recommends improvements in the integration and interoperability approach for Medicaid development projects. A common interoperability approach is needed for each state Medicaid Enterprise internal project, and recommends a more assertive stand on integration and interoperability on all projects funded by CMS (such as Medicaid IT projects or CMMI) along with the move to EHRs and systems with Meaningful Use 2 and 3. Each organization funded needs to create an Integration SOS Master Plan and to define the integration points used. The organization should be encouraged to

- Define what ONC is calling "Public APIs" that use standards when available
- Make recommendations for standards when necessary
- Share the experience
- Create reusable assets that have resulted from government funding

A repository of integration actions and results should be created to define

- Past events and their outcomes
- Opportunities for improvements
- Future new "integration events" and integration points
- The links to related standards and "pilot research" projects

Time frame: Establish a detailed 2017–2018 plan by January 2017 with bi-annual updates and an interoperability scorecard.

1.9 Interoperability

The level of interoperability that has been achieved to date is spotty at best. Some states and regions have done well, such as Maryland, New York, New England, and the Indianapolis regional health exchange, but many more have been grappling with leadership issues; ways to sustain the Health Information Exchange (HIE) after the initial grant has expired; and ways to connect to the many legacy HHSs systems.

ONC is looking to jumpstart improved interoperability with a more focused initiative. Chapter 4 defines the keystone integration and interoperability platform for both administrative and clinical data. The platform includes hubs, logical channels, and Public APIs with a phased value-driven approach. This approach with a common interoperability architecture needs to define bi-directional communication among patients, their population types, and provider types (including the medical home), and the set of provider experts supported by researchers and disease management-focused non-profits, the National Institutes of Health (NIH), and a recommended ONC–CMS sponsored interoperability pilot research and shared services development program. A phased incremental modernization approach is needed. Initial Public APIs at the basic, intermediate, and advanced capability levels should be provided along with service-based ontology-enabled interfaces that use open standards, but provide a methodology and governance approach to evolve from the "stovepipe" legacy system to a network of SOS. This network should be able to be tailored to the "patient" and to the "provider support community" that is adapted and extended based on the selection and tailoring of logical administrative and clinical channels and use of smart API end points. This approach has been used in finance, telecom, and in intelligence and defense applications, but will require leadership, investment, and new approaches for healthcare IT. A recommended use of Medicaid as the core for defining this approach is described in Chapter 5 as one of the key MITA version 3 extensions. (Massachusetts is using this approach now, and 17 other states have shown interest in similar approaches that can become shared services used by all.)

1.10 Analytics Integrated into Fact-Based Decision Making

Better integration and interoperability can facilitate better decision making. A decision making framework for healthcare policy, payment, and clinical decisions can be a tailored version of the James Taylor Decision Making Framework (Chapter 8—Footnotes) and the Clinical Decision Support thinking from HL7. A draft is shown in Chapter 8.

> Time frame: This will occur in the 2017–2021 time period, but the standards effort must start now so they are ready to support the next wave.

1.10.1 Reference Model: L Value-Driven Bi-Directional Business-Knowledge and Integration

There are many methods to look at the healthcare system. But for many years the patient was not the focus. The organizations developing the models were the healthcare providers: Kaiser, Mayo Clinic, Cleveland Clinic, and Intermountain Health, and lead by "doctors with an IT-engineering" focus. Patients and providers of healthcare are now equal players in the bi-directional transfer of information. The SOS that must connect between the patients and providers must cross what have been traditional boundaries. There are many great technical approaches and new enablers like Business Process Management Notation (BPMN), service oriented architecture, ontology engineering, and new ideas of business artifacts, but all need to have a bi-directional patient-to-provider viewpoint. The value must be delivered to the patient, and it must make the life of the providers easier, more effective, and more efficient. These goals must involve the bi-directional tying of systems of systems together.

What is missing is a generic bi-directional Roadmap and the ability for federal agencies, states, and large numbers of healthcare organizations to create an Integration–Interoperability Roadmap that aligns with the federal, state, and regional elements needed to provide and evolve an integration–interoperability backbone. While the backbone will require collaboration and standards, the real benefit will occur with innovation and new approaches that can occur with the coopetition that can be fostered.

Chapter 8 provides the generic bi-directional backbone and the types of questions and planning steps needed for creating the individual organization's Roadmap and aligning with the state, local, regional, and national initiatives (Figure 1.9).

The bi-directional channels that will be defined are a set of logical pathways. These pathways can be based on disease-focused management information that can be exchanged between patients and providers for that specific disease. The bi-directional channels can define improvement recommendations and links of improvements. The channels can have a regional focus and can be defined by regional collaborative organizations. The value of information delivery networks can reflect the "regional formation" based on local leading hospitals or the partnering of key leaders who form

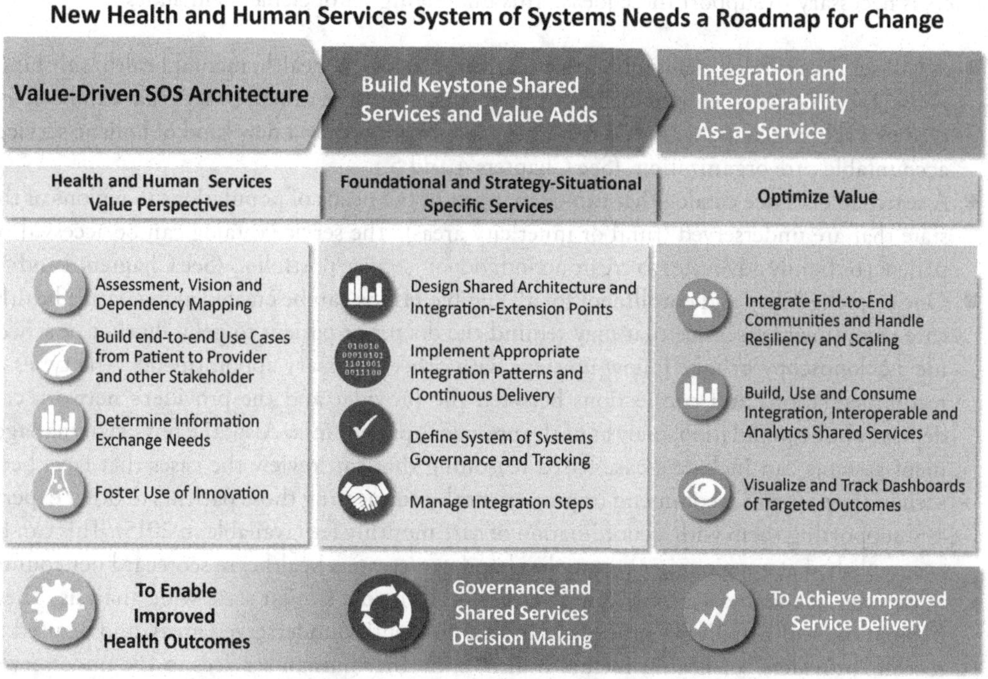

New Health and Human Services System of Systems Needs a Roadmap for Change

Figure 1.9 Simple iterative process for each quarterly release to connect the SOS together.

accountable care organizations or coopetition agreements. Funding approaches for care coordination or handling of types of patients with the best available services or identifying beds for mental health patients in crisis or "e-bola-like responses" can all work with a value-chain of providers all providing linked delivery services.

1.11 Creating Integration and Interoperability Solutions and Implementing Shared Services Projects

ONC and the related FACA and workgroups can do more than create plans; they can create a set of incremental frameworks similar to the recent interoperability project defined as the JASON study and workgroup (Jason is a non-profit lead by MITRE and other companies) and work with a collaboration of those who are willing to create open source shared services. This collaboration can start with government-sponsored programs, but can work with any healthcare organization, state, or regional group.

Innovation and improvement must be fostered within the planning, analysis, and architecture time frames, and must create a reusable shared service approach. Some efforts have been made to define and create a unified set of services between HHS agencies that are aligned at the federal, state, and local levels, for example, New York with its Medicaid Redesign Project and the early 2010 ONC initiative to integrate HHSs. A number of states agreed to this approach—Minnesota, Oregon, Utah, West Virginia, and Illinois. A number of agencies called this project START—Strategic Transformation and Reusable Technology. The anti-ACA politics killed the proposal, but subsequently there has been an awakening of interest in the START proposal. Also, the Robert Woods Johnson and Brookings Institute Engelberg Center, with Dr. Mark McClellan, are advocating for "Communities of Health." An underlying set of elements that will be described in later chapters is necessary to support these ideas. This underlying set of elements includes

■ An all services catalog that will bundle services into logical health, mental health, substance abuse, food, housing, employment, training, education, and other services that can be delivered by HHSs agencies with case manager support or used by a new kind of holistic services accountable care organization. (See Chapters 4 and 5.)

■ A searchable service catalog that can be mapped to the needs of populations in regions of the state that are underserved (rural or inner city areas). The service catalog can be accessed by patients or family advocates to create an individual "service portfolio." (See Chapters 4 and 5.)

■ One stop eligibility and enrollment for all eligible HHSs can be created along with a healthcare recommender service that may remind the doctor or patient to get a flu shot or schedule a colonoscopy or take follow-up steps with other necessary appointments. The types of recommendations and connections between the provider and the provider's network can depend on the population analysis of the provider's patient mix. Also, the physician management systems can include a case-based reasoning that can review the cases that have been seen in the past and recommend improvements by connecting those patients to other experts and supporting them with a coordination of care monthly fee (available in 2015). This can be accomplished at a regional or county level and can create a healthcare scorecard per county. Wisconsin has such a system. New York has performed a similar state-wide analysis. These population health analytics processes can help to identify underserved areas, and be used to recruit "providers" of health, mental health, and other human services to the underserved areas and be linked to the provider portal (See Chapters 6 and 9).

1.12 Intercloud Framework for Patient–Consumer Linking to Value-Driven SOS for Government and Community Health Architecture and Shared Services Analysis

In other complex systems, different SOS approaches have evolved. Many of them are evolving into their own cloud services. Unfortunately, unless the Intercloud standards are applied in a consistent manner, there will be islands of interoperability and integration. Fortunately, Intercloud standards (P2302) and other management standards can be leveraged to create the Intercloud framework defined in Chapter 10.

While there are some translations necessary, much can be learned and leveraged from other complex systems. The many systems of systems that represent both the government and the communities of healthcare providers and hospitals can be grouped together into value-delivery networks using a logical set of software defined networks. This SOS can link together the many organizations that need to both agree to work together and that need to share information, plan together, and actually share payments and work on continuous improvements together.

The perspective taken is based on defining value to the patient by defining a network of providers and their related systems, and connecting them with information sharing and interoperability. Each path of bi-directional information exchange must provide some value. Historically, healthcare has looked at each encounter and billable event individually. It was driven by a "fee for each service" perspective. Healthcare has to look at value from the perspective of the patient. Each individual is a patient and goes through a "life course"—from pre-natal to birth to all the early health checks to accidents and the evolution of chronic conditions. What is the value of healthcare delivery during your life course? Today, each system has a "healthcare information crumb" about some event in a person's life. Each emergency room or doctor's visit is not connected together. They are all small "bread crumbs" along our life course that can tell a picture of our health.

Diseases are like hidden criminals that are often difficult to diagnose, and it is often even harder to create a prognosis; prevention of certain diseases and chronic conditions is also difficult. Today, we watch and track criminals and suspected terrorists; but often "diseases" are our personal terrorists and lurk for years. Some of these "diseases" today are revealed and understood because of our genetics. But connecting the "dots" between symptoms is often obscured because the patient moved, had different symptoms and, in the rush, no one would delve into the problem. Almost everyone who was eventually diagnosed with multiple sclerosis has a number of weak signals and incorrect diagnoses occurring before getting the appropriate diagnosis and treatment. Cancer patients and many others find the diagnosis by the doctor who asked that extra question or had the other information available from another system. The value delivered SOS requires that all those doctors and hospitals and lab results can be linked into a Personal Value Delivery network. Ultimately, each person or at least the high utilizes will have their own topics of interest and a set of bridging agents that will simplify their access. This may be the 20-year goal. The focus is to create communities of interest that provide a value delivery by integrating and providing interoperability for "patients-like-me." The cystic fibrosis (CF) community has done this with its own network, and other value-delivery networks are piloting and evolving. However, building these value-delivery networks for each rare disease that affects 30M patients and numbers about 1200 rare diseases would be very expensive unless the improvements in care, such as those discussed by the twenty-first Century Cures and demonstrated by CF, can be used widely. Although a set of shared services and APIs for everyone or every disease management-focused group would be very expensive, a common interoperable reference model and shared services/APIs can create the key elements of the integration and interoperability platforms.

The government in its acquisitions process can require a set of end-to-end business scenarios that align with the ONC interoperability plan. For instance, as part of the 18 or more states requesting interoperability funding from Medicaid, joint proposals or individual SOS architectures can be submitted, and the best features in these proposals can become extensions to the Medicaid IT architecture. States can agree to build or reuse shared services.

Analysis of these proposals can be accomplished allowing CMS Medicaid state programs and the supporting industry groups to compare and align a set of steps that are similar for all states. The steps can include the following:

1. Conduct an assessment and establish a coopetition approach with the balance of collaboration and competition–innovation that will both standardize and foster innovation.
2. Start with the target value of new healthcare that is integrated and interoperable.
3. Define the communities of interest and types of patients and the type of value that can be delivered with healthcare IT enabled processes.
4. Clarify the desired end state with a series of patients to provide end-to-end scenarios with value outcomes. Create a value-based use CASE repository for sharing healthcare cases and being able to find specific patients or cohorts for research studies.
5. Determine information exchange needs and define a data-information integration model and experience from Justice-Intelligence such as the ISE and the National Information Exchange Management (NIEM), such as the information sharing IEPS toolkits and their 10-plus year experience and 90% coverage throughout the United States and Canada. What can we use from DIRECT and CONNECT open source software developed by ONC, but now supported by an open community of participants? Can there be a similar open source environment created for the states with HIEs? Use Medicaid as a shared service cloud for public services, and also for hospitals and vendors at a reasonable fee.
6. Review the state of the innovations (CMMI, ONC-sponsored Beacon community grants).
7. Establish Strategic Health IT Advanced Research Program (SHARP) grants for four areas: area one—SHARPS-Security and Health IT; area two—Patient-Centered Cognitive Support—collaboration and usability; area three—Healthcare Application and Network Design; and area four—Secondary Use of EHR Information.
8. Create a set of standards that is the core in interoperability standards profiles and identify the next actions expected by the Standards Organization. Define a simplified end state for Wave 2 that reflects the use of these standards.
9. Create a value concept model focused on how to improve the delivery of value to patients: define how the linked information, not repeating tests, and providing a more complete information view can help with patient care, and improve with interoperable exchanges.
10. Define a value-delivery network for patient or rare disease operational networks describing the concepts or how such networks will work including their benefits. It will describe the new integration and interoperability capabilities and provide personal or disease-focused groups with the ability to integrate into and make situational specific and strategic extensions to a common integration and interoperability platform. Determine as a key element how bundles of services can provide "integrated value to a patient and family group." These bundles of services will be tied with having a master, regional, and local service catalog and with a bundling approach. This bundling approach will also require new individual payment changes, such as paying for coordination services that will begin in 2016 by providing "service groups" related to the types of "needs" and "populations and case analysis" in a regional population area. This regional population area can be related to hospital referral

regions initially, but each area can have a "service catalog" that can be a key integration capability.

> Time frame: This will occur in 2016 with a presentation at the Annual Medicaid Enterprise System Conference (MESC) in August 2016. The baseline integration and interoperability services and Public API will be implemented by 2017. The year 2020 will bring an updated version 2 and beyond, with shared services and improved APIs.

1.13 Building Keystone Shared Services and Ability to Adapt and Extend with Value Adds

Interoperability needs to have a common set of elements of keystone shared services to advance value adds such as those presented in Chapter 9. Patients, family, and advocates can connect with a registry and repository of topics and logic channels. A standard identification and enrollment process can be defined along with a common set of identity–trust-network information. One approach the authors are developing is a common integration and interoperability ontology that can be used by a family of SMART APIs. This ontology addresses one of the issues noted by the ONC Interoperability Working Group and the ontology is described in Chapter 6.

> Time frame: Interoperable architecture and Public API piloting will occur during 2016 along with Medicaid initiatives and the HL7 FHIR initiatives. These should be ready to support the Medicaid interoperable projects described in Chapter 5.

1.14 Information Sharing Services

Building and reusing information sharing services must be linked into a reference model such as that shown below. It may be necessary to form a governance structure and a non-profit and open service-based organization. But many of the initial information sharing services can be basic identity and security services and very simple information exchanges. These information sharing services would be funded by all government healthcare contracts that must each contribute to an open Information Sharing Service registry and repository, and also use, or consider using, shared services that appear within it. A government directive from the Office of Management and Budget, support from the General Services Administration (GSA), and the sponsorship of program managers and leadership at the Medicaid program, CMS, the NIH, the Food and Drug Administration (FDA), the Centers for Disease Control (CDC), etc., will ensure the viability of this shared services system (Figure 1.10).

> Time frame: Interoperable architecture and Public API models and governance approach need to be defined. The United States General Services Administration (GSA) has a shared services initiative that can be tailored and adapted to healthcare along with using the NIEM Healthcare Interface efforts that have begun. Work with groups like National Association of State Chief Information Officers along with the standards organizations, Object Management Group (OMG), Healthcare Services Specification Project (HSSP), and HL7. This will occur in 2016.

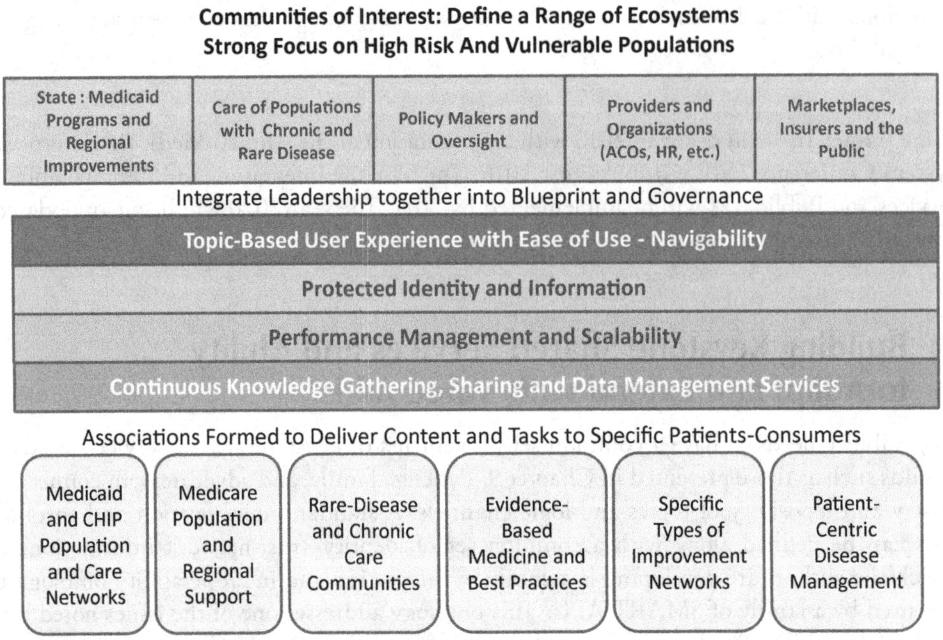

**Communities of Interest: Define a Range of Ecosystems
Strong Focus on High Risk And Vulnerable Populations**

State : Medicaid Programs and Regional Improvements	Care of Populations with Chronic and Rare Disease	Policy Makers and Oversight	Providers and Organizations (ACOs, HR, etc.)	Marketplaces, Insurers and the Public

Integrate Leadership together into Blueprint and Governance

Topic-Based User Experience with Ease of Use - Navigability
Protected Identity and Information
Performance Management and Scalability
Continuous Knowledge Gathering, Sharing and Data Management Services

Associations Formed to Deliver Content and Tasks to Specific Patients-Consumers

Medicaid and CHIP Population and Care Networks	Medicare Population and Regional Support	Rare-Disease and Chronic Care Communities	Evidence-Based Medicine and Best Practices	Specific Types of Improvement Networks	Patient-Centric Disease Management

Figure 1.10 New architecture reference models with a focus on systems of systems or enterprises that are part of an ecosystem of interconnected enterprises.

Defining Discovery Services with a Service Catalog Aligned with Communities to Establish a Health Ecosystem that is Integrated with Patients and Family Needs

In a few states, much discussion has occurred on creating a Master HHS registry.

Time frame: Initially create a reference model and service interface for briefing paper on HHSs Open Service Registry/Repository (May 2016). A working group will be formed and complete its standards submission (February 2016), with a pilot project during 2016. Shared services are targeted for early 2017. Development tools similar to those used for the ISE can be tailored for each set of information exchanges to and from each ecosystem. Each ecosystem area will have a "society" or task force that will define the service model. The task force will support common services for creating, updating, discovering, linking, and aligning services to meet "case-population type." The task force will also provide the ability to find services in a region (health service regions—initially aligned with the hospital referral region).

(Part of the ONC Interoperability portfolio)

Open Public APIs will be used to connect across the administrative and clinical ecosystem elements and the related public data sources, such as CDC, FDA, NIH, and CMS (Figure 1.11).

Define the Patient Service Needs catalog and provider services, and place them in a "Service Master Registry" based on standard meta-model (Figure 1.12).

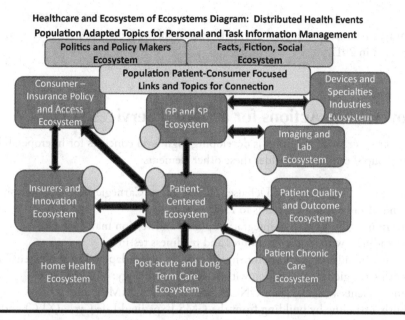

Figure 1.11   Patient becomes the center of the healthcare ecosystem: but the complexity of the ecosystem must be managed for all stakeholders.

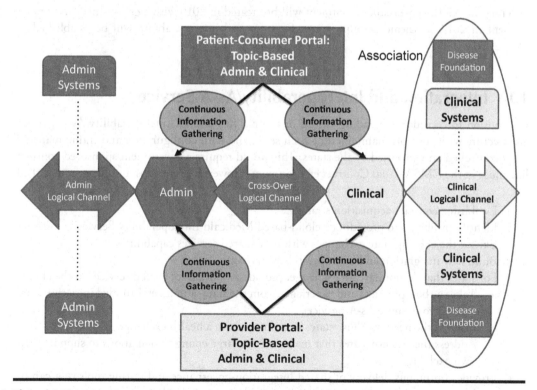

Figure 1.12   Many organizations have a portal, but there is no common portal to communication reference model: draft a conceptual vision (add service catalog with two views).

Time frame: Bi-directional logical channels using a software defined network approach will be established in 2017.

1.15 Governance Actions for a Shared Services SOS

An ONC governance working group is developing high level concepts for interoperability governance. That group should also consider these other elements

1. Translate the (Department of Defense (DOD)/SEI at Carnegie Mellon University [CMU]) SOS and ultra-large scale systems to HHSs
2. Create an integration map of integration points and version management
3. Track readiness with quality attributes and readiness testing
4. Establish a foundation package for shared services with adaptability and extensibility
5. Establish strategic transformation with reusable technology: Version 2
6. Use components available from ONC, CMS, and the CMMI grants
7. Establish a baseline by building from the CMS Expedited Life Cycle (XLC) and its shared services usage

Time frame: The governance document will be created in 2016 with a governance environment in 2017. Medicaid state programs for improved interoperability will be established in 2018.

1.16 Integration and Interoperability/As-A-Service

One option to consider is blending the 18 or more states into an Interoperability/As-A-Service architecture with controls maintained by each state, and with configuration and traffic management controlled and governed by the states. This would require a government-sponsored contract like those in the CMS Virtual Contract environment. However, a few steps must be accomplished

1. Establish a contract acquisition strategy.
2. Identify inhibitors to providing a cloud-based Medicaid Interoperability Service.
3. Extend the existing state exchanges with new shared services capabilities.
4. Build new integration and interoperability services.
5. For states that do not have an exchange, provide an option for shared services in the cloud:
   a. Take the best practices and experience from the state- and federal-funded initiatives, and create two or more As-A-Services
   b. Address the needs of those states that do not have a health exchange
   c. Address the western states that may not have large enough populations to support their own exchanges
6. Provide continuous delivery of shared integration-governance and testing tools that can be used by states or by communities or other healthcare organizations.
7. Improve integration and readiness to save money for the government and the healthcare industry (similar to Center for Emergency Response and Threats (CERT) organizations).

8. Provide reusable elements in a repository to support all three major elements, but also address the resiliency, scalability, and protection and threats needs that can be handled better as an industry (SEI CERT-like function).

Time frame: Create a scalable interoperability cross-regional pilot with a service design and pilot contract in 2017.

1.17 Pilot Bi-Directional and Improvement Networks for a Rare Disease Collaborative

Regional networks and those with Medicaid Interoperability As-A-Service are two types of networks that are useful for patients, providers, and healthcare organizations in general. High volume health users, like in the United States, also need integrated and interoperable health information with a bi-directional communication approach. The CF community uses such a system. An explanation of this type of approach is described in Chapter 9. A reference model is shown in Figure 1.13. The Office of Rare Disease Research-NIH (ODR-NCATS [National Center for Advancing Translational Science]) could sponsor an architecture study and pilot project with the creation of additional open service elements, such as rare disease registry, ontologies, and information extraction agents (Figure 1.13).

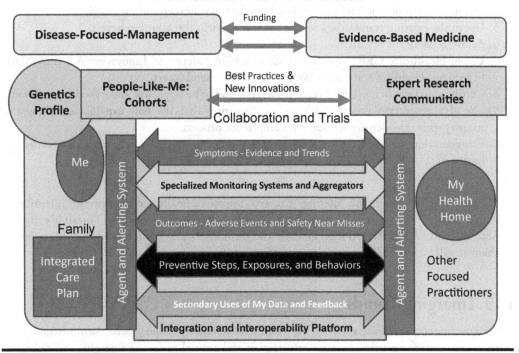

Framework for Common Bi-Directional Communication: End-to-End Patient-to-Provider Models

Figure 1.13 Logical patient and provider model for bi-directional managed collaboration.

Time frame: The NIH rare disease architecture study will be conducted in 2016, and a pilot project with one or more rare disease associations will occur in 2017.

1.18 Building in Protection: Policy-Based Machines, Data Segments, and Layers of Protection

Protection needs to be built-in, and not added on, with the use of healthcare security, privacy, and identity profile and shared services. Much research has come from programs like SHARPS and the National Institute of Standards and Technology (NIST) activities and industry workgroups. However, profiles, shared services, and certification of products and processes should be performed in a consistent manner for all the government programs. Some of the recommended actions include the following:

1. Protection analysis, shared services, and certification of products and end-to-end service readiness for deployment.
2. Use of the current research and the protection approaches coming from NIST, SHARPS, and from other industries.
3. Incorporation of shared services and certification of products and processes from the beginning, and protection agents with Healthcare CERT and Safety Center.
4. Provision of a legal safe harbor where safety issues and interoperability gaps can be discussed and resolved without legal penalties. Provision of an approach to working through the privacy policies and definition of ways to negotiate through privacy barriers in high risk cases and to define protection reference models and standard exception messages.
5. Use of the existing standards, keeping options open, and tracking progress.
6. Acceleration of the research.
7. Use of Healthcare CERT and Safety Center, FDA Safety and Innovation Act (FDASIA), FDASIA—Usability and Safety Workgroup recommendations.
8. Certification for systems that are ready to integrate and be interoperable under specific conditions.
9. Use of a protection process with agility. Ensuring that the new capabilities follow the security–privacy–identity service and compliance process.
10. Consideration of Insider Threat Management. Leverage CMU SEI activities related to healthcare.

Time frame: "Protected with Sharing" Era with improved health security, privacy, identity shared services will be defined in 2017. In addition, an Health Insurance Portability and Accountability Act (HIPAA) legal analysis and recommendation of the needs for legislative changes will be identified.

1.19 Emerging Trends

Many government agencies, such as the National Aeronautics and Space Administration or defense and research agencies, have a strategic plan and annual review of emerging technologies. They identify technology gaps and create investment plans.

When fostering innovation in healthcare delivery, it is necessary to review emerging trends and focus on specific technology reviews that are ready to be leveraged today. Innovation needs to be linked into the health organization investment cycle and can include the following steps:

1. Identify the status of innovations. Semantics and business process modeling and even agents are available to support the dynamic and often rapidly changing needs of healthcare.
2. Focus on opportunities to leverage identified high potential capabilities.
3. Leverage what has been important in integration and interoperability in other industries, such as banking, telecom, and the defense SOS integration approach.
4. Assess the status and leverage the ONC Community grants called BEACON grants and SHARP grants. Summarize and identify key approaches to be leveraged.
5. Use standards profiles and accelerators. Keep it simple; the complexity will come.
6. Arrange a series of meetings with an "Eye to the Innovators," specifically, White House Innovation Fellows and others.
7. Overcome the resistors to interoperability. Provide a process and keystone platforms of shared services based on government contract work.
8. Use software defined networks for topics and communities.
9. Use original agents and ontologies, and integrate with constraint logical models (Figure 1.14).

Time frame: Annual cycle with activities in each quarter. Fit with the government budget cycle.

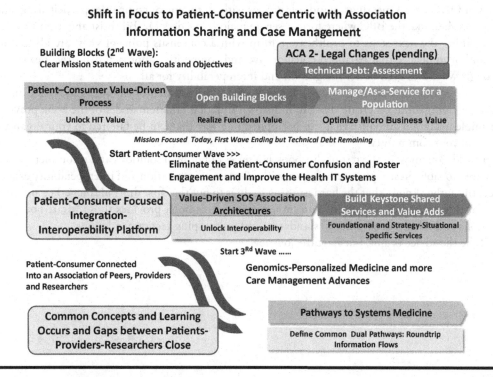

Figure 1.14 Working in parallel with the next Wave (2) and the future Wave (3) in a series of overlapping activities.

1.20 Conclusion

If a common approach to integration, a more focused interoperability effort, and a way to focus on analytics and decision support for both administrative and clinical information that is integrated into all clinical activities does not exist, the system will remain disparate and uncoordinated. Every organization can try to solve its own integration–interoperability–analytics problems, but that endeavor is very expensive and will create a "special code" that will have to change as the world evolves. Those many integration steps that may be individualized for each organization will be fragile, and will have to be updated as others change. There will be a regular crisis situation in each organization because each organization is impacted by others. The lack of planning and architecting systems correctly will result in small changes having large ripple effects. Stability at the interfaces and new governance practices are hard to establish and implement, but the alternative is either chaos or having "hero technology integrators" who fix each problem, and seem to be on call "24-7" until they quit from exhaustion. We do not need technical integration heroes who work through the night to figure out how to get two or more systems integrated.

Integration needs to move to a "plan-architect-verify" driven change process. But there are many forces fighting this integration. Other industries have found a balance between competition and collaboration and moved toward coopetition. That balance will have to occur in this joint world that includes government and medical providers partnered with a range of health IT companies. There are still weekly announcements of new technologies, and standards are moving along. But many organizations that are focused on their own installations and projects that went live in 2014 are trying to determine where other organizations are, where they are going, and developing a vision that fits within the multiple ecosystems of which the organization is a member. The recent series of ONC FACA meetings, standards groups with all the major companies participating, and policy studies, like the BPC where former senate majority leaders Dr. Bill Frist and Tom Daschle are defining the next steps to healthcare reform with a consensus point of view, are all leading the author to believe that balanced collaborative and competitive approach can drive healthcare through Wave 2 to even better integration and interoperability for all.

Each organization needs a strategy, architecture, and Roadmap of its own. Chapters 2 and 3 can help an organization create those to fit its own situation. The remainder of the book provides the implementation guidance that can be applied in a way that can be tailored to your organization and your community.

In addition, most of the rest of this book is a series of notional solutions and recommendations that are probably presumptuous; however, with 40 years of integration and interoperability experience, the author knows that the hardest thing to do is to put that first draft idea together and then present it to others for refinement and improvement. This book provides those "draft notional" solutions and other related process, standards, and prototyping recommendations.

Take the advice or not, but start the journey!

Chapter 2

Steps Needed to Plan and Design a Patient–Consumer-Driven Architecture for Wave 2

Abstract

Wave 1 represents the functions and facilities perspective and the use of IT from those perspectives. Wave 2 needs to step back and take new patient–consumer and provider-community caseworker perspectives and align around neighborhoods and disease-related communities. This does not have to replace the current systems but to focus on the topics and information and service needs of patients and consumers and bring in technologies that can reduce the complexity, build bridges at the people to people level, the episode and care level, and to manage the aggregation, increase the many sign-ins to portals and systems, and provide translation of new research and best practices to local practices and to the patients at any level of health, language, or financial literacy. Health IT must think about the users and hide all the neat technology under the service and build the system for change. All the pieces must be integrated and tailored to the unique needs of each individual. Simplicity is not the focus!

2.1 Introduction

Many organizations started Wave 1 with limited planning and architecture efforts and with very little thought to what should be done after the initial investment and installation of the EHR system. If an organization had only put a strategic foundation in place, or if it had not taken the many short cuts, that organization would not have to stop and pay the "technical debt" that has accumulated. But every transformation seems to suffer those issues and has also had to make a shift to make the systems both more consumer friendly and easier to update and maintain. This has been seen in banking and telecom. In addition, there is always a learning phase. Now is the time for these shifts. However, there are also critical new drivers necessary to create a new paradigm, that is, a new approach that turns HHSs to the patient and consumer focus. This chapter discusses the shifts and pausing to move in the new patient–consumer direction.

2.1.1 The Big Challenge: Meeting the Needs of Patients and Consumers Using Health IT and New Innovative Approaches

Many healthcare organizations used the ARRA-HITECH incentives and the changes to the ACA to try to keep pace with national and regional leaders by jumping into the "install first and plan and architect later" Wave 1 changes.

- Often these efforts have been vendor or system integrated as a partner-lead effort. That may result in vendor lock-in.
- While the ONC certified some vendors, because of the mixture of successes and semi-successes that need to be assessed, a new direction must be developed, especially interoperability, usability, and patient–consumer centric focus.
- Many organizations may need to pause and "create a new plan and architecture."

To be patient–consumer driven, the system will need a new type of user interface and an approach to hide the complexity and provide new health IT capabilities that aggregate and integrate services and content together. The system must take a new population health approach that opens new opportunities to be innovative and tailor each organization's solutions to the needs of its community and population mix. This can provide a special opening to the vulnerable and underserved populations such as those with disabilities, rare, and complex diseases, and can address health inequities by delivery throughout the country with innovative use of telehealth.

One of the key steps is to look at the drivers for the next phase and determine whether they are correct. The concern is that the focus has been extensively on the provider-healthcare organization stakeholders, and a new patient-centric approach is needed. This is a central tenet along with the breaking of the silos with a new SOS approach. What will result as we continue is a new patient–consumer driven approach with new integration–interoperability planned from the patient–consumer's needs. We must especially address the high cost, highly vulnerable populations, and, by meeting their needs with better services, better quality, better outcome, and better information, we will also break down the "cloud of confusion" that surrounds the fragmented healthcare and human services delivery process.

The confused and unhappy patient and consumer of today needs to have a new type of system that can be built from their viewpoint. Figure 2.1 shows that the unhappy confused patient, consumer, advocate, or family caregiver is blasted by fragmented services, confusing bills, unclear insurance information, and professional terminology that makes decision making so difficult. Many healthcare organizations have brought in the latest EHR and now can start optimizing its use. But that still does not address the critical element of the patient–consumer who keeps getting left out of the problem analysis and solutions. Currently, the average Medicare patient sees seven providers and each one may offer a portal and EHR, in addition to the patient's visits to multiple hospitals and many labs. Each can offer a portal, but keeping track of sign-ins and consolidating information from specialists introduce more confusion. Something needs to be done.

We need to understand the needs of the patient–consumers, the populations served. All patients are different but they can be grouped together as shown in Figure 2.2. Each patient–consumer has his or her own profile and his or her own topics of interest and if a complex disease or disability is involved, the profile will be more complex. But this can be simplified and hidden from the user.

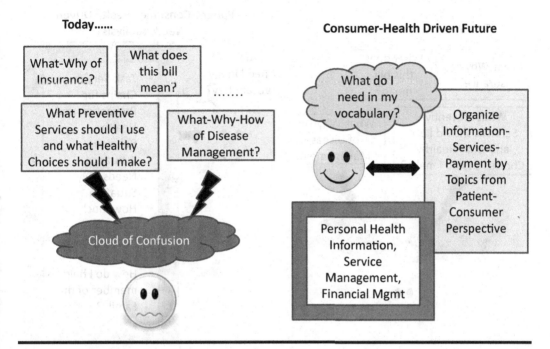

Figure 2.1 Unhappy and confused consumers need to become the new drivers for a new happy consumer future.

Creating for the patient–consumer a needs-driven set of profiles, adaptable user templates, and related use cases can provide a key to changing confusion to user satisfaction. These profiles and user experience templates have to be generated with a consumer focus. The profiles must use a consumer vocabulary. They need to be driven by an articulated set of simple questions that, when answered, clear the "cloud of confusion." The doctor or nurse must be engaged, but many of the questions can be answered once or a few times and be ready for patients. An alliance of providers can provide a cooperative response to those with rare, complex, or a variety of disabilities.

But the key is to understand and focus on reducing the frustration from fragmented HHSs. The patient–consumer may receive the best care, but have a frustrating experience. The nurse or doctor can provide a personal caring touch, but if the billing is confusing, and the medication directions are not understood, confusion and danger can result.

The sick or disabled often call on family and friends to fill the confusion gap. This confusion gap is being filled by family caregivers who are tired, confused about their own situations, not being paid, and just plain frustrated. In the case of someone who is disabled or has a chronic condition, the patient–consumer or caregiver may spend far too much time:

- Locating services
- Struggling with bills
- Fighting to understand a complicated insurance policy
- Remembering the doctor's instructions or
- Wondering if the condition is the result of the illness or a side effect of the medication

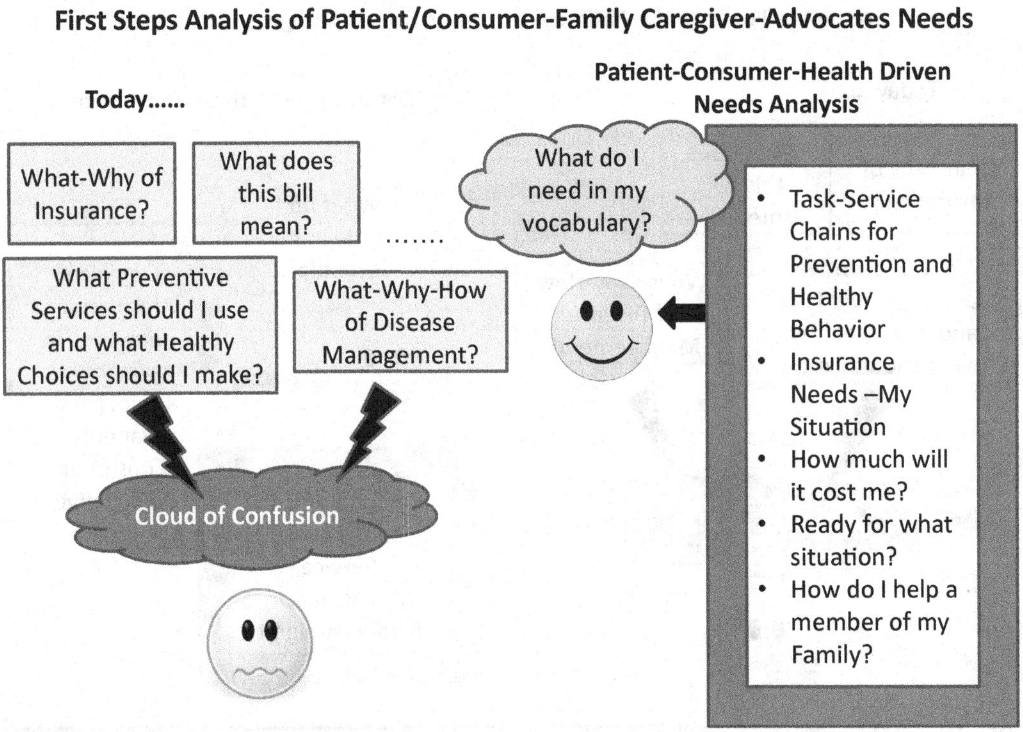

First Steps Analysis of Patient/Consumer-Family Caregiver-Advocates Needs

Figure 2.2 Patient–consumer health driven needs analysis.

Patient–consumers may search for information on the Internet, getting much good and many false leads, and search for peers who have faced similar problems. They ask peers questions when they should be asking their doctor. Or they get tired, depressed, or resign themselves to being confused and not being smart enough to understand. They have the right to understand their care and have access to their health information.

Articulating those many needs and factoring them into the next wave of planning and architecting takes collaboration between the patient–consumer advocates and the providers such as the Associations Alliances of Support. This takes creating a library of needs drivers for that next wave of planning (the on-line version is available on the associated book website).

A general framework for topics and patient–consumer needs is shown in Figure 2.3. This framework can be for a general health population, but the topic template and the underlying "hidden services below each button" can be adapted to each population type. Development of a set of templates is now underway, with tailoring for those with disabilities and rare diseases. Each population type can be represented by a set of personas that can be analyzed using a set of characteristics and scenarios of wishes and frustration (use cases). These sets of personas can be used to drive the federal, state, community, and healthcare organization needs. Today, we are driven by a policy maker, a politician, a visionary doctor, but with very little vision of how to improve care. Now there are efforts like those of the Cystic Fibrosis Foundation and their improvement initiatives. Many other disease-patient advocate groups are doing excellent work, but they are not providing a consistent "voice of the patient–consumer." Tim Pletcher, a thought leader, has advocated a use case factory. Rita Landgraf has been leading a Delaware Patient–Consumer group that includes

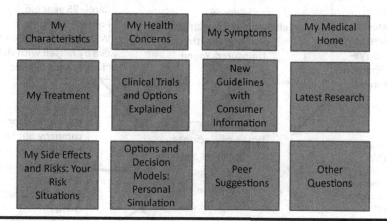

Consumer: Touch and Explore- "Find me some more like this"

My Characteristics	My Health Concerns	My Symptoms	My Medical Home
My Treatment	Clinical Trials and Options Explained	New Guidelines with Consumer Information	Latest Research
My Side Effects and Risks: Your Risk Situations	Options and Decision Models: Personal Simulation	Peer Suggestions	Other Questions

Figure 2.3   Building a population patient–consumer specific needs model library.

strong voices such as Ann Phillip from Delaware Family Voices. However, those stories and needs should be consolidated into a library that can be built to assist in this effort.

Personas can drive the general template, and a related set of personas in a similar spectrum can be defined for each disability: cerebral palsy, rare disease, multiple sclerosis or chronic condition, or diabetes. An ensemble library of these types of personas, related to the user tailored interfaces and underlying services can evolve (see Appendix B for the start of those personas) (Figure 2.4).

The result of this needs analysis, along with understanding the many systems of systems (Figure 2.5) that exist and can be extended, adapted, and integrated, can be a Roadmap for change. Done at the state level, this can be the incubator of change, but with some alignment at the federal level, or more likely with a non-profit that is focused on the type of population that needs the services. Hopefully, in other chapters, the steps to set up such a population-focused association and improved delivery will be revealed to you.

But where are innovation and the drivers for change coming from? The states, or even regions in the states, in cooperation with the federal government and with the local community leaders need to bring these changes (see Figure 2.6). There will be 50 Plusinnovation and improvement organizations that can learn from each other, especially if during their planning process they create a common strategic set of templates, measure, and share their successes and lessons learned. There are between 12 and 20 such initiatives throughout the country that, if they follow a similar approach, can leverage and create a set of shared services. The innovation investment can be magnified by sharing, but this will require changes by both the granters (CMMI and others) and the grantees (many states and regional initiatives that are locally funded).

2.2 Challenges, Controversies, Coopetition, and Issues

The ONC and CMS have been working on their strategic plans and have requested public comment. This process is open and transparent. However, often ideas are not able to be communicated in the last 5 or 10 min of the public comment sessions. This section summarizes one observer's view of creating a 10-plus-year strategic Roadmap. What are the challenges in Don Berwick's Triple AIMs (Care, Health, and Cost)? What are some of the key controversies? How can the

Create a Series of Patient-Consumer Personas

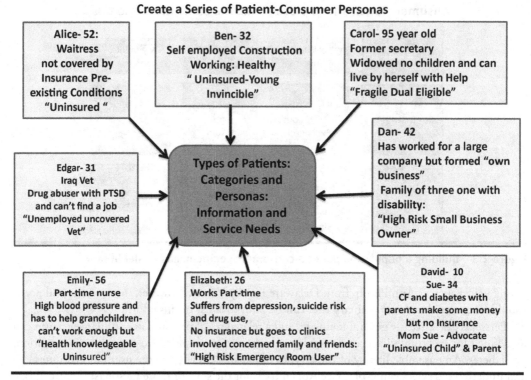

Figure 2.4 Defining a general persona for a population types and driving the use experience templates and underlying services and content services.

Patient-Consumer Services-Information-Payment-Situational Specific Categories: Consumer Needs Model Library

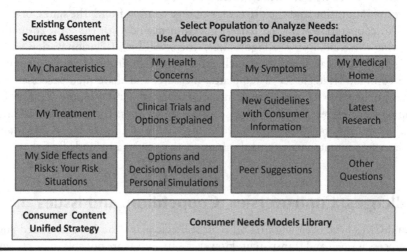

Figure 2.5 Each user experience must be focused on the selection and analysis of a population and creating a consumer needs model and strategy of unifying associations that focus on that particular population.

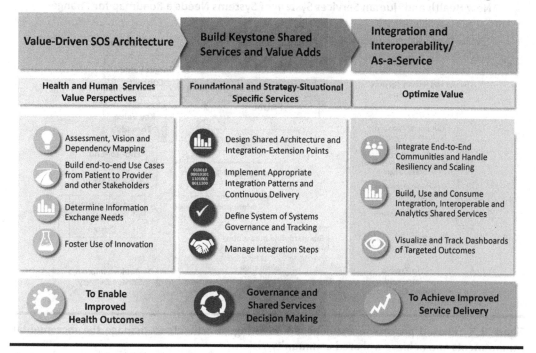

Figure 2.6 **Thinking outside healthcare boundaries is difficult and needs an agreed-upon and simple set of processes and artifacts.**

strategic direction create the right balance between collaboration and competition areas that are the coopetition directions? Which issues can be resolved with time and piloting?

In a high-level representation, Figure 2.7 illustrates the alignment of these many change initiatives. A working group that goes beyond the ONC's narrow interoperability focus will be needed to create the overall transformation Roadmap. But the Roadmap can break the silos with an SOS architecture and an integration and incremental commitment and change process that can include a national alignment on an annual basis.

Providing this context will help to understand the solutions and recommendations made in Section 2.4.

2.2.1 Challenges: AIMs—Care, Health, and Cost

- Fragmentation and lack of interoperability are problems, but what does the new vision look like?
- The IOM has been creating a series of reports on the problems for years; however, the planners and architects have not taken on creating a vision because there are multiple visions.
- A communication approach based on a simple architecture framework needs to define the business impact of CMS and healthcare policies based on the results of the last few years of innovation projects.
- Sharing with the healthcare industry (HIMSS 2015) is not based on a common concept of operations; a concept of operations is often used in defense or other complex systems

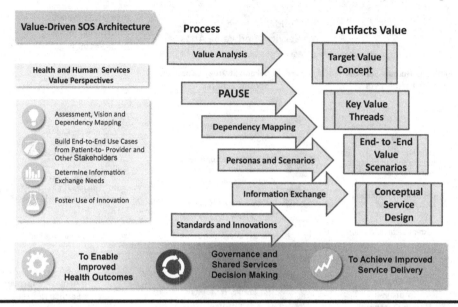

Value Driven System of Systems Architecture for Process and Artifacts
New Health and Human Services System of Systems Needs a Roadmap for Change

Figure 2.7 Phased process assessment and creating of artifacts to manage the incremental commitments and achieve a shared community vision.

to explain the operations during a normal day, a crisis, or peak situation, or after a major improvement has been made.

■ CMS does not want "one size fits all"; however, rulemaking gives that impression.
■ A communication process is needed; we are trying to address this.
■ Reports and attestations are needed to receive incentives based on Meaningful Use, but these may not be aligned with key organizational goals, and often may not communicate the "why." Health IT activities may be misaligned, not communicated clearly, and not clearly meet the organization's "intent."

Time frame: Define challenges and AIMS with a strategy map based on the ONC FACA Open Group Meeting (February 10–11, 2015) with a joint workshop sponsored by HIMSS, AMIA, HL7, and ONC.

Recommend a new health and human services approach that is patient–consumer driven—Spring 2016.

2.2.2 Controversies

■ Can the slow evolution process based on standards and the establishment of many "points or small networks" of interoperability, be addressed by a "coopetition healthcare interoperability" defined by a government–industry joint strategic game plan?
■ Repeal the ACA or improve it. What has worked and what hasn't?

- There are unclear directions and best practices in the areas of user experience, safety, scalability, resiliency, integration across the enterprise, and with the regional and national systems. This will require an implementation guidance document to be created during 2015.
- Organizations are in the "find and fix" and "blame" game, rather than working to make systems operational. Is it time to pause and regroup?
- Who is responsible for being the integrator, and how does integration align with the strategic goals?
- What kinds of problems need to be anticipated?
- How are health IT solutions or products going to be improved? Can these solutions and products fit with other products? Does an organization go with one vendor suite or go with the best of breed?

Time frame: Next Steps Policy workshop with think tanks such as the Brookings Institute, Rand Health, CMS CMMI, and IOM working with the government to provide "fact-based" advice on what can be addressed next for healthcare reform and legislative recommendations. Spring 2017—Legislation 20176 after the next presidential election.

2.2.3 Coopetition: Defining the Mix of Collaboration and Competition

Coopetition is a strategic concept that has been developed to describe the impact of changes in many industries defined as that balance of collaboration on key standards and interoperability elements, and competition on adding new features, improving usability, and integrating analytics and evidence-based decision making into healthcare environments.

Definition: Coopetition occurs when companies interact with partial congruence of interests. They cooperate with each other to reach a higher value creation if compared to the value created without interaction and struggle to achieve competitive advantage (*Wikipedia*).

Other industries have found that they have reached a tipping point, for example, with the telecom standards or the standards for PowerPC, cell phones, and others. Some of the ecosystems within healthcare are now moving close to coopetition tipping points with standards involvement and considerations of open source-based shared services. Over the next year, coopetition may become a new approach.

2.2.4 Issues

Many issues need to be addressed during this healthcare IT transformation; but these issues can be scheduled and assigned to standards organizations, and can also have a government lead assigned to each issue.

Define government-research-standards leaders to address issues:

- Assignment of responsibility for providing guidance. The ONC or CMS or standards organizations, and what are they doing?
- EHR standards and use of common reference models and design patterns

- Lack of large integration experience among consultants: most consultants have focused on installing the current selected product
- Lack of good SOS and integration and resiliency methodologies for the new era of dependable interoperable health and human care systems

Time frame: Issues should be assigned to a year and quarter target date at least a year before the solution is needed. A set of standards organizations can be involved and aligned with these issues in Spring 2017.

2.2.5 Solutions and Recommendations

These next sections provide those "draft notational" solutions and other related processes, standards, and prototyping recommendations. These solutions and recommendations can only be viewed as starting points with the need for a value-driven improvement process. Far too often, solutions are refined or improved or derailed based on the skewed opinion of the most vocal person in the group. A value-driven analysis approach is needed that allows all stakeholder opinions to be considered. This approach will provide a multi-valued decision-making process to be captured in decision rationale templates that can be baseline with the governance groups. The decision rationale templates can be open for reconsideration as experience and additional information become available.

2.2.6 Multiple Attribute Value Analysis and Decision Making

While the market and consumers may decide many system features and innovation projects found within CMS CMMI projects, how are winners and losers selected? Design rationale templates need to capture multiple attributes or design aspects (Appendix C), and choices must be provided to governance organizations.

Some of the system attributes to be considered include:

- Breadth of sharable community
- Robustness: ability to prevent, mitigate, and recover from harmful changes
- Survivability: ability to recover from expected failures and provide a restore point for unexpected changes
- Changeability: ability to support frequent and often shallow changes with automated support, and to provide a process and support tools for deep and epoch changes
- Versatility: ability to support many use cases within and across ecosystems
- Viability: to withstand various types of expected long life cycle evolutionary changes

A business services scenario should be driven with the stakeholders clearly defined.

Time frame: Define attributes for version and epoch management of shared services, Public APIs along with test and verification tools—May 2017.

2.2.7 Meaningful Use 2 and 3 with a Series of End-to-End Scenarios

The attributes and key characteristics have been loosely defined by defining Meaningful Use characteristics. As we move forward, more formal multi-attribute decision templates and related end-to-end scenarios need to be defined.

Decision Management Notation for Healthcare Policy Making:

■ End-to-end scenario process with a series of integration points that must be aligned to deliver complete HHSs needed, such as shelter for homeless, job training, etc.
■ Definition of common business needs from patients to providers with definition of value-adds and gaps to be closed for each "regional" community of health or service zone related to the hospital referral region.
■ Definition of a service catalog of HHSs needs, and recommendations for bundles that can be integrated by public agencies at the federal, state, and local levels.
■ Use of a set of personas for common cases of needs, and description of the types of providers based on the types of services provided and their relationships, their referral and partner networks, and their location perimeters. Identification of the service area and the number of similar service providers. Identification of underserved areas.
■ Definition of common capabilities with ability to adapt and extend. Sets of linked services can be bundled based on review of cases and referral patterns.

Timeframe: Review Meaningful Use 2 and 3 from ONC–CMS—August 2016.

2.2.8 PAUSE Assessment

As healthcare organizations complete Wave 1 of their projects, it is time to pause to assess the current situation and to identify the next steps. Assessment has been used in improvement initiatives for many years; the SEI Assessment is an assessment that has been used by many. PAUSE is also an acronym:

Plan the strategic focus of the healthcare organization
Assess the maturity and the technical debt
User experience review based on the populations supported
SOS mission threads and logical channels and common integration steps and interoperability services
Establish the baseline Roadmap and create an open environment with a phased incremental modernization approach

This acronym is used to reflect key concepts as part of the three workshop steps:

1. *Workshop 1* is focused on establishing the strategic focus of each healthcare organization. Workshop 1 considers identifying key partners and competitors. It also identifies whether the organization is in a very active area or a laggard area. This strategic workshop is a necessary step, and it is critical to have the engagement here of senior leadership and boards of directors. This workshop is the place where the leaders of the healthcare organization can

reflect on their positions and ascertain where they want to go in the future. It also presents the opportunity for them to come to a common agreement:

   a. Consideration of area of expertise in the community—high quality services for cardiology, pediatrics, maternity, care in some rare disease, etc.
   b. Understanding of where the healthcare industry is going is often difficult and may need outside help
   c. Creation of a consumer needs model library to focus on the population being addressed by the individual state, organization, and community

2. *Workshop 2* looks at the business process, the automation tools and issues, and use cases where integration and interoperability need to be addressed. There may be many mission threads and end-to-end use cases that are identified before Workshop 3. A review and understanding of the direction of the current vendors and solutions that will deliver strategic value are defined. This step will often lead to a portfolio of not only integration and interoperability services, but also those value-adds that can be enabled by being interoperable. An agreement on where the community or industry will cooperate and where they will compete can actually be defined in a coopetition strategy that can be signed by all.

3. *Workshop 3* selects the solution elements and the time frame in which they will be delivered, and expected outcomes and improvements from the point of view of clinical, quality, safety, human factors, and other attributes. Those decisions will be captured in a multi-attribute decision rationale template, and those with issues will remain open and choices made when issues or additional facts including market needs are determined in the future. Workshop 3 will kick off a continuous ongoing governance process and the individual organization's Roadmap. That Roadmap may have alignment points with federal–state–local or other key alignment integration points, but often many of the Roadmap elements will be within the organization or with its partners. At the end of the third workshop, the association of service providers and content providers that are focused on a specific population type can create a basic association alignment agreement.

One of the key steps for leaders of one of the "healthcare ecosystems" is their strategic selection and commitment to collaborate in standards activities and open innovation projects, and in their determination of how to compete. This selection, commitment, and determination will have to involve most of the major health IT companies, but also the leading and recognizable names (Mayo Clinic, Cleveland Clinic, Intermountain Health, Kaiser, Johns Hopkins, The CORE Institute, etc.). It will also require that some of the standards groups work together and accelerate their standards process and align with some of the standards that other groups will define. Some groups, like the Joint Commission, HIMSS, and HL7, seem to be moving toward "coopetition"; but others are still more lobbyists or advocates for their own narrow applications. Additional study of the coopetition pathways for healthcare is needed. The authors are now working to create a more detailed analysis of healthcare coopetition and to recommend steps that can lower the barrier to coopetition (Figure 2.8).

Time frame: Conduct 2015–2016 series workshop. Conduct survey of key initiatives with which to be aligned. Gather regional plans.

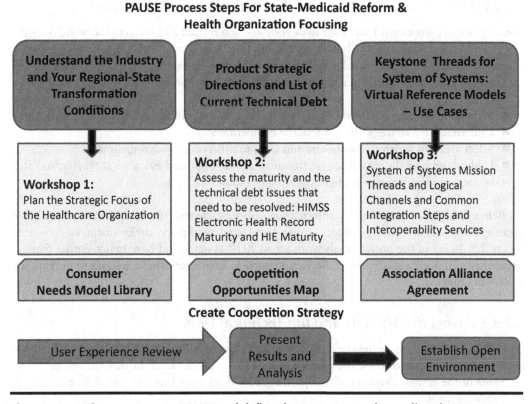

Figure 2.8   Using a process to PAUSE and define the next steps and new directions.

2.2.9 *Process for Assessment*

Workshop 1 can involve both a gathering of information by health organization staff and brainstorming by senior management. Much can be accomplished in a single session if the tone has been established and the members of leadership put on their "strategic" thinking caps.

Create an assessment checklist and strategy map:

1. What is the reputation and what are the competencies of the healthcare organization based on major "health centers of excellence." What are the best doctors and hospitals?
2. What are the major health events of the organization, providers, services, and the types of patients?
3. Why is this level of competency needed?
4. What is the population analysis in this region?
5. What resources are needed to improve the level of competence?
6. How can we collaborate with local healthcare organizations?
7. How can we partner with nationally recognized healthcare organizations?
8. What are we inspired to become?

2.2.9.1 *Plan the Strategic Focus of the Healthcare Organization*

The output from Workshop 1 will have to be reviewed and revised and taken to the board of directors. To make real decisions, the board will have to know the cost and the solution elements and alternatives. High-level conceptual solution elements can be created.

Cost estimates and the business cases can be organized into portfolios:

■ Set common strategic goals and select from those unique to your region and using your strengths
■ Understand the strategic direction of the competition
■ Select areas on which to collaborate and areas to differentiate the organization
■ Understand how the workplace environment can be improved based on surveying and also by seeking ideas for improvement from organization members

Before the planning workshop, information will be collected and related to the healthcare organization's location, competition, current focus, and workplace environment as shown in Figure 2.9. Many of the professionals work across EHR systems and have many similar frustrations; they also need a similar but tailored approach to their user experience and to provide the underlying support.

2.2.9.2 *Assess the Maturity and the Technical Debt*

One of the key steps is knowing the results of what was accomplished in Wave 1, and understanding what is maturing and where the problems exist. This is often called the technical debt.

Some of the related elements of this position post-Workshop 1 and pre-Workshop 2 include the following steps:

1. Use HIMSS-related assessment tools on maturity.
2. Create an "as-is" architecture and get feedback from key stakeholders.
3. Identify issues that need to be resolved. Create both a patient–consumer topic and interests as discussed before but also a simpler professional interface as shown in Figure 2.9.

Figure 2.9   The provider-professional support community will have a parallel topic structure approach.

2.2.9.3 *User Experience Review Based on the Populations Supported*

During Wave 1, the building block phase, many functional departments and leaders were involved. This is a good time to gather the early user experience and review the ideas and those silent complaints not previously voiced. Each stakeholder is a part of the population supported by the processes and automation systems, and they are the customers. Gathering customers' opinions can be unnerving to those who have spent such energy completing Wave 1; but this information is essential to determine the next steps.

Some of the steps that need to be accomplished are defined below:

1. Select the populations and the needs templates from the patient–consumer needs library.
2. Divide the users into population groups, and gather concerns and feedback based on the task and usage of these populations.
3. Use a process like Task User Reference Framework as a user centered design evaluation approach along with just simple listening, asking users about the ease of use, providing them training, and being open to new ideas and feedback.
4. Define the user information gaps and health literacy of the population. Create a consumer health vocabulary.
5. Define a touch and easy access service, information, and payment management approach.
6. Address confusion and frustration points.
7. Create a simple set of service models and define integration approaches with shared services.

2.2.9.4 *SOS Mission Threads and Logical Channels and Common Integration Steps and Interoperability Services*

Ultra-large-scale systems, like the air traffic control system, the many military command and control systems, weather systems, homeland intelligence systems, and other commercial systems, like banking and healthcare, have been defined as SOS. The SEI at CMU has been working on the process for SOS Engineering, and it is recommended that many of these concepts be adapted by healthcare organizations. This section provides a summary with the detail in Chapter 3.

Healthcare transformation can learn much from the experiences of these other large-scale programs. It is important to (1) define a set of mission threads that cross the systems boundaries and (2) define a set of capabilities and features and a logical flow of information and controls that require the integration either very tightly or in a more loose fashion.

In an SOS, there is often information sharing and control sharing services at the integration points. Healthcare has many integration points that often are hidden. Only now are some types of coordination paid for in experimental projects. Healthcare needs to define a set of key and secondary mission threads (may have to call these keystone threads or, as David Harel, in the reactive systems and scenarios approach calls them, behavior threads or b-threads). It is important to create a set of overall maps between systems that define the capabilities and the interfaces, and that describe the context from the user perspective.

In January 2015, the International Council of Systems Engineering (INCOSE) and OMG conducted a workshop on SOS modeling. There should be multiple maps defining the links between systems, the functions and the context that fit with the user perspectives, and the types of interactions that are necessary. In other high risk areas, there are both simple graphical mapping diagrams and more formal models for critical high risk and safety characteristics. For healthcare, where coordination and alignment are critical to prevent handoff problems and to reduce redundancy of tests and imaging, similar critical linkage systems analysis will be needed. These critical behavior threads can also ensure that the concerns and requests of the patients and the findings by the provider community are communicated at the same time to the next provider in the chain and to the patients–family–advocates. Healthcare is a dynamic business process that must adapt to new information, new findings, and new requests by patients. Fortunately, the next generation of business processes is addressing these kinds of dynamic business processes, often with agents at the coordination and integration points.

Time frame: Define a set of innovation action plans for the healthcare and standards community for the 2017–2020 time frame—mid-year 2017.

2.2.9.5 *Establish the Baseline Roadmap and Create an Open Environment with a Phased Incremental Modernization Approach*

Workshop 3 is the point where the baseline is established and the agile, iterative governance process begins. While many early projects have established their own open environments and started a phased incremental modernization effort, the common processes have been missing.

An organization like the SEI/CMU or others could establish a common process illustrating ways to establish a baseline and evolve incrementally. Some of the issues that could be addressed include:

1. Defining integration and mission threads capabilities together, also linking to the health information exchanges.
2. Determining if the DIRECT and CONNECT open source features from the ONC and the community might also use other disease and community registry technologies along with healthcare mission threads.
3. Getting to Meaningful Use 2 or 3 mission threads. Creating a set of keystone mission threads based on the coordination of care and transfer of patient research.
4. Reviewing existing Medicaid interoperability proposals and defining the issues that many of the states have.
5. Reviewing CMMI innovation projects and determining the healthcare organization barriers to interoperability.
6. Determining the standards gaps.
7. Creating a framework such as that defined in the JASON task force sponsored by MITRE and reviewed by an ONC Work Group to review the 2014 JASON report.
8. Setting up an ONC interface committee that will work to close the gaps in standards.
9. Defining the future of DIRECT and CONNECT, and simplifying its use with an improved starter kit. Using this and other government projects to establish an open environment for integration and interoperability.
10. Working with SEI and others to explain ideas on incremental modernization:
    a. Shaping the plan and a set of foundational steps
    b. Defining quarterly incremental transformation steps
    c. Fostering the use of shared services
    d. Defining common design integration patterns as the bridges between existing products and new solution elements

11. Defining the fundamentals of interoperability basics for all vendors:
    a. Defining an interoperability manifesto.
    b. Requesting that all certified vendors sign a commitment letter.
    c. Asking each vendor to define its interoperability approach, from new service interfaces to providing tools to users and training on "integration gluing steps."
    d. Requesting that vendors provide their interoperability strategy progress reports on an annual interoperability progress and capabilities report. Currently, there is an annual ONC Report, but there needs to be a government–industry report on interoperability status, including the level of interoperability across the country in each state and hospital regional area.

> Time frame: New shared services SOS interoperability standards profile and decision templates—mid-year 2017.

2.2.10 Define Integration and Extension Points

Integration needs to be defined with common artifacts and processes. Some of the areas to be considered include the following:

- Creating BPMN with its extension with an ontology-based set of medical ontologies and related clinical information models with integration and extension points. Using those that exist but filling in gaps and recommending to standards groups.
- Building on the existing architecture elements and joining them together.
- Standardizing APIs and defining gaps.
- Using a semantic ontology and linking-based API approach.
- Reviewing the Federal Health Architecture (FHA), MITA, HL7, etc.
- Ascertaining whether an integration–interoperability reference model can be linked across these.

> Timeframe: Post FHIR 2015 mid-year. Define gaps to be addressed—2016. Present new standards—mid-year 2017.

2.2.11 Define Key Value Threads and Shared Services

Multi-attribute decision making must continue through the development cycle and must consider the benefits of the key value threads and the reasons why shared services are so important.

A set of design attributes and models must be refined to integrate shared services throughout the life cycle. Some of the steps include the following:

1. Ensure transparency and access to information based on multi-attribute decision-making templates:
   a. Create an example, such as using and extending Bluebutton. Bluebutton is an open source project that began with the Veterans Administration to encourage the veterans to download their EHRs, share them with their doctors, and understand their diagnoses and

their care plans. Bluebutton has reflected a shift in sharing data with patients. Projects similar to Bluebutton, such as OpenNotes (also open source), show the connections to all clinical and administrative information and the cross mapping of that information into a life-course plan for a patient and his or her family members.

  b. Define other examples such as Medicaid.

2. Define administrative threads and their relationships to channels.
3. Define clinical threads and their relationships to channels.
4. Define payment threads, and note ways that administrative, clinical, and payment threads need to converge as key "gating" points so that coordination of care can occur.
5. Define the portfolio of value threads through the health and human services ecosystem model.
6. Define basic integration–interoperability platform of services.
7. Use Medicaid hub or health information exchange (best practices).
8. Select approach to be used by states and regions with health exchanges: can they support the vision?

  a. Can Medicaid support most of the needs? Identify some of the 18 state proposals.

  b. Where is the advanced planning approach going that is used in the Commonwealth of Massachusetts, including Medicaid?

9. Define the cloud option. Can "as-a-service" services be stored and used in the cloud, or can more than two be used with resiliency, and can backup be created (profit making or non-profit making usage of open source shared service capabilities). The intent should be that every government-funded project should use, revise, and contribute to one or more related open source projects.

Time frame: Extend federal CIO shared services—mid-year 2016—and tailor to government-partner FHA—January 2017.

2.2.12 Define Data–Information Subject Areas for Integration and Interoperability of Administrative and Clinical Information

Interoperability has to be bi-directional and often multi-directional with convergence and integration points needed to integrate the administrative, clinical, and payment information that must be aligned. This convergence of the logical administrative systems and clinical systems can relate clinical and administrative message types that can be organized based on topics and the keystone threads that need to be integrated together. The logical cross-information that must be aligned and harmonized must be defined. This can be a limited amount of core information that is often called a Universal core (UCORE). This core information will allow the coordination of care, the handoff and patient transfer, and the linking between administrative enrollment and payment systems and the clinical records (EHR, imaging, lab, prescribing, and fulfillment systems). The patient portal, related to the administrative and clinical systems from the patient's level of health literacy and expected understanding, can be aligned with the provider portal and the providers' viewpoints (Figure 2.10).

During the last year, a key understanding has evolved that healthcare IT needs to address more than just healthcare, but also address human services. If a patient is diabetic, but is also homeless,

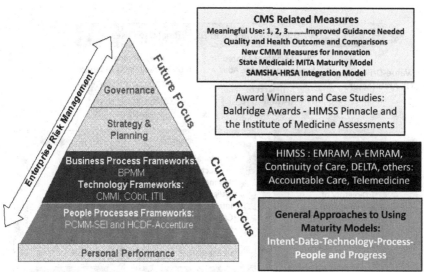

Figure 2.10 Align healthcare with other strategic improvement initiatives and clarify government involvement.

both conditions have to be addressed. A new set of human services with common definitions needs to be defined with "service definition standards" and a common service catalog created (Figure 2.11).

Information sharing for healthcare can follow approaches similar to the Intelligence Agency and Homeland Security National Information Exchange Model (NIEM) practices. These approaches can be combined with the patient–consumer needs driven approach and allow the users to learn from experts and peers.

HHSs can learn much from the experience of the intelligence, homeland security, and defense systems, from the common information exchange packet descriptions, and from the initial efforts to define information sharing for HHSs. The new health IT strategy, released as a draft in 2014, and the interoperability Roadmap need to align with a set of standards efforts from those of many different organizations (MG, HL7, HIMSS, etc.) to a FHA or, as the Justice Department defined, more of a general reference model. A health and human services reference model for government and industry could be defined by a group such as OMG. Some of the steps that need to be accomplished include the following:

1. Adapt and extend the information sharing architecture, and fit with the HSSP/FHIR approach.
2. Define subject ownership and governance by federal agency and "standards teammates."
3. Note the limited number of areas needing harmonization. The harmonization of those standards can be limited to core-only areas that address common identifiers, such as who, what, where, and why identifiers.
4. Note what is standardized today, and accelerate standardization efforts with government support, piloting the activities with government projects.

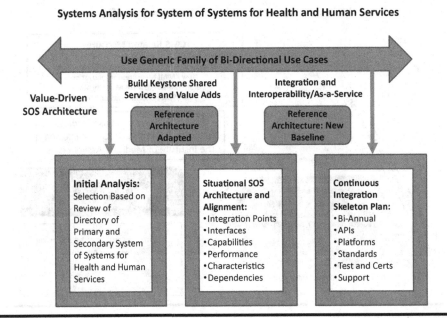

Figure 2.11 **Create a series of aligning activities based on healthcare use cases driven by health events and the information that needs to be integrated, to create a continuous integration skeleton with which healthcare organizations, states, and regions can align.**

Time frame: Create a health interoperability standards profile with basic, intermediate, and advanced capability that is similar to the profile used in Smart Financial Data by OMG—2016 and 2017.

2.2.13 Define the UCORE of Identity Information

Data and information modeling is often the orphan of enterprise or solution architecture, and there is either a tendency to try to harmonize everything, or to hope the extraction, transformation, and loading tools can handle it. A healthcare data strategy is needed, one of a number of alternatives need to be reviewed, and data integration strategy and data alignment reviews need to be conducted before integration. Two interesting approaches have been used: DOD created a data integration model and defined a UCORE, while the Open Group has defined a Universal Definition-like approach. These and other approaches should be reviewed and a strategy selected. Also, defense has been collaborating on new integration, modeling, and governance techniques that can be simplified and adapted to HHSs integration. This will be discussed in more detail in other chapters.

Time frame: Define a set of data integration and alignment patterns and services, and a data strategy policy for healthcare. Create a repository of key universal identifier information and examples of data integration across the keystone threads, along with related examples, data review, and certification process—2016–2017.

2.2.14 Logical Channels and Interfaces

Two sets of channels can be defined: one for administrative functions and one for clinical functions. Both sets have to deal with systems of systems, and common logical paths have to be defined. A set of logical business process models with related knowledge views (ontologies) must also be defined, along with the use of agents for flagging conditions of interest, either administrative alerts (if the planned budget and the estimates are exceeded) or clinical alerts (about potential adverse events and need for follow-up).

The streams of information have to be bi-directional, and include both clinical and administrative information, and that information moving together, so that the alignment of administrative and clinical information and its mapping can occur. Far too often a patient receives a bill that cannot be clearly related to the clinical event ("I didn't know that doctor was consulted"), and it may or may not fit within the patient's budget. Both payment and cost transparency, and the understanding and closing of the gaps of health literacy, are key to approaches that these channel frameworks can address (Figures 2.12 and 2.13).

Some of the steps that need to be undertaken by an interoperability group include the following:

1. Using the bi-directional clinical and administrative information channels, specific business process modeling, like end-to-end use cases, will be created, along with the ability to integrate them with crossover channels.
2. Breaking all messages into logical groups from communities of interests to the consumers and related stakeholders.
3. Starting with FHIR and administrative message.
4. Picking common scenarios—appendix with the detailed value end-to-end scenario models and
    a. Eligibility and enrollment
    b. Child health and foster care
    c. Ability to find a specialist across state boundaries and get cross-boundary care coordination
    d. Rare disease new practices
    e. Referrals and feedback
    f. Recommendation for HHSs to share the information: enter once—use many times
    g. Electronic Health Records (EHRs) that can be detected by a bridging agent and sent to safety check points, to analytics aggregation services or areas such as public health
    h. Finding best practices and other cases with a call to the community

Time frame: The ONC will work in parallel with the FHIR groups and one of the key results will be a set of logical channels that can be managed by Public API and information sharing platforms or health information exchanges—2016–2017.

2.2.15 Integration and Interoperability Platform: Services and Capability Models

One of the key steps is to define and provide an open source integration and interoperability platform and set of services and capabilities, and will involve a project like Medicaid interoperability, where the following are defined:

■ Basic: administrative and clinical hubs and API end points are created.

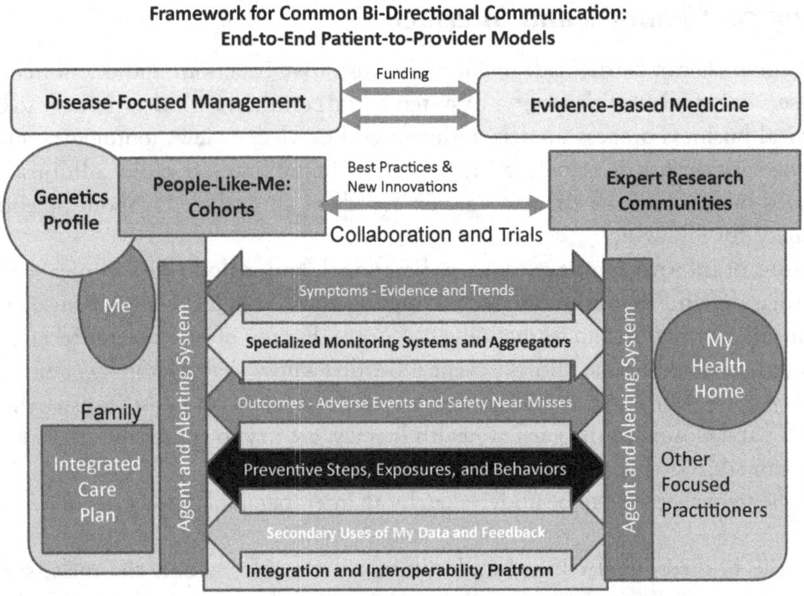

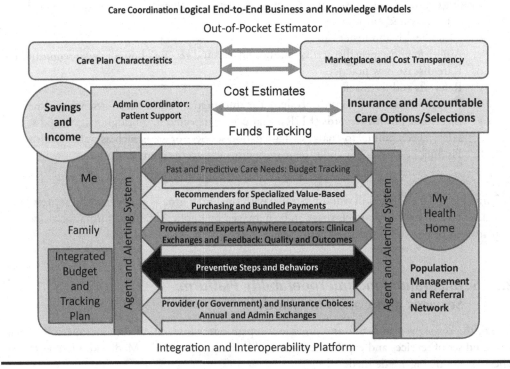

**Framework for Common Bi-Directional Communication:
End-to-End Patient-to-Provider Models**

Funding

Disease-Focused Management

Evidence-Based Medicine

Genetics Profile

People-Like-Me: Cohorts

Best Practices & New Innovations

Expert Research Communities

Collaboration and Trials

Me

Symptoms – Evidence and Trends

Specialized Monitoring Systems and Aggregators

Outcomes – Adverse Events and Safety Near Misses

Preventive Steps, Exposures, and Behaviors

Secondary Uses of My Data and Feedback

Integration and Interoperability Platform

Family

Integrated Care Plan

Agent and Alerting System

Agent and Alerting System

My Health Home

Other Focused Practitioners

Figure 2.12   Define the types of logical communication channels: high level.

Care Coordination Logical End-to-End Business and Knowledge Models

Out-of-Pocket Estimator

Care Plan Characteristics

Marketplace and Cost Transparency

Savings and Income

Admin Coordinator: Patient Support

Cost Estimates

Insurance and Accountable Care Options/Selections

Funds Tracking

Me

Past and Predictive Care Needs: Budget Tracking

Recommenders for Specialized Value-Based Purchasing and Bundled Payments

Providers and Experts Anywhere Locators: Clinical Exchanges and Feedback: Quality and Outcomes

Preventive Steps and Behaviors

Provider (or Government) and Insurance Choices: Annual and Admin Exchanges

Family

Integrated Budget and Tracking Plan

Agent and Alerting System

Agent and Alerting System

My Health Home

Population Management and Referral Network

Integration and Interoperability Platform

Figure 2.13   Similar representation that ensures that administrative and payment information flows and converges with patient information and clinical information.

- Intermediate: business process will be connected with knowledge and translation between the patient and the patient's understanding of the administrative-cost information. The health information will include ontologies and the linking between specialist vocabulary and lay language, to address one of the key concerns: miscommunication on either the administrative or clinical side or both at once.
- Adding the individual organization's own extensions and advance capabilities.
- Special standard registries for categories like rare diseases or outcomes or clinical trials.

Time frame: This activity can be accomplished in 2016–2017 period.

2.2.16 Development and Integration of Shared Services and Creating a Master Roadmap and Negotiation Process

One of the only ways to move forward is to have one or more agencies and states create the open shared services elements for the administrative and clinical hubs and the API end points, along with creating the strategic and governance tools and SOS life cycle models. Those shown on the left of Figure 2.14 must create a common foundation that the states and the healthcare associated

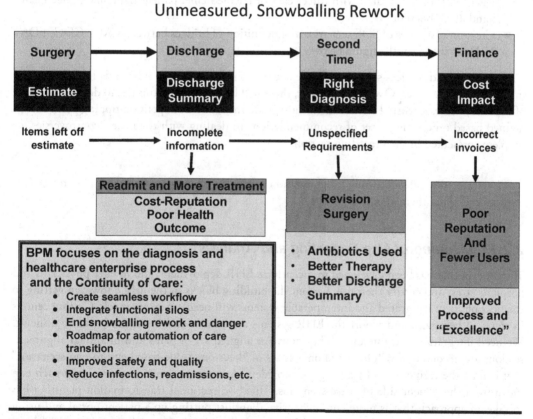

Figure 2.14 Defining the risks and prevention steps using end-to-end integration resulting in reduction of rework for a range of integrated services.

administrative and clinical organizations can build and extend. A set of shared services can be aligned with the government-wide and GSA-lead shared services requirements in government contracts, and can result in a portfolio.

But shared services for improved health interoperability need to focus on improving the coordination of care for common health services, such as surgery, shown in Figure 2.9.

The end-to-end flow of the patient must include the closure of incomplete information, a clear understanding of what is expected by the patient–provider, and ensuring that follow-up paperwork, including the invoices and other "gaps," can be addressed with a common set of shared services. Extensive end-to-end SOS analysis will need to identify a common set of shared services that can be used by government and industry. Often a non-profit organization leads the creation of such shared services for healthcare; it can be one of a number of such organizations: Joint Commission, HL7, HIMSS, or some other new entity.

A set of projects should be reviewed as the sources of the initial development projects that can seed the Open Integration and Interoperability Repository. Similar projects should be required to use this Repository. Some of the candidate areas include:

■ Medicaid interoperability and joint sponsorship with ONC, CMS, and other government agencies, such as the Administration for Children and Families (ACF)
■ Creation of a series of scenarios that can be addressed: cross-state eligibility and enrollment, fraud prevention, child health and foster care, getting to the "Centers of Disease Experts" wherever they are located with direct care or telemedicine, patient handoffs, public health handoffs (e-bola) or
■ Creation of a series of SOS scenarios and definition of bridges between CMS–CDC–FDA–NIH, as shown in the figure below

A set of shared services solutions will be needed to turn healthcare fragments into end-to-end interoperability services. Over the next year, there will be many opportunities to define a basic set of shared services. A trusted environment must be defined, and a coopetition tipping point can be defined based on creating a set of recommendations in dealing with the issues, controversies, or problems presented in the preceding section.

Timeframe: Provide a training program and outreach to share ideas on creating shared services and using them effectively—2017.

2.2.17 Meaningful Use Reporting and Analysis

The concept that has been developed to incentivize EHR deployment, and to have physicians and hospitals attest and certify their use, has put the building blocks in the field. However, getting to the next phase of integrated and interoperable systems will need a new approach. Getting centers in states to help with and report the EHR systems assessment and installation will be difficult. We need integration and interoperability now. An aligned set of plans and bi-annual alignment sessions are needed that will be based on a series of "keystone value-based end-to-end scenarios" that can be the recipes used by a range of providers. A common "patient-centric" approach can move from the patient side of these scenarios. This bi-directional transformation planning has to take an approach that is more comprehensive than just putting up a patient portal and using Bluebutton or another simple guidance. This transformation planning all depends on the local situation, that is, ascertaining what steps can be taken when, and which steps have the most value for each individual organization. However, some of the value-based end-to-end scenarios shown in Appendix A can be a good starting point for any organization's consideration:

■ Explain in terms of value-based end-to-end scenarios and patient–provider improvements.
■ Provide a skeleton target concept of operations: a series of life events from the patient's perspective can be used as the "integration points":
  − Preventive medicine health checks
  − Family history and genetic assessment
  − Diagnosis and gathering of biomarkers and findings
  − Chronic care management
  − Episode onset
  − Ambulatory surgery or other outpatient engagement
  − Tests and results
  − Medication reconciliation
  − Discharge summary and pending test results
  − Follow-up treatment
■ Fit with the latest "rule" and ensure that the organization's technologies and its integration–interoperability are "fit for the purpose"
■ Define and agree on key principles for data management and integration:
  − Examples of the principles include:
    1. Use solutions that are fit for the purpose
    2. Define the source of the information and related decisions and level of certainty: decide when the information needs to be reused and retested
    3. Capture data when first generated and route with provenance tagging to the secondary uses
    4. Control the data with a set of "data quality attributes" and flagging and data improvements: flag uncertainty and provide the ability to note problems
    5. Build in and leverage automated data quality checks, notification, and alerts
    6. Control the quality at each stage
    7. Conform to regulation and guidance
■ Find a business-driven architecture plan that is attuned to the strategic approach to the HHSs needs of the population being served. Note whether the foundational automation design tools are put in place to support the testing and readiness. Use some of the experience from **Britain's National Health Services** and the experience of other countries.

Time frame: Meaningful Use 2 and 3 will be tested—2016 and 2017. Pilot the training and reporting area on selective high interoperability areas around the country and update to ensure that they fit together—2017.

2.2.18 Emerging Trends

To move to the next stage, we have to work from an integration and interoperability perspective. We must focus from the patients' and providers' perspectives on:

■ Improvement in disease management for chronic conditions (CMS is funding a number of new grants in this area).

- Cost containment (new projects are being funded and programs like the Healthcare Readmission Program are showing good progress in slowing the cost in Medicare).
- The ability to get ongoing collaboration and sharing. A new continuous information and collaboration approach that builds on the "channels of communication" is established in Section 2.3 (Figure 2.15).

There is an extensive amount of advanced research and many papers on the next steps by groups like the American Medical Informatics Association, the Society of Clinical Data Management, HIMSS, and HL7, but there is not much practical action on ways to integrate the many pieces of healthcare together and to support a dynamic and rapidly changing industry.

Time frame: Create a panel discussion or workshop with the ONC or with joint standards activities—until 2020.

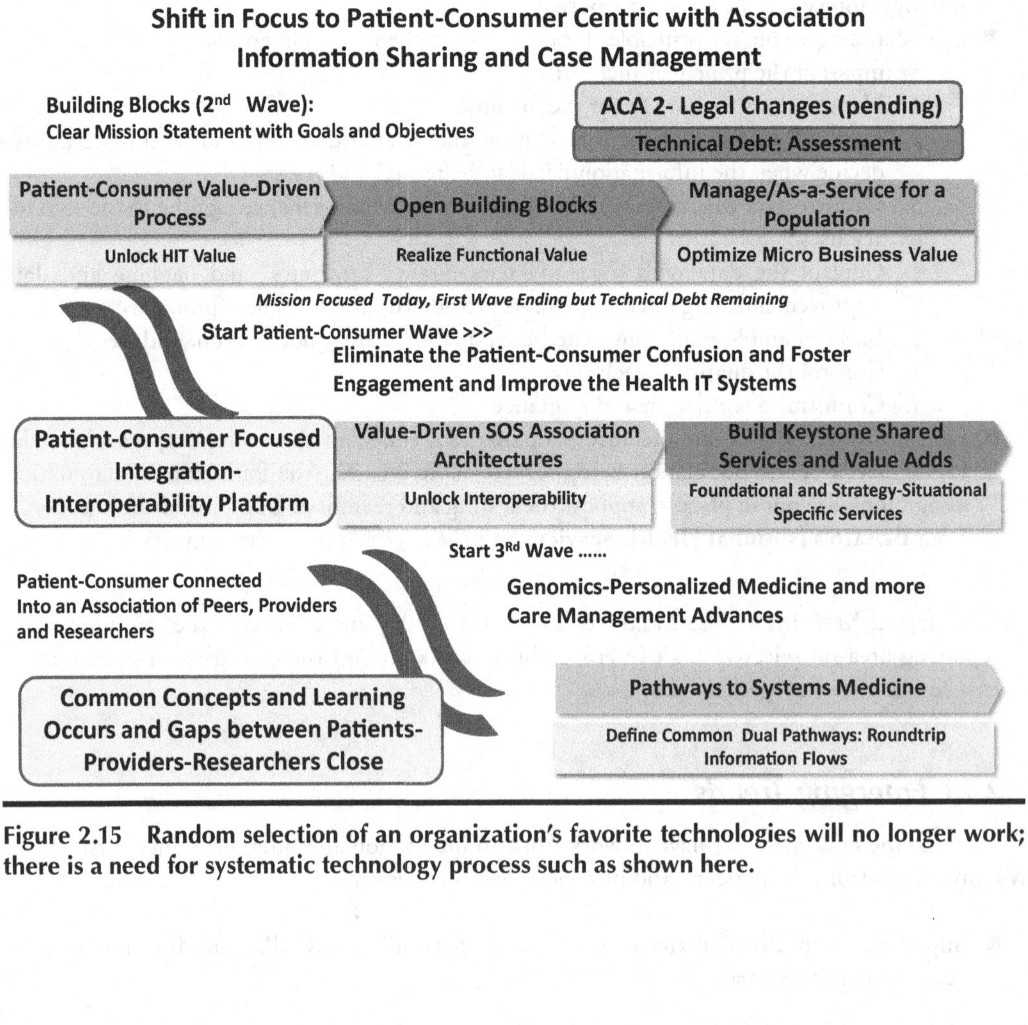

Shift in Focus to Patient-Consumer Centric with Association Information Sharing and Case Management

Building Blocks (2nd Wave):
Clear Mission Statement with Goals and Objectives

ACA 2- Legal Changes (pending)
Technical Debt: Assessment

Patient-Consumer Value-Driven Process	Open Building Blocks	Manage/As-a-Service for a Population
Unlock HIT Value	Realize Functional Value	Optimize Micro Business Value

Mission Focused Today, First Wave Ending but Technical Debt Remaining

Start Patient-Consumer Wave >>>
Eliminate the Patient-Consumer Confusion and Foster
Engagement and Improve the Health IT Systems

Patient-Consumer Focused Integration- Interoperability Platform	Value-Driven SOS Association Architectures	Build Keystone Shared Services and Value Adds
	Unlock Interoperability	Foundational and Strategy-Situational Specific Services

Start 3Rd Wave ......

Patient-Consumer Connected
Into an Association of Peers, Providers
and Researchers

Genomics-Personalized Medicine and more
Care Management Advances

Common Concepts and Learning Occurs and Gaps between Patients- Providers-Researchers Close	Pathways to Systems Medicine
	Define Common Dual Pathways: Roundtrip Information Flows

Figure 2.15   Random selection of an organization's favorite technologies will no longer work; there is a need for systematic technology process such as shown here.

2.3 Conclusion

Interoperability won't happen unless someone is responsible, and reports and dashboards are required, and unless the benefits are clearly understood. The ONC has been working on this project for 10 years. Over the next 10 years, the plan and incremental results must be clearly visible; there must also be congressional oversight with positive feedback and negative-improvement recommendations. Positive feedback from Congress is hard to visualize during 2016, but we can hope.

Chapter 3

Wave 2: Integration Using System of Systems Health and Human System Model Integration Process with Integration Maps and Risk Management

Abstract

Integration has often been an afterthought but now must become a central approach to heath IT transformation. A representation of the integration approach is shown in Figure 3.1. Major issues in establishing patient–consumer centric and information-centric Wave 2, described in Chapters 2 and 4, respectively, require defining a new services and information architecture and providing an integrative approach. We cannot build a totally new integrated patient–consumer-information-centric architecture from scratch and get to a connected Health and Human Services shared services (HHSs) approach. To achieve that goal, we must evolve in an incremental fashion. However, if our vision is centered only on the providers and hospitals, and their host systems—as the current approach, and we don't turn the focus to patient–consumer interactions and their content-information and service needs, we will still have great complexity and the wrong focus. Healthcare improvement has to be about better quality, more efficient, and less confusing care. Today, health IT systems are focused on the providers, the hospitals, the labs, etc., and automating their functions. That step is necessary, but like all industry transformation, the focus needs to shift to the consumer in balance with all stakeholders. Providers practice transformation and improvement must focus on ease of use, interoperability, and new capabilities for care coordination, with mental

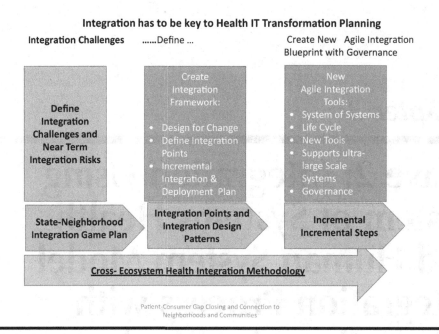

Figure 3.1   Following the integration process.

health integration; however, new patient–consumer-information-centric approaches are needed. That shift must take place with a set of managed integration planning steps.

This shift provides a major integration challenge, and needs to use large-scale integration approaches. It will require evolutionary incremental steps that require alignment at many levels. Federal, state, community, and healthcare organizations, in addition to small practices and, most important, consumers must be part of an integration strategy. A set of aligned integration strategies must be open and transparently developed and managed. The many patient advocacy groups must act as the voice of patients and consumers, and leadership from State Innovation Models and CMMI must support alignment. The host-based focus must turn to an SOS with an information-centric network that has patients–consumers as the key endpoints.

New SOS and information-centric methods must evolve. The set of external systems and the cross ecosystem has to be an early focus of the next wave of transformation. Figure 3.2 shows the very high level integration method that needs to be used to overcome the many difficulties now faced. A brief discussion of service-block diagrams, information-centric needs analysis, the use of integration maps, and the integration points are provided. The results of this integration planning and use of common integration design patterns can be an agile and evolving integration approach.

Interim Step 1 will contain interim architecture points that use both HIEs and DIRECT and CONNECT with bridging agents.

Interim Step 2 will include defining a Personal Data Cloud and human service capabilities as linked services.

Interim Step 3 will have a network of data and information sources that will use the new information-centric networks that are being piloted and standardized.

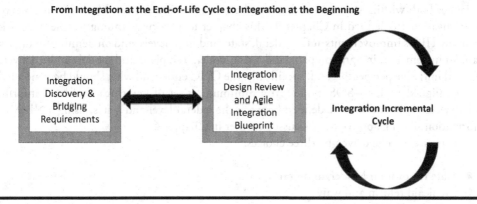

Figure 3.2   Simple integration model.

All interim architecture will introduce both value and risks. Risk must be managed and reduced with open reviews and transparency. Risks can be reduced, and a visible approach to delivering capabilities and evolving the system can be part of quarterly and annual delivery cycles. A simplified version of the defense and intelligence community SOS incremental commitment approach is proposed. This version includes a virtual chained set of models, patterns, and shared services that are evolving in use in complex defense and intelligence applications, but have not been used in healthcare. The existing applications are resulting in better and better stovepipes. The next generation of integrated HHSs and integrated information can use a modified (simplified) version that can be managed at the federal, state, and community levels. The question is who provides the middle of the chain? There are two alternatives in states with an existing HIE that can provide the infrastructure backbone. Others can use Medicaid or an adaptable-evolution layer using direct-connections that can be created with shared services.

3.1 Introduction

Many organizations have begun Wave 1 with limited planning and architecture. Initially, there was a push to automate, to install an EHR system, and to become more competitive. Wave 1 for Medicaid used a function-business services approach, and faced implementation involving an advanced planning document and an incremental evolutionary approach based on MITA. More than 10 years ago, one of the major problems was the inconsistency of planning and funding approval; even the concepts and terminology were different from one state to the next. It was said that if you knew one Medicaid system, you knew one Medicaid system. MITA, and the basic concepts that it embodied, was an early business-driven service-oriented architecture that created new common terminology, common planning, and a basic set of business services that could be adapted and extended. It did not have an approach on how to integrate and deliver the complete service needs of the patient and the family. However, there were a series of attempts to reach out to other federal government agencies, such as ACF, and there was actually a similar MITA-like model created with the Substance Abuse and Mental Health Agency (SAMSHA).

Now a number of states are either using State Innovation modeling grants or Medicaid waivers to address the reform initiatives. The reform and innovation studies have identified many initiatives both within Medicaid and across the states that are critical. More details observed on the innovation are defined in Chapter 9. This chapter focuses on planning for the integration of the many HHSs improvements at the federal, state, and local levels, and on defining an integration plan, an incremental integration plan, and a risk model. The plans and model can be delivered by a federal initiative perspective and, specifically, the ONC effort and what should become a federal-partner aligned HHSs—SOS model. At a minimum, a set of key threads of both information and services chains need to be defined between the federal level and states, using a NIEM-based information sharing approach—discussed further in Chapter 4.

Integration can be driven by three choices:

■ State Innovation Models and grants
■ Medicaid reform and waivers
■ Policy–politicians–patients and providers set of improvement recommendations that can be integrated together

3.1.1 State Innovation Models

There are 11 states that have received grants from the CMMI. Some of the aspects of improvement that these states are addressing include:

■ Clinical coordination of care across provider facilities
■ Behavioral health and primary care integration
■ Practice transformation
■ New payer models
■ New insurance oversight and transparency
■ Clinical quality measures and improved outcomes
■ Opioid and substance abuse
■ Outreach to high risk populations and underserved areas

3.1.2 Medicaid Reform Including IT Updates

A number of expansion and non-expansion steps have looked at both integrating the Medicaid population with a more integrated set of HHSs, and also at establishing medical homes, value-based purchasing, and other alternative payment approaches, and at modernizing their old legacy IT systems.

Wave 1 Medicaid started with a limited strategy, but with a push by all states to automate and refresh their systems with a sizable federal investment. The vendor community had been performing the same steps and had failures, and a new services perspective was introduced. Commonality was discovered with the ideas of adaptability with business process models, rules, choice selection tables, and the ability of states to extend and innovate. A group of consultants conferred, and a process was adopted to MITA-size the products; one new vendor came forward with innovative approaches. The mini-Medicaid industry saw a push to automate also reflected in a large set of mergers and acquisitions. The industry is now at a new tipping point where a refresh is desperately needed.

Today, Medicaid is expanding and being integrated with mental health and opioid dependencies, and with the dual-eligible population. Medicaid has to fit with the new vision of ACOs and medical homes, and has to use population health and SOS thinking.

The landscape for medical services is growing with all the hospitals, facilities, and even physician practices coming online; some of these organizations have individual patient's EHRs that are spread across facilities. This chapter provides an approach to integrate these many diverse elements into logical SOS that can evolve together by following a time-phased set of integration maps. While there may be a national integration map that is maintained by ONC–CMS, the integration map for the region–state–local area and individual organizations can include the interoperability features, the services capabilities, the focus of knowledge, and the patients-population supported by each network.

Value is achieved by strategically networking in a systematic incremental manner. The linking of SOS needs a set of high-level systems analysis methodology that defines the pathways between systems, their connection to users, their context for usage, the detailed description of functions performed, and the information that is passed from system to system. The steps that a function should perform can trigger a services call through a system-to-system defined interface, and be monitored based on behaviors, including constraints based on risk and safety factors. For example, a common risk is a broken connection. Some of the linkages are extremely critical, and a detailed model of the underlying integration and interoperability information need to be defined in a very formal manner with agreements between all organizations involved. There are common interface and integration patterns that can be shared, and a common approach to handling exceptions and problem conditions can be defined in a high reliability platform. A common high reliability integration and interoperability platform can be built as a shared service, and can support those states that do not have existing integration messaging capabilities. Many states or regions of the country have not created their own HIE, but with the added capabilities of a value-delivery network approach, can connect to all the systems that fit with an ACO or medical home or the disease management networks.

3.1.3 Ad Hoc Changes on Annual Basis

Every governor and many legislatures seem to take on an annual quest to find the silver bullet to how Medicaid can be eliminated. The set of improvements and recommendations need to be put into a Medicaid Waiver, a Medicaid Advanced Planning Agreement, or a State Innovation grant, or submitted as a one-off recommendation. There are many common issues from the states, and there is a desire from the federal level to create shared services that can be used by multiple states. But integration is still needed.

All states need to have basic integration–interoperability capability. This can be accomplished by Medicaid systems (17 are proposing new capability) or by creating shared cloud-based logical channels that can be shared by all. A set of clearly defined standards and a planning-architecture approach are needed along with a transparent Roadmap to show the integration–interoperability progress across all counties and states in the country. In addition, it is essential that the SOS have the ability to handle a range of diseases to get to the best care and the best evidence and experience, wherever the patient resides.

Where is Medicaid now? Stuck between two worlds and needing a new direction!

Medicaid is at a tipping point where the Wave 1 MITA has to be refreshed, and a new patient-population and SOS approach creates a new planning, architecture, and governance process leading the way to an open shared services environment. There have been hints of that need voiced at the MESC in 2013 and 2014, by discussions at the National Medicaid EDI Health Work Group, and at the National Medicaid Directors' conference. The author has had discussions with CMS personnel about the waves of change and where Medicaid fit into those waves. *A refreshing is needed now!*

The name of MITA can change, but a refresh process is needed to create a new baseline framework that can foster state innovations.

The refresh process should follow the steps below:

1. Agree that it is time to change. Create a change manifesto and change working group charter.
2. Analyze the current planning and architecture: list the problems with the current planning, architecture, and governance.
3. Define new concepts that need to be employed—integration, interoperability, analytics, population health, new services concepts, such as Medicaid ACOs, medical homes, mental health and substance abuse integrated care, etc. Create a series of concept white papers and briefings.
4. Define the Next Generation of MITA, using SOS representation.
5. Define integration–interoperability and related analytics platforms with an open service platform architecture and set of open APIs as bridges between HHSs and from federal to states.
6. Define the data access models and services: health and human services data artifacts and data integration services model with the UCORE of common data elements.
7. Create a shared services state baseline plan that fosters the use of open service elements.
8. Refresh and replace all MITA documents.
9. Create and use a new governance process.
10. Build a Medicaid repository and Medicaid integration and test environment.

Time frame: Create a Medicaid "Need to Change" announcement and integration–interoperability policy statement, and begin an accelerated Wave 2 MITA—August 2016 with results by August 2017.

Connecting patients, doctors, specialists, and the experts consulted in special cases can be a complex ever-changing activity, or it can be well defined. One approach that has been advocated and used successfully in other industries has been to define an enterprise architecture. But the first questions are

■ What are the boundaries of the enterprise?
■ Who are the customers and communities that are being served?

The Medicaid Enterprise Conference initially discussed a very confined MMIS, and did not use the word "enterprise" until 2006. Over the last few years, the Medicaid Enterprise Conference has taken on broader health, enrollment, and eligibility data needs, and, in MESC 2014, addressed more of the broader physical health and mental health needs. Some states are looking more at the broad needs of the citizens. (Cindy Mann presentation at 2014 and National Association of Medicaid Directors (NAMD) 2013.) Medicaid can be used as the umbrella to address many of the broad HHSs needs in a more holistic way. Good health is about more than just visiting a doctor's office; it is about wellness, that is, eating well and exercising regularly, and avoiding toxins and smoking, obesity, and drugs and alcohol.

This chapter looks at some of the enterprise architecture efforts that have been defined at conferences like HIMSS and HL7/OMG, and the limitations that those approaches have. An SOS cross-ecosystem approach is proposed and described as one of the next steps needed in planning for Wave 2. The Medicaid systems and other related systems can be put into an SOS architecture:

■ Using a government-to-community SOS approach that goes beyond the 2004–2006 enterprise architecture used by the author in defining MITA.

- Using the models from the INCOSE SOS for healthcare, but it is critical to understand the key behavior threads. Additional value-delivery models will be needed.
- Identifying the healthcare organizations that must be aligned and the combined value proposition that must be defined.
- Updating the current architecture elements to define an SOS approach that can create a government-to-community partnership with a new generation of MITA and by alignment with a new FHA and alignment of MITA with State HHSs, SAMSHA, CMS, and HHS EA (enterprise architecture). Healthcare and the complex systems must use a new approach. As one of the creators of the old EA approach, the author believes that the approach and the reference models need to be changed.
- Some providers have started: HIMSS conferences…Intermountain discussions.

There are well-documented stovepipes and limited usage in some cases like Healthcare.gov. The next generation of healthcare systems must take an SOS value-delivery approach that builds upon the older approach, but also integrates planning and architecture with an integration plan and value-driven governance approach that fosters the use of shared services.

3.2 Challenges, Controversies, and Issues

Every siloed health, mental health, and human service organization has created its own set of case workers who solved problems with their own set of services. A broader set of services needs to be defined and aligned at the federal, state, and local levels. This approach can give many more "one-stop" services, and ensure that the bundled services are complementary and complete. This broader set of services can be used both for public series and for new forms of accountable care and service organizations.

The new ecosystem that is created by connecting the SOS together will need a consistent set of cross-cutting pathways, and the value of the connection has to be defined. In addition, those creating the SOS must illustrate a clear benefit to patients and ease of use for providers. Gaining the stakeholders cooperation will require payment incentives like monthly coordination payments and medical home payments (Figure 3.3).

3.2.1 Integration Challenges

New EHR systems need to address interoperability; however, the focus has been within provider networks and within states, but not across provider network and state boundaries. Also, the focus has been on provider-to-provider with some excluded, such as nursing homes and mental hospitals. The limited consumer focus wants the consumer to sign into each provider's portal, and discovering new specialists, receiving feedback, collecting information in a personal information model, and activating services are not integrated. Patient–consumer focused integration is not addressed. But the patient–consumer is where the information, services, and changes in behavior are needed.

Many of the Medicaid systems still have the 1980s development approach, and it has been a challenge during the last 10 years to change that. There are two varieties of system, either fee-for-services or managed care, and none address the new types of ACOs, new forms of value-based purchasing, alternative payment models, and the need to integrate the mental health, medical homes, coordination of care, and the linkages to human services needs of the high risk and underserved Medicaid populations.

Integration of Information and Services from a Patient/Consumer's Perspective: Integration Points

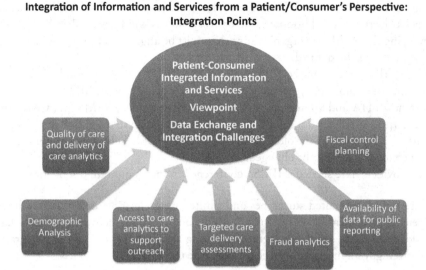

Figure 3.3 Shifting to patient-centric integrated series of services presents many challenges.

A significant amount of money is spent each year on Medicaid systems, but the following negative properties still persist:

■ Often Medicaid systems are not following a shared services approach
■ Often shared services are not effectively used
■ The cost model for shared services, the reuse and cost of integration, and need for common cross-information channels are not defined
■ Interoperability is treated at the message level, and not the business-stakeholder level
■ Shared services and common integration patterns are needed
■ Focus on delivering services to the patient–consumer with integrated information and services, especially for the disabled, those with chronic conditions, those with rare and progressive diseases that require extensive care management, and frail dual-eligible population

Time frame: SIM and Medicaid reform must be worked together and recognized as the key backbone to healthcare, human services integration, and an adaptable-exploratory interoperability layer that can be self-managed by communities of interest. This will eventually require federal programs to align but much can be done by state innovation and reform initiatives. A federal and state set of HHSs interfaces and shared services can be defined with CMS, Medicaid, SAMSHA, ACF, Food Stamps, NASCIO, and other human services to be integrated. A service catalog and set of integration patterns and common integration points can be defined. Each of the state innovations and Medicaid reforms can contribute shared services capabilities. These services may not support the complete needs of other agencies and states, but the reuse can be valuable for all. Some types of integration can include the integration of HHSs into one portal. This one portal would link to health, mental health, substance abuse, and other human services with an integrated delivery set of services that have chained SOS service capabilities—2017.

3.2.2 Controversies

Healthcare IT, and Medicaid in particular, seem to be controversial topics. Finding common ground needs to be addressed in a year between elections, like 2015–2016. But politics has not recognized the positives that are happening in many states, and getting press coverage on anything that is successful is critical. Positive stories, such as those from Delaware improvements—presented by Health Secretary Rita Landgraf as "Stories from the Ground" in Appendix F—illustrate the type of success that needs to be shared.

Healthcare and human services integration is complex and does not lend itself well to political sound bytes and take time and commitment. Governors and political leaders have been very effective in presenting the case and working the issues, but that requires a simple combining of the integration Roadmap, the resource-cost model, the value-achievement-success stories, and extensive collaboration. Some state innovation and Medicaid reforms prove that it can be achieved. But the information has to be simplified, explained, and packaged so that it can be used for a range of political alternatives and innovation can be fostered.

Some of the issues that could be addressed by a bi-partisan task force include:

- Politics and the schedule pressure and belief that innovation can win over planning
- Lack of large-scale experience and initial budget pressure
- Short cuts
- Blame versus work to make the SOS operational
- States that lead and those that won't take responsibility
- Medicaid decision by states: innovation, but with political issues

Time frame: Secretary of HHS creates a bi-partisan task force: to find the Medicaid reform strategic directions; to combine a set of state innovation best practices; and to define the common ground of alignment among federal, state, and community initiatives. Report— September 2017.

3.2.3 Issues

A number of issues must be addressed in improving MITA and in advanced planning and program management. A consistent federal–state–regional Roadmap must be provided that includes:

- Assignment of person/entity responsible for the project and the integration points
- Creation of an integration master plan, integration process, integration templates, and governance with risk modeling
- Definition of integration model with both simple block diagrams and use of integration patterns, shared services, and emerging SOS standards and reference models
- Addressing of the lack of large integration experience among consultants
- Addressing of the lack of good methodologies for the new era of digital health and human services integrated transformation

Time frame: State innovation and Medicaid reform issue report should be presented to the secretary of HHS and integration of health and human services government oversight committee—Summer 2017.

3.3 Solutions and Recommendations

This section provides draft recommendations that can be used by the CMS Medicaid state program office and the associated advisory committees as a starting point for discussion.

Integration can start from many places but the key is to shift the focus to the patient and consumer. One method is to create a set of patient–consumer focused scenarios and to use a simple SOS block diagram approach with some areas using a more formal Unified Modeling Language (UML)-based Systems Modeling Language (SysML) representation. A series of simple block diagrams (such as Figure 3.4) can be created and used by many. Over the next few years, the defense SOS initiatives will mature along with SEI and OMG standards, and more formal models can be developed. But for now a simple set of graphics, with some additional notes and markings along with simple integration templates, can be used.

3.3.1 Process Step for Integration and Interoperability Shared Services

The complexity of HHSs has not been recognized and an integrated viewpoint does not appear to be identified. The top of Figure 3.5 shows the legislative and policy makers' triggering of actions and changes without any integration planning. The siloed health or human services systems often remain fragmented, or another system is created, or integration costs or last minute gaps are identified, and overruns result. This could reflect the immaturity of the HHSs "market," but could also reflect the over-simplification of legislation that does not look at the range of differences in needs and the lack of consensus on what needs to be done and how it can be done.

The legislature makes recommendations and often even defines implementation with dates and defined goals, but in some cases, with solutions that cannot be implemented. Those recommendations are then turned over to a government organization and often supported by a working group of

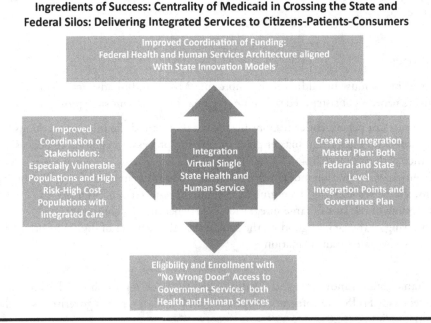

Ingredients of Success: Centrality of Medicaid in Crossing the State and Federal Silos: Delivering Integrated Services to Citizens-Patients-Consumers

Improved Coordination of Funding: Federal Health and Human Services Architecture aligned With State Innovation Models

Improved Coordination of Stakeholders: Especially Vulnerable Populations and High Risk-High Cost Populations with Integrated Care

Integration Virtual Single State Health and Human Service

Create an Integration Master Plan: Both Federal and State Level Integration Points and Governance Plan

Eligibility and Enrollment with "No Wrong Door" Access to Government Services both Health and Human Services

Figure 3.4 Patient–consumer to provider: service-block diagram and integration points.

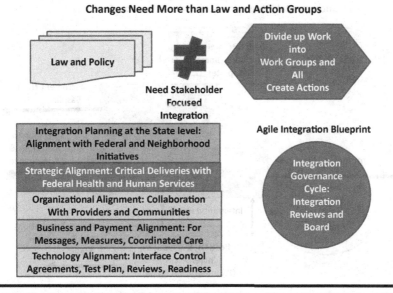

Figure 3.5   Federal laws for both health care and human services reflect new policies, but do not provide stakeholder integration.

experts. A development contract is then given to the lowest bidder with no integration plan. Then, we watch as the government agency or contractor testifies on what went wrong. There is insufficient planning in the new legislation on ways that the new policies fit with the existing or evolving industry packages, such as the EHR. In addition, there is limited feedback on the feasibility of how the pieces fit together and whether integration is possible. As legislation is being composed, a preliminary integration plan can be developed and a set of concern areas, integration risks, and assumptions can be defined. An honest dialog could ensue on the risks and benefits, and alignment with the key partners can be pursued. An agile integration blueprint can be created that shows the federal, state, and other stakeholders, and, most importantly, the patient–consumer usage, features, and benefits.

This type of agile integration blueprint as shown at the bottom of Figure 3.5 can foster a set of alignment steps, and create multi-year, annual, or quarterly alignment maps with a set of integration baselines. The integration baseline and focus on both the high assurance level and the rapid change level focus on an approach where integration is a key enabler and concern area. Key aspects include:

Tests of integration points and concerns:

■ These early integration verification and validation steps can provide early successes or identify risks that can be resolved prior to critical dates. All requirements are not equal, and by identifying the risks early, the most critical elements can be addressed.
■ The step of iterative integration baselining and governance steps is shown in Figure 3.6.
■ High assurance capability should use READY technology that is proven and ready.
■ Rapid change level should have features that the end users can change and tailor to their needs without long wait times until subsequent releases.
■ Developers believe that they can solve any problem, but the solution may come with incredible personal cost, with contractor cost overruns, or with excessive delays. Risk must be visible, and not seen as "evil" or a "personal or corporate failure," but as something to be expected and worked through.
■ A transparent risk process is shown in Figure 3.7.

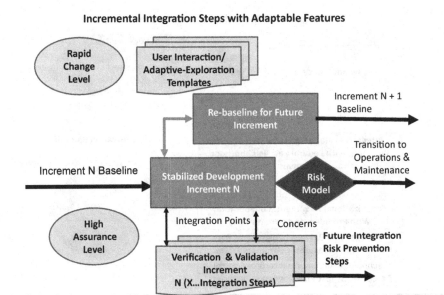

Figure 3.6 Multiple integration baseline for high assurance and rapid change fitting together.

3.3.2 Integration Mapping

Each state (as of August 2014, 18 states had proposed interoperability projects) should go through a shared services analysis that will define a set of processes, build a set of artifacts that can be shared between states, create an open service repository, and foster reuse (Figure 3.8).

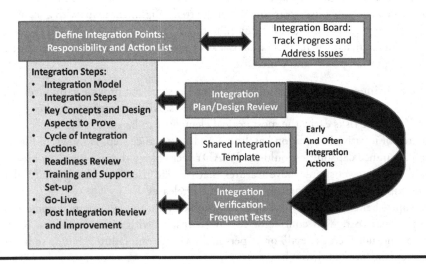

Figure 3.7 Each integration point introduces risk and addresses one or more concerns.

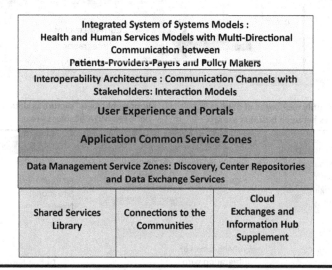

Figure 3.8   Reference model to define and categorize shared services and APIs.

3.3.3 Breaking the Silos with a Keystone Interoperability and Integration Platform

One of the initial intents of MITA was to address interoperability and integration issues. A clear concept of these issues must be drafted that can present the business value of interoperability to governors, legislators, policy makers, and public advocates interested in the Medicaid population (Figure 3.9).

Time frame: Release of data briefing on new shared services for integration, adaption, and information exploration based on experience from initial state innovations and Medicaid reform, and convergence of new reference model.
Present to CMS state innovation and Medicaid policy makers—Summer 2016.

3.3.4 Define a Reference Model for Key Threads and Services Needed

Interoperability for Medicaid can be defined with an interoperability reference model, a set of standards used, and a clear identification of any gaps. Medicaid industry groups can define such an approach by August 2016 (Figure 3.10).

Time frame: A MITA integration–interoperability–analytics reference model extension can be developed and reviewed—present at the Medicaid Enterprise Conference August 2016.

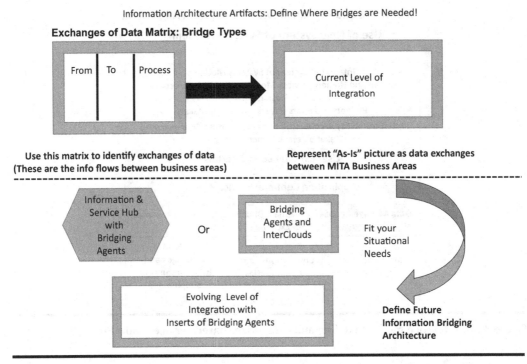

Figure 3.9 **Conceptual thinking about the strategic goals for the integration and interoperability platform.**

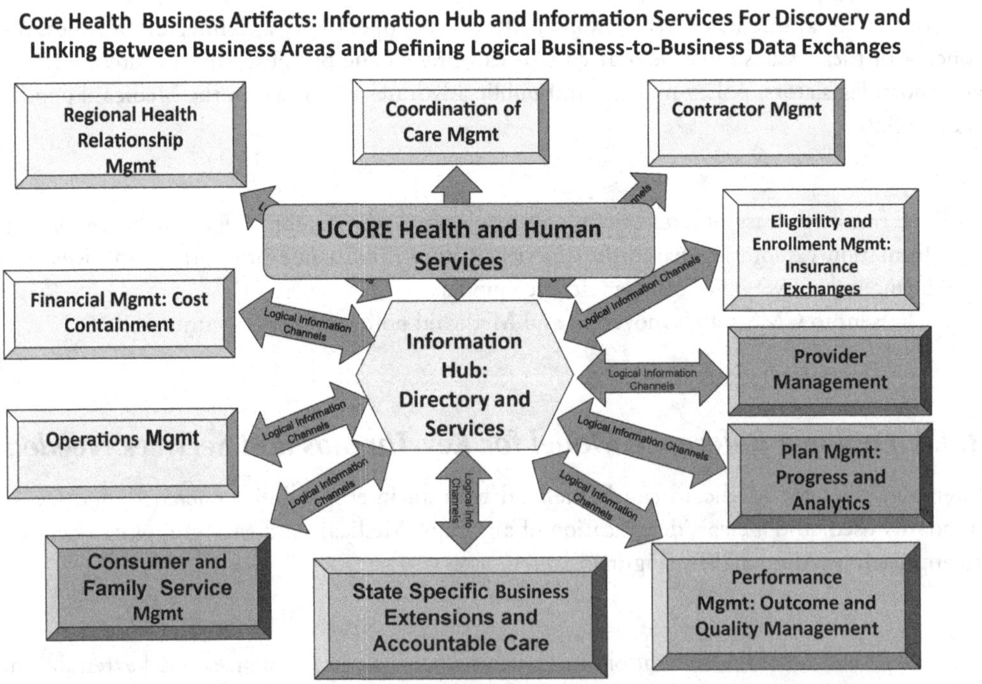

Core Health Business Artifacts: Information Hub and Information Services For Discovery and Linking Between Business Areas and Defining Logical Business-to-Business Data Exchanges

Figure 3.10 Defining interoperability reference model that can extend MITA.

3.3.5 Define the Data–Information Subject Areas

The specific application of the Medicaid system to other systems, like eligibility and enrollment, and the connection to related human services will need to be addressed so that shared services can be consistent. A common core and business area data–information model can use an approach such as that shown in Figure 3.11.

MITA needs an integration and interoperability shared services project. The project can follow the UCORE and data services used by information sharing as shown in Figure 3.11. It can also provide a cloud-based set of logical channels supporting the other Medicaid states that want to use a common platform, but that do not have the leadership to address this key issue. Solving the issue once, and letting all states adapt and extend it to their individual needs, makes a lot of sense. It would also ensure interstate communication, and ensure that all states and counties could access the integration and interoperability platform. An architecture and cost tradeoff study for these two alternatives should be investigated during the spring of 2016.

The following steps should be included:

1. Define the UCORE of identity information for patients, services, and locations
2. Define an information hub and a set of directory and translation services
3. Create a set of integration and interoperability scenarios
4. Allocate shared services development to one state, and have a peer review state that will work on compliance and will be the first outside user
5. Present the results and readiness user to a large group of states
6. Create version and change control
7. Conduct a quarterly update plan for all basic services
8. Provide ability to adapt and extend the shared services with more capabilities and more advanced optional capabilities

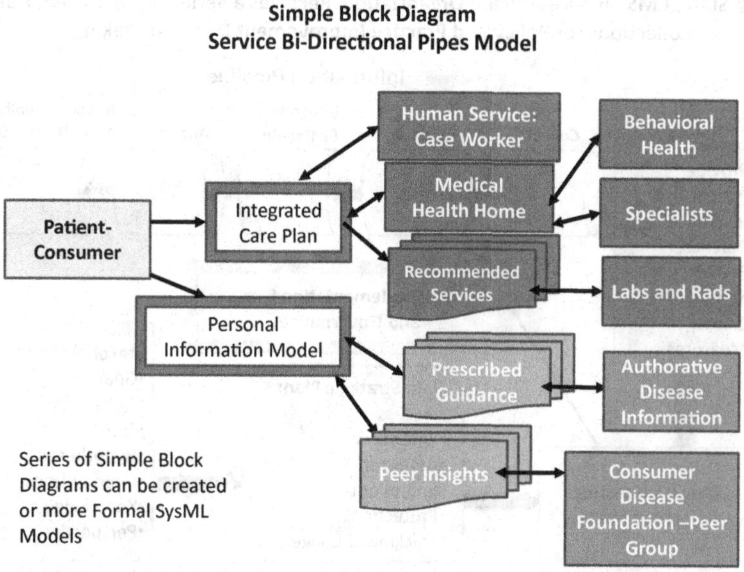

Figure 3.11   Defining a set of universal identifiers that cross pipelines of information and service areas.

9. Define and publish logical channels and interfaces to be included in an open service repository
10. Include a data pipeline model to show how data and reports are shipped to CMS or other research partners as shown below
11. Create a complete reference model diagram such as shown below
12. Define services and capability models
13. Integrate a master Roadmap and negotiation process (Figure 3.12)

One of the next key steps is to take the existing approaches like MITA (which the author defined about 10 years ago), and change it to a patient–consumer driven approach with new types of provider services, new cross-channels of communication, and new business models. A conceptual view of this new shift is shown in Figure 3.13 with a set of defined "channels" as patterns for the many services, and for necessary information, payment, and care integration.

For many years, each state has built its own capabilities. Medicaid has been living with the myth that each state is so different. While there are differences between states, there are many commonalities that can be leveraged to manage costs more efficiently. These types of changes may be allowed to follow a waiver process not requiring legislation. However, to provide the same options across the country, legislation may be necessary to get value-based purchasing and bundled payment to be offered across all states. The states are showing that they have many innovative ideas, but they all need to address integration and interoperability. Now is the time to address this in a consistent manner.

Time frame: Create an update for MITA for integration, interoperability, and shared services—January 2017.

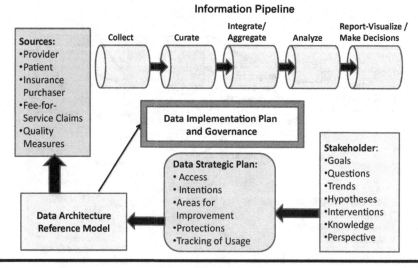

Each State, CMS, and Healthcare Organization Receives a Series of Healthcare Data Collections for Policy and Practice Improvement Decision Making

Information Pipeline

Figure 3.12 Defining state-to-health organization information pipelines and related data strategy, implementation, and governance activities.

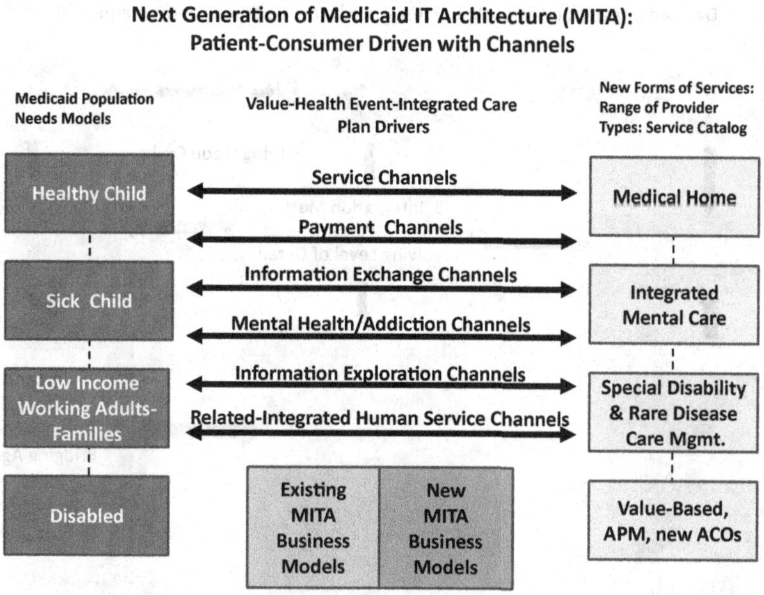

Next Generation of Medicaid IT Architecture (MITA):
Patient-Consumer Driven with Channels

Medicaid Population Needs Models	Value-Health Event-Integrated Care Plan Drivers	New Forms of Services: Range of Provider Types: Service Catalog
Healthy Child	Service Channels ⟷ / Payment Channels ⟷	Medical Home
Sick Child	Information Exchange Channels ⟷ / Mental Health/Addiction Channels ⟷	Integrated Mental Care
Low Income Working Adults-Families	Information Exploration Channels ⟷ / Related-Integrated Human Service Channels ⟷	Special Disability & Rare Disease Care Mgmt.
Disabled	Existing MITA Business Models / New MITA Business Models	Value-Based, APM, new ACOs

Figure 3.13   Defining a next generation of MITA reference model with each type of patient–consumer as the focus and not just functionality.

A process that begins with integration and interoperability together is needed. A more detailed representation of an integration process is shown in Figure 3.12 and it can become the start of a new process for integration by all major systems.

This process can begin with Medicaid and the state Health Information Exchanges within each state or regional areas, but it should apply to each disease type that can be a natural grouping. The patient can be referred to one or more disease groupings and his/her health records can result in ongoing cohorts of "patients like me." Achieving this goal will require the following set of common steps. Six of these steps are shown in Figure 3.10, along with a common set of solution elements (darker boxes) like those shown in Figure 3.11. This reference model shows the blending of process with solutions that can be used to move to a national–state–regional integrated and interoperable environment. It also includes a strong focus on disease-focused integration and dashboards to track progress across the country. Interoperability must be clearly visible; otherwise the result will be the slow progress seen in connecting states for public health reporting. After nearly 20 years, all states and all counties are still not connected. A phased approach is necessary, but integration and interoperability must reach all corners of the country.

The vision in Figure 3.15 will require a systematic integration approach with bridging agents that can either be stories with an information-service hub or distributed across the patient–consumer and provider-community caseworkers or within a service support cloud.

3.4 Emerging Trends

Integration and interoperability are discussed at all levels of the industry and at government meetings. Meetings may not be an effective way to achieve the commitment necessary to achieve the essential goals. The industry must reach its tipping point to clarify "coopetition." It must

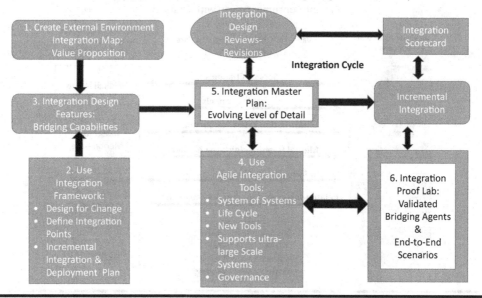

Figure 3.14   Detailed multi-step process with iterative integration cycle.

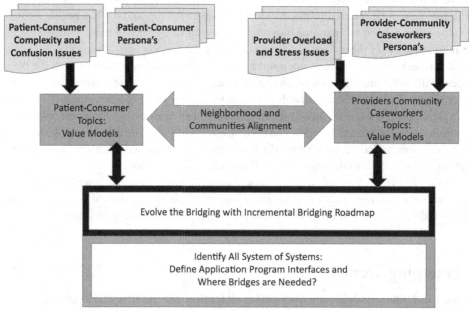

Figure 3.15   Integration planning is crucial for health IT transformation and Medicaid reform.

specifically define collaborative standards and a set of competition factors, such as usability and analytics. The next year can bring that tipping point and can affect the necessary industry changes with an annual cycle of interoperability reports required by Congress as part of the 2016 "Cromnibus" appropriation board.

Some of the key items that must be addressed annually, especially over the next 12–16 months, include:

1. Work with the FHA to expand its capability to be a HHSs architecture, going beyond the federal level to reflect government, define shared services, take a patient–consumer focused point of view, and align with state innovation on new reform, payment, and coordinated care concepts for a new generation of Medicaid and MITA
2. Create an SOS methodology tailored to HHSs integration and use that methodology for Medicare, Medicaid, and MITA
3. Define an integration risk scorecard and a set of integration verification and validation measures, integration patterns and shared services, and integration planning and governance tools
4. Establish basic measures for national, state, and community (e.g., each hospital referral region) and county (or neighborhood)
5. Create an integration mapping process based on disease types, and define a set of logical channels and communities of interest that are focused on patients–providers who are aligned together
6. Establish a MITA integration–interoperability reference model with a set of shared services (tradeoff study in spring 2017)
7. Use a number of API appliances, such as those of IO-informatics, IBM DataPower, Layer 7, with one cross silo, linked to many systems, such as the mental health to Medicaid medical home scenario. Adapt the Argonaut API in summer 2016
8. Also consider how coordination of care can help the Medicaid population with special focus on disabilities and behavioral health integration (Figure 3.16). An integration approach that can be used for Medicaid, State Innovations or any regional, neighborhood or community approach is shown in (Figure 3.16). A set of bi-directional interactions between patient–consumer and provide-community caseworkers can focus on data, service and community integration and a incremental integration planning process.

Time frame: Define high value use cases—June 2016. Review at NAMD—October 2016. Create focus groups on key business cases to be added—2017–2020. Define virtual HIEs with a set of software defined networks in clouds with a set of policy-based attribute access management features.

3.5 Conclusion

3.5.1 A Next Generation of Medicaid and MITA Need an Integration Approach

A new approach is needed to Medicaid and MITA. The approach can address interoperability first, but it must go beyond that. A new approach can have as its primary mission to provide the

Evolving to Meet Immediate and Long Term Needs: Subject Area and
Bridge-Data-Service Integration Roadmap

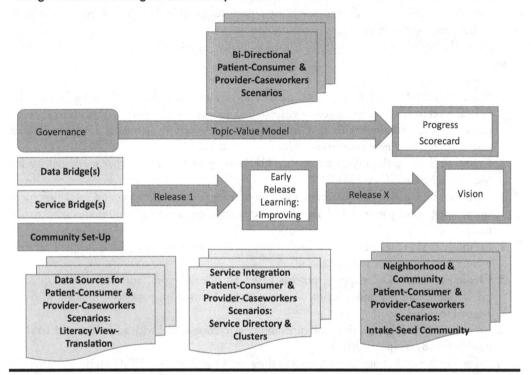

Figure 3.16 Using integrated end-to-end scenarios and focus on bridging between data, services and communities.

framework for commonality and spur state innovation. Wave 2 MITA and related elements can be the catalyst for Medicaid reforms. Over the next year and a half, a Wave 2 MITA can become a reality. More details on the integration, interoperability, and analytics approaches are described in the next few chapters, and fundamentally improving state Medicaid systems can be key to rejuvenating other state and community systems.

3.6 The Practical Stuff

There are many practical steps that can be applied to solving each interface with its unique approach to using common integration and interoperability patterns:

- Create a series of new concept white papers
- Create a working group and respark the innovation of the community
- Conduct an SOS Medicaid analysis
- Define a core set of interoperability capabilities, but encourage states to make extensions by adding new capabilities that fit the organization's state or enterprise needs as long as they support the adaptation models (such as rules or parameter controls)

- Create a set of mental health, Medicaid, and other services with a service metadata and chain of linked services that are stored in the repository
- Create a business process model that can be a basic "coordination model"
- Show that the technologies exist, and note that the main issues are funding and working together
- Show how an SOS has worked in criminal justice across federal and state boundaries and environment systems
- Establish basic shared services; turn conferences into workshops; create "shared services" hackathons; and create an open services governance and test environment that is shared by *all*

Time frame: Create NEXT WAVE State Innovation and Medicaid panels, and encourage states and contractors to recommend and share integration and interoperability best practices at each MESC annually and at the NAMD. Summarize the "best practices" and candidates for shared services. The State Innovation Models and the Medicaid reform activities and other CMMI successes have to be packaged, and the good news on how the improvements have affected the lives of Americans has to be sent as "stories from the ground." Statistical improvements also need to be shown.

A FACA-like Board and set of committees can be established similar to those used by ONC. Start in 2016.

Chapter 4

From Host-Centric to Patient–Consumer-Information-Centric Interoperability Enabling New Care Coordination and Analytics Building Blocks

---

Abstract

The functional building blocks of EHRs now exist in most hospitals and providers' offices. Some states have connected the many·host systems from the healthcare organizations together and used HIEs as their interoperability solutions. Some states like New York and groups of states like New England and Maryland–Delaware–DC have their host-centric HIE models using a common shared approach. This message-to-host and back interoperability is very focused on providers, hospitals, labs, pharmacies, and radiology facilities, each connecting to and through the state-based innovation hub. They are dependent on each state following through and getting onboard. Even if money has been provided, this is difficult. But with cloud technology and the emerging information-centric networking approaches, an alternative interoperability approach can be defined. The EHR systems will still have to support host-to-host-centric approaches and evolve to a patient–consumer-information-centric interoperability architecture, leveraging new standards.

However, these EHR systems now need to fit with the unfulfilled promise of HIEs. This chapter summarizes the state of the current Wave 1 technology, and then presents "draft" ideas for new patient–consumer-information-centric enabling technologies that will leverage a set of new standards from Internet Engineering Task Force (IETF) and a series of interim patient-consumer-information-centric solution architectures, patient–centric-information-centric APIs (see definition box), and an integration set of design models and library of shared services.

Background: Interoperability Perspectives

In the very early days of EHR, a number of regional HIEs were started as pilot programs in California, Arizona, New England, and in the Indianapolis area. There was only a limited penetration of EHR, and the health reform movement was not moving very rapidly.

While some of these exchanges had enough support from the local region or group of states, some of them were not sustainable. But much about the technology of that early experience has influenced the standards effort.

HIEs: State Based

As part of the HITECH Act, other states sponsored exchanges, and their initial focus was to integrate all hospitals together.

States have received early grants and have connected major hosts together.

State	Year Started	Current Status	Next Steps
Delaware	Delaware Health Information Network (DHIN)	Operational in all hospitals	Evolving to patient–consumer portals and focus on inequities
Maryland	Chesapeake Resource Information Support Program (CRISP)	Operational in all hospitals	Strong focus on nursing homes and home health care capabilities
New York	State Health Information Network Environment (SHINE)	Completely covered with a series of regional networks	Key to Medicaid reform with Medicaid medical home and behavior integration
Other states			

These efforts were started at the right time and now have a cooperative customer base, but have all had a limited or invisible effect on the patient–consumer, and will need to research new approaches in the future such as Intercloud Standards.

Direct-Connect Interoperability: Very Basic with Plans for the Future

In 2010, ONC proposed an alternative approach to connect the doctors and hospitals directly together with DIRECT-CONNECT. As an intermediate standard, this approach will have other search, discovery, and favorites, and other capabilities. This could be part of the solution for the small practice or rural office or within a state that does not have an integrated health information initiative.

Build into Procurements: Defense and Veterans Administration and Congressional-ONC Oversight

There are a number of interoperability forcing factors coming from government programs such as Defense Health Service Management. This system is estimated to be worth over $18B over the next 10 years as all the military systems upgrade to the Cerner systems under the contract with

Leidos and Accenture as the lead integrators. IBM bid EPIC, and Computer Sciences Corporation (CSC) with Hewlett-Packard (HP) bid the Allscript tools. An important key was not only interoperability, but also strong knowledge of the existing Altha-based legacy system.

One of the strongest roadblocks to interoperability has been the EHR vendors who divided into two camps: vendors with large market shares that wanted interoperability among their hospitals, enjoyed "vendor-lock-in," and used lack of standards as an excuse to not investing; and vendors with large procurements like the defense hospital systems who have been forced to address interoperability, including the veterans' hospitals. But maybe the key was the interoperability reporting required by Congress and ONC that requires ONC to report blocking, and to describe the industry response to the need for interoperability demands. Early signs show that vendors are now playing "well" with each other, and determining where they can compete and where they must cooperate. The industry may come to a "coopetition strategy" where the foundation can be shared by all, and the new value-adding features can be added by each vendor.

Require Electronic Health Vendors to Offer Interoperability

But the pressure is mounting for interoperability. The Congress is holding hearings on the enablers and barriers to interoperability. ONC is defining a 10-year interoperability Roadmap and standards profile, and reporting to congress on the vendors' interoperability capabilities and identifying those that are not supporting health interoperability.

These approaches must overcome barriers, and create and extend motivators that are part of the CMS incentives (Meaningful Use 2 and 3 (see definition box)). The solution architecture elements must include features that moderate stakeholder resistance to using these integrated–interoperable environments for the key building blocks. It is possible that the concept of HIEs came too soon before EHRs and other systems were put in place, and before the shift from the "fee for service" mindset to "coordination" and "medical home" concepts with new payment approaches. But HIEs may not have the design aspects, adaptability, and extensibility that is necessary to allow the broad range of changes to be compatible without falling into the "one-size fits all" trap. An incremental roadmap of suggested actions is included throughout this chapter:

- Patient sign-on portals allow patients to see their results and receive e-mail or cell phone notification
- None of these provide the necessary interactive user experience and the information–data-centric exploration and connection across multiple providers and mobile access

Key Concepts for a Patient–Consumer-Information-Centric Approach
Definitions:
Meaningful Use is a term that describes a set of criteria for the use of EHR systems by which healthcare providers can improve patient care. The initial meaningful use criteria involved the installation of an EHR system in a Medicare or Medicaid provider office and the use of that system in a "meaningful" way, such as with electronic prescriptions. This is called Meaningful Use 1 and is effective through 2016. Meaningful Use 2 began in 2015 and will be in effect until 2019 with more focus on interoperability, and will work across hospitals and provider networks. See the Appendix for more details.

Patient–Consumer-Information-Centric
Application Programming Interface:
An *application programming interface (API)* is a set of routines, protocols, and tools for building software applications. An API expresses a software component in terms of its operations, inputs, outputs, and underlying types. An API defines functionalities that are independent of their respective implementations, which allows definitions and implementations to vary without compromising each other. A good API makes it easier to develop a program by providing all the building blocks. A programmer then puts the blocks together. See the Appendix for more details.
Shared services describes the provision of a service by one part of an organization or group where that service had previously been found in more than one part of the organization or group. Thus, the funding and resourcing of the service is shared and the providing department effectively becomes an internal service provider. The key here is the idea of "sharing" within an organization or group. This sharing needs to fundamentally include shared accountability of results by the unit from which the work is migrated to the provider. The provider on the other hand needs to ensure that the agreed results are delivered based on defined measures (key process indicators [KPIs], cost, quality, etc.). See the Appendix for more details.

4.1 Introduction

This chapter summarizes the key aspects of Wave 1 of Healthcare Transformation that some leaders have already experienced; others are waiting to complete Wave 1, but are asking about next steps. During Wave 1 and early Wave 2, there have been extensive innovations within hospitals, within regions, and even across a disease-social movement, like the innovations and improvements within the CF community. Now a series of strategic actions is necessary that will move to more integration, interoperability, and to a patient–consumer-information-centric approach.

This chapter addresses the following questions for individual organizations:

- Patient–consumer to provider B-directional information-centric analysis
- Emerging information-centric networking
- "What's next?" patient–consumer-information-centric interim solutions and emerging standards
- Although there are "Meaningful Use 2 and 3 standards," there are existing problems, and I'm not sure where my organization's goals fit into the system
- Are the standards and technology ready? IETF
- Is my vendor going to be a leader or a reluctant player in the more interoperable world?
- What is the government doing to help, or are they just going to confuse me?

One of the key enablers for change could be the translation of the FHA which is currently being revised and updated along with an interoperability plan. This chapter recommends that an even broader approach is needed to define a federal government HHSs architecture and an interoperability platform of shared services, including basic, intermediate, and advanced services, and related Public APIs.

4.2 Patient–Consumer to Provider B-Directional Information-Centric Analysis

An aligned Roadmap is required through which the organization and the "context-region-types of disease services they provide" are aligned in both a top-down manner with ONC and CMS providing a master schedule, and a bottom-up manner through which the individual organization provides the focused improvements that are important to that organization, that is, the shared services improvements projects (Figure 4.1).

4.3 Emerging Information-Centric Networking

The success of the Internet-host model proved that there had to be common elements such as domain naming servers and common browsers. But the solutions and add-ons to be content managed add significant complexity. Research and demonstration systems have been developed for initial patient–consumer to provider integration.

For healthcare interoperability, there must be common elements that provide the "middle-out" approach. These common elements will provide the key resources for integration and interoperability between the entities within individual communities. In some places in the United States, HIEs provide those kinds of information sharing resources. However, in other areas, there is a need to create information integration–interoperability hubs, and to support open "innovation and marketplace driven changes."

This chapter also recommends building a next generation of patient–consumer-information-centric end points and new protocols supported via Next Generation MITA. These approaches can

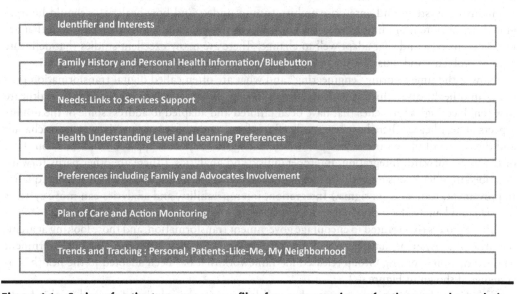

Patient-Consumer Centric Profile

- Identifier and Interests
- Family History and Personal Health Information/Bluebutton
- Needs: Links to Services Support
- Health Understanding Level and Learning Preferences
- Preferences including Family and Advocates Involvement
- Plan of Care and Action Monitoring
- Trends and Tracking : Personal, Patients-Like-Me, My Neighborhood

Figure 4.1 Series of patient–consumer profiles for user experience for the general population and for each unique population type.

be expanded to reach out to the "communities of interest" with strong focus on patient–consumer-information-centric end-to-end information architectures.

A network of such PC-I Channels with Cloud support services can be expanded, be scaled across the country with adaptability and extensibility for each state, be aligned with the community, and be population tailored. A patient–consumer-information centric "HHSs ecosystem architecture" can evolve by creating these open and standards-based shared services used across the country with Medicaid support. This HHSs ecosystem architecture would have open patient–consumer-information keystone platforms or virtual Cloud-based information exchanges that can be adapted with a flexible and evolutionary approach, and have "enough" standards, yet still foster innovation. A series of new interim solutions are described in Chapter 11.

There are a number of paths forward. However, a simple set of reference paths forward and integration-alignment points (that occur during the July 1 to September 30 time frame) can create a set of incremental "linking of the healthcare fragments" together with a drive to focused integration–interoperability with a fact-based analytics approach.

4.4 Ecosystems Tying Systems to Systems and Information-Centric Paths of Progress

Healthcare has been treated as a practice or set of processes with underlying training; but, for years the practice of medicine depended on the doctor's training, his mentor or fellowship director's style, or the variants of regional practices that are part of that medical culture. This was similar to the ways that factors were managed before industrial engineering. These practices lead to safety issues, deaths, preventable adverse events, and inconsistency illustrated by great cost differences.

Over the last 15 years, healthcare has been introduced to systems engineering, business process reengineering, and EHRs and IT, resulting in improvements. However, an overall systems approach is needed that looks at the healthcare process in the context of the "enterprise" of which it is a part, the regional ecosystem, and the related ecosystems that exist. Organizations should use the industrial systems and enterprise architecture to understand how healthcare should be integrated into a system or an SOS with the connections between and across the ecosystem that are loosely connected and that adapt well to change. There are many excellent studies that delineate current problems and illustrate the move to put in the building blocks described in Wave 1.

Now is the time to bring "engineering" and what are often called digital transformation processes into healthcare. This chapter describes the steps to introduce to medicine and healthcare new "engineering" approaches that have been tailored and adapted to address some of the unique aspects of healthcare. There have been early efforts from a number of perspectives, but this chapter and the next pull those various viewpoints into a healthcare systems approach and focus on three of the paths forward: integration, interoperability, and analytics. (There are other paths forward described in other books that will be included by reference: business process improvement, quality improvement, lean, and six sigma.) Integration, interoperability, and analytics can move systems forward and benefit the individual and organizations, and result in evolving ecosystems.

Those groups that wanted to encourage government transformation, and those looking at architectures for ecosystems, have been making some progress. In May 2014, the OASIS Government Transformation Working Group released its framework that has been adapted to the health ecosystem and shown in Figure 4.2.

This figure focuses on key aspects that will be used in the solution described in this book. In particular, this framework will provide some guiding principles for Wave 2. It will provide

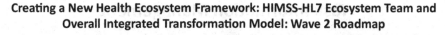

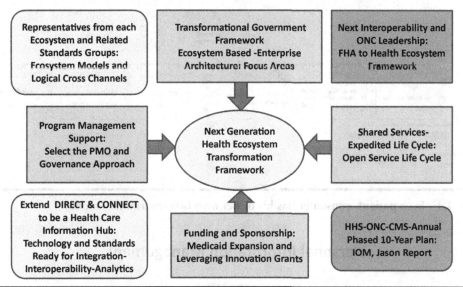

Figure 4.2   Roadmap for elements of transformation.

business management and service management concepts that align and extend the government-related enterprise architecture efforts of the FHA, CMS Enterprise Architecture, and MITA. The framework also provides concepts on governance that cross organizational boundaries with the focus on integration, interoperability, and creating an open service-based health analytics framework with the same analytical goals, measures, trends, and monitoring dashboards that will leverage the "vast" amount of government data that is now being released for public use.

There is a set of common interactive functions shown in Figure 4.3 that are right below the surface; these can provide key functions for task functions and personal information management as shown in Figures 4.4 and 4.5. These general functions can be adapted and extended to meet the personal preferences and address special needs such as those from a disability population or

Patient-Consumer-Advocates Focused Interaction Management

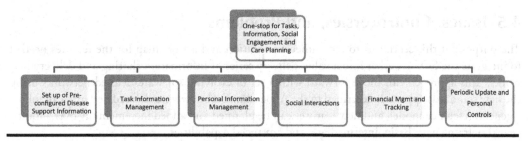

Figure 4.3   Family of user experience interaction models for the patient–consumer that can be reused, adapted and extended for a range of population needs.

Task Information Management

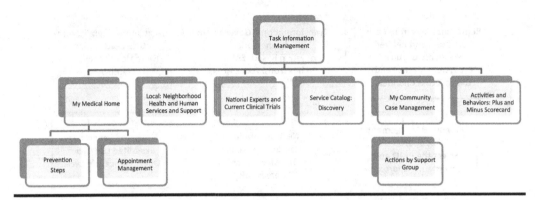

Figure 4.4   Each patient–consumer has his or her own task information model.

Personal Information Management

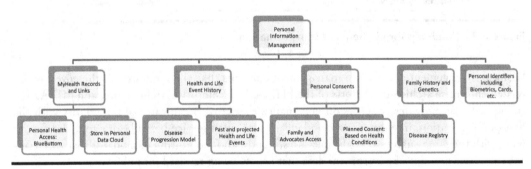

Figure 4.5   Each patient–consumer can have his or her own logical personal information model that can be stored in a local server or in a personal information cloud.

those peers with an association of services in web service location or data and information from other related websites. These sites can be associated with common security, privacy, and consent practices discussed in detail in Chapter 11.

4.5 Issues, Controversies, and Problems

The purpose of this section is to recommend a solution and a Roadmap for the features needed to integrate the SOS together into a value-delivery series of information sharing and delivery networks. This approach can move forward with a set of evolving software-defined networks using the new standards approach described in the Appendix. Each software-defined network can follow a general reference model, and new features can be planned and added incrementally over a multi-year timeframe with basic, intermediate, and advanced capabilities.

The timeframe should be a living time line showing the capabilities and features needed in the current year plus 2 or 3 years into the future, with the approximate availability date, at least in terms of the quarter of the year (e.g., new attribute-based security features will be available in the third quarter of 2018 or sooner). The key to establishing any solution or Roadmap is ascertaining the current situation regarding the building blocks, EHR systems, and other healthcare IT systems, and the HIEs that are part of Wave 1.

A holistic picture of a fragmented industry is difficult to obtain. One attempt to study the feedback of stakeholders from an early HIE was the work of Robert Rudin in his 2011 MIT PhD thesis, "Using information technology to exchange health information among healthcare providers: Measuring usage and understanding value." Subsequent work was performed by others in Rand Health IT studies. Now, we can also take the SOS approach that is based on high-level SOS diagrams used by the INCOSE SOS Healthcare Workshop in January 2015: capability maps, functions, and context diagrams that will vary depending on where in the country you are (i.e., the Maryland maps and Alabama maps will differ, but they can give a good baseline of the current state, and show how the elements can be linked together). For planning purposes, additional value-delivery maps and risk-safety and integration maps can be created. Those concepts will be introduced later. But the point is that techniques are necessary to show commonality in a simple process, but flexibility in the planning, because of the great variability found in American healthcare. We must first recognize the differences, and then move to commonality on fundamental items like vaccinations, public safety, and the ability to access the best care no matter your zip code. But that will take overcoming some hurdles.

4.5.1 Controversies, Motivators, Barriers, Moderators, and Issues

The activities of Wave 2 have begun, but often without the assessment discussed in Chapter 2. Some areas, like Medicaid in Chapter 3, offer a sustainable element that most early exchanges have lacked.

Some organizations are still focused on installing their EHRs in their hospital or clinic, deploying their connections to partners, and gaining acceptance by doctors and nurses who work within a given subject area. ONC has convened meetings to discuss the challenges. This involvement will reinvigorate "long-time" advocates, but new approaches are needed.

Wave 1 and even previous precursor pilots have often started with limited business-technical architecture and business case development. It seemed evident that healthcare IT and communication would have a positive impact, as they have in so many other industries. However, healthcare has resisted. Maybe the technologies or standards were not ready, or the healthcare IT change agents did not speak enough medical terminology. Or maybe the common ground controversies weren't addressed.

So, it is appropriate to step back to understand the controversies and the motivators behind stakeholder involvement in integration–interoperability; stakeholders need to achieve their goals, like coordination of care or integrated analytics. Some studies have identified barriers to healthcare IT and business process reengineering. Rudin talks about "moderators," which have been considered necessary features or design aspects that must be addressed as part of the solution architecture. The moderators are stepping stones that can be used by all to move to a common approach. One of the benefits of shared services or well-defined APIs is that they move everyone in a specific direction. But these moderators do not have to be inflexible. The moderators have to include a change management and deployment process, and support feedback where issues can be resolved. The complete solution must include those related support elements.

The roadblocks have been discussed in the press and in congressional committees. Senators Lamar Alexander and Patty Murray held a series of panel discussions during the summer of 2015 and parallel sessions have been held with the 21st Century Cures work by Congressmen Upton and DeGette. One of the most interesting is the presentation by Paul Black from Allscript where he described both the barriers and enablers of interoperability.

"I was invited here today to speak about interoperability and concerns about information blocking, and as more independent doctors use our software to treat patients than any other commercially available product, I'm pleased to share recommendations with you on this topic. This is important for two reasons: if a stakeholder were to intentionally get in the way of information exchange, (1) it would be bad for patients and (2) it could be anti-competitive.

Congress and the American people have wisely made an investment in the advancement of health information technology, all oriented around one goal: ensuring that this country's citizens are receiving the best possible care—both from a quality and cost perspective. Robust, open information exchange across a multitude of vendor platforms and care settings is critical to ensuring that we meet that goal for America's patients. An increased level of transparency and cooperation is needed to meet this challenge—health information technology developers, caregivers, employers, payers, pharmaceutical companies, health systems, and the government must all work harder *together* to solve this problem. Tomorrow's healthcare networks won't be built by one company alone, or even by health information technology developers alone, but by all of us."

Paul Black also provides a succinct to-do list that we will revisit in later solutions sections.

"There are many factors that need to be addressed for us to ultimately be successful:

- We need to expand the standards development process, building on the real progress underway with guidance from government, and allowing the private sector to continuously develop, adopt, and modify new standards.
- Key constituencies, such as public health registries, labs, state HIE organizations, and others who are not following available standards in their work, should be required to do so.
- State laws and regulations must be harmonized, particularly those related to privacy and security, patient consent and other similar topics.
- Legal and liability concerns among providers about how the data will be used outside of patient care must be addressed.
- We need to get beyond the focus on how data is transmitted and agree on what and how data is stored.
- Activation strategies are needed to increase use of healthcare IT by patients and their caregivers, while also generating accountability for their health outcomes.
- We need a national patient matching strategy—a way to identify each individual patient. This is a real challenge to both robust data exchange and patient safety, and Congress needs to stop blocking progress on this critical issue.
- Finally, generally, greater transparency around interoperability and healthcare IT among virtually all stakeholders must be achieved."

Much of the ground for interoperability has been plowed by state programs like New York's SHINE-NY, Michigan-MiHIN, Maryland–Delaware–DC-CRISP, and others. These have focused on the health of the citizens within those states, but now the issue is what happens when a patient goes from one state to another. When will we get a national HIE and what should it look like?

One place the controversies surface are in the battlegrounds of the standards committees and Section 501C corporations that have been formed to support the common issues. But executives, politicians, and procurement officials pushing and talking about interoperability is a key to progress. Now how much can they learn from similar information sharing environments that have been started and successfully deployed in intelligence and homeland security? I hope a lot.

4.5.2 Controversies

The government role is critical in addressing these key elements. However, there is controversy between those who see the government as the problem and those who see the government as the solution. Ultra-large scale systems of systems have all had some degree of government involvement, including the Internet which started out as Arpanet. Change can create some leaders who do not want standards. However, the coopetition needs to find the right balance between collaboration and competition. Where is the common ground? Over the next year, industry/government can define the tipping point for healthcare integration and interoperability.

The standards process is very time consuming and, depending on standards committee participants, can have a narrow vendor approach or a broad approach. Healthcare standards efforts have tried to create universal healthcare solutions and have gotten bogged down. ONC is moving to accelerate the standards process and to foster innovation, but the incentive program is running out of funding. The next phase of incentives may really come from accountable care organizations, the need for medical homes, and the integration of Medicaid and mental health.

The market is very active and there are many companies and standards efforts like West interoperability and the FHIR initiatives which are taking a more phased and incremental approach. More description and tracking of FHIR are defined in the Appendix.

One of the issues that arises is that of multiple standards groups and limited alignment. Some of those groups are formed by cooperating groups, such as the CommonWell Health Alliance, or HealtheWay—now renamed Sequoia Project, or the HL7 and HIMSS initiatives. However, during 2015, the ONC created the master list of Standards Advisory Document (May 2015) that has many standards, but has not yet been put into a usable profile.

4.5.3 Motivators

It often looks like there is no alignment of motivation: everyone wants to go in his or her own direction. But the limited studies have identified key motivators and, as this transformation moves forward, we need to gather more aligned information on goals and motivations.

The market will dictate if all the EHR vendors will play or will simply announce that they intend to meet and comply with all standards. The true test will be the buyers' and payers' insurance companies, government Medicare and Medicaid and large insurances, and we the patients and parents, insisting that the EHRs be findable, searchable, and delivered in a timely manner. Getting from talking and attending meetings to action really requires work, but many of the basic elements are READY Technology that can be leveraged. We are at a point where coopetition will be reached, where interoperability will become the foundation, and where vendors will find new places to compete; locking in information will no longer be a threat.

4.6 Continuous Stakeholder Engagement and Shared Services Development

A healthcare transformation governance council is needed to ensure that all stakeholders are engaged in a constructive manner. Today, political headwinds make a fact-based conversation difficult. There are FACA committees run by ONC that are addressing many of the key elements, but the key participants are not always present. Communication, outreach, and the willingness to work on practical and pragmatic approaches require attendance by all stakeholders.

Some of the necessary steps include the following:

- Patient–consumer needs analysis.
- Information-centric source and discovery analysis.
- A strong foundation on the importance of stakeholder engagement must be provided, along with a series of points on engaging stakeholders in a collaborative way. That collaboration must occur at multiple levels: national, state, and regional, and it must reach the level of supporting those who are disease management focused, and acknowledge the effects on each patient and family.
- Acknowledgement that the appropriate starting perspective is that of the end user, that is, the patient. What are the actions and the tasks that each stakeholder has to perform?
- An assessment of the current complexities and problems. Can they be fixed as we move forward?
- A demonstration showing how doctors and administrators have engaged differently in this new world.
- Patient portals: Creating all these websites and ensuring that the information is presented in a way that can encourage patients' understanding and good decision making, and engage them in good buying practices. Unfortunately, many of the websites are not well done, and, because of the lack of consistency of information and user systems design, responses have been negative.
- Provider portals: How can we simplify the life of the provider and clarify his or her payments and incentives? Appropriate explanation to physicians and their staff is critical. Confusion will result in tremendous resistance; the State of North Carolina, for example, has put pressure on the contractor, and the American Medical Association has voiced its displeasure. Key players have strong influence if the systems do not work as specified.
- A specific focus for a cross ecosystems information model. What is the essential information required in the model?
- Acknowledgement that the SOS will be designed for change: the laws, policies, regulations, and best practices will change over time.

Open service-based applications need to include: (1) a behavior model for each interface and (2) a series of information flows and control flows that represent a series of benchmarks. These benchmarks can represent a series of "test as we go" verification steps that can build verification and validation planning into the overall development plan.

4.7 Patient–Consumer-Information-Centric Interoperability and Continuous Delivery

Web services must evolve and be able to handle both shallow and deep changes. Shallow changes must be supported incrementally with automation. Some of the key concepts that must be discussed on a state or regional basis include:

- Acknowledgement of the size of the problem: identity management is a key issue for healthcare
- Challenges: risk and "data" usage. Understanding of the problem and optional solutions
- Scope of the problem

- Understanding of the standards and technology
- Definition of a shared service environment
- Provenance and consent must determine the identities of those who are permitted to use the organization's information and the reasons for that use
- Continuous integration-continuous delivery and continuous verification and validation point to research and IBM UrbanCode Package and related new DevOps activities, and the need to have continuous validation of open service-based applications (continuous integration documents)

The state or regional communities must come together and create their own plans to connect their related SOS with a very pragmatic approach to interoperability. States working together as in New England and the Maryland–Delaware–DC HIEs or the buddying collaboration between Michigan and Illinois illustrate the possibilities and can save money and share risks. Patients' care crosses organizational boundaries and the patient may live and work in one state or another or get sick on travel. Care delivery and information delivery must be seamless under all those conditions. Most of the fundamental processes and even the capabilities defined in the next section will be common.

4.8 Process Steps: Shared Services and SOS Capabilities

The current process approaches do not support shared services and SOS capabilities. Their development activities in these areas are being addressed in Defense, SEI/CMU, INCOSE model-based systems engineering and SOS project, along with research at the MIT Enterprise Systems Division program, SERC lead by Stevens Tech, and in a series of research initiatives in Europe.

Each organization should include the 12-step process for defining how its solution fits in the ecosystem. Meaningful Use 2 and 3 emphasize connecting with all the key elements.

1. What is happening in your region? Is there an existing exchange? Is Medicaid going to provide an exchange?
2. Who are the critical patients–consumers and what services-information are needed?
3. State and healthcare, human services populations that are focused on improvements?
4. What are similar organizations doing? Note regional competition and similar organizations' best practices.
5. What provides the organization with the most competitive advantage? Define the value proposition and the value model today and an incremental set of steps for value improvement.
6. What vendor relationships does the organization have, and is the organization's vendor an "interoperability advocate" or delaying the process? HIMSS and HL7 interoperability is pushing and ONC Meaningful Use is pulling. (Identify the drivers for interoperability.)
7. Is the organization focusing on the business-clinical integration use cases, and creating a Roadmap for the next two years? Define a set of administrative-clinical use cases; select some from Appendix A.
8. Is the organization using and creating reference architecture and approaches that are independent of its vendors? Show the vendor what your organization wants, and do not just look at what the vendor wants to sell you. Focus on defining the set of open service-based application interfaces. Look at research examples like SOLOIST (Bianculli) and other WS-COL and WS-Agreement and the need to have a set of end-to-end benchmarks and verification tests.

9. Are you focusing on these improvement approaches?
   a. Cross organization and state–regional integration
   b. Key decisions that support your goals, questions, trends, and data availability
   c. Create a hub or an appliance that fits with open standards-based interoperability: DIRECT and CONNECT (next set of standards)
   d. Lean business process models
   e. Quality and outcome measures
   f. Safety and reliability
   g. Systems engineering for healthcare
10. Are you creating a Roadmap of future steps?
11. Have you used regional networking and collaboration?
12. Are you noting national and international collaboration: making the vendors listen with "collective buying power?"
13. Have you tracked your progress monthly based on integration concepts of operations and dashboard of improvements?
14. Did you continue to refine and improve the plan, the architecture, and the Roadmap?

4.8.1 Barriers

The focus is on the existing providers, hospitals, and the related health information technologies and the interoperability capabilities. Refocusing on the patients–consumers will require a new mindset. A patient–consumer focus needs to have a set of patient advocacy organizations that are vocal advocates for a shift in approach and demonstration created in one or more states. (Proposal for states—see Appendix D.)

Meaningful Use 2 and 3 must have a practical timeline and must not undermine the efforts that have already been expended. Interoperability must be realistically achieved in all states and a phased approach offered. The barriers must be documented from the point of view of each of the stakeholders including:

- Financial incentives
- Understanding what Meaningful Use means
- Plan-architecture that fits Meaningful Use
- Over-promises of vendors
- Vendors that aren't promoting interoperability
- Unclear direction from government
- Hating government direction, but wanting and needing it

4.8.2 Moderators

A series of common ground elements that need to be defined include:

- Value-delivery network
- Integration map
- Integration connection point
- Integration timeframe
- Common interoperability shared services
- Integration certification and assessment

4.9 Issues

Integration and interoperability issues can be resolved with studies, prototypes, and piloting, and creating models or standards that fill the gaps. One of the problems in solving these issues is that the architects, systems engineers, quality engineers, and business process designers do not know the practice of medicine and vice versa. An interdisciplinary approach is needed, which the process controversy should address.

One of the issues is to recognize that medicine and healthcare can try to reinvent those design aspects of similar SOS approaches, or they can borrow, tailor, and extend existing systems, with changes based on the unique aspects of healthcare. Issues have to be collected from many different viewpoints such as the integrators, researchers, and the medical CIO to provide a multi-disciplinary, multi-attribute approach, and clear set of issues:

Issue	Approach	Responsible Parties
Value-delivery network	Combine the value-delivery model with the software delivery network model and the type of "healthcare topics" and the linking of end points together	OMG, HL7, HSSP
Integration map	Define a set of logical integration maps that are focused on key improvement goals and represent the next few years of activities	ONC with the SEI/CMU
Integration connection points	Provide templates and formal models for integration and their verification and testing	OMG—model driven architecture or integration planning team
Integration timeframe	Provide a master schedule and way for many systems to link in and manage the integration risk and the design aspects of the integration steps	ONC with the SEI–CMU
Common interoperability shared services	ONC–CMS and GSA agreement of the shared services and APIs needed over the next phase to achieve Meaningful Use 2 and 3	GSA shared services project and the HHS CIO Council

The issues are just an initial start for an approach and recommendation of a joint government–research–industry team to solve.

Issue resolution will need to leverage previous industry experience and healthcare pilot project experience. Scheduling and coordinating these resolutions will need the continued involvement of veterans in the field and recruitment of new change advocates.

There are a few cross-communicators who can speak the language of medicine and these other disciplines, but there need to be many more. This section is designed to define that common communication ground and to define actions that can address some of the most immediate pressing needs.

A common process and pathways to move forward are delineated here, and the types of invest-ments described that were made by the early healthcare transformation leaders and those from other industries that have paid off. Wave 1 installed many of the building blocks, but Wave 2 is the natural optimization and improvement phase. Each industry has needed to go through its own Wave 2. Once a basic set of tools for automation have been installed, those tools need to be revised to improve quality, to eliminate waste, and to improve the safety of the operations. This is often defined as lean or six sigma process.

There are now groups within HIMSS, University Industrial Systems Engineering and Enterprise Architectures, and a few physicians–computer scientists–engineers who have learned more about medicine. However, these are disciplines that are "across" campus from one another or even across town or across the state, and they have to bridge the concept and communication divide. We are looking for healthcare–architecture–planning–engineering, a "hope" to create a baseline of common understanding. That common ground especially needs to focus around three specific areas: integration, interoperability, and analytics. There are other areas where common ground is needed that will be summarized later.

It is essential that each organization review where it fits in Wave 2 using a vision-strategy ses-sion where a portfolio of changes can be created. Some of the Roadmaps may include pre- and post-surgical care coordination, mental health and physical health integrated care models, and support of a chronic condition, such as that for CF that have been used with great success. The approach described takes that CF improvement approach, along with the early experience in the patient-centered outcome research initiatives (PCORI), and looks to create the elements that can be leveraged to address other rare diseases and many chronic conditions. Every rare disease does not need to reinvent the CF or other disease-focused approaches; but all can benefit if the common infrastructure can be defined. A common rare disease integration and interoperability approach can get us closer to the "21st Century Cures," as discussed at a series of bi-partisan hearings dur-ing 2014, and could be part of proposed legislation. (See the Appendix for more detail.) A "21st Century Logical Infrastructure" could be a centerpiece to meet the cures for the nearly 30 million patients with one of the 7000 rare diseases. This chapter discusses these disease-focused networks, and the associated chapters will also provide key guidance on the many options that can be chosen as each organization's Way Forward is created (Figure 4.6).

4.10 Information Sharing Reference Model: Integrated Views for Improvement

A number of groups are working on interoperability specifications and addressing key challenges like identity management, dynamic consent, and cross EHR provider integration. These groups include CommonWell Health Alliance and the ONC Interoperability Portfolio Working Groups. CommonWell (formed at the HIMSS13 conference) has made good progress, and is led by the vendors, except for EPIC, who is the largest vendor. They have recently defined key concepts in a document (October 21, 2014), and have created Service Specification 2.0 and Use Case 2.0 with post-acute care and ambulatory surgical care. They have also looked at the initial standards that exist, and since they have been in existence for less than 2 years, are in a deployment and outreach stage. This review is very much focused on the core, and is now beginning to address the key challenges, such as consent, complexity, and consistent identity management; the ONC initiative addressed certification and many related secondary uses of information sharing, such as public health, quality and outcome measurements, and support for research. So that these initiatives

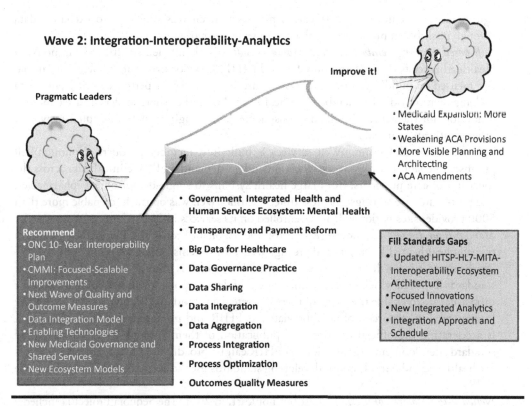

Wave 2: Integration-Interoperability-Analytics

Improve it!

Pragmatic Leaders

- Medicaid Expansion: More States
- Weakening ACA Provisions
- More Visible Planning and Architecting
- ACA Amendments

- Government Integrated Health and Human Services Ecosystem: Mental Health
- Transparency and Payment Reform
- Big Data for Healthcare
- Data Governance Practice
- Data Sharing
- Data Integration
- Data Aggregation
- Process Integration
- Process Optimization
- Outcomes Quality Measures

Recommend
- ONC 10- Year Interoperability Plan
- CMMI: Focused-Scalable Improvements
- Next Wave of Quality and Outcome Measures
- Data Integration Model
- Enabling Technologies
- New Medicaid Governance and Shared Services
- New Ecosystem Models

Fill Standards Gaps
- Updated HITSP-HL7-MITA- Interoperability Ecosystem Architecture
- Focused Innovations
- New Integrated Analytics
- Integration Approach and Schedule

Figure 4.6 Wave 2 forces of pragmatic leadership and resolutions to improve and not regress.

don't become two or more ships passing in the night, more focus needs to be placed on "alliance," and it has to become clear that these specifications will become key components of the next wave of acquisitions.

A set of bi-directional pathways can be defined and related to the topics of communication between the patients and the providers that support both general and mental health coordination. These pathways can also support a topic related to a specific type of "care and cure" on which the patient is focused or on which the patient should be focused. The set of "care and cure" paths can use a common set of integration and interoperability standards, and use software agents to ensure that the information is exchanged to and from the primary sources and the secondary uses of the data.

Jitin Asnani—Executive Director of the CommonWell Health Alliance on August 4, 2015 summarized the "Five private sector interoperability initiatives to watch" on Managed Healthcare Executive website:

1. *"Hub-to-hub exchange.* The eHealth exchange is the oldest of these initiatives, having formed in 2006 as a federal-led effort known as the nationwide health information network exchange. In 2012, the eHealth exchange was reformed as a public–private effort under the non-profit entity 'The Sequoia Project,' with a continued focus on enabling hub-to-hub exchange of data, especially between hubs set up by very large provider organizations and HIEs.

2. *Push-based exchange.* DirectTrust.org was formed in 2012 as a non-profit to carry on the work deferred by the Direct Project initiated by the ONC. DirectTrust.org focuses on shared

agreements and a uniform certification process that enables providers to exchange data through push-based protocols, much akin to secure e-mail.

3. *Pull-based exchange embedded into providers' software.* Launched in 2013, CommonWell Health Alliance is the first and only health IT (HIT) vendor-driven interoperability initiative focused on building working infrastructure and services for person-centric health data exchange nationwide. Its members are healthcare IT market share leaders and technology innovators for the acute, ambulatory, post-acute care, imaging, laboratory, pharmacy, and other healthcare segments.

   Since access to CommonWell services is built into member products, CommonWell promises to enable seamless record location and on-demand 'pull' of clinical data across the spectrum of care providers, from large health systems to single-doctor offices, pharmacies, and post-acute care settings. At press time, CommonWell was on track to enable more than 5000 provider sites nationwide to be enrolled on its services in 2015.

4. *Standards for discrete data exchange.* In 2014, the Argonaut Project was founded by a handful of major healthcare IT vendors and prestigious health systems. Argonaut is focused on defining the standards for the exchange of 'discrete' data, which is in stark contrast to the current standards for HIE, which focus on 'documents' of data. Argonaut will not build any specific infrastructure to enable the usage of these discrete data standards (known as fast healthcare interoperability resources, often abbreviated as FHIR and pronounced as 'fire'). Rather, it is accelerating the official creation and publication of them through HL7, an accredited standards development organization, so FHIR can be broadly used by organizations across the healthcare industry. It is also developing standards for the access of FHIR data from the EHR.

5. *Network-to-network connectivity.* Last but not least, in 2014, The Sequoia Project launched a new, separate initiative called Carequality under the assumption that, at some point in the future, the industry will be composed of a number of separate networks that will need to connect with each other. As such, Carequality is creating the policy and trust frameworks to enable such intranetwork exchange, led by healthcare IT vendors and healthcare provider organizations."

6. "*Patient–consumer-information-centric network option* is to define an information centric network of networks with software-defined network technology and to use these as complementary pathways forward." (Relate to Internet classification number [ICN] network and standards.)

7. With a patient–consumer-information-centric interoperability game plan over the next year or two, the ICN must fit with health standards efforts from Sequoia, CommonWell, and HL7-FHIR, and allow multiple pathways forward to be used. But a nationwide network of networks can be the key target.

Time frame: Patient–consumer-information-centric-information sharing reference model—mid-October 2016.

4.11 Standards Profile and Accelerating Gap Closure

A standards profile must be created showing existing standards and the gaps in those standards. Material must be gathered from the CommonWell service specification. ONC 2015 standards define the current HL7 standards, but have not addressed how healthcare can use business process modeling, decision modeling, case modeling, XML Business Reporting Language (XBRL) reporting, or looking outside the healthcare practice areas. These items can provide a valuable addition and will be recommended for inclusion. Other reference models are needed to build upon FHIR and related smart platforms to provide a "care and cure value-delivery network." Also, MITA needs to add new interoperability, accountable care organization, quality measures and outcomes, and a reporting approach. One of the biggest gaps is defining how the SOS can be integrated together. Again, looking outside of healthcare is recommended. Healthcare IT can leverage approaches similar to battle management languages and interoperability, using an approach that is patient-centric, rather than soldier-centric.

Time frame: Compile standards profile and define an accelerating approach to gap closure by identifying standards development organizations and timelines—May 2015 with updates by November 2016.

4.12 Information-Centric Network-Software-Defined Networks Aligned with Patient–Consumer–Healthcare Value Models

In other areas, such as science, open grid forum standards have been defined, or in telecom itself, software-defined networks have been defined as the underlying part of the infrastructure. For healthcare, there are many message level standards, but no networking standards. The FHA or company–government–partner network architecture can use software-defined networks with value models, and create a "draft standard" that can be presented to one or more standards groups such as OMG and HL7.

Time frame: Consider how the software-defined networks can be used as part of health interoperability and identify any gaps—January 2017.

4.13 Patient–Consumer-Information-Centric Public APIs: Open APIs with Governance Process

Interoperability discusses Public APIs, and the rule-based wearable mobile agent can provide a patient with a smart end point that can adapt to network conditions and handle failures with its own workarounds. Those smart end points must be trustworthy and resilient. If a problem occurs, including a security threat, the mobile agent must know the surroundings. The patient should be able to safely send the information or not while sitting in Starbucks. Also, when a failure occurs, the types of fixes and workarounds must be defined. All these high reliability features are needed for the future value-based network applications. Those types of smart endpoints will be the enablers of trusted mobile applications that will be supporting doctors, patients, and those monitoring their own health. The high risk patient should be able to move around and his or her vital signs will be monitored and relayed back to his or her personal health store without being visibly connected. Current implementations of DIRECT and CONNECT have used API appliances, such as IBM DataPower, or Layer7 in the case of Defense Military Health and VA information exchanges. However, there does not seem to be a clear Public API reference model. The new Argonaut API from HL7 should allow those rules to be installed according to the patient's conditions, preferences, and privacy concerns. These new APIs will allow the patient to connect and have trusted bi-directional community with providers and the support of social communities and research communities of which the patient is a part.

Time frame: Define the design standards and pilot one of the API capabilities—October 2016.

4.14 Shared Services: Design–Development–Deployment and Governance

ONC–CMS and other federal agencies can design and follow the federal implementation guidance for shared services (April 2013), along with other new GSA shared services initiatives. A set of proposed interoperability shared services can build upon the DIRECT and CONNECT experience, and on new ONC working groups and industry groups such as CommonWell. Vendors such as Cerner are fostering a strong partner program, while Allscript is encouraging application stores to be created on their open API.

Time frame: Review the GSA proposed standards with a strong focus on how the healthcare logic channels and networks can evolve. Draft shared services candidate list. January 2016 with a complete specification—November 2016. (Use CommonWell when applicable.)

4.15 Governance Tools: Integration Plan along with the Management of Shared Services

Defining a transparent and centralized governance approach is one of the most important tasks of establishing this level of integration and interoperability. Initial studies of governance were performed in the Fall of 2013, but many gaps existed. A new set of governance tools that can align with the SOS maps, and can provide support to each virtual delivery network will need to be created.

This common partnering approach can be used to define a common approach to "care and cure" value-delivery networks. They have to define a design process, use a set of governance policies, and have a collaborative process that links to its stakeholders, and can follow a systematic series of process steps shown briefly below.

Time frame: Review the existing governance and review the new evolution tool concepts like those for information-centric network and open interface management of SOS. Recommend a governance process and simple set of tools to be used. SOS for patient–consumer-information-centric tools, methodology, and governance—Spring 2017.

Patient–consumer-information-centric network with a number of varieties, such as the "care and cure" value-based service delivery networks:

1. Define the population that this network can support with "care and cure" services.
2. Define the population for this "care and cure," and create a panel within your practice or region of support.
3. Define care services based on "Best Practices and Medical Guidelines."
4. Define the research and clinical trials based on most of the members supporting the research agenda for curing or improving the practices and developing new research or medications, etc.
5. Define the prediction steps for the populations supported. Ascertain how many patients need this type of "care and cure" services.
6. Define the prevention steps that can delay or reverse the disease progression or postpone its clinical realization.
7. Define an approach to personalizing the specific care.
8. Define the payment approach with a mix of value-based patients and traditional fee-for-service patients.
9. Define a "care and cure" tracking and performance dashboard.
10. Develop a set of "care and cure" value-based service delivery shared services that can "co-evolve" and integrate with other service delivery networks.
11. Support with a governance approach and decision support process that supports the financial management and clinical care processes.

The SOS Governance Structures and Process are a Key Element Needed to Meet the Healthcare Transformation in Wave 2 and Wave 3.

4.16 Patient–Consumer-Information-Centric Pathways and Local, Extendible Architecture with Integration Points

How can these underlying integration and interoperability elements be created in "open source" that can be leveraged for an "extendible product base?"

Time frame: Develop an extendible architecture with integration points concept paper and conduct a workshop—February 2017.

4.16.1 Integration Certification and Community-Problem Resolution

CommonWell has defined an approach using levels of links certification that will allow EHR vendors to use edge capabilities and common shared services, and to provide new extensions that encourage innovation. The new service specification was released October 21, 2014, along with a concept document, and will take 6–9 months to mature. This is already aligned with many of the integrated health environment standards, is very patient-centric, and defines some basic shared services.

> Time frame: Recommend a certification and community-problem-solving and resolution approach—March 2017.

4.16.1.1 Integration Master Plan

Already there is an indication that a more resolved and pragmatic approach is underway. The hardline resistors still exist, but "bi-partisan" improvements to legislation are being discussed in Congress. States that resisted Medicaid expansion, such as Virginia and Florida, are having policy battles, and political battles are being taken to the voting booths. But there are also underlying changes, such as the ONC 10-year plan. During the first half of 2016, the integration steps will need to be refined. Hopefully, the ideas here can help guide that effort (Figure 4.7).

> Time frame: Create a healthcare shared service Wiki and master schedule alignment for 2015–2020 with quarter-by-quarter identification points—Fall 2016.

4.16.2 Integration Master Plan and Integration Points

Healthcare.gov and the many new EHR systems in the healthcare IT organization have resulted in islands of automation, and there have been problems with integrating the pieces together to move forward to the next phase of interoperability. This type of ultra-large scale integration is very

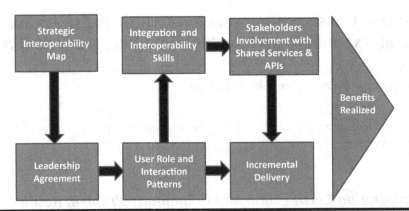

Figure 4.7 **Defining the steps from strategy and reference models to meet the organization's needs.**

different from the small projects and individual IT projects addressed by government agencies involved in healthcare or in insurance claims processing companies.

The healthcare IT industry needs a new perspective that can leverage the ultra-large scale experience of air traffic control systems, intelligence information sharing systems, and many military mission-oriented systems. This kind of SOS integration is one of the approaches taken by the US DOD, but it will need to be translated into appropriate approaches for healthcare.

Integration must become a key discipline and must be the driver for ultra-large scale project management that works on an annual enrolment readiness cycle, provides an incremental modernization of systems, and is driven by a set of value-driven transformations. The Roadmap to integration must focus on a set of cost effective, efficient improvements that can be delivered to patients. The macro improvements and integration steps must fit with the "small-scale" patient–provider integration around a disease movement-focused effort, such as that of CF, which can result in focused and quantifiable improvements.

The following are challenges to integration:

- First, it takes time to plan and architect the pieces and get everyone on the same page
- Version 1 of anything is not very good, and accepting that fact and moving on is politically difficult
- The practices of large-scale integration with ultra-large scale systems and the integration of SOS have only been studied by CMU/SEI, universities (like Penn State University, Stevens Tech, and University of Southern California), and only with limited focus on medicine and healthcare
- Integration of SOS must define an integration Roadmap, define a process for integration tracking, and create an integration timeline and set of tests
- Experience can be found in the large government programs from air traffic control to space, weather, and intelligence systems, and experience in the health systems of other countries

Time frame: Provide training on methods for individual organization's participation, and add capabilities to the open service environment—October 2016.

4.16.3 Creating a Regional or State Transformation Integration Plan

Currently, there are some states and regions that have a basic set of capabilities. However, some states have no HIEs, and they will have difficulty meeting the Meaningful Use 2 or 3 requirements.

Review the major state initiatives and create a goal-oriented use case factory of health exchange examples, like those of Tim Pletcher from the Michigan Health Exchange before the Senate Health Panel. Build upon a set of health exchange shared services and use National Association of State Chief Information Officers (NASCIO) as a state shared services advocates group.

Those states without the basic capabilities should be taking a new approach. Chapters 5 and 6 will provide a virtual service infrastructure that can be used in the next phase of regional or state transformation. Planning for the transformation can be formulated with the 12 steps defined below.

12 Step Transformation Process:

- Establish a state or regional leadership council.
- Ensure that the key government and key commercial stakeholders are engaged and patient–consumer advocates are represented.

- Determine where your organization competes and where it cooperates. Profit making and non-profit activities have to be established.
- Create accountable goals and objectives as part of strategic vision.
- Create a non-profit cooperative that will manage the cooperative elements: HIE, patient–consumer portal, provider and case worker portal and collaborative groups for both neighborhoods and "care and cure networks" related to a disease or chronic conditions and to share open services across state and federal boundaries.
- Establish a transparent governance process and an agile integration blueprint that will allow multiple organizations to share and support evolution over time.
- Create a solution reference model with a patient–consumer population focus and an open set of interfaces as integration points.
- Define the key linking elements: use a set of standards profiles and an approach to create "gap fillers" that can be clearly adapted and extended to meet the bridging needs between components and organizations.
- Define a value and benefit business case approach that can show the investment, benefit by sharing and reusing services, and used to make incremental commitments and track progress.
- Create a release plan with quarterly releases related to the evolving reference model and delivery of value and business case solutions.
- Define a concept of operations which includes long-term cost, sustainability and deployment, and continuous planning process.
- Define and communicate periodic results, review to understand lessons learned and to recognize individuals and organizations for their hard work and success. Say thank you as part of the annual progress report!

Time frame: Create a state–regional–local capabilities assessment and planning template, working with NASCIO and other non-profits—October 2016.

4.16.4 Connecting to the Current Capabilities: Integration and Extension Points

One of the next key steps is to clarify the roles of CMS, ONC, the states, and the many related healthcare organizations to ensure that their roles are aligned. This alignment must be implemented at the strategy level and also at a level that creates a "community-based" network that can focus on integration and interoperability, and include in its focus the clear identification of issues and assignment of responsibilities to resolve those issues (Figure 4.8).

Time frame: The federal healthcare IT strategy and related CMS strategy and architecture are too internally focused. They need to consider the people they support, the population groups, and the regions of the country, and not approach everything from only the federal perspective. A guide on a community-based set of alignments can be created for review—November 2016. Updates and getting outside the beltway can take another 6 months—March 2017.

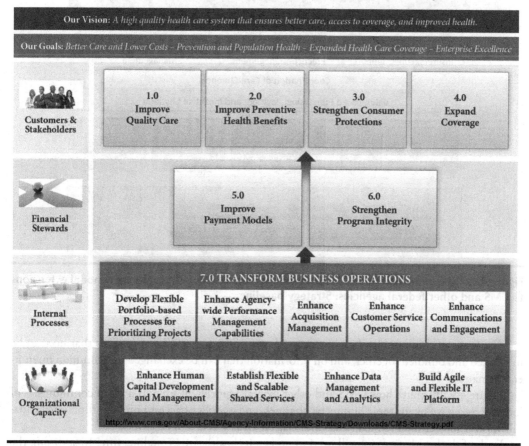

CMS Strategy: The Road Forward (2013-2017):

Create a Government-Healthcare Ecosystem Map.

Figure 4.8 Recommending strategy and reference models extensions to CMS: Strategy baseline.

4.16.5 CMS Patient–Consumer-Information-Centric Enterprise Architecture Needs to Extend to the Ecosystem and Communities of Interest

Enterprise architecture has been required by the federal government for more than 14 years. Some agencies and states have focused first on breaking down the internal silos, with strong focus on defining the current systems and understanding their opportunities for improvements. The federal and state healthcare agencies and the major healthcare organizations need to focus on evolving to more of a community-of-interest approach. These federal and companion state HHSs agencies can be aligned to deliver government services to citizens and businesses, and can also provide these services internationally, or to other governments.

CMS and other federal health agencies and the FHAs need to combine to become a government/partner/communities-of-interest architecture such as that shown below.

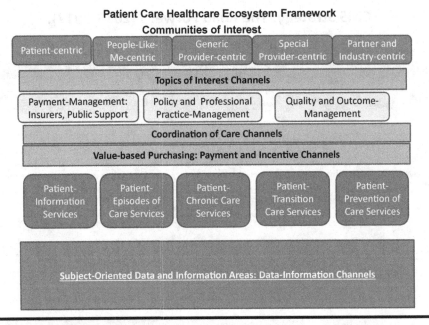

Patient Care Healthcare Ecosystem Framework
Communities of Interest

| Patient-centric | People-Like-Me-centric | Generic Provider-centric | Special Provider-centric | Partner and Industry-centric |

Topics of Interest Channels

| Payment-Management: Insurers, Public Support | Policy and Professional Practice-Management | Quality and Outcome-Management |

Coordination of Care Channels

Value-based Purchasing: Payment and Incentive Channels

| Patient-Information Services | Patient-Episodes of Care Services | Patient-Chronic Care Services | Patient-Transition Care Services | Patient-Prevention of Care Services |

Subject-Oriented Data and Information Areas: Data-Information Channels

Figure 4.9 Recommended new CMS/community outreach-focused reference model extensions to CMS and other federal agencies: Strategy baseline.

The focus of this combined architecture (shown in Figure 4.9) is on services that need to be integrated and bundled together, and on information that can be exchanged in a common interoperable manner.

Figure 4.9 illustrates how CMS and other federal agencies all support a set of communities of interest, and have major topic of interest channels and a series of access points to functional capabilities and subject-oriented data and information areas.

Each of the health agencies will need to update its healthcare IT architecture. In addition, the FHA will need to be changed and aligned incrementally with a set of parallel activities shown in Figure 4.10.

Figure 4.10 shows a set of paths forward that provide incremental modernization steps; however, there is often a lack of clarity on what is expected at their destination.

Because of the many activities to introduce new EHR technologies, new benefits are introduced through health insurance marketplaces (Healthcare.gov, state marketplaces, or new Medicaid expansion in many states); debates about the subjects are introduced in others.

Underneath the visible waves are extensive initiatives that are critical to making progress, with the focus on these four paths forward and many others. Each stakeholder engagement path has illustrated a focus on improving user interactions and increasing involvement of patients. Providers and insurance companies are creating portals to fit "people-like-me," whether for a more general approach or for a specific community of interest, such as CF. Better user experience is being created by determining the type of user of the portal and by defining a set of use cases with a persona, a set of background knowledge, and a clear set of actions. The SHARPC-funded projects have focused on usability and improved collaboration across teams of providers and patients. These research initiatives have promise, but there is still extensive complaining about the EHR systems and their usability and collaboration.

Series of Paths of Progress: EA Ecosystem

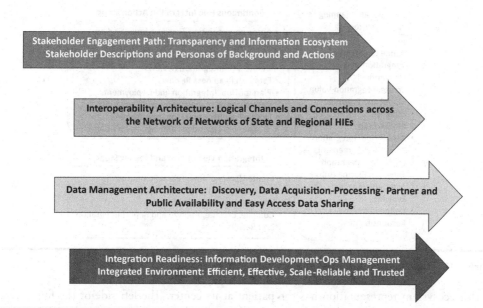

Stakeholder Engagement Path: Transparency and Information Ecosystem
Stakeholder Descriptions and Personas of Background and Actions

Interoperability Architecture: Logical Channels and Connections across
the Network of Networks of State and Regional HIEs

Data Management Architecture: Discovery, Data Acquisition-Processing- Partner and
Public Availability and Easy Access Data Sharing

Integration Readiness: Information Development-Ops Management
Integrated Environment: Efficient, Effective, Scale-Reliable and Trusted

Figure 4.10   Skeleton roadmap of paths forward.

Interoperability architecture is also a work in progress for standards organizations, and continues to be a major area of concentration for the ONC which, in May 2014, released a new 10-year plan that provides a strong focus on what will drive Wave 2. The new EHRs will support not only primary data usage, but also secondary usage that can drive public health and quality and outcome measures, and also support many clinical trials and research activities. Although we have many years of data standards efforts and master data management, a more incremental phased data quality and standards alignment Roadmap can now be defined if government, states, and commercial vendors can provide the right leadership. The last path forward can illustrate a method to integrate EHR systems that are not interoperable and the many stand-alone systems.

In the past, integration seemed like an after-thought. However, since all of the systems of systems must be linked, integration and the regular schedule of updates for the next year or two are critical. Integration must be part of the overall planning and architecture process. Some regions that have health information systems (like NY-SHINE, MD-CRISP, or New England's HIEs) can be critical elements for integration and the Meaningful Use 2 and 3 projects "coordination" of patients across facilities.

For these and other paths forward, the key will be how each organization's initiatives fit with the others in its own area of the country, and how that organization compares with the best practices throughout the country. Wave 1 talks about where we are now and opportunities for improvement, while Wave 2 will provide the Roadmaps that can be selected and built upon.

While each organization can set up its own integration plans for its ecosystem as shown in Figure 4.11, a set of common shared services can be used in many "care and cure" value services delivery networks. These shared services must be defined with a coopetition based on collaboration between industry and the government definition of standards, and on the ability for competition based on competitive value-added service features.

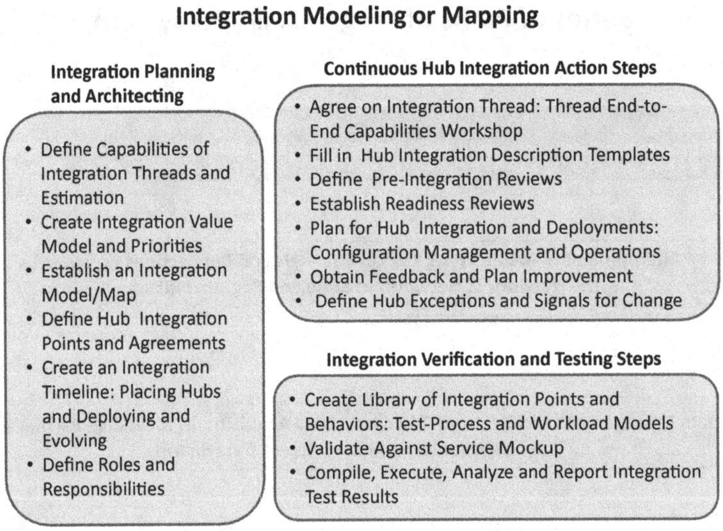

Integration Modeling or Mapping

Integration Planning and Architecting

- Define Capabilities of Integration Threads and Estimation
- Create Integration Value Model and Priorities
- Establish an Integration Model/Map
- Define Hub Integration Points and Agreements
- Create an Integration Timeline: Placing Hubs and Deploying and Evolving
- Define Roles and Responsibilities

Continuous Hub Integration Action Steps

- Agree on Integration Thread: Thread End-to-End Capabilities Workshop
- Fill in Hub Integration Description Templates
- Define Pre-Integration Reviews
- Establish Readiness Reviews
- Plan for Hub Integration and Deployments: Configuration Management and Operations
- Obtain Feedback and Plan Improvement
- Define Hub Exceptions and Signals for Change

Integration Verification and Testing Steps

- Create Library of Integration Points and Behaviors: Test-Process and Workload Models
- Validate Against Service Mockup
- Compile, Execute, Analyze and Report Integration Test Results

Figure 4.11 Interoperable shared services and API portfolio.

This ecosystem representation has the patient at its center. The left side of the figure represents how the organization receives insurance. The patient's disease support organizations, such as the CF Foundation and many others, can be the surrogates in the policy meetings, leverage grant funding, and create disease-tailored interfaces connecting to healthcare systems to improve care and promote cures. These disease-tailored interfaces can provide learning and information from the experts to the primary care providers and the special providers who address the patient's "care and cure" needs. The disease advocates foundations (such as the CF Foundation) can create disease progression models, identify the types of health events to expect, and provide guidance for the episode recovery or chronic care services needed to prevent those episodes.

The insurance and primary care ecosystems are driven heavily by perceptions of the state of healthcare today and where it can go in the future; these important perceptions are those of the insurance regulations, the ACA marketplaces and rules, and state and local politics and policies. There are those optimists who can see a new healthcare system, and there are those who see disaster occurring. However, most people, once introduced to the facts, recognize that, like other industries (banking, telecommunications, cell phones, e-retail, etc.), the healthcare industry will have changes, and we can work to set the stage for improved healthcare. Young doctors will demand changes to fit their i-Pads and i-Phones, the new genetic-based medicine, and the availability of the latest clinical evidence. The new "baby boom generation" will have a mixture of patients and providers who are very health-literate and knowledgeable about computers and the Internet. In addition, there are others who unfortunately did not have good health insurance for years. All the other ecosystems must feed into the care of the patient, including the large pharmaceutical industry and the new forms of home care, acute care, and nursing homes. These must all fit together with transmission of information into an integrated picture of the care of the patient, care for the population in a region, and care for the population of the nation.

Time frame: Define the interoperability shared services and development plan for use by CMS—2016—and other agencies—2017.

4.16.6 Using Simple Semantics Ontologies Today

Interoperability will need to use a new data approach, such as the use of ontologies.

Time frame: Leverage the research progress from e-science and review the progress from the European "Semantic Healthnet" and the clinical information modeling efforts project—Fall 2016.

Figure 4.12 shows the key paths and the secondary information paths from Medicaid patients to a set of keystone and secondary pathways that can perform the information integration in a consistent manner with less human involvement.

Time frame: Research program building on the National Library of Medicine (NLM) ontologies programs and research—February 2019—and standards efforts—2020.

4.16.7 Strategy and Principle Agreement and Mapping

One of the key programs is each regional network creating its own policies. (Start with a skeleton diagram and work on agreement with the key stakeholders.)

Figure 4.13 creates a platform of an open ecosystem with shared services and open API and presents a graphic similar to that used by Medicaid to represent the planning and architecture process.

Goal and Functional Integration From Many Perspectives

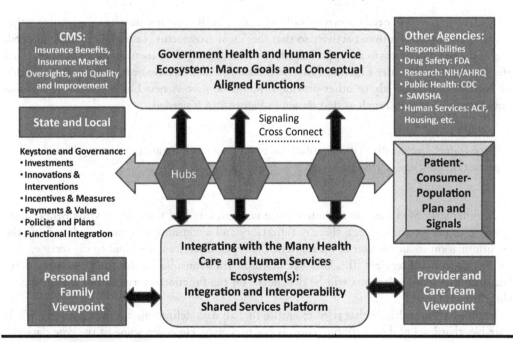

Figure 4.12 Chronic care focused patient moved to the center: total needs are center for health, mental health, and human service alignment.

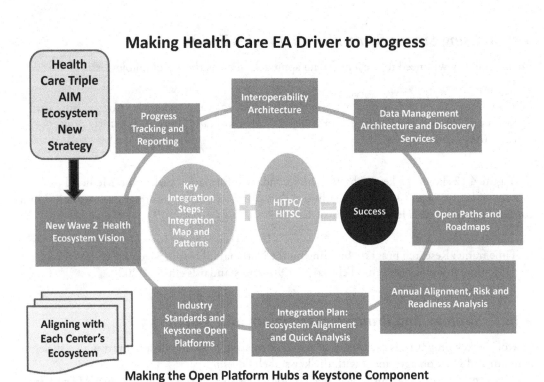

Making Health Care EA Driver to Progress

Making the Open Platform Hubs a Keystone Component
of the Health Ecosystem Improvements.

Figure 4.13 Updating key concepts to align with Wave 2 needs.

Each ecosystem will need its own overall strategy. These Roadmaps must be integrated together and have an annual alignment activity so that the "cross ecosystems" or the SOS can be aligned. One of the key differences in the approach advocated is making the patient an equal partner in any reference model. The older EHRs or functional reference models have been all from the provider, the labs, the radiology lab, or other providers' points of view. A new bi-directional patient and provider reference model such as that shown in Figure 4.14 is needed.

Time frame: Use the NIST policy machine to create a set of regional common sharing and protection policies—2018.

In other large SOS, such as the intelligence systems, criminal tracking, environmental management, or the weather system, there is a directory and a common approach to identifying the key information about the user of the services, the types of services, the input to the services, and the outputs from the services. This UCORE of information must be standardized, but many other data and information elements will be dependent on the functional services and the ecosystem where they are used.

Far too often, healthcare has tried to ensure that all data definitions are in agreement. While desirable, that level of data harmonization is not necessary. However, some of the core data elements do need to be aligned. This is a key step to the success of this next wave of integration and interoperability.

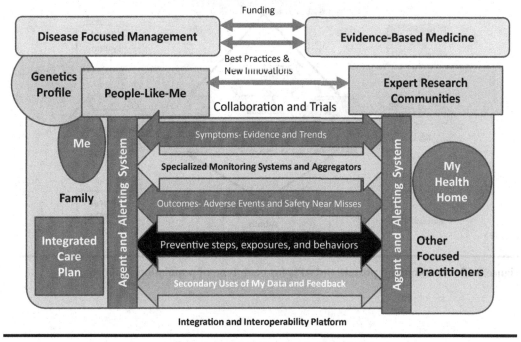

Figure 4.14 Patient–provider aligned with bi-directional communication.

Analytics need to provide the right information, at the right time, with a clear understandability of actionable information. Analytics have to be more than reports, and will have to be integrated into all patient care processes and into all oversight and management processes. An analytical process framework will be described on how the framework can be used for decision making and tracking the integration–interoperability progress. The analytics framework can be integrated as a set of services tailored to the type of "information-decision" making needed by the patient, the providers, the payers, the policy makers, and the public; this will decrease confusion, allowing transparency on what is decided, and on how the decision was made and why. The portals and APIs must not only share information, but must link to tokens related to payments and align the payment, administrative, and clinical data as shown in Figure 4.15.

Using Public APIs that are defined by standards organizations and developed by government or industry to be shared as open sources-open services capabilities that can be used and extended by industry.

4.17 Leveraging Emerging Trends

SOS architectures:

The HL7 FHIR and the HSSP standards activities can be driven by the new congressional mandates for interoperability along with the potential interoperability stack being considered by ONC as shown in Figure 4.16.

Planning that FHIR is available and can be widely used as part of Meaningful Use 2 and 3 will require that during 2016 the government–industry and standards committees must work closely together. ONC

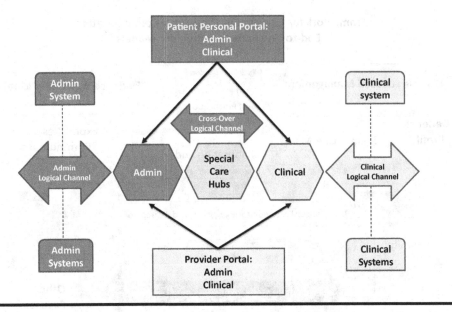

Figure 4.15 Recommend portals and APIs for each type of population supported.

JASON Example Architecture
(With proposed mapping to standards)

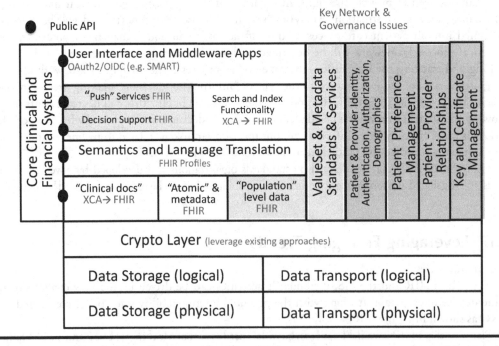

Figure 4.16 Using JASON diagram with MITA, FHA, and the agency enterprise architectures.

can become the standards driver in agreement with one or more standards organizations. The year 2016 can be the tipping point for standards collaboration that has been shown in other industries. Standards will make progress and some elements will be used in Meaningful Use Certification in 2017, and by 2020, the standards will be complete and the full deployment will be widely available.

A key question now is how much action does the government take on standards, and how much action is the responsibility of industry?

Government-funded programs like the Defense Medical System Modernization (DMSM) and Medicaid and other projects can insist on integrated and interoperable FHIR solutions. The federal government is paying for it. Other governments and other organizations can require compliance as well.

Perhaps, many of the old ideas that died as part of the artificial intelligence "winter" should be considered, made more practical, and aligned with the current XML, Service Oriented Architecture (SOA), Resource Description Framework (RDF), and other technologies.

Information-Centric Models, Standards and Demos

Parts of the ecosystem will have common elements, but may also have special elements; 20%–30% of the elements will be different and unique.

4.17.1 Fitting the Individual Organization into the Related Networks

Each organization will need to create a strategy and an approach that shows, from a business point of view, how it can work with national and local leaders, and how each individual healthcare organization can be a leader and leverage best practices.

Some of the elements that have to be created to link an organization's strategy into related network partners are shown in Figure 4.17.

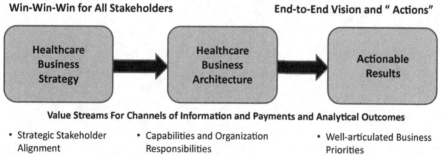

Putting Healthcare Business Architecture Into Action

Figure 4.17   Recommending SOS thinking and process steps for all health and related human services needed.

4.18 Conclusion

Wave 2 needs more planning and architecture to achieve the key goals; this means that a real strategic–architecture–planning process with a clear set of value propositions is required. Who will be driving this? The organization's CIO, CMO, and the newly appointed chief medical information officer will be providing the organizational leadership. However, if the organization is a small or one-person provider shop, that one-person performs all of those functions; the organization needs to define partners and to pick a strategy that fits within the region and within the ecosystems in which the organization must survive.

Chapter 5

Using New Medicaid Reform with Next-Generation MITA for Patient–Consumer-Information-Centric Health and Human Services Interoperability Architecture and Shared Services in the 2018–2020 Time Frame

Abstract

After a demonstration project that results from Chapter 4 and Initial State Innovation Model Deployments in a number of states, a set of patient–consumer-information-centric shared services and cloud-based capabilities can be supplied as shared services and through the patient advocacy disease foundations as part of the neighborhood and community national programs. Also individual patients who want to manage their own care with improved techniques can be brought on board and supported with bridging agents. Both neighborhoods-communities and bridging agents are discussed in more detail in Chapter 10.

When the basic interoperable shared services and Public APIs are available, the next steps illustrate the ways that Medicaid can connect to human services, mental health, and related human services. Medicaid can also use medical homes, community-based services, and rare and chronic care management to assist with decision making and to include analytics. This connection between Medicaid and these other services is the preparation for the real value-added phase.

Time frame: Chapters 5–9 do not have as much detail and will require more refinement and alignment of innovation projects over the next 2 years. This health IT transformation journey will be supported with additional articles and artifacts shared through a Health IT Transformation LinkedIn Group and involvement in working groups such as those of ONC, HL7, HIMSS. Please join and support and provide feedback and improvements.

5.1 Introduction

Aspects of Medicaid IT characteristics are described and ideas are shared at the Annual Medicaid Enterprise System Conference (MESC) and the NAMD Conferences. Over the next few years, a panel discussion and workshop at these events can be used to provide a community-based approach to sharing innovations.

Some states are leading the interoperability agenda (14 states have requested funding). Other states' programs (New York's Medicaid Reform, Healthy Washington, Minnesota Health, and other projects) need to be shared with additional states and moved toward a shared services approach.

5.1.1 Background

The MITA was designed with the initial concepts developed by the author in 2004–2006:

- To be the common business-driven framework for Medicaid strategic planning
- To support Medicaid evolution with a service-based approach
- To foster a lower risk, less big-bang approach
- To move toward incremental modernization

This service-based approach did not focus sufficiently on interoperability, and has been waiting for health interoperability standards and health information exchanges to be refined. MITA has evolved, but it still has some key elements that need to be updated to create the Wave 2 MITA. Over the last few years, the author has been asked what he would do differently. This chapter addresses some of those gaps, and the ideas will be presented as change requests to CMS.

One of the key capabilities that is missing is an analytics framework that looks at the past, current, and future measures as shown in the conceptual diagram in Figure 5.1.

5.2 Challenges, Controversies, and Issues

5.2.1 Challenges

The basic elements of MITA have remained in place since 2006, but it is time for a pause, and a determination must be made on the way that Medicaid can address the following issues:

- Principles and patterns must be addressed for business capabilities that can be aligned to related linked services, while identifying the gaps and areas needing improvement.

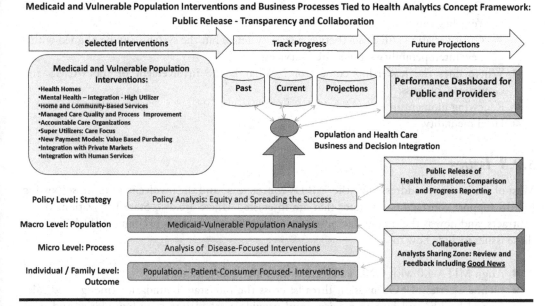

Medicaid and Vulnerable Population Interventions and Business Processes Tied to Health Analytics Concept Framework: Public Release - Transparency and Collaboration

Figure 5.1   Recommending analytics policies and interventions feedback and analysis.

■ The NAMD has shared many innovations that are working at the middle level across all state boundaries; however, many of their ideas have not been included within MITA.

■ MITA has not been linked with ONC and other human services issues. How can shared services be developed based on many state innovations that can be cost effectively managed with shared services and Public APIs?

MITA does not include ACOs, medical homes, or value-based purchasing, though some of the states have proposed those approaches. A new set of reference models with shared services should be defined.

5.2.2 Controversies

States now fall within two categories, those with Medicaid expansion and those without expansion; however, there are some common problems with both categories. Resolution is needed in the following areas:

■ Pure data modeling has failed in trying to harmonize the data models globally across all systems. But in other systems, like the military, a set of key common identifier information and core information has been harmonized into what is called a common core or UCORE.

■ Some Medicaid states are aggressive in expansion, and interoperability has to be addressed consistently now.

■ All states should be aggressive in improving efficiency and effectiveness.

■ Medicaid is the stepchild.

■ Implementation and development issues exist:
  – Short cuts: making the minimal changes to the legacy system and saying it is MITA compatible.

- Can integration and interoperability shared services be integrated into a main frame? Yes, they can.
- Great variation still exists (between state systems) but the systems can be aligned with a new interoperability set of shared services.
◼ Where does the leadership come from? What is the involvement of states-CMS and Governor-Congress?
◼ Renewing momentum.
◼ Herd mentality.

5.2.3 Issues

Most of the issues are addressed by the "MITA contractors" and the involvement of those existing MMIS support contractors for states that are interested. There are also State Innovation Model contracts, and now is the time to factor innovation and improvements back into MITA. Some of those issues include how to

◼ Align MITA 4.0 with ONC's FHA and interoperability strategy.
◼ Define a series of SOS mission threads: cross the interstate boundaries among Medicaid, mental health, and human services, and provide a set of intrastate boundaries and message exchanges for eligibility and enrollment, sharing past activities, and also supporting a Medicaid patient who needs to travel to a center of excellence for treatment that is not available in the patient's state for a given type of rare disease.
◼ Establish a common set of universal data elements based on a simplified terminology, the "literacy-based ontology," aligning the translation from expert providers and their scientific concepts with a simpler terminology that the patient–family–advocates can understand.
◼ Expand MITA principles to address design aspects that connect to new concepts like the ACOs, medical homes, integration with mental health and substance abuse, and other new concepts that can be loosely integrated along with other state innovations with a common approach to integration and extension management.
◼ Provide a data integration model and intrabusiness model including external Medicaid with mental health/behavioral health, human services, and marketplaces.
◼ Provide a set of state and local–state–regional–national analytics framework capabilities, and describe the types of decision making that new business intelligence (BI) and Big Data capabilities can address:
  - Define a set of Big Data use cases that are aligned with the NIST Big Data reference models and the CMS Big Data approaches
  - Define a set of use cases and a set of Medicaid Big Data storage and access to similar cases of project innovation and improvement performed by others, so they can be used for comparison between states

Spreading innovation may require identifying similar attributes and sharing information on what did and did not work well, and sharing among the communities across the country. For example, there are many commonalities and common challenges among rural and urban areas, but there are also unique elements, like Brooklyn where there are more diverse languages than almost any place in the world. Understanding the make-up of the general population, and also the specific population of the practice or the ACO or the zip code, will require a common set of population dimension and characteristics.

Each state, as part of its Medicaid Advanced Planning Document, must use the new extended MITA reference model, and include defining the shared services and APIs to be created and used as part of their upcoming projects:

- Who is responsible? Can Medicaid and states' HHSs organizations then define those they will create, and identify the shared services gaps? The objective is to create an open services library that can be shared among those states addressing similar projects. One of the initial steps will be to create shared services and APIs that provide integration, interoperability, and analytics capabilities.
- The planning should use a set of standards and reference models that need to be identified for Medicaid and shared with ONC. ONC can use MITA 4.0 and beyond, and the many Medicaid innovations, as a key investment going forward.
- One of the key elements is to translate the DOD, intelligence, and other large SOS experiences to the health IT consulting community, and to present the approaches to new and traditional health IT vendors. The SEI/CMU has supported other large complex projects, and now they need to be leveraged by healthcare transformation projects.

The integration process has not been well documented in complex systems. System integration practices have not been shared, but now is the time for the community to define good integration–interoperability practices, and to show how analytics methodologies can be integrated into these large-scale complex projects. A set of best practices and illustrations of ways to link the outcomes of the many projects can be created by a group such as the American Council of Technology and Industry Advisory Council. Other groups, such as the INCOSE, can define a systems engineering, integration, and tracking process that can be used in this new era of integration–interoperable medicine.

5.3 Solution and Recommendations

Medicaid has been in a reporting mode for years, and the Medicaid Statistical Information System (MSIS) state reporting statistics data warehouse has had problems supporting the program management and tracking capabilities of Medicaid systems, population health, and quality measures and outcomes. States have used many different reporting formats, and it has been difficult to compare progress and results across the states. MITA needs to have a performance reference model and a set of common performance outcomes on the efficiency and effectiveness of the Medicaid investment architecture and plans for improvement of the architecture. A set of agreed-upon goals/questions is needed regarding improvements–efficiency–effectiveness and "community health," and Medicaid patient types for quality, safety, and outcome measures. The National Quality Forum (NQF) and the CMS Clinical Quality and Standards measures can be part of a set of BI-based data warehouses, as shown in Figure 5.1, by reviewing the methods for developing, integrating, and deploying the selected Medicaid interventions across the state and across the population.

The objective is to understand how the innovations and improvements for Medicaid can be analyzed based on the CMS State funding and payment policies, the Medicaid population in a state, and a comparison with other states. How are patients with rare or chronic diseases managing their health issues? How does healthcare IT allow for other health capabilities needed to support the patient and the family? How can healthcare IT be linked to other family related social and economic issues? This is especially important to the integrated care model among mental health, substance abuse, and related primary care health needs, along with the related human service needs. Many states are finding themselves with an epidemic of care needs for methadone and opioid addiction in rural areas, and cocaine and heroin in urban areas. Economic and cultural disparities must be addressed along with the large cost of healthcare. Of key importance is understanding how the disparities are addressed on a fair and consistent basis, and understanding what works and why. This will require analytics that include more information than traditional Medicaid systems have had in the past.

5.3.1 New BI Analytics Framework Needed

For years, Medicaid did not have enough information or enough facts, and many policies were made without the BI that can now be part of a common framework. This framework will provide state-to-state or region-by-region data, and illustrate how some interventions worked and others did not.

Many states have tried to move toward improved reporting as part of the ten-state pilot T-MSIS, but have had great difficulty because the pilot lacked an overall data collection and reporting framework. A process model needs to be built, with the information flow from reporting to the data warehouse, with a clear set of business scenarios that support a set of goal–question–indicator–trends common decision-making steps. Figure 5.2 shows a life cycle approach to decision making and the types of decisions. Each state can have separate goals–questions–indicators–trends–dashboards, but they can all use the common set of question–answer templates and common macros that can be shared with CMS and with other states. The question–answer templates can be used across all states, can be used with different underlying tools, and can be represented in the Predictive Model Markup Language (PMML) that is a standard used across all the major BI tools.

Chapter 6 addresses this in more detail.

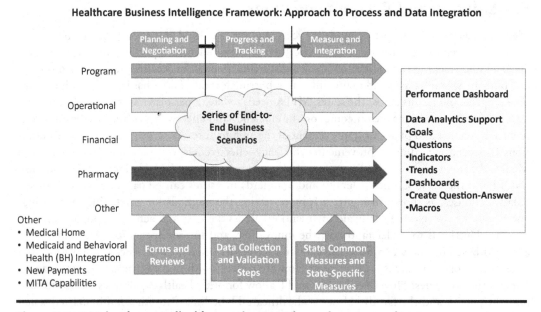

Figure 5.2 Moving from Medicaid reporting to BI for each program change.

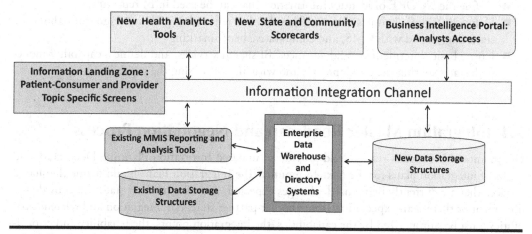

Overall Show a Blend of Earlier Reporting(e.g., MMIS for Medicaid) with New BI Reporting and State and Neighborhood Scorecards:
Discovering Best Practices and Issues of Equity and Underserved Needs

Understanding the Types of Questions, Measures, Analytics, Indicators, Trends and New Analytics Needed by States, Medicaid, Neighborhoods

Figure 5.3   Extending MITA with a mini-BI reference model.

Figure 5.3 shows a conceptual level and Figure 5.4 shows a more detailed logical framework and the linking of data across both old approaches and the types of BI tools.

Reports will not be totally eliminated and, as a transition step, the existing reports (shown in Figure 5.3) will allow each report to be compared with new BI analytics tools and a script approach.

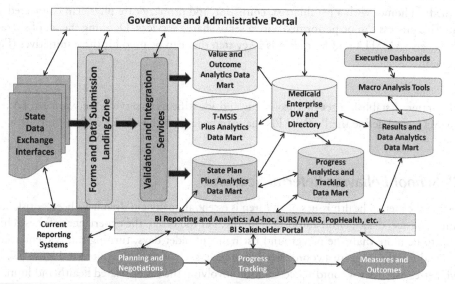

New Integrated Medicaid Enterprise Business Design and New Ability to Trace and Analyze Program Decisions and State Funding Unified BI Architecture and Integration Points

Figure 5.4   Detailed MITA BI logical architecture of shared analytics services.

A detailed update to the MITA reference model that will include a connected BI model, rather than previous reporting capabilities, will need to

- Define how Medicaid BI will fit with the health ecosystem model
- Define the data/information subject areas that can be linked to the BI
- Define the UCORE of identity information that can be used in BI reporting
- Define BI logical channels and interfaces that can reflect data gathered from throughout the state, data shared with CMS, and comparative benchmarking
- Create basic, intermediate, and advanced BI shared services, and define a capability model with states sharing the development, and with all states using the capabilities

5.4 Integration Master Roadmap and Negotiation Process

On an annual basis, each state should provide an updated Integration Planning Document, and status of integration plans for the next 18 months. The Integration Plan should define the shared services that are currently being used, changes expected, and whether that state will provide the document or there is an expectation from another partner state. All integration and related capabilities must be summarized by the capabilities, the integration points, the reliability and criticality of that integration, along with funding source, governance approval and change steps, and the methodology for design, verification, certification, and integration testing.

5.4.1 Cross Clinical and Administrative Coordination Scenario: Mental Health and Medicaid Alignment with Integration and Interoperability Shared Services

The first type of health event has both dual enrollment and a personal identification event between mental health and substance abuse; in addition, the patient is enrolling in Medicaid and creating a "dual-medical home" with a psychiatrist, counselor, and primary care physician connected to the patient. This process can be performed with a set of shared services. Defining the set of shared services between SAMSHA and Medicaid is a key step that can be used for these initiatives (Figures 5.5 and 5.6).

Time frame: Establish a set of enrollment and identification services between MITA and SAMSHA, and define the Public APIs that can be used at the service edge—June 2015.

5.4.2 School Behavior Referral Scenario

Addressing the mental health issues of children is essential; many children have been at risk because of family violence, drugs, child abuse, or bullying. Far too often, the experiences of these children turn out to be more than the playground fist fights of older days, turning into violent school or family incidents that require a coordinated approach, such as that illustrated in Figure 5.7. Using such vignettes can drive a coordinated solution involving the set of related health and human service events and the exchange of information in a reliable and safe manner.

Mental Health (MH) and Substance Abuse (SA) Final Rule - Major Medicaid Impact

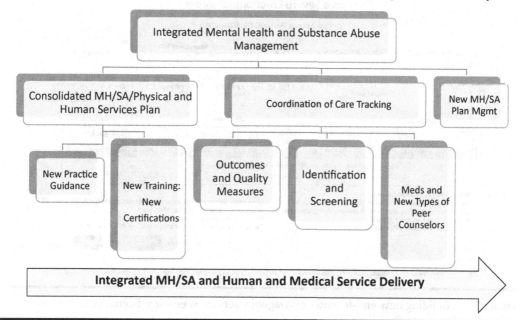

Figure 5.5   Recommending strategy and reference models extensions to CMS: strategy baseline.

Mental Health and Substance Abuse Final Rule – Major Medicaid Impact

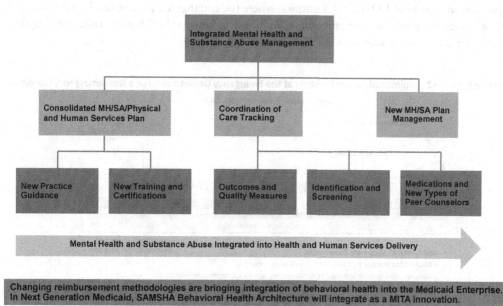

Figure 5.6   Recommending new integrated MITA and SAMSHA alignments.

Example Scenario 1 – Child Presents at School with a Behavioral Health Issue Eventually Diagnosed as a Severe Emotional Disorder

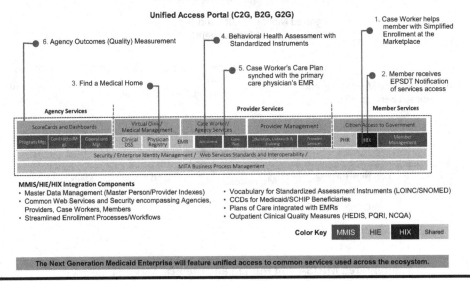

Figure 5.7 Building new end-to-end cross-agency service scenarios: Scenario 1.

5.4.3 ED Set-Up of Mental Health and Medicaid Connections

Frequently, first responders arrive at a scene to see a situation that calls for either mental health treatment or physical health treatment that will be covered by Medicaid. Today, because of the Global Justice Information Network, a new message format can be created to link police/first responders to a hospital ED to find a hospital where the endangered patient can be safely treated. In most states, the patient can be enrolled in Medicaid and mental health programs, and coordination of care can begin as shown in the vignette shown in Figure 5.8.

Example Scenario 2 – Uninsured Person Presents at the Emergency Department For a Non-emergency Condition

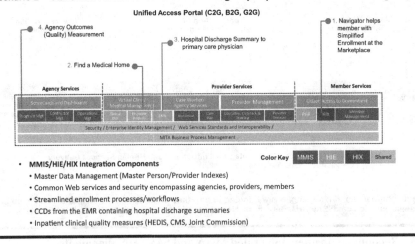

Figure 5.8 Building new end-to-end cross-agency service scenarios: Scenario 2.

5.5 Emerging Trends

Over the last few years, the states have introduced many new ideas, and now is the time to update and create a MITA 4.0. MITA 4.0 must be tied to mental health, and especially to substance abuse and overdoses. Unfortunately, the Medicaid population does not have the advocacy groups that Medicare does, but Medicaid can become the common bridge across the states and to the federal agencies. The CMS state program (with the support of NAMD and MESC) need to achieve the following during 2016:

- Use an SOS modeling approach based on INCOSE Workshop and extensions along with more formal models of critical "integration points" where safety and resiliency are critical, such as follow-up appointments or alerts when a lab test shows specific conditions
- Create a new MITA integration reference model and a UCORE MMIS marketplace and mental health and human services link
- Use a service meta publishing capability like the OASIS Business Document Exchange with related OMG/HL7 HSSP standards
- Accelerate the standards efforts with the development of open shared services that are shared between CMS and state programs
- Collect a set of goal–question–indicators templates related to the performance information from the patient-centered point of view along with the point of view of the Medicaid provider community
- Create an integrated care model with similar goal–question–indicators templates, an integrated view of the Medicaid MITA and SAMHSA behavioral health reference models
- Define a set of integrated health and human services scenarios

A technical approach is needed to define how related services can be integrated and enabled with the use of software agents. Software agents can collect the data and integrate a BI-based set of capabilities. Agents can represent a given perspective and support a type of user—either patient or provider. User agents can profile the many types of data to an integrated view of a Medicaid population, and a population can be aligned with the set of services and the population's needs by zip code area.

An overall integration model can show how the system of systems can fit together with integration points, links between the system capabilities, and color-coding and annotations of the types of links. Also, a data collection and software agent that includes a feedback information channel can define a set of messages that can travel across a software defined network identified as a performance logical channel. The SOS map will show the links across the service capabilities for integrating Medicaid or behavioral health systems together into a value delivery network. These concepts are shown in Figure 5.9.

5.6 Moving the Medicaid Systems to a Patient–Consumer Focus

The next generation of the Medicaid systems must shift focus from a 1970s functional model to a patient–consumer engaging model as shown in Figure 5.10, where engaging, improved ease of use can create a patient-centered approach to the range of Medicaid subpopulations. The large Medicaid population can be divided into categories. There has often been a myth that those in the Medicaid population did not want or care about their health. My contention is that, because of

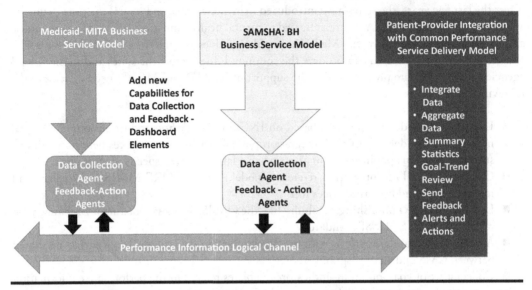

Figure 5.9 Performance data collection, analytic, and feedback from the patient/provider-centric delivery perspective: adding new capabilities to business services.

these people having so many inequity issues and food, housing, and financial problems, they were too overwhelmed to address their health and wellness issues. In addition, the information has not been delivered to the Medicaid community in a format they could understand. It may be advisable to borrow ideas from Education's Title 1—the approach to low income students.

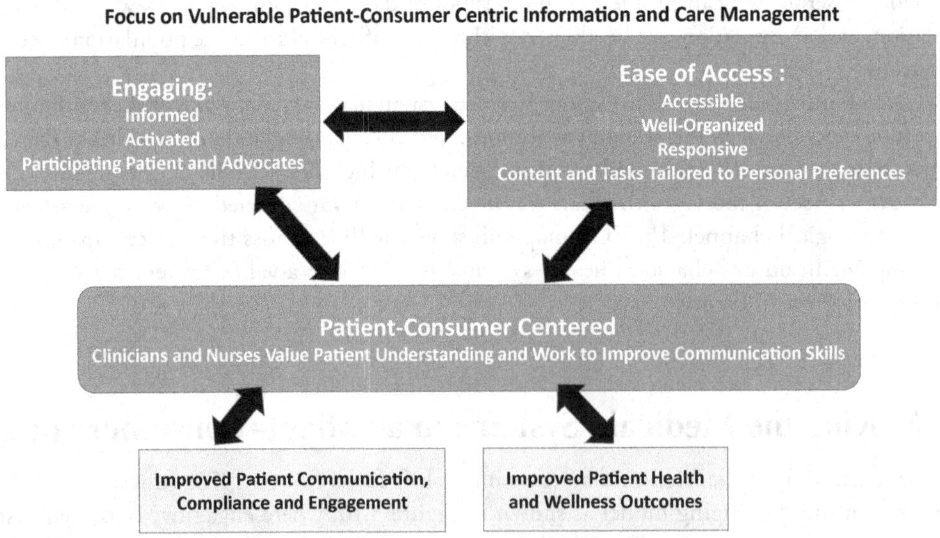

Focus on Vulnerable Patient-Consumer Centric Information and Care Management

Engaging:
Informed
Activated
Participating Patient and Advocates

Ease of Access :
Accessible
Well-Organized
Responsive
Content and Tasks Tailored to Personal Preferences

Patient-Consumer Centered
Clinicians and Nurses Value Patient Understanding and Work to Improve Communication Skills

Improved Patient Communication, Compliance and Engagement

Improved Patient Health and Wellness Outcomes

Figure 5.10 Patient–consumer engagement can become a critical part of engaging the Medicaid population.

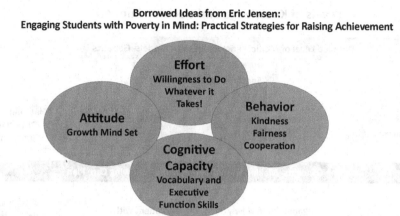

Figure 5.11 **Patient–consumer engagement borrowing from processes used in Title 1 education.**

One of the key steps to engaging Title 1 children, along with their parents and grandparents, in education or in their health is to get them to believe that they can learn about healthcare and wellness, and that their learning is very important to their well-being. That critical step of getting over "I can't learn that" and "I don't want to ask dumb questions" is essential for improving healthcare delivery and for gaining compliance with medical directions. Many individuals without a high school education are very intuitive, and can function well with the assistance of friends and family; however, they need to overcome their own attitudes. Nurses and some very people-oriented doctors get this naturally, but others must be trained on health literacy concepts, and learn how to present vital information in small cognitive chunks, often using culturally translated material with strong visual infographics (Figure 5.11).

Like leveraging any other field into healthcare, adjustments must be made to support the Medicaid or disabled population. Some of the early translation ideas are shown in Figure 5.12.

The overall concept of creating a set of common scaffolding, and not overwhelming anyone with technical information, may actually be foreign to the doctors themselves who pride themselves on their medical school survival skills. But a patient–consumer-centric approach may need to have an incremental delivery of new concepts, verifying that the patient–consumer understands

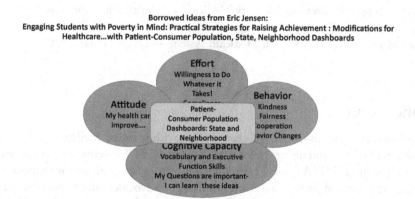

Figure 5.12 **Patient–consumer engagement tailored to the Medicaid subpopulations.**

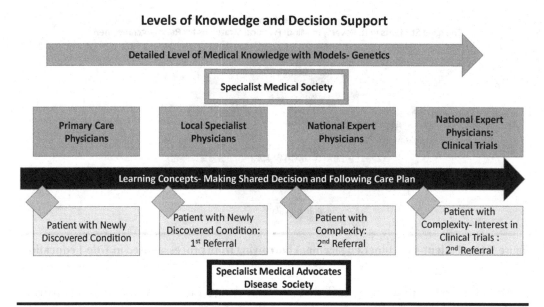

Figure 5.13 Patient–consumer engagement requires consumer-focused categories of knowledge.

the information before decisions that rely on that information are made. This new concept is shown in Figure 5.13.

The perception that the Medicaid population was not interested in learning about health has been a key roadblock. Health literacy involves correcting the misunderstandings regarding key concepts about health, and explaining the benefits of diet, education, and taking one's medication even when one feels perfectly well. Having the patients–consumers learn these concepts, and integrating their learning into new practice transformation, can be part of a Medicaid reform initiative like the initiatives seen in a few states like New York (Figure 5.14).

Another key roadblock to Medicaid change has been the "hard design" of the data model, and the lack of a new dynamic data model like is shown in Figure 5.15 with the ability to evolve to it in an incremental fashion.

> Time frame: A team of previous industry Medicaid IT consultants, who have discussed the need for a next-generation approach, will convene a workshop during 2016 to leverage these and other ideas to shift the focus on Medicaid systems—Target January 2017.

5.7 Conclusion

There is evolution to a patient–consumer-centric focus with involved Medicaid patients and their advocates that will take a fundamental reform of the Medicaid IT systems to what I have described as the Next-Generation MITA, a new culturally complete, respectful, and incremental learning model. Engaging Medicaid patients and their families and advocates must begin now. At the same time, we must move from a system of isolated, siloed service delivery to a system that integrates all of the needs of a patient or a family unit. Medicaid reform can be the lynchpin of reform across

Developing a Strategic Learning Direction:
New Concepts, Approaches and Tailoring to Workplace Factors
Strategic
Government- Fed-State-Local Drivers
Strategic
Medical Association & Ecosystem
Drivers and Focus Areas
Population
Analysis:
Needs and
Trends
Defining Organization
Strategic Direction:
Coopetition and Value
Delivery Networks- Change
Initiatives
Provider
Satisfaction
and
Concerns
Workplace Factors
Practice
Structure
Geographic
Location
Patient
Population
Working
Environment
Relationships
with Co-Workers
Perceived Quality of
Patient Care
Electronic Health
Records
Physician-Support
Staff Incomes
Health System
Changes

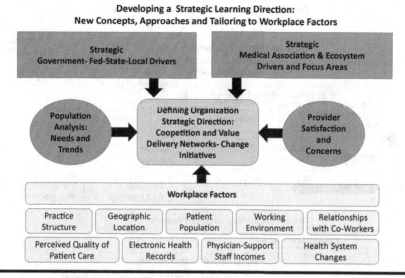

Figure 5.14 Patient–consumer engagement must rely on performing a Medicaid subpopulation analysis and understanding population support in each individual state and in communities within the state.

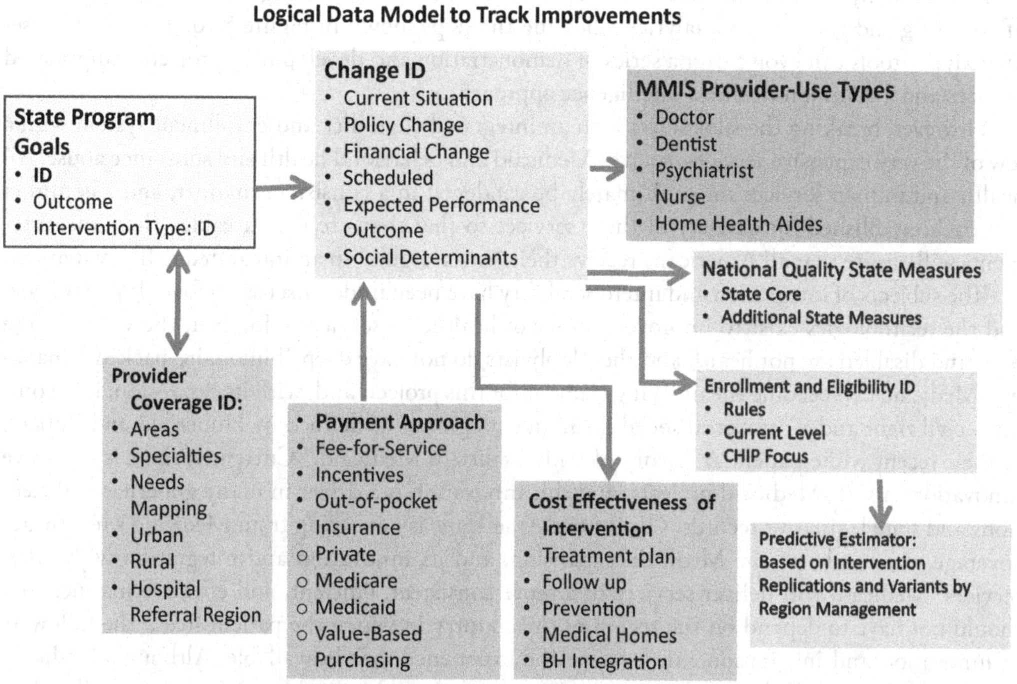

Logical Data Model to Track Improvements
State Program
Goals
• ID
• Outcome
• Intervention Type: ID
Change ID
• Current Situation
• Policy Change
• Financial Change
• Scheduled
• Expected Performance
Outcome
• Social Determinants
MMIS Provider-Use Types
• Doctor
• Dentist
• Psychiatrist
• Nurse
• Home Health Aides
National Quality State Measures
• State Core
• Additional State Measures
Enrollment and Eligibility ID
• Rules
• Current Level
• CHIP Focus
Provider
Coverage ID:
• Areas
• Specialties
• Needs
Mapping
• Urban
• Rural
• Hospital
Referral Region
• Payment Approach
• Fee-for-Service
• Incentives
• Out-of-pocket
• Insurance
o Private
o Medicare
o Medicaid
o Value-Based
Purchasing
Cost Effectiveness of
Intervention
• Treatment plan
• Follow up
• Prevention
• Medical Homes
• BH Integration
Predictive Estimator:
Based on Intervention
Replications and Variants by
Region Management

Figure 5.15 Next-generation Medicaid can align with other new changes and begin with a new data model that supports evolutionary data modeling.

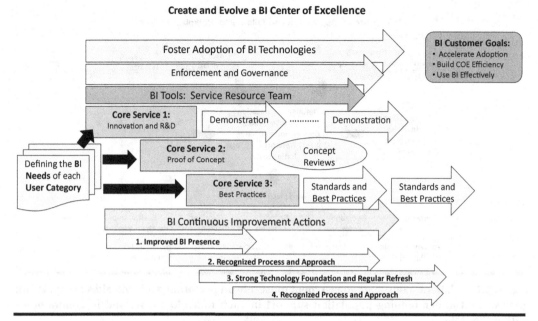

Create and Evolve a BI Center of Excellence

Figure 5.16 Incrementally building business intelligence (BI) into all processes: Not an add-on.

the country, and not the stepchild. One of the key changes that is needed for Medicaid reform is to build in analytics and business intelligence into each program change with a consistent form of reporting and goal-driven analytics following the steps shown in Figure 5.16. The common set of analytics tools can evolve over a series of demonstration and development projects using shared services and a common business intelligence approach.

However, breaking the silos starts with an integrated eligibility and enrollment system with a few of the very expensive services, such as Medicaid and behavioral health and substance abuse. All health and human services must ultimately be cataloged in a consistent manner, and a common approach established for delivery of these services so that they are measureable. These measurements will ensure that all Americans receive their "social rights" in an integrated delivery manner.

The subjects of integration and interoperability have been under discussion for at least 10 years, and the technologies exist to improve delivery of healthcare services. However, the voices of the poor and disabled are not heard, and their lobbyists do not have deep "billionaire-backed" financing. Medicaid can become the unifying element for this project, and, with its expansion, is becoming a civil right and a "universal social insurance program," as defined by Huberfeld and Roberts in their recent white paper, "A Theory of Universality in Medicaid." Currently, there is extensive innovation in state Medicaid projects, and this innovation is a driver in many gubernatorial elections and state legislative records. One in five Americans is benefiting from Medicaid's healthcare coverage, the results of the Medicaid expansion, and its innovation and integration with other services. Medicaid will deliver services in a more consistent, efficient, and effective manner that should not have to depend on the region of the country in which the patient lives. The followers of innovation and integration can leverage the experience that is available. Although Medicaid directors and many others may know the success of the new Medicaid programs, especially when politics are involved, good news and success stories in this field are not "breaking news." Medicaid can be a collaborative success story that helps pull people out of poverty, so that they will not have chronic conditions or cancer or birth defects that could force a family into poverty and often bankruptcy. Medicaid can be the social insurance program and "sleeper program" that does not get the recognition it deserves.

5.8 The Practical Stuff

Working with one or a number of non-profit independent organizations can be a practical step to providing the public relations for Medicaid and to defining some basic building blocks for collaboration:

- Using Medicaid innovation and associated HHSs improvements
- Leveraging and adapting success from other states
- Creating an open services governance approach
- Encouraging more states to work together; this has shown progress and results to date

Starter kit for delivering Medicaid expansion and alignment activities: behavioral health, dual eligible, homeless, foster care, etc. Innovation can be driven by collecting the many ideas and shared services from all the projects shown in Figure 5.17. These projects can then seed a repository of ideas and shared services.

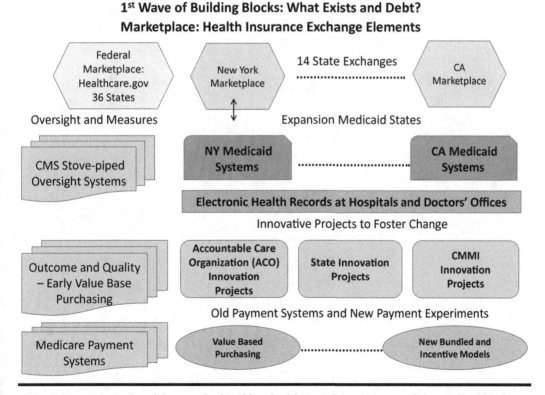

Figure 5.17   Innovation driven at the local level with state innovation models, Medicaid reforms and accountable healthy communities.

Chapter 6

Fostering Innovation and Integration, Alignment and Continuous Planning into Your Evolutionary Life Cycle

Abstract

Healthcare transformation will need innovation and continuous integration planning that aligns with legislative and policy changes. Healthcare has been stuck and the fee-for-service models and the government shadow of Medicare and Medicaid pricing structure have held back the innovation level of healthcare. As new Health IT models focus on patient–consumer-information centric technologies and use new standards, the key is to foster innovation and share those success stories in an open transparent manner. Innovation from State Innovation Models and Medicaid Reform seems to be migrating across state boundaries while new "stories from the ground" have to be created. Collecting good news and success stories and getting them to be leverage will take a new innovation incubation process. It will take new innovative business processes and use of "fast smart ready technology."

6.1 Introduction: Fast Smart Ready Technology

New fast smart use of technology must pick the ready technology and place it into a continuously evolving plan and into a culture that fosters innovation. There are many differences between healthcare where the long-term research funding on new cures need to be funded by agencies like the NIH and their institutes along with the philanthropy of Disease Foundations such as Cystic Fibrosis Foundation, Multiple Sclerosis Society, American Heart Association, or American Cancer Association, or many of the other rare or common diseases. Innovation can happen at the cusp of the challenges faced by the patient—the advocates and the frontline providers and the researchers in what can be called "Care and Cure Networks." Innovation also requires funded experimentation such as those sponsored by the CMS Center for Medicare and Medicaid Innovations or the Robert Woods Johnson Foundation and the many small and regional improvement initiatives that are addressing big and small challenges. Fostering innovation needs incentives, a new innovation governance structure, new innovation economics, and a process where the technologies that can be used by a series of innovation can be formed. Innovation is not just one giant leap head but a series of small challenges that can be integrated into a continuous innovation–integration plan. Healthcare Transformation can be treated as the present day Apollo Moon shot and requires similar planning and leadership. The planning for Health Transformation can use the older Apollo mission approach along with ideas from futurists like James Canton: *Future Smart—Managing the Game-Changing Trends That Will Transform Your World—2015* and Steve Androiles pragmatic new paradigm on how to identify and select *Ready Technology—2015* are blended together into a continuous innovation and integration planning cycle with the right mix that was used successfully in the Apollo project to encourage daring and innovation. First, today where fear and threats have become the norm on any government project. Innovation will require the engagement of the future smart consumer and advocates that care about their health and spend so much time on their own health or the health of a family member with a rare disease. While the ACA triggered and enabled many experiments by organizations and states the dissemination and alignment of these many improvements will need a visible innovation and integration continuous planning that fits into an SOS life cycle.

Today, there are many innovation projects but no process to capture those innovations and share them. An Health IT innovation community such as a LinkedIn community can gather the success stories as shown in Figure 6.1. Others can be collected in a conceptual framework shown in Figure 6.2.

The technology and business innovation need to part of a cycle of innovation that address the large challenge that are broken into a series of smaller incremental challenges that reflect stepping

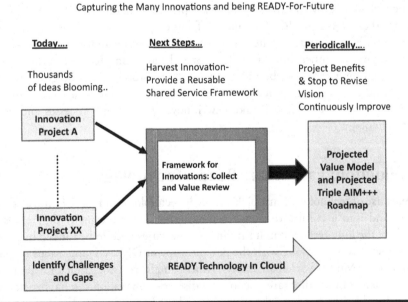

Figure 6.1   Capturing the many innovations and being ready-for-future.

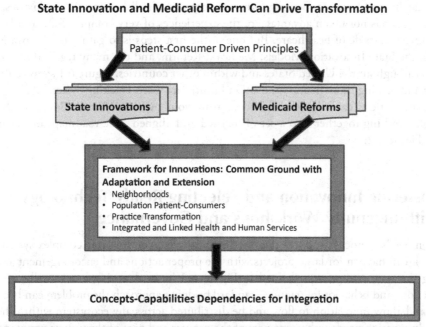

State Innovation and Medicaid Reform Can Drive Transformation

Figure 6.2 **Shows the recommended process for both investigating the work of the health policy and process visionaries and health IT visionaries, and leveraging the best practices and experiences with information sharing and integration across large industry segments and across complex systems like those of defense and intelligence.**

stones that can be replicated and adapted throughout the country. Those mini-challenges can be risk reduced by leveraging ready technology.

An innovation process must be built into the process and connected to the bridging technology with low-risk approach based on ready technology that is cloud-based, has open application interfaces, and built in security and privacy protections.

Each year healthcare organizations have to select the technologies that can be used and create a portfolio of innovative projects that can be linked to a set of successful innovation projects.

6.1.1 Innovation Manifesto

- Innovation must be requested and bred into the culture—"we got a man to the moon" so we can do this but it takes good engineering with high integrity management that provides *straight talk* and choices based on goal-value-risk analysis
- Innovation and risk do not have to be associated as long as a ready technology is selected and pilot tests are prepared
- Complex system of systems integration needs to follow a common bridging approach and use a agile and rapid life cycle process with focus on integration
- Ready technology concepts based on Steve Andrioles—2015 book and the evolutionary integration, interoperability, and goal-driven analytics and federated data strategy using bridging agents and common information approaches to simplify the integration tasks
- Innovation is a social process that requires openness and encourage, and recognizes the successes and shares the lessons learned

Fortunately, healthcare can leverage what has been accomplished in other industries; but, up to this point, it has not taken advantage of the experiences of very complex SOS and large integration projects outside of healthcare. But one of the first steps is to gather the innovations that are within the State Innovation Models, Medicaid Reform, and the many regional improvement initiatives throughout the United States and within other countries. Figure 6.1 shows a process of gathering and sharing those in an "Innovation Healthcare Case Tracking System."

These innovations can then be used in creating your own state, community, or alliance of associations working together into a set of focused and aligned agile roadmaps or blueprints as shown in Figure 6.2.

6.2 Fostering Innovation and Selecting Ready Technology with Ingenuity Workshops and Governance

Innovation needs a process and just does not magically happen for large complex system of systems. But it can happen for large projects with the proper actions and encouragement and nudging along the way. The process defined in Figure 6.3 looks daunting but actually with many human actions and behavior following a standard bridging approach the problem can become less complex and allow innovation to flow and be distributed across any ecosystem within the health industry. Innovation needs to become part of the process and part of the way not only individual companies work but also how innovations are aligned and integrated together. Industries also need help from their "associations" to foster innovation and government agencies can be great enablers

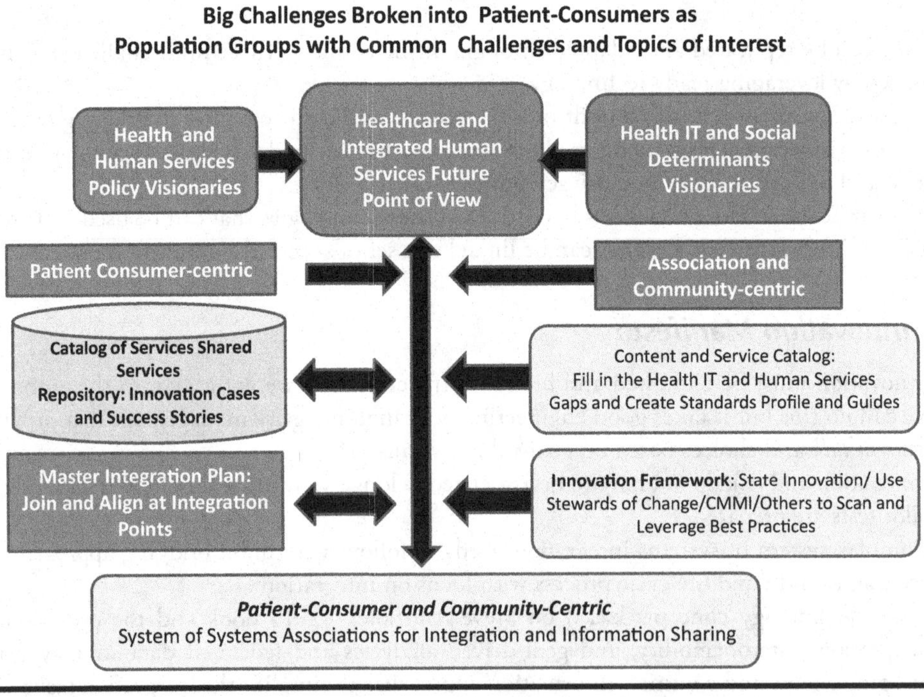

Big Challenges Broken into Patient-Consumers as Population Groups with Common Challenges and Topics of Interest

Figure 6.3 Scanning and leveraging experience and practices from other industries and filling the IT gaps.

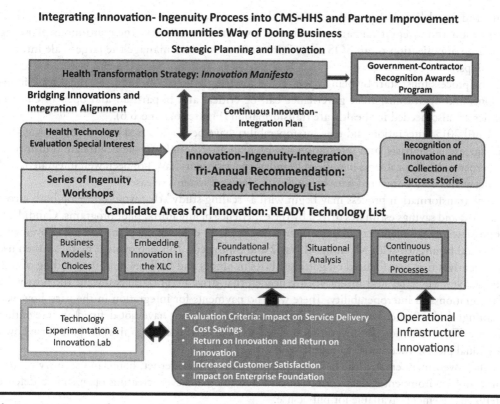

Figure 6.4 Process for managing innovation: Three levels strategic-integration level and ready technology level.

or roadblocks to innovation. There are many futurists who ignore the hard work and process that is needed. Government can learn from Silicon Valley and an innovation economy can be fostered and government contracts can create their own innovation springboards.

A pragmatic process that is shown in Figure 6.2 includes a strategic level at the top and ready technology level at the bottom with actions in the middle that involve workshops, governance, and most importantly integrating the innovation projects into the master plan. Innovations must be connected to strategic goals and be categorized into (Figure 6.4)

- *Strategic innovations* that reflect new ways of doing business
- *Bridging innovations* that show the linking between people, processes, and information across the silos of functionality
- *Operational infrastructure innovations* that reflect the cloud, the software defined networks, the mobile application, and the range of linked data and semantics that go beyond the current web technologies

6.2.1 Moving Innovation and Integration to a Primary Focus and Placing in Life Cycle

A solution implementation team has experience in the earlier water-fall life cycles and often has experience in agile version such as CMS expedited life cycle (XLC) an example of an agile and rapid life that includes none of them has factored in innovation and integration. Innovation and integration can be treated as goal-driven elements. The continuous planning of a large organization or an SOS must foster innovation and manage the large-scale integration steps.

The process must start by being open to and fostering innovation. Industry, the disease foundations, and open-transparent governance can be critical and bi-partisan and open to choices. Politics are also needed for healthcare transformation (Figures 6.5 and 6.6).

Until 2015, integration and true interoperability have been addressed on a small message-by-message exchange basis, and integration has been an afterthought in the healthcare transformation process. Many problems have been found as those systems have not been well integrated, and the delay and undocumented fixes break during the next systems release.

The transformation process may begin with a "scaling study" that would develop both a cost to deploy, and savings estimates driven by the experience of any initial pilot programs. Candidates for possible improvements could be put into a master target deployment plan. These improvements also could be aligned with Meaningful Use 2 and 3 projects. This deployment plan can then use the incentives that first focused on getting EHRs in offices and facilities, and the funding of that project. New vignettes and incentives are needed that drive organizations toward the next wave of integration and interoperability. There were no payments for integration in the past; however, Meaningful Use 2 and 3 are really focused on this subject, but have not defined an integration strategy. There may not be any common elements defined if each organization pays for its own individual pieces. There must be incentives.

The government created the basic building blocks of the Internet, homeland security protections, and environmental data collection and now they are even creating open-source defense intelligence elements available for public use.

To share information and help the integration steps through a network of industry-research advisors, the government can

1. Define the integration steps from planning to the actual integration; these are lost in the budget hole
2. Create a clear understanding of who is paying for which elements: government projects are required to have reusable shared services
3. Identify the innovation steps and select the ready technology
4. Define an innovation–integration life cycle and a set of integration patterns and models that can be reused and leveraged
5. Using open application program interfaces and intercloud technologies to discover and create network of networks that cross ecosystems boundaries
6. Define policies and protections across the integration points
7. Define an SOS set of logical channels
8. Define a patient and provider portal as the initial user interaction and integration experience that can eventually be personalized based on the users' special task and service needs

This chapter describes how to use a set of integration, interoperability analysis, design, and operational management models. These models use semantics, ontologies, linking of business processes, data, and decision grids that will bring integration, risk, and readiness thinking into the set of related SOS projects.

Agile-Innovative XLC: Integration-Innovation in each Project and Encouraging Open Choices and Fostering Strategic, Bridging and Operational Infrastructure Innovation

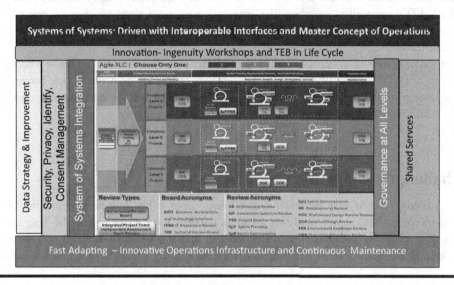

Figure 6.5   Integrating innovation throughout the life cycle.

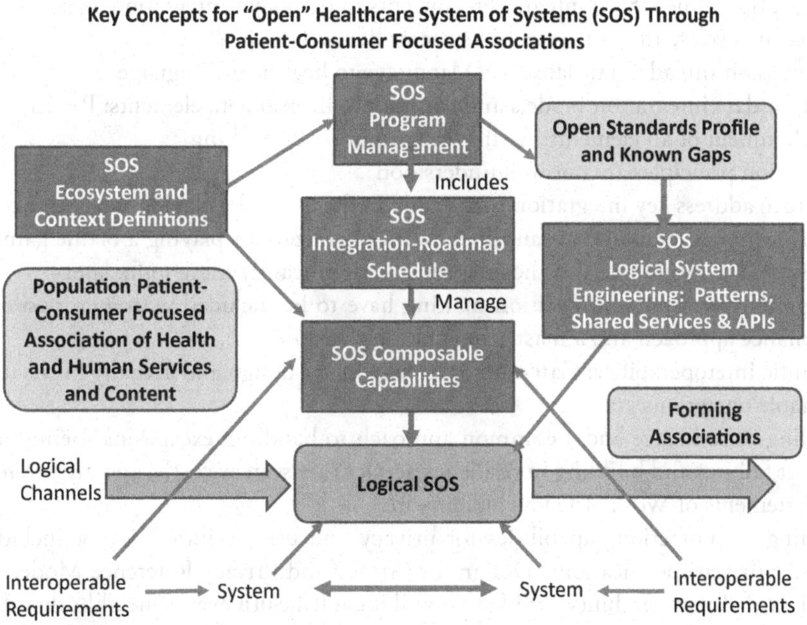

Figure 6.6   Innovation integrated into a system of systems framework.

6.3 Leveraging Capabilities: Ready Technologies

Because this process has occurred in other industries in other ultra-large-scale systems, defense and intelligence have focused on the SOS integration sets of projects that need to be aligned with each other. The SOS for multiple services (e.g., army, navy, air force, and even other governing bodies like NATO) must all fit together. This integration required a process change, new systems engineering, and new software engineering disciplines; this integration experience can be leveraged by healthcare.

Integration of system of systems has not been well defined. There have been some recent documents from SEI/CMU, and 10 years ago, a book was published on Continuous Integration, Enterprise Integration Patterns. However, the "integration shops" do not encourage documentation, and, in addition, each experience has been very difficult.

6.4 Challenges, Controversies, and Issues

The real challenge is not just presenting experience from other complex areas, but showing the relevance to healthcare. To illustrate that relevance, we must speak the language of healthcare and relate the complexities and experience and the second language and terminology. It takes speaking in both terminologies, and also finding the common ground between them.

6.4.1 Challenges

- Introduction of new SOS integration concepts to the major integration agencies
- Project life cycles, and not system of systems life cycle
- SOS mission threads: translate DOD language to healthcare language
- Need for data integration models and common universal data elements: Patients, providers, and alignment of all elements: we like to harmonize everything
- Integration principles are not well understood
- Failure to address key integration issues early in the life cycle; playing the "game of chicken," that is, who will be found at fault first. With organizations playing a blame game, integration issues are found late and those issues cost significantly more to fix later
- Integration planning and decision making have to be included with a cross-siloed system governance approach and a master integration schedule
- Semantic interoperability: Can ontologies help in the design and actually in the use of more adaptable operations
- Building in resilience and a common approach to handling exceptions. Being prepared to support failures and building in resiliency services are seen as costly, and are not required by the Statements of Work. The low bidder wins
- Building in protection capabilities for privacy and other "-ilities" is not included in the business-driven specifications. Design for Privacy and Privacy Reference Model and create a Standards Interoperability Profile that will include health events, neighborhood and communities and bridging agents to shift the focus to the people-centric approach and not be facility focused

EVERY STATE HAD TO MAKE SOME CHANGES TO MEDICAID ELIGIBILITY AND ENROLLMENT TO MEET THE ACA REQUIREMENTS: SUCCESS AND BEST PRACTICES

From CMS Presentation by Jessica Kahn—March 12, 2015

In 2013, Healthcare.gov received tremendous negative publicity. Often good news and good practices do not get the same level of attention. On March 12, 2015, CMS Lead, Jessica Kahn, Director of Data and Systems Group, Center for Medicaid and CHIP Services, summarized the experience and lessons learned in a presentation, "Modernization on Demand: Addressing Changing Eligibility Requirements."

The overall takeaway is that CMS did an excellent planning and staffing job, planned for contingencies, and conquered many issues by working with each state and with the states' many contractors. The change could have negatively impacted the 72 million patients under Medicaid and CHIP. However, the success allowed 10+ million more to receive healthcare service, and also allowed all the states to move into a modern and consistent approach to eligibility and enrollment. Forty-one states had to replace their old IT or paper-based systems and do verification with the Healthcare.gov data hub. The effort required planning for risks, and also required all states to develop and manage a mitigation plan. It created a flexible matrix oversight organization, with CMS government employees taking on additional responsibilities while still continuing their regular duties. The steps required extensive communication and a partnering attitude by federal employees and states and their many contractors. It required cooperation and teamwork by many government employees given extra assignments. Many people stepped forward to go above and beyond their normal daily assignments. There were lessons learned on

- Requiring mitigation planning by all
- Communicating and listening to the needs and concerns of each state
- Having clear lines of communication between each state and CMS with a federal matrix management approach

CMS good practices should be recognized, and each person should be thanked for his or her contribution. The CMS folks cared and delivered for the 10 million new enrollees.

6.4.2 Controversies

- Shared Services Acquisition and Reuse: Too many architecture short cuts. Because the low bidder wins, bidders do not include integration and do not create shared services
- Government is the integrator, but they have no process, limited skills, and no integration architecture: Integration Center of Excellence based on SEI/CMU
- Healthcare Integration Plan is not anyone's deliverable. The pieces will fit together, but the industry is not open/transparent. The healthcare industry needs to leverage experience from telecom and finance as they went through transformation based on defining a common set of standard communications
- There are great variations in integration approaches, and the problems are at the interfaces; services and common shared services can be used, but they have not been used effectively or widely

- Where does the integration leadership come from?
- Defining a new approach: Leveraging the SEI System of Systems Integration approaches, but tailored to a agile and rapid life cycle

6.4.3 Issues

The Department of Health and Human Services needs to first create a set of issues and get all of its operating divisions engaged not only in government programs, but also in supporting the "defragging" of the industry, and in creating new information, integration, and interoperability platforms, shared services, and Public APIs:

- Who is responsible for integration? That responsibility should not rest with a contractor or with a contractor that has not had experience—small business set aside
- Standards and reference models for integration
- Integration points
- Lack of large SOS experience among the consultants, and new and traditional vendors are not providing less risky options
- Lack of good integration–interoperability and analytics methodologies for the new era of Integrative–Interoperable Medicine

6.5 Solutions and Recommendations

Classic web services and even the trendy REST Patterns have not really addressed the integration issues.

One of the problems has been that web services have not considered integration, continuous improvement, and the changes occurring on both sides of the interfaces. Integration needed to be inspected and not tested, and most of the service governance tools have not been connected to the life cycle development processes.

The first generation of the web services stack did not factor in change, the semantic interoperability issues of both sides of the ecosystem, and the SOS scale problems. This lack of factoring is shown in health transformation where each project was on its own life cycle, and the readiness and risk of the end-to-end ecosystem was not examined until it went live. Long-lasting systems that are connected together, like the air traffic control system or the intelligence networks, consider how the introduction of changes will impact the operations. Healthcare transformation cannot become rigid; the alternative is to design the change management aspects into the system, and to create an adaptable integration process with a new generation of semantic interoperability and continuous integration test and development models and processes.

Prior to the ingenuity workshop a set of innovation preparation steps are needed as shown in Figure 6.7. These may be a starting point but other ideas will be captured during the workshops and investigated and tracked for their readiness to be used.

6.5.1 Integration and Interoperability Continuous Delivery and Integration Process Steps

The capture of innovation ideas and their alignment with goals and their planning in the integration master schedule are shown in Figure 6.7.

Concurrent Planning for the Integration and Interoperability of the System of Systems and the Continuous Delivery and Integration

New Health and Human Services System of Systems Needs Resiliency and Scalability

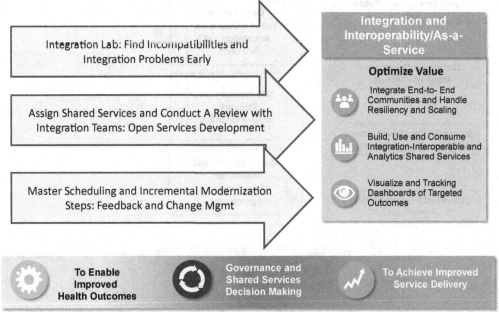

Figure 6.7 Continuous integration and deployment and planning from the start.

Develop a continuous integration and deployment plan that includes the following elements: ability to discover the data elements, their sources, their policies, and establish an open API to be used. Over the last 7 or more years, the Open Grid Forum and the other e-science world has created new integration with open API and now a federated management of clouds. Healthcare will follow e-science starting with research and with disease foundations that can connect their focused communities with partner cloud technology and using intercloud technology. These cloud technologies as presented in the series of NIST Cloud Technology Workshop briefings July 7–10 highlight the maturity and the gaps that still need to be addressed.

6.6 Continuous Integration Process for Health Ecosystem Model with Patient–Provider Exchanges

Health events need to "semi-automatically" coordinate the linked set of services that are triggered based on the patient's consent and desired interoperability "health event artifacts," and the transmission of that data to the primary providers and to the secondary public health, clinical trials, research data stores, and any quality and outcome data stores. Both the stores and the secondary data collections should be created without the need to route information. This level of automation should be built into the daily process flow.

Events can be identified or deidentified based on the patient and provider permissions and consents. The health events will trigger a set of "event correlation" tokens, consent tokens, safety-alert

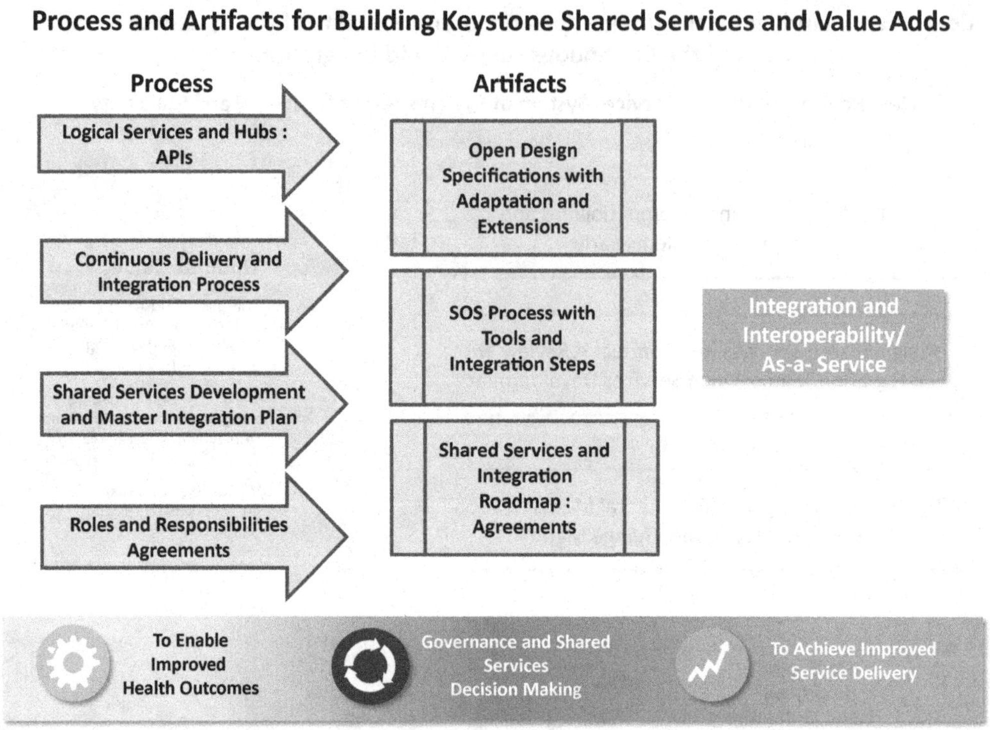

Process and Artifacts for Building Keystone Shared Services and Value Adds

Process	Artifacts
Logical Services and Hubs : APIs	Open Design Specifications with Adaptation and Extensions
Continuous Delivery and Integration Process	SOS Process with Tools and Integration Steps
Shared Services Development and Master Integration Plan	Shared Services and Integration Roadmap : Agreements
Roles and Responsibilities Agreements	

Integration and Interoperability/ As-a- Service

To Enable Improved Health Outcomes

Governance and Shared Services Decision Making

To Achieve Improved Service Delivery

Figure 6.8 Continuous integration and deployment and planning builds artifacts that are living and align with integration and interoperability services from the start.

tokens, payment-value tokens, and secondary use tokens. These tokens can be managed across the distributed set of services, and provide tokens for auditing and distributed agent-based controls. More detail on this approach is under development by the authors.

Health Event Data Domain—will include an event data model based on the events that are common for all population categories and for special episodes, such as surgery, cardiac events, and other health events flows, based on chronic or rare disease operational contexts.

Common health events can be used by patient care managers who are part of medical homes and care coordination roles. Health events can be defined based on clearly specifying why health event information needs to be exchanged and for what purpose. Event-driven technical standards can be aligned based on the patient-population needs. An integrated set of semantic ontologies can be new enablers that provide the vocabularies for sharing and that support the provider-to-provider, but also patient-to-provider, communication. One of the difficulties is ensuring that the semantic meaning is clearly defined at many levels of understanding and that the context of the data is not lost during transition and transformation. Technical capabilities provide the architectural context within which the exchange is executed. All of these components focus on the interoperability framework.

A set of high-level goals and series of hubs can become the initial connection points that can be bridging innovation technology. A conceptual representation of the process to foster ingenuity and innovation is shown in Figure 6.8. Innovation is really occurring at the state and regional level but also must be done by the federal government and innovation must be a consideration in all new bids and proposals and not merely "low-bidder wins."

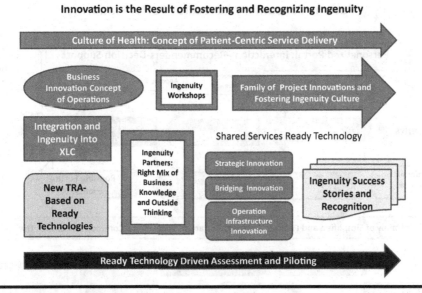

Figure 6.9 Innovation has to be presented and approved by governance boards: there are no bad ideas—all ideas have to be discussed and made visible.

The actual data constructs that define the event-driven data exchange content model and related alerts-notifications include the following:

- Mechanism for identifying and categorizing patient–provider assets for sharing
- Framework for capturing data elements and the relationship between them (semantics); the patient's expertise health literacy level; the provider's expertise and relationship with the patient; and the conditions/event being addressed
- Method for structuring the data, the standards used, and methods for exchanging the data/information so that users are able to both access and use the data/information
- Technical standards to design and implement information sharing capabilities into a health information sharing SOS network
- Approach for documenting exchange patterns
- Data/information flow to include the tagging of the data, discovery, and retrieval
- Principles, roles, and responsibilities for data management and stewardship

One of the keys is to create a collaborative environment for patients and their advocates as shown in Figure 6.9 that will think about innovation from the point of view of their needs and the needs of the types of health issues that happen and those that can be prevented.

Providers need to use tools such as the provider portal ideas in Figure 6.10 that can help connecting them not only with their patient population but also with their local and expert network of colleagues. The portal must provide value and usability in supporting the provider and his immediate group practice along with the population-community and provide connections to local improvement and new medical research initiatives.

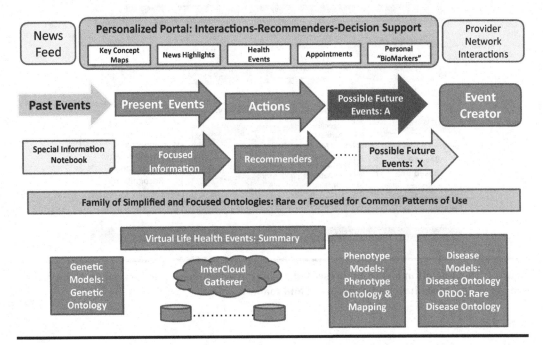

Figure 6.10 Patient–provider collaborate on information, new approaches, and best practices for given types of health events.

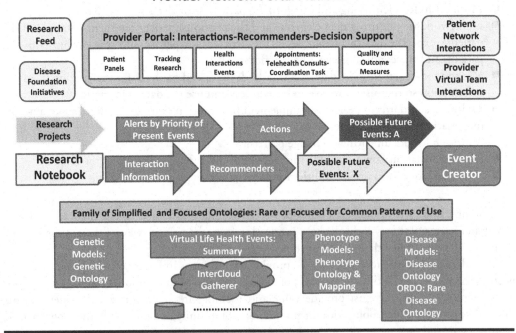

Figure 6.11 Connecting providers with patients and their network of collaborators.

6.6.1 Managing Based on Health Events

The set of health events will need to evolve with a common integration approach, such as that shown in Figure 6.12. Each health event is connected to patient–consumer to provide-community caseworker interaction and has associated data, services, and resources that are within a neighborhood or disease community. The health events are associated with bridges and an associated bridging agent. Those agents can check for safety conditions, protection and consent, can translate between medical professional language and consumer vocabulary and can reduce the confusion, complexity and information overload. More details are in Chapter 10.

6.6.2 Continuous Exchange and Alerting between Patient and Provider

One of the key aspects of dependable coordination of care and controlled processes will depend on reliable and safe delivery, guaranteed feedback, and alerting services that ensure that all critical steps are completed. One way to ensure that delivery, feedback, and alerting is to create a common set of health events that link to chains of services. This set up is critical and can follow the concept shown in Figure 6.12.

Each community of users that supports health events will need to follow a process to align the populations or related community by location or by specific disease type. The community support administrator will follow a series of steps shown in Figure 6.13.

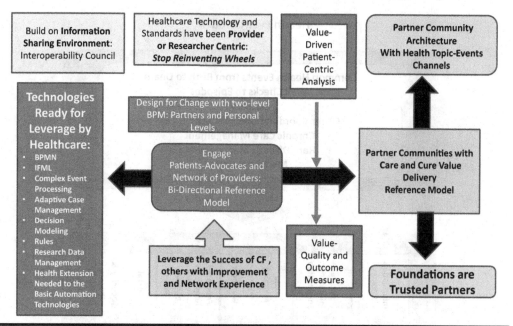

Existing Technologies Can Meet Healthcare Value Delivery Needs: Information Sharing Environment and Patient-Centric Approach

Figure 6.12 Defining and building event exchange patterns and workflows that drive a systems integration model.

Disease-Specific Focused Network & Analysis Framework
• Create a Strategic Roadmap and Collaborative Patients-Supporters-Providers and Researchers Network – along with Pharma & Government Researchers
• Define a Baseline and Goal-Oriented Quality and Outcome Measures
• Establish Value Delivery Networks with Value Payments and Bundled Payments
10-Year Strategic Disease Improvement Plan
Population Disease Specific Focused Group
Sponsored Research
Pilot Projects
Disease Registry
Trusted Connections
Improvement Initiatives
New Meds & Practices
Evidence Base
Value Delivery "Care and Cure" Network
Shared Genetics and Knowledge Network
Individualized Analytics: Tracking
Predictive and Disease Progress Models

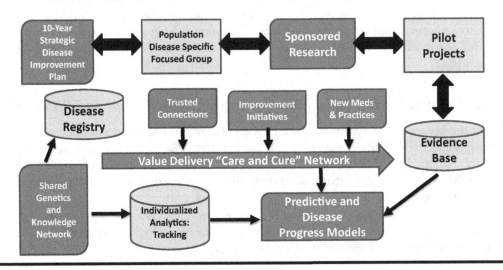

Figure 6.13 Creating a disease specific event flow model defining a care and cure delivery network.

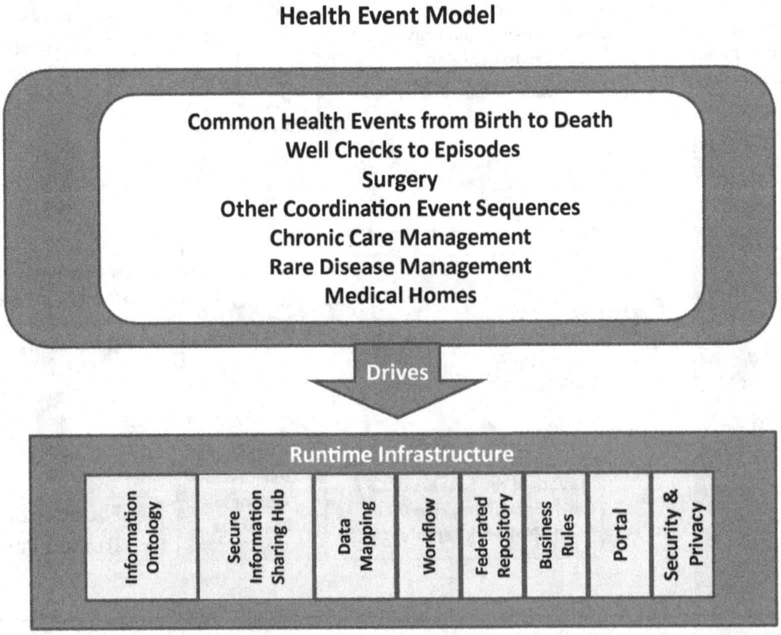

Health Event Model
Common Health Events from Birth to Death
Well Checks to Episodes
Surgery
Other Coordination Event Sequences
Chronic Care Management
Rare Disease Management
Medical Homes
Drives
Runtime Infrastructure
Information Ontology
Secure Information Sharing Hub
Data Mapping
Workflow
Federated Repository
Business Rules
Portal
Security & Privacy

Figure 6.14 Configuring the links from patient to medical home and related provider teams.

6.7 Creating Health Event Information Hub

Managing these many pathways will need both a patient-centric viewpoint and a set of provider viewpoints. A representative model for the configuration of these health information hubs is shown in Figure 6.14. The provider and patient information spaces are connected to one or more gateways with a set of agents that route, filter, enrich, and provide safety and health event alerts and notifications.

6.7.1 Creating a Patient and Provider Analysis Portal for Specific Diseases and Communities

Patient–consumer and providers and community case workers often talk past each other using different vocabularies and having different levels of focus. Today, talking past each other and the patient–consumer being confused is accepted. It should not be and there are ways to bridge that divide with consumer health vocabularies, with infographics, and with built in e-learning. We are now in the era of isolated portals that everyone has to sign in too. The average Medicare patient has seven different providers and may go to one or more hospitals. There is interesting information on each but they are not aggregated and integrated together. Just remembering all the sign-ins and receiving the e-mail traffic can introduce new frustration to the patient–consumer, and the providers are stuck in the same multisite problem. There has to be a bridge or gateway across the patient–consumer where not only health records flow but also understanding gaps and confusions can be closed. A representation is shown in Figure 6.16.

Health Event Information Integrated Landscape View w/ Life Events

Common Approach (Artifacts)	Common (Standards) Profile	ISE Interoperability Framework (I²F)	Industry Standards and Specifications
Business Performance Security	Reference View	Business/Operational Capability	Requirements Definition
			Representative Standards
Applications/Systems Security	Technical View	Technical Capabilities	Technical Standards
		Exchange Patterns	
Infrastructure Data Governance Security	Implementation View	Exchange Specifications	Interoperability Standards
			Implementation Framework
Service Design Principles – Assured Interoperability			

Health Events Ontology

Figure 6.15   Reference model for event-driven health information sharing hub.

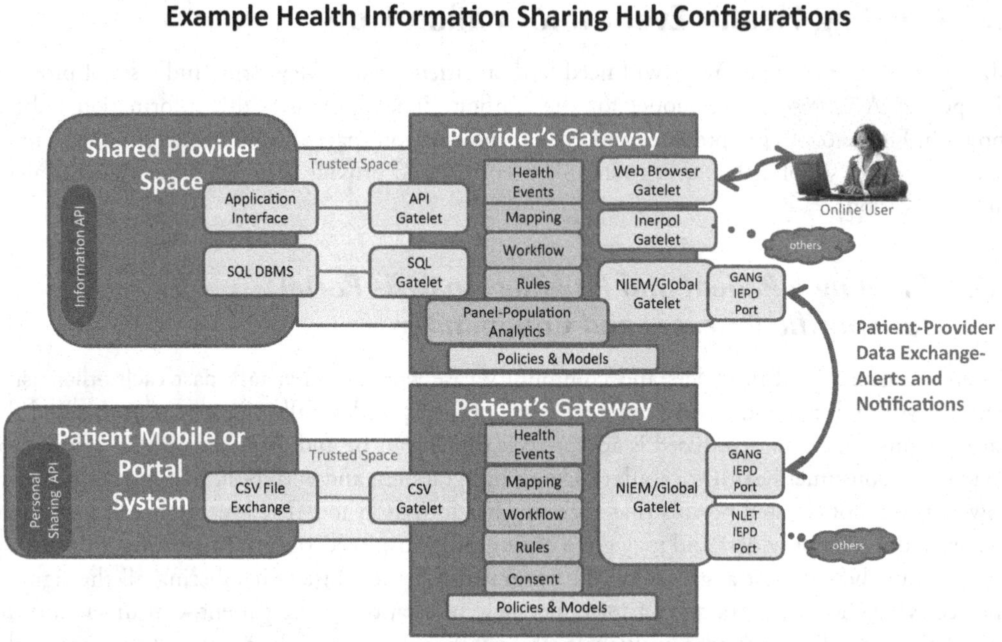

Example Health Information Sharing Hub Configurations

Figure 6.16   Integrating the provider and patient's gateways together.

6.7.2 Continuous Pathway Integration Readiness and Risk Scorecard

Defining the set of pathways and the vignettes and scenario-driven models can drive the integration steps below:

1. Define the patient and related health events to medical homes and providers
2. Use one or more scenario-driven end-to-end integration vignettes for planning and architect. Conduct no blame reviews and test early and often
3. Define the types of events to be handled. Define exception handling approach and a set of resiliency tests
4. Define health events, failures that could occur, and steps that must be handled, including guarantees, with a set of safety condition rules: "what happens if" conditions
5. Define how changes can be made with a rapid change and deployment process
6. Define "never happen" highly controlled conditions to meet critical conditions
7. Deploying this ready technology to close down the gaps actually takes a plan, such as shown in Figure 6.17

6.8 Emerging Trends

6.8.1 An Integration and Interoperability Research Project Needed

Many of these concepts have been applied to the military in an efforts to provide consistent information for battle. However, that experience was time consuming and difficult; but the lessons learned and the many concepts underlying that experience are being summarized as part of

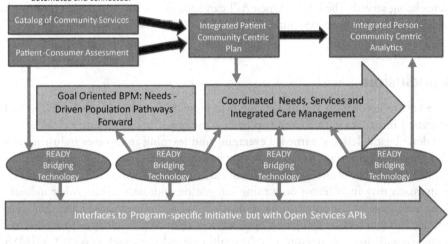

Figure 6.17 **Bringing ready technology into the federal, state, and community effort to create an Integration Blueprint.**

this continuing research. There is also extensive research in the next generation of choreographic end-to-end service design and the use of models and their self-adaptive and dynamic capabilities.

New approaches to address the integration and interoperability with neighborhoods, communities, and bridging agents are defined in Chapter 10. There are also other issues to be addressed, such as

- Use of semantic ontologies and new platforms like the Semantic Integration Agent-Based API Appliance to create an integration design and operational set of integration agents
- Creation of an information SOS Integration Mapping and Governance Decision Making Tool—Shared Service evolution

People-Centric Integration and Provider-Centric Integration—today a preset portal is set up for patients and providers at best and the ability to integrate in new services and define the types of interactions that meet a patient or providers personal needs is limited. This will require turning the integration problem on its head to address it from the end-users perspective. An analysis approach as described in Figure 6.17 shows the parallel analysis for both the patient–consumer and the alignment with the provider and community caseworkers. A bi-directional modeling tool connected to an Open-source Interactive Flow Modeling Language an draft OMG standard using a tool Webratio to create templates that can allow users or service providers to provide a range of user access methods that fit a range of situations and types of users from the first-time to the expert or the occasional visitor. The key to success of health IT transformation is the ability of non-programmers to provider the analysis and basic design of user interactions, workflows, and the ability to define neighborhoods, communities and create bridging with the heavy cost of programmers and the ability to reuses templates and models from common repositories.

Healthcare Federated Cloud and Open API Initiative is needed to build upon and move the HL7/FHIR, Agronaut projects to the cloud and include the intercloud and define the service level agreements, the federation management and to provide the ability for the patients to expand their interfaces and providers to build out their network to form networks that can meet immediate patient needs and can evolve to meet the population-service strategy that is adapted based on the patients being served. The OCCI Open API can become a basic foundation that can become translated to the healthcare ecosystem.

6.9 Conclusion

One of the keys to innovation and integration is to present ideas that can be leveraged by healthcare integration initiatives with a clear step by step process. It must include a clear benefit statement and describe any lessons learned. Leveraging and learning from other industries is a major cultural change. It is important to recognize that healthcare does have unique elements, but often they have not made it out of the "research chasm" to be implemented by the mainstream industry. Today's approach may involve not only using integration approaches from other industries, but also taking advantage of the opportunity to dust off and reengineer those ideas that were ahead of their time. This will require using new open services technologies, along with mobile SOS apps architectures; it will also require groups in the healthcare industry, such as AMIA, HIMSS, HL7, etc., to be open to learning and revisiting and repackaging old ideas.

6.10 The Practical Stuff

Integrators have to work with the medical-computer science research community to define a new set of hybrid integrator-medical-computer science solution architects and managers. They need to have a blended perspective that should include

- Viewpoints for project managers and solution architects: integration leaders are needed
- Defining a test-driven approach with documented integration risks and assumptions
- Defining reused and shared services packages and their APIs: API Lab and API Appliances
- Defining a common approach to handle cross-interface errors
- Focusing on resolving the problems, and not focusing on who is to blame

Chapter 7

Analytics Framework for Range of Health Services

Abstract

One of the first capabilities that integration and interoperability can support is a new approach to tracking analytics that can fit the individual organization and its regional and state perspectives. But the analytics have to be simple and delivered to the providers that are transforming their practice and delivered to the patient–consumers. Yes, there can be places for the real-analytics lovers and policy wonks but this has to be graphical, easily understood information that makes healthcare and the economic impact easy to understand. Think about this as the graphics on the front page of the *USA Today* or how to track your success on the fantasy football league. Just because it is statistics and risk factors—it can be presented to the patient–consumer and the local provider who wants to improve the care delivery. These new forms of simple-graphical analytics can also support the range of new innovative organizations. ACOs and new forms of value-network delivery will have to create analytic frameworks that can be aligned so that random nonintegrated measurements do not occur. Measures have to be integrated with each strategic improvement goal.

One of the key steps forward is to have an analytics environment that can be shared, comparisons shopping by patient–consumers, and benchmarking by providers who are undergoing transformation. One of the keys to the transparency of pricing, quality, and outcomes will be delivering the information to the patient–consumer with limited health or statistics literature. This can be done with a modified set of health-tailored infographics. The providers who are overloaded with information want to have the information also delivered in rapidly consumable byte-size chunks that are directly related to the transformation actions and the "scorecards" promoted in their neighborhood. Providing a transparency process, architecture, and shared services for both the doctor–caregiver side and visibility by the patient–consumers will be one of the key steps in health transformation.

7.1 Introduction

This chapter summarizes aspects of the health and social determinants for analytics that are key to Wave 2 of healthcare transformation. The key is to integrate analytics into the strategic, tactical improvement, and daily operations of the healthcare organization. Far too often integrating analytics is an add-on. Integrating analytics and decision making based on facts are a critical step in any industry's transformation.

Analytics have to fit into a large framework of integrated care management, illustrating how healthcare fits within the state–region and how performance can be tracked. A proposed framework is shown in Figure 7.1. The measurements must be able to determine how the many new concepts (the left arrows (orange)) can be measured as part of integrated care, and how they can align with the goals of the organization and the community of which the healthcare organization is a part. The Triple AIM +++ represents the reflection of the expanded and aligned goals of your organization with the state and federal goals. One issue cited has been that the measures and related analytics have both tried to measure everything and not allowed for a specific approach related to the improvements and interventional changes being made by the organization or the regions. Large amounts of data are collected based on NQF measurement sets, but they are not organized into what the organization can use. Fortunately, dashboards can be created to focus on the measures of interest for you, your state, and your region.

Those measures can be shared and comparisons can be made on your improvements, the trends and indicators of progress or regression, and your progress over time can be tracked and collaborative improvements made.

Integrated Care and Social Services Model with Health Events and Life Events including Prevention Actions with Quality and Outcome Measures with Transparency: New Patient-Consumer Metrics

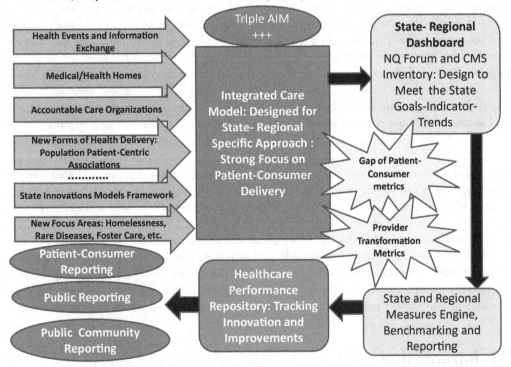

Figure 7.1 Common approach needed to support benchmarks of local, regional, and national perspectives analytics policies and interventions feedback and analysis.

This chapter will drill down on this top-level conceptual framework with the logical elements that need to fit together. This is intentionally "vendor neutral" architecture which can be aligned with many of the well-known vendor products that can be mapped against these capabilities. The vendor products can provide more capabilities, but the key is to support a common set of input or output data models. Today an organization's analytics staff may support a number of products. With mergers and acquisitions constantly occurring in healthcare organizations, every organization probably has one or more of those products. The data have to be integrated without having to replace all analytics tools. This requires that a logical analytics model be aligned with an industry standards reference model. A set of analytics can be integrated to one product family or, more often, to an ensemble or tool kit of analytics products that fit together. A logical reference model and defining interface–integration points for analytics will allow analytics and decision-making services to be integrated into the organization business process.

7.1.1 Leverage Analytics Frameworks and Early Health Analytics

Healthcare analytics have been accomplished with few standards or reference models. However, there have been some recent elements that can be leveraged (Figure 7.2).

7.2 Challenges, Controversies, and Issues

BI came out of manufacturing and Wall Street, and was driven by the ideas for balanced scorecards and strategy mapping. However, healthcare rarely worked as a business. The patient and the payer were two or more different stakeholders, and the policies and payment practices were not conducive to innovation. That is all changing, and, as new approaches are introduced, new BI approaches need to be introduced in a systematic manner.

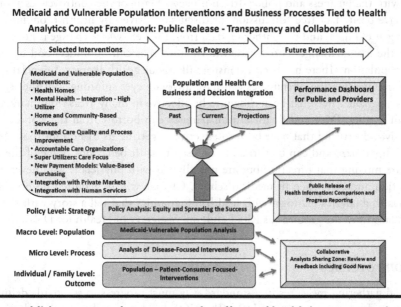

Figure 7.2   Establish an approach to measure the effects of health improvement interventions and policy changes.

7.2.1 Challenges

When Medicare and Medicaid were introduced in the mid-1960s, computers were not widely used, and paper fills and paper reports were the norm. Because of this early paper implementation, government and industry became used to reports, and the report formats were actually included in the Medicaid systems and delivered to what was then the Health Care Finance Administration, now the CMS. Healthcare first saw data warehouses and data marts in clinical trials and research, and only recently have vendor offerings shown how analytics can be integrated with business process.

A health analytics process was starting to evolve outside the vendor offerings with the ideas of Jason Burke, Health Analytics-2013, and the issues and ideas presented at a series of HIMSS Clinical and BI Communities of Practice and working groups. Analytics has been a strong vendor focus, but has had little focus in the standards arena or within academic research programs, such as North Carolina State University, Northwestern University, and others. At this time, there is not a lot of effort in open sources and standards efforts in health analytics, though more attention has been paid to clinical decision support systems (CDSSs); however, the market has not integrated decision support with workflows or business process models. They have failed to find the integration points that are needed to make the recommendations and alerts relevant to the doctors' practice experience.

However, medical decisions are affected by the flow or lack of flow of money (coordination of care payments that do not occur or other incentives). These decisions are also affected by taking a new "value-driven" and integrated approach to coverage and to preventive care and payment reform matters. Defining new performance-management models, and creating quality and outcome measures, are affected by the "data collection, annual reports, and comparisons" by the CMS CCSQ and the collection of Innovation Comparisons on each innovation sponsored by the CMMI. Some states, such as Wisconsin and California, have defined regional scorecards, and the Dartmouth Health Atlas has created useful studies and reports that have helped shine the light on the great variants in care and the geographic disparities; these analytics have not been integrated with the business and policy driven process. Many of the controversies about care and financing have been "fact free" discussion, or discussion driven by health economists who have been looking at old data, and not gathering data from the field where change is now occurring.

One of the key challenges is to create information that can be understood by the patient–consumer population. There has been extensive talk about health literacy, financial literacy, and certainly some presentation of statistics can have anyone's eyes spinning. But the telling of data stories with a personal twist has been shown to be effective in many areas from marketing to fantasy football leagues. Price and financial transparency can borrow from the world of marketing and persuasive advertising that have been so effective at getting us to stop for those McDonald's fries or pick up a pizza and can be turned to be used to shift behaviors. Some of the weight loss adds now are moving that direction but are not aligned with physicians who never were taught about nutrition and diet when in medical school. Change will be required on both sides and a common health analytics platform with health infographics that tell a story with both data and a "personal face from the ground" as Rita Landgraf, Secretary of Health for Delaware discusses.

7.2.2 Controversies

Aligning and gathering measures in a standard way must progress to standards definitions, and must integrate those measures into EHRs. The NQF has been working diligently since passage of the ACA, along with evidence-based medicine for PCORI, and with more data collection from CMS CCSQ and their service-based data collection, reporting, support for near-real-time research, and benchmarking.

The government has started to gather data and create standard quality and outcome measures for physicians quality reporting, hospital reporting, and end-stage renal disease. They have also begun to collect data on cancer centers, ambulatory care centers, and psychiatric facilities. However, they are working to improve and compare the facilities, and to allow for benchmarking and comparisons. Early results are positive and show great progress in measures such as hospital readmission rates, and some ACOs are doing well, while others are struggling with measures and providing analytics.

Now that the data are starting to roll in, states, researchers, policy makers and, at some point, politicians and the public, will be able to look at the healthcare industry and make decisions based on information and predictive analytics.

But, as changes occur, the BI approach will have to integrate with decision making at the policy, strategic, operational, and individual patient level. One of the concerns has been on health literacy, financial literacy, and vocabulary that is not consumer friendly. Why bother to try to explain it to "those people"—just tell them what to do! We may be "those people" or our friends and family may be and we all should demand to receive information in a more simplified format that should include:

- Our statistics—our risks—our predictive health information and our potential cost impacts
- We should be able to compare which hospital has the highest success rate, or the highest infection rates, and do comparison shopping for that joint replacement or other elective procedures

- Use of new health infographics and a clear learning path forward and an honest answer like "I don't really know what is wrong" and "Medicine does not understand that yet" maybe very helpful

Making the graphical easy-to-understand patient and consumer information will require a graphic style guide and the use of a consumer medical vocabulary and a health-statistic literacy level and prototyping with a variety of personnel. This will require a set of studies similar to those sponsored by the SHARP-C user interaction research funded by the Office of National Coordinator but also involvement by the newly forming ONC Consumer Task Force.

Now is the time to create a more comprehensive BI framework approach and to link to other reference models.

7.2.3 Issues

It is difficult to improve what you cannot measure. Measurement is new to medicine, and there are many issues, as shown by the clouds and blocks representing possible actions in Figure 7.3. There are many groups that have taken up the cause, but there is a need for a public–private leadership with the NQF receiving public funding, and with the CMS CCSQ and CMMI and a set of Health Improvement Initiatives that are networked together (The Network for Regional Healthcare Improvement [www.nrhi.org]):

- Taking the early seeds of improvements and analytics and spreading them with a process, an architecture and visual in both a patient–consumer and provider understandable approach
- Defining a new NQF aligned set of measures that can be adapted and used for not only facility measures but also for patient–consumer measures that can be understood by all

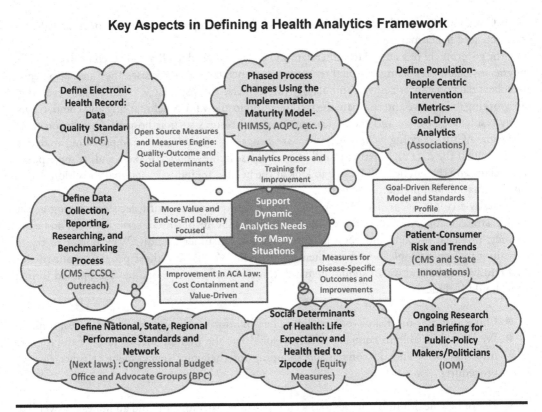

Key Aspects in Defining a Health Analytics Framework

Figure 7.3 **Many analytics and possible improvements for "Medicine Meeting Measures" have to be integrated together.**

- Providing a collaborative industry user-interactions portal experience to gather and review their reports, and receive incentive payments
- Use new health infographics and simplified statistics presentation
- Introducing new value-based purchasing and research partners all having a patient–consumer focused approach and not just geared to the physicians involved

CMS is also making the data quality and outcome for hospitals, physicians, and a range of other specialty centers available to the public, allowing near-real-time policy research. HIMSS has focused on training, processing, and defining maturity models. There are still many standards that need to be aligned. Two of the biggest issues are addressing the medicine-to-measurement literacy issues and the integration of performance measures into a national approach that is consistent from individual facility to local regions, to states to nation-wide metrics.

The good news is that there are many actions being taken; however, they are not coordinated. Recently, ONC has begun a measures initiative, but has not yet created a vision and roadmap.

7.2.4 Challenges of Analytics Integration

One of the key changes necessary for analytics integration is to shift from periodic reports to ongoing dashboards that support goals–questions–trends indicators, yielding an action approach that gives near real-time feedback and fact-driven decision making. This process needs to move toward what has now been popularly called BIG Data, but be tailored to the range of healthcare and medicine-based decision making and evidence-driven policies. The problem is that the analytics need to be collected together, but that collection cannot create a gigantic data warehouse with all patients–providers–resources, and cannot track all health events. Rather the collection of data must be converted to an analytics SOS method of thinking in which analytics aggregation and auditable-trusted processes are used. A set of logical analytics trails can be defined, and open services measures engines, aggregators, and predictors used, with an integrated CDSS and the business process and decision-making modeling approaches from business, and alignment with new payment reform systems.

7.2.5 Challenges of Stakeholder Engagement: Vendors with Abstract Services Layer

All of the participants need to be gathered together with a convening group (IOM), and the vendors have to form a health analytic open service layer. While all vendors can create their own interfaces in the form of APIs, they still might not fit together seamlessly. A new initiative, such as the HL & Argonaut API project, can provide the environment where cooperation can be achieved. This is similar to the tipping point found in other industries, especially if that cooperation is driven by new cooperating initiatives, such as those by the BPC, ONC, HL7, ACOs, and the use of the experience of other industries.

7.2.6 Challenges of Interoperability and Analytics

It has taken years to achieve cooperation among leaders in the banking, security, and insurance industries. Healthcare can follow a path like the financial industry that created the Enterprise Data Council, and worked through the OMG standards organization to define a "smart data" initiative for the financial industry. They have also used the XML Business Reporting Language (XBRL) to converge together into an integrated analytics and reporting approach. A similar approach will be needed as new value-based purchasing and other bundled payment models are created for healthcare. OMG has discussed creating a similar initiative for healthcare with extensions to XBRL to reflect dashboards for individuals, patient panels within a practice, and disease-focused dashboards. An XBRL for healthcare can be created and aligned with a subset of quality and outcome measures that are selected from the NQF, but linked to organizational goals and related to improvement initiatives.

It will take a few years to coordinate all stakeholders to create a detailed roadmap for interoperability and analytics, but the 2017–2020 timeframe will require that a new framework be in place.

The NIST Big Data Reference model and other ideas presented later can be piloted in selected states and regions that have already shown leadership, and extension outreach and involvement can begin.

7.3 Solutions and Recommendations

One place to start is to integrate "business intelligence and interoperability" thinking into the Medicaid state programs, and to track ways that the planning and negotiations that occur with the state advance planning document can be linked to the Medicaid and CHIP program management. In this way, there will be a shift from reporting to more integrated progress and tracking, not only of the intervention at the individual program change level, but also connected to other related initiatives:

- A standards performance dashboard can be defined
- Common concepts related data analytics can be linked between goals
- Specific types of questions can be answered
- The indicators of progress and trends and common dashboard shared services can be created

This is summarized in Figure 7.4.

Time frame: Recommend an analytics project to a set of states to create a Medicaid performance dashboard and pilot projects with a number of states involved—June 2016.

7.3.1 Analytics Reference Model

Key to this integration is the creation of a healthcare organization BI analytics step to present to a standards organization. An early draft should be presented, and a separate document explaining all the elements is needed (Figure 7.5).

Time frame: Create a draft document and related request for information (RFI) for standards such as OMG, and get a number of analytics companies to participate—2017.

7.3.2 Analytics Data Model: Common Identifiers

Analytics must support a range of goals, questions, and metrics, but the key is to use a common set of identifiers for the information sources, including tracking the interventions, their goals, and

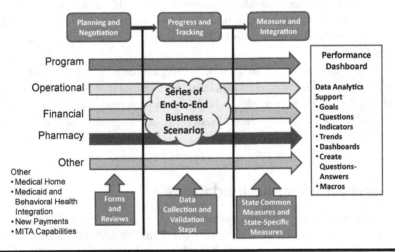

Figure 7.4 Building analytics into process improvement and change cycle.

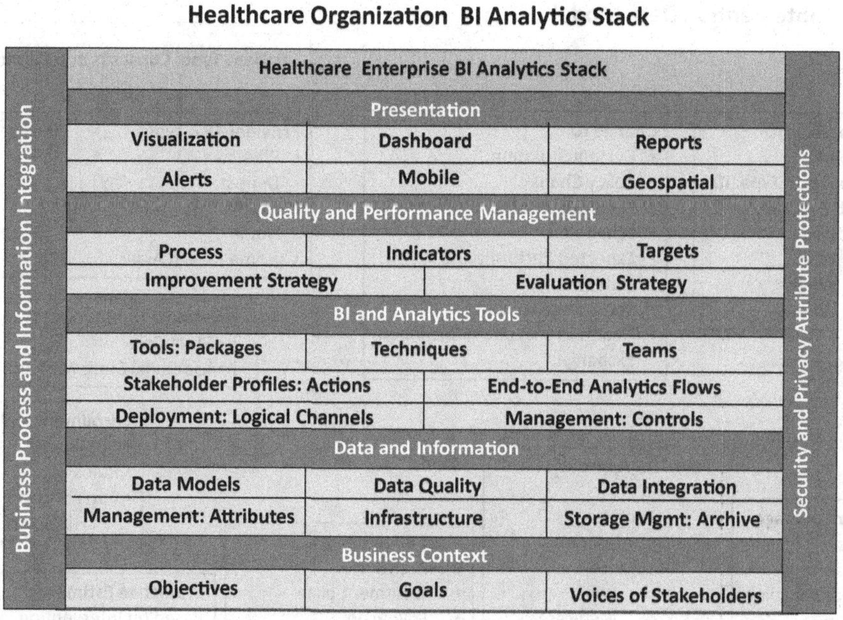

Healthcare Organization BI Analytics Stack

Business Process and Information Integration	**Healthcare Enterprise BI Analytics Stack**		**Security and Privacy Attribute Protections**

Figure 7.5 Analytics framework for health analytics.

the types of interventions and health events that are to be measured. An earlier draft of common identifiers for health analytics and improvement intervention is shown in Figure 7.6.

> Time frame: Create a common data model that can be linked with the NQF data model and the CCSQ Data Model—Fall 2016.

7.3.3 Predictive Process Models: Immature but Needed Now

Those who have worked with healthcare analytics have mostly considered past data and made comparisons between regions of the country or different practices. Very little predictive modeling has been done, though there is a recent set of conferences and new tools coming from entrepreneurs. In addition, health economists are becoming a known entity.

Some of the tools are using the Predictive Model Markup Language (PMML), but there has not been a strong process focus. This modeling and language provide a draft, and will need to mature; however, a more appropriate approach is needed now. See the draft ideas in Figure 7.7.

7.3.3.1 Fitting into the Surrounding Environment

Include the 12-step process for defining how the individual organization's solution fits in the ecosystem: Meaningful Use 2 and 3 emphasize connecting with all the key elements:

1. Note what is happening in the individual organization's region
2. Ask what similar organizations are doing
3. Discover what provides the individual organization with the most competitive advantage

Intervention Data Model

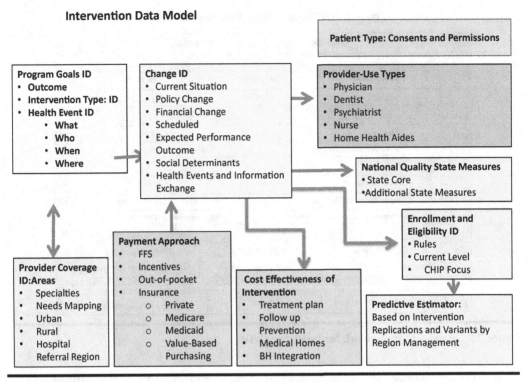

Figure 7.6 Standardized data elements for analytics identity and tracking interventions.

Predictive Analytics Process Models

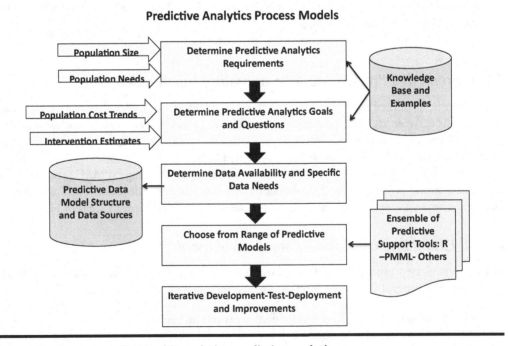

Figure 7.7 Recommending health analytics predictive analysis.

4. Note what vendor relationships the organization has, and whether these vendors are "interoperability advocates" or procrastinators?
5. Focus on the business-clinical integration use cases, and create a roadmap for the next 2 years
6. Use and create reference architecture and approaches that are independent of vendors, that is, show the vendors what you want and do not just look at what they want to sell you
7. Focus on the following improvement approaches:
   a. Cross organization and state-regional integration
   b. Key decisions that support your goals, questions, trends, and data availability
   c. Create a hub or an appliance that fits with the Open-Standards-Based Interoperability: DIRECT and CONNECT—(next set of standards)
   d. Lean business process models
   e. Quality and outcome measures
   f. Safety and reliability
   g. Systems engineering for healthcare
      Patient and consumer transparency and support for shopping for the best quality care. Provider information for the physicians and the professionals that are transforming their practice for benchmarking and comparing their improvements with their peer-providers
8. Create a way forward roadmap with analytics delivered to both the patient–consumer and the providers
9. Network and collaborate regionally
10. Collaborate nationally and internationally: make the vendors listen with "collective buying power"
11. Perform monthly tracking based on integration concepts of operations and dashboard of improvements
12. Continue to refine and improve the plan, the architecture, and the roadmap

Time frame: Update the prediction model and align with usage scenarios showing use as part of improvement activities—Fall 2016.

Common Dashboard Structure and Style Guide including elements such as:

1. Provide a top-level dashboard and easy drill down on the far right
2. Upper left: map components
3. Upper right heat map with easy identification of key elements
4. Information table with detail on the left
5. Associated graphical representation on the right
6. Use consistent graphic style and common terminology
7. Support context sensitive help
8. Support the back button and provide easy links to other websites: use common banners and headers and footers

A standards guide with sponsorship by HIMSS or the federal and state CIOs and other professional groups is necessary so that user analytics experience becomes common and reduces the confusion in presenting important information (Figure 7.8).

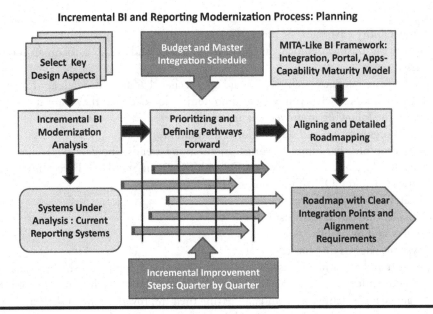

Incremental BI and Reporting Modernization Process: Planning

Figure 7.8   Improvement related to change life cycle: build in tracking and measurement.

Time frame: Work with ONC on a measurement roadmap with bi-directional measures for the professionals and the patient–consumers—July 2017.

7.3.4 Relate Analytics to Needs of Community of Interest, and Ensure Analytics are Goal Driven

A number of states and regions are focused on the healthcare of their citizens, and one or more quality measurement and discovery studies can be conducted that can fit with a state or region. The concept is shown in Figure 7.9.

Time frame: Create a MESC or NAMD white paper and presentation based on work with one state with a focus on patient–consumer analytics and transparency—Fall 2016.

7.3.4.1 Define a Set of Health Infographics and Their Usage for Both Patient–Consumers and Providers

There are a number of techniques used in other fields that have not been brought to either the patient–consumer or to communicate to the busy provider. One of the key techniques is infographics. Randy Krum in Cool Infographics: Effective Communication with Data Visualization and Design tells about how he could see data patterns but he found that most of his business customers "just wanted to understand the conclusion" but liked that the conclusion were based on data but wanted to understand how it related to their business or their consumers. He found Infographics to be the solution. His definition of "Infographics—a large graphic design that combines data visualization,

Propose a Quality Measurement Review and Discovery Study

Example of a Measurement Matrix

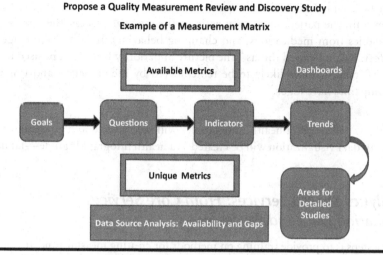

Figure 7.9 Create a set of measures that align with goals–questions–indicators and tracks key trends.

illustrations, text and images together into a format that tells a complete story." There are a few info-graphics in healthcare but the telling of the good stories are not a part of the culture of medicine.

Today, medical advice is one of the most searched for topics but the results do not follow the best practices of infographics that tell a complete story. This would include

- Objectives to inform, to entertain, and to persuade and audience
- Provides data in a visual form
- Includes a conclusion and a call to action

Each major medical conclusion can be presented with two sides of the story:

- The patient–consumer side
- The provider–physician side, nurse, or other professional

This can all be derived by the experts that are reviewing the evidence and do great detailed data analysis and make the discoveries and care management recommendations that need to be translated into the highly visual world of the consumer.

Today, we want to share the decision making with the consumer but in many cases, we want to persuade them to do the right thing. In some areas, there has been disinformation like in the cases of smoking and cancer or vaccines and autism. Or the hype of the pharmaceutical vendor that makes it seem that taking this miracle pill means you do not have to worry about diet and exercise.

A dual-persuasive structure can be created following a common persuasive structure:

- The key message
- What is the health problem addressed?
- What is the danger if not addressed?
- What is the solution?
- What can both the provider and the patient–consumer do?

These can be coupled with visual explanations that can explain the approach and idea in more depth, explain the patient–consumer actions, the medical process, the disease progression, the delaying tactics from medications, and changing behaviors. It can also leverage the picture superiority effect. Krum defined this as "The picture Superiority Effect can be used to make *visual* information 650 percent more likely to be remembered by the audience, and this is the major reason that companies have logos."

During 2016, a collection of health infographics will be collected and guidelines on how to use them with data visualization will be created as a health infographic guide—January 2017.

7.3.5 Analytics Shared Services: From Core Services to Sharing Data and Processes

One of the key steps is to provide training on methods for creating measures and analytics outcomes using shared services. These types of services are often combined into what is called a center of excellence. The center of excellence can drive the BI usage and create common reusable elements. The center of excellence can provide introduction to analytics; link processes to medical measures and outcomes; be the focus areas for business-design consulting with healthcare IT; and include training, policy formation, use of evolving shared services and reference models, and use of analytics APIs that can allow shared data to be stored in a range of tools: SAS, IBM, Oracle, and support of the integration of data with federated queries. The creation of the BI Center of Excellence is shown in Figure 7.10.

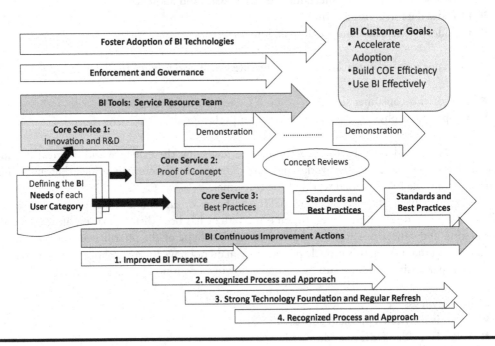

Figure 7.10 **Plan for creating BI center of excellence and support to states and regional initiatives.**

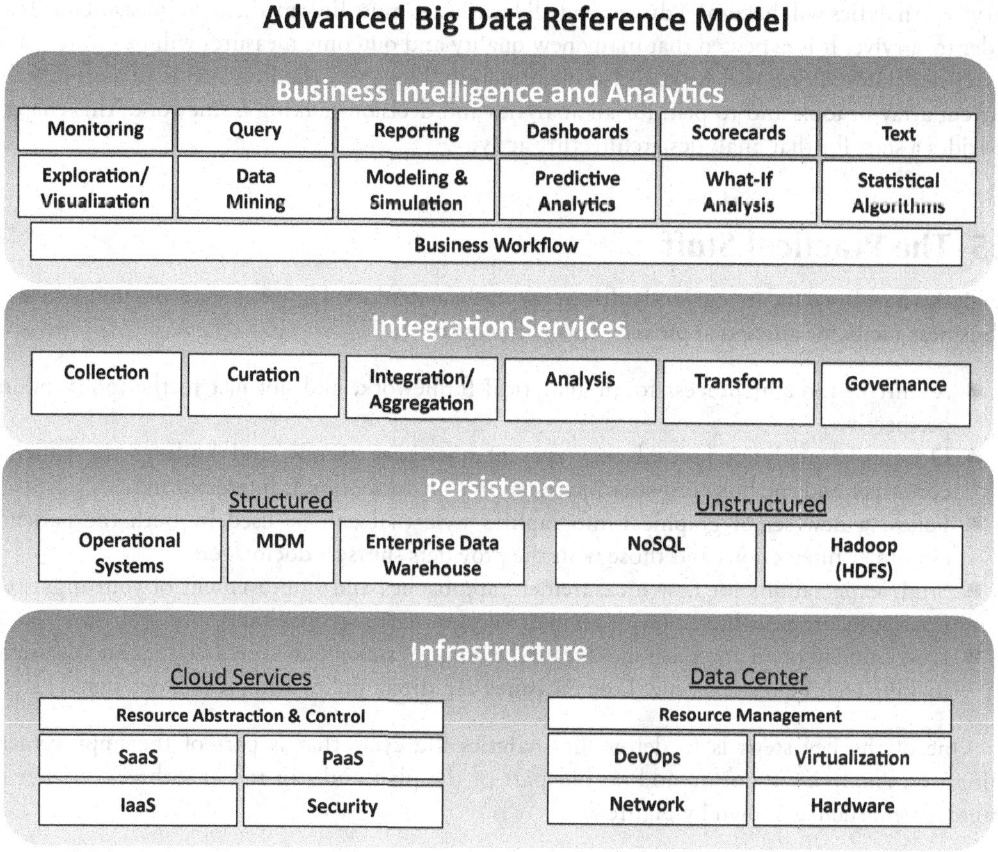

Advanced Big Data Reference Model

Business Intelligence and Analytics					
Monitoring	Query	Reporting	Dashboards	Scorecards	Text
Exploration/ Visualization	Data Mining	Modeling & Simulation	Predictive Analytics	What-If Analysis	Statistical Algorithms
Business Workflow					

Integration Services					
Collection	Curation	Integration/ Aggregation	Analysis	Transform	Governance

Persistence

Structured			Unstructured	
Operational Systems	MDM	Enterprise Data Warehouse	NoSQL	Hadoop (HDFS)

Infrastructure

Cloud Services		Data Center	
Resource Abstraction & Control		Resource Management	
SaaS	PaaS	DevOps	Virtualization
IaaS	Security	Network	Hardware

Figure 7.11   NIST big data reference model and use cases: needs more healthcare involvement.

7.3.6 *Emerging Trends of New Analytics and Big Data*

A portfolio of paths must move forward with a strong governance approach. A set of reusable shared services analytics elements needs to be shared among healthcare policy makers, operational decision makers, and clinical decision makers. In addition, the link between the research community and the operational community has to be provided. One of the key focus areas is Big data and healthcare and medicine; these specialized areas can leverage initiatives such as the NIST Big Data Reference Model shown in Figure 7.11.

A system medicine framework is being designed and will be described in e-Book 2 of this series.

7.4 Conclusion

Wave 2 needs more planning and architecture to achieve the key goals. A real strategic-architecture-planning process with a clear set of value propositions needs to be created. Who will be driving this? The CIO, CMO, and the newly appointed Chief Medical Information Officer will be the working organizational leadership. However, if the organization is small or is a one-person provider shop, the one person carries all of those responsibilities, and needs to define partners and pick a strategy that fits within the region and within the analytic ecosystems in which it must survive. Analytics will become a driver, and all healthcare must link medicine to measurements in order to survive. It is expected that many new quality and outcome measures will be created, and better decision making will be key to transformation. However, the first step is to assemble the current array of tools and to plan for an analytics and decision-making framework. This chapter provides a start for that analytics architecture activity.

7.5 The Practical Stuff

Analytics and Big data are currently driven by product vendors. However, everyone must turn to a business-medicine aligned approach. This will require

- A shift in thought process to an analytical framework, and not just to the tool vendors' perspective
- Design the analytics around the types of questions, trends, and findings the patient–consumer and the busy provider interested in transformation is interested in
- Follow a new set of graphical-infographics style that can be used by both the patient–consumer interactions and those with the providers–nurses–doctors, etc.
- Study expectations for new measurement approaches and improvement of your organization's measurement literacy with an internal resource or a consultant
- Development of an approach to educate the range of stakeholders on analytics and decision-making techniques and how those measures can direct policy and process decisions

One of the key steps is to define an analytics life cycle that is part of the improvement initiatives. Analytics is not an add-on but part of the plan and can reflect a three-level tier of improvement such as shown by Figure 7.12.

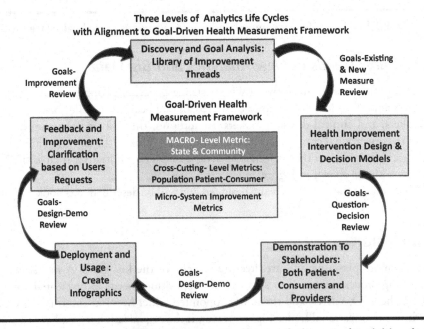

Figure 7.12 All improvements will have an interlocking analytics set of activities that will be planned throughout the agile development and integration process.

A set of new reference models, data standards, and process approaches will be needed over the next few years. Achieving this goal will require

- Creating a basic analytics framework and starting to create some early results
- Defining a predictive process and linking to tools and techniques
- User-interactions guides that can align but tailor the information exchange between providers and patient–consumers using tailored health infographics
- Mapping the current ensemble of products and understanding the direction of those products toward the future
- Defining short-term improvements and an immediate approach to integrate the analytics tools with the business process and create a set of goal-oriented dashboards that can easily be changed
- Noting the importance of fostering involvement in understanding the problem and explaining what the data reveal
- Defining new data techniques and new predictive modeling algorithms that can leverage the real-time data from CMS, support the update based on constantly arriving data, and reflect the impact of the spread of innovation
- Starting now with the data that the organization currently has, answering the organization's current nagging questions, and creating a data inventory and data wish list; analytics can evolve
- Supporting the natural extension to new phase 2 ACO models and new forms of delivery reform
- Linking the analytics framework with a set of value-based purchasing and bundled payment options

Incremental Commitment Planning, Governance, and Tracking Value-Risk-Integration

Abstract

"If we got a man on the moon, we can do this." In fact, the author, who in the early part of his career worked on the Apollo mission, heard exactly that at the end of his career, as a complaint from a CMS customer. We agree with that sentiment; however, there are major differences today. There is actually a book, published in 2009, titled "If We Can Put A Man on the Moon...Getting Big Things Done in Government," authored by Eggers and O'Leary; that book defines some sound principles represented here with concepts based on Business Transformation and large IT projects. One of the simple techniques that the Apollo mission employed was to have each launch have its own focus and its own recognition and achievement awards. We need to take a similar approach to each incremental commitment given a mission focus thematic tag-line and to recognize the accomplishments of that mission with an achievement award and thank you party. People work not only for pay, but also for a feeling of accomplishment.

But one of the key concerns is what are the forcing factors that drive the change of such ultra-large scale SOS that represent the healthcare communities? Well, the drive should be the patient–consumer populations and their drivers by topic areas with the focus on the key integration points. The providers and many stakeholders will have to also be aligned around the capabilities they need but the key is delivering care, content, and services to the patient–consumer populations. Otherwise, the question is left to each alliance partner to integrate from their point of view but they have not been aligned. An Agile Integration Roadmap will be updated each quarter as a series of critical and partial alignments occur as the HHSs community moves forward to their shared and unique subcommunity goals. Each Apollo and other space mission selected from many objectives and learning opportunities and the downselection and alignment process was critical. A similar incremental integration process is presented in this chapter.

8.1 Focusing on Goals and Implementation

Creating legislation is a messy business, often focused on achieving a result independent of other legislation. Creating an IT solution with only broad requirements is also messy business. However, when the legislation passed to date implicitly assumes that "IT Magic" can occur, and is easily accomplished, then the outcome is just messy, not a good outcome. Legislation that depends upon leveraging IT technology needs to incorporate and reflect those dependencies. The risks associated with integration and interoperability can be addressed within the legislative process and the budget, but each piece of legislation and program initiative must identify and consider dependencies so that solutions can be developed with integration and interoperability included, based on shared services. But integration and interoperability have to be focused. The focus is around the patient–consumer along with the population and topics and services that need to be integrated and the alignment to the providers with their related services. There has been a legislative shift with the twenty-first century Cures bills and the discussion by ONC and CMS on being more patient–consumer centric but the plans are still aligned with delivering "functions and capabilities" to meet everyone's needs. Someone has to be the priority and the approach described here shifts that focus to the patient–consumer.

That legislative plan and master integration roadmaps must include elements such as the following:

- Defining the patient–consumer needs and capabilities and prioritizing their evolutionary improvement.
- Defining the integration and interoperability shared services (the hub) and the analytical framework that can support a range of decision making for policy makers, quality- and production-focused care delivery leaders, and, most importantly, a range of episodes of care.
- Defining your healthcare and human services Transformation Roadmap.
- Defining a legislative strategy map with the goals and objectives and the proposed implementation plan on a quarter-by-quarter basis, could be a bridge between the legislative and congressional oversight committee. Congress can understand the risk of the legislation they are proposing, along with the value and priorities of the executive branch, and "collaborate" on implementing a sound SOS with an integration roadmap. If the American people are the end customers, the members of Congress are the requirements engineers and planners, but there still must be some degree of systems engineering from the beginning.
- Rethinking the legislative process is probably impossible, but after the legislation is sent to the White House, or shortly before, the executive policy makers will create the basic planning documents and start implementation following an integration roadmap and series of performance dashboards for tracking progress. This will start the legislative oversight on a more sound footing.
- Focusing on the implementation of two or three items each quarter and incrementally making more commitments and evolving an Agile Integration Roadmap.
- Planning and architecting incrementally:
  - Evolve the concepts and detailed logical design incrementally based on improving the patient–consumer capabilities and those of the other provider stakeholders.

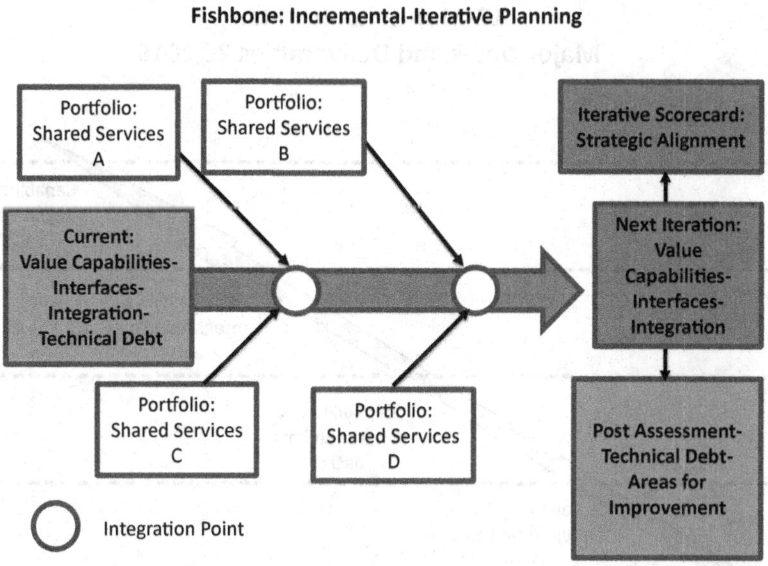

Fishbone: Incremental-Iterative Planning

Figure 8.1   **Fishbone diagram to move from current state to next major increment.**

- How much is enough? Each iteration will refine the plan, the architecture, the implementation, and deliver more capabilities. Making sure the foundation is in place and the scope of the effort is defined, including creating peak scenarios of usage, selecting shared services to use, and identifying ones that are needed.
■ Developing a transparent and open development process, especially ensuring that user-centered design is applied. It will create an actively managed strategy map and implementation plan that can be used to support a consistent end-to-end value chain.
■ This plan can be used by congressional/government oversight reviews and also used by the Government Accountability Office in their audit and review process.
■ Those plans can be revised on an annual basis with results, lessons learned, and plans for the next 18-month plan that includes a series of specific integration points and the target end points.

Some examples of such simple representation are shown in Figure 8.1—fishbone integration diagram and portfolio arrow diagram in Figure 8.2.

8.2 Background: Finding a Realistic Target

There are many healthcare policy makers who believe that they are responding to a vision, and there are as many visions as there are visionaries. Vision is about aspiration—the possible. It is often somewhat simple, yet powerful. Complex situations, such as healthcare often seek to create a standard to pursue a vision, looking to deal with the complexities in a consistent way. Although that seems logical, if there is not a consistent unified portfolio of "linking standards" that can create a common profile, integration chaos can result. The integration chaos has a number of common properties. Each effort is independent of the others, everybody is "doing their own thing," and adding to the complexity. Everyone has the solution to integration, but there is no common

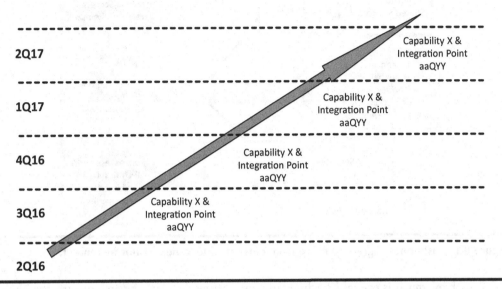

Figure 8.2 Representing each process-information portfolio with a deliverable arrow diagram.

solution. Integration is achieved over one hectic weekend or it takes months, but soon breaks again and again. Everyone wished there was a standards approach, but there was not time to accomplish that the first time, or even the third time or the fifth time. Integration chaos repeats over and over! Leadership and standards provide the structure to deal with the complexity, while it is critical that we not lose sight of the vision.

But there is a real vision of a seamless EHR system. There are also what appear to be closed systems supporting healthcare, such as those of the Veterans Health Administration and Kaiser, Geisinger, Intermountain, and Mayo, which can become more open, and provide the ability for information sharing. The advanced vision for integrated and interoperable medicine must be implemented and deployable across all parts of the country. ONC has been in existence for 10 years, and is now developing a realistic roadmap for the next 10 years.

8.2.1 Principles of Incremental Modernization: Incremental Commitment Planning

The field of healthcare is massive, and a roadmap must be created that supports incremental modernization of healthcare IT. By introducing a new incremental modernization roadmap:

■ Systems will go beyond a project focus and provide an overall incremental modernization agenda; it will be driven by patient–consumer value-based guidance with a focus on one or more population types and the related provider stakeholders.
■ A definition will be created for a new incremental modernization project life cycle, and not SOS life cycle; each quarter will address the next increment along with a two to three quarters look ahead.

- An approach will be defined that uses the concepts of SOS mission threads to focus health-care on patients; as the capabilities are expanded more support studies will be conducted including proof of concepts pilots and studies to keep the risk low.
- Legislation often shows these great jumps of completion. The strategic and implementation plans discussed in the previous section must align the assignments and responsibilities that are often divided between government agencies, or that are not clearly defined. A clear role is provided so that all stakeholders for each focus area can at least clarify who will be using the services and the benefits expected.
- The integration incremental roadmap will create a realistic risk balance finding the level that is lower risks—not too little or too much. The legislation often includes release dates—that may or may not be realistic. Some of the "must make" dates should be interpreted as "guidance" and the government and contractors must use an incremental scheduling and estimation process to report back to HHSs leadership and if necessary congressional oversight to come up with an evolving but lower risk plan. I know how difficult can be as I had to report on a high risk space shuttle program where all other contractors said they were all on time and had no risk. Once, I reported that the mandated dates could not be reached—all the others confessed. I actually delivered my piece early. Sometimes being fearless works out.
- A Strategic Implementation and Agile Integration Roadmap that connects the SOS together will be created at the conceptual level and then refined each quarter. The many communities of HHSs can align the capabilities with other health organizations, states, and regions to align their planning within the national–state–local timeframes on a quarter-by-quarter basis.

One approach discussed in Chapter 4 is to conduct the PAUSE assessment that would include a bi-annual PAUSE update to ascertain whether all organizations are heading in a beneficial strategic direction and to identify early integration chaos situations.

A workshop should be created with the other SOS transformation areas with leaders from the SEI and Stevens Tech SERC, presenting alternative approaches that have been used in other complex industries, and also presenting the best practices from the SOS evolution paths refined to fit healthcare needs.

Leveraging Best Practices for Transformation: Industry advisory work group—Summer 2016.

8.3 Integrated Strategic Direction and Resource Planning

A set of strategic goals, although difficult to define, must be used to provide a common direction. The starting point and priority has to be the patient–consumers and the population that they are members of. Prior efforts have given the priority to the best voiced stakeholder with the most power. For example, the healthcare standards address is driven by the Mayo Clinic, Kaiser Permanente, Intermountain, and others that are part of the leadership and visionary. That may have been effective in the Wave 1 but they do not have the "voice of the disabled, those with rare diseases, the Medicaid population, etc." Actually the voice of the patient–consumer is often represented by a few non-profits like American Association of Retired Persons (AARP) or a disease foundation but they often do not get heard.

Key problems are identifying: the patient–consumer needs and capabilities, how the patient–consumer threads cross existing systems, what resources exist today, and what resources are needed to update them. Currently, all silos look at their own changes and do not collaborate to see how the whole fits together. An integrated strategic direction and resource planning process is needed with a set of high-level SOS diagramming techniques similar to those being proposed by the INCOSE SOS workshop in January 2015, with some additional integration and value-risk diagrams.

Present to INCOSE the Patient–Consumer Integration Process—as soon as possible—2016.

These goals will include ensuring that all stakeholders can come into alignment with key pathways forward and with the creation of value models and strategic action plans for each pathway. The problem with strategy is making it implementable and adaptable to change. Healthcare transformation will take many twists and turns, but adjustments will be needed with a governance process. Governance for an SOS and set of value-delivery networks will require managing a set of concurrent activities.

An overview of the concurrent activities is shown in Figure 8.3.

Strategic alignment needs to have the involvement of multiple strategic levels, including

- Politicians and leadership who select the key strategic directions and the strategic dependencies
- Those involved in the improvement initiatives with a basic efficiency and effectiveness that make the integration and interoperability implementable
- Definition of a set of processes, information perspectives, and the current state, including a review of what competitors are doing and the best practices of the industry

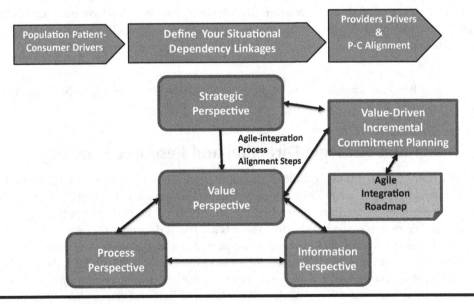

Value Relationships between Perspectives: Agile Incremental Integration Planning

Figure 8.3   Strategic alignment and value-driven incremental commitment.

- Definition of a set of collaborative and competitive projects with new value-capabilities-interfaces and integration with key partners
- In some areas, each organization may decide to collaborate with others, to lead selective initiatives, or to wait for others and then become a fast follower
- Each organization's style selection may depend on its own situation and its readiness to commit
- There are a number of evolutionary paths that are part of a portfolio approach. Using Incremental Commitment models, each organization may be on a number of different paths moving forward, but at a different level of commitment; the path may be strong, phased, weak, or investigative
- Different evolutionary paths and different levels of commitment will allow options and choices to be kept open
- As each quarter progresses, some commitments will be strengthened and others weakened or withdrawn
- But the key is to take a new patient–consumer viewpoint and prioritize the capabilities needed and the alignment
- Timing is critical! Otherwise newer silos will be created
- The situation will dictate the timing, and a mixture of patience and persistence will allow the organization to be alert to move forward at the right time; then it can pursue the common elements of the shared services and new Public API. Each major process or information perspective must be tracked with its own portfolio scorecard that can be tailored to the strategic perspective as shown in Figure 8.4.

Propose a new Community Portfolio Approach for Shared Services—Summer 2016.

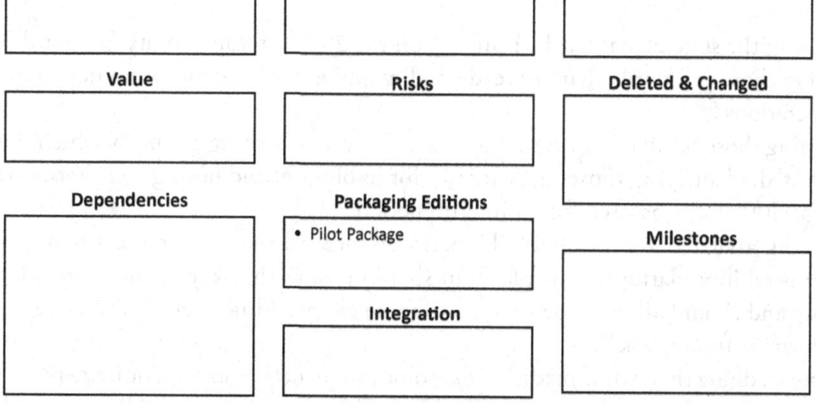

**Scorecard: Advancing a CMS-Community
SOS Ecosystem: Incremental Commitment Model**

Pressures	Capabilities	Added
Project • Industry •	Current Progress • Project Goals	

Value	Risks	Deleted & Changed

Dependencies	Packaging Editions	Milestones
	• Pilot Package	
	Integration	

Figure 8.4   Scorecard for the community or process-information portfolio.

8.4 Challenges, Controversies, and Issues

Creating a roadmap that spans multiple election cycles is difficult. Politicians may not be elected by suggesting the value of taking a long-term approach to solving problems. Americans want action; however, complex problems require a patient and persistent approach, a position that can be counter to the interests of elected officials.

8.4.1 Challenges

An open transparent process, like that of the ONC work groups, must include sessions that share more results. In addition to close stakeholders, the public and patients also need to understand what is happening; they are key stakeholders, too!

All stakeholders must understand the challenges:

■ It is important to know what others are doing, to understand best practices, and to acknowledge that this does not have to be a time-consuming and painful effort. The goal is to prevent integration chaos and to provide information on expectations to all stakeholders on a phased basis. Healthcare experts believe that healthcare IT is unique; however, there is common ground, and many difficult questions can be answered by observing the experience in other fields of endeavor.
■ Information overload exists. It is advisable to provide only the information needed for the next phase or focus area so as not overwhelm stakeholders. Most people do not want to know the entire strategy; they simply want to know that a strategy is in place.
■ A rigid approach is not necessary, but a foundation can be created that is adaptable and extensible, leaving options and choices for the future. It is important to note lessons learned and the experience of getting stakeholders involved.

8.4.2 Controversies

Healthcare is at a tipping point where stakeholders need to decide their level of "coopetition," that is, where key organizations will collaborate, and where they will compete. This tipping point will be key to all industry players including ONC, HHS, CMS, and legislators, and must involve responding to priorities such as

■ Defining the state of standards. Building on the 2015 Interoperability Standard Advisory
■ Testing those standards that are ready and mapping with a conceptual design and concept of operations
■ Defining those standards gaps that must be resolved, assigning a time by which they must be addressed, identifying those that can wait for resolution, and noting any alternative bridging approach that can be used for an interim period
■ Defining a virtual and adaptable IT pathway forward that can frame a basic integration–interoperability platform; this platform should ensure that key vendors provide interoperability and should allow those vendors to more easily add new capabilities to a common IT platform or framework
■ Acknowledging that, while medicine has some uniqueness in its IT requirements, many stakeholders believe that much can be learned from other industries and other standards efforts

- Defining a decision-making process that helps provide guidance regarding when to REPAIR one or more systems needed over the next increment, and when to move on to newer products or services
- Deciding whether to use agile development versus a strategic roadmap or a little bit of both
- Focusing on the present, but with a strategic longer term focus: ensuring that the foundation and infrastructure provide a stable base with which to move forward
- Acknowledging that mistakes can be made and rework will be needed; understanding that this is the way of progress, iterative, learning from what does not work, not just from what does work. Using a combined agility with an enterprise approach; features from Barry Boehm's Incremental Commitment Management can be used, as well as related SEI and DOD SOS Guides
- Modernizing incrementally with quarter-by-quarter focused outcomes, with some paths forward that have long lead times
- Leveraging the SEI SOS integration approaches tailored to the CMS XLC that is updated with a new strategic-value-driven incremental commitment approach
- Acknowledging that the more strategic life cycle must include a portfolio management approach that leverages shared services and SOS linked capabilities

8.4.3 Issues

Not all of the standards and integration approaches are controversial. However, these approaches do need to be assigned and addressed, not waiting for the standards process to evolve. The priorities of the standards groups align with the healthcare priorities. The ONC Standards Advisory is a good initial start, but it needs to address broader end-to-end process standards. ONC is in the process of establishing a close working relationship with industry and advisory groups. Government projects can be a driver for change, but the healthcare organizations must be smarter interoperable purchasers. The current DoD procurement requires interoperability, and similar requirements for Medicare, Medicaid, Indian Health, and Veterans Health can put buying power behind healthcare interoperability. It is still incumbent on each health care organization to understand and answer questions such as

- Who is responsible for integration? It is a community activity!
- How are the priority issues addressed with a governance process that involves not only senior leadership, but also all levels of the organization? It must evolve incrementally with the right balance of new capabilities and critical improvements
- Are strategy maps in place and what are our areas of attention? Must be delivered to meet the needs of patients–consumers and population groups
- Do we have a focused scorecard? Progress must be tracked and stories must be told with visual infographics
- What are the foundational elements for everyone to adopt? Intercloud GWs and security and privacy approaches must be built in, discussed in Chapters 11 and 12
- Can the commitment be sustained? Keeping the alliance intact must require that all stakeholders see the benefit and creating the right type of collaborative balancer
- Are the process and information capabilities mature enough to be used? There are a lot of standards and technologies that can be used. It is time to change the governance and integration approach

■ Are the standards really ready? The second year of the ONC Standards Advisory and the many other open standards are ready but the patient–consumer focus can determine where the focus to close the gaps can be made

8.5 Solutions and Recommendations

Need for Focused Delivery and Ensuring that the Feedback and Adjustments are made with Incremental Planning

Implementing a strategic plan requires a disciplined process that is continuous and that occurs iteratively over an extended period of time. This iterative process is shown in Figure 8.5.

Recommend an Open Service Virtual Interoperability Library that can be used in Meaningful Use 2 and 3—Fall 2016.

8.5.1 Value Perspectives from Your Organization and Your Dependencies

After the initial workshops defined in Chapter 2, additional design-deployment artifacts are needed to show how the value perspectives are translated and become operational (as shown in Figure 8.3), as well as how they are regularly updated to meet the constantly changing local and national scenario.

Focus on Patient-Consumer Centric: Integration and Interoperability Building Blocks

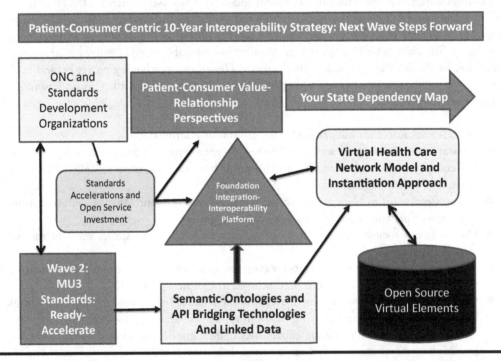

Figure 8.5   Iteratively translating strategic intent mapping into committing the actions using a semantic ontology integration and interoperable mapping tool.

8.5.2 Define a Set of Value-Driven Virtual Models and Services That Can Be Integrated

There are many opportunities for improving healthcare, especially by connecting healthcare services as a related bundle of services. Making the selection between the many alternatives is not an activity to be performed once a year, but must involve a continuous government and incremental commitment process.

The strategic choices must be mapped to value-driven business-decision models and related to the underlying services that are integrated as shown in Figure 8.6.

Recommend a service application virtual environment model—Fall 2016.

8.5.3 Integration Incremental Commitment Spiral

One of the most difficult steps is to gather the many stakeholders that are needed to address a patient–consumer population and the related stakeholders. A conceptual roadmap can be created for the patient–consumer population type and represented in a graphic style like Figure 8.7. It will require setting the overall architecture, defining the keystone shared services along with the group if shared integration and interoperability share services. This picture alone needs another 10 pages. But I need to meet my deadline.

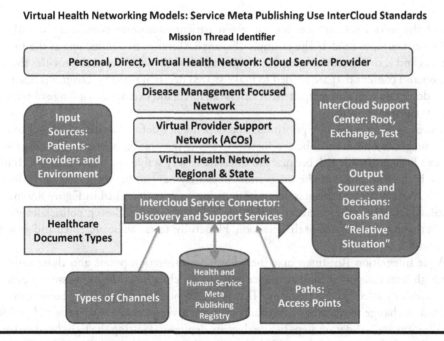

Figure 8.6   Iteratively translating strategic intent mapping to committed actions using semantic ontology integration and interoperable mapping.

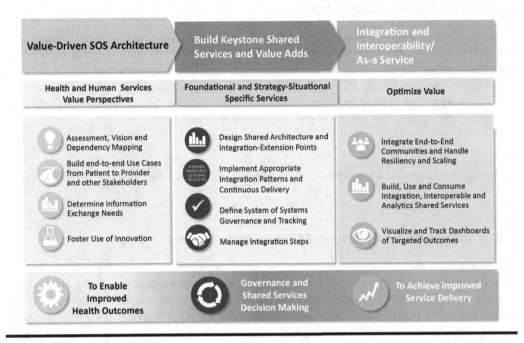

Figure 8.7 High-level integration map based on patient–consumer first but addressing the variety of stakeholders strategic goals can be including the conceptual picture.

One of the next level artifacts for the given patient–consumer population would be the patient–consumer pipes model. The example (Figure 8.8) shows two forks, one at the top showing the tasks and activities of the integration care model while the lower path provides the related information and content that are needed to make shared decision making. Diagrams like this can be used as design pattern and template that can be adapted and extended to a range of population and patient–consumer needs.

Once the capability needs are prioritized and dependency defined a risk assessment of each of the major integration point must be conducted. Crossing integration points and linking elements together can have negligible risk because the interface is very stable and well defined with moderate or very high risks. Some of the integration steps may have to be postponed until the risk is manageable. A graphical representation and discussion such as described in Figure 8.9 may need to be used. The facts can be discussed with high-level leadership and even politicians about the level of risk that can be accepted in this iteration. Hopefully, facts can be presented and a moderate risk iteration can be defined.

An Agile Integration Roadmap may include many integration points and those categorized into two high-level categories: high assurance and rapidly changing. The high assurance elements and interfaces can affect many elements. This is represented in Figure 8.10. Some capabilities are designed to change frequently while others are high assurance and must be tested and follow more verification and validation steps before they are deployed. Getting the right balance between design for change elements and the stable base will require extensive visibility and judgment. We cannot change too fast or take too long.

Simple Block Diagram Service Bi-Directional Pipes Model

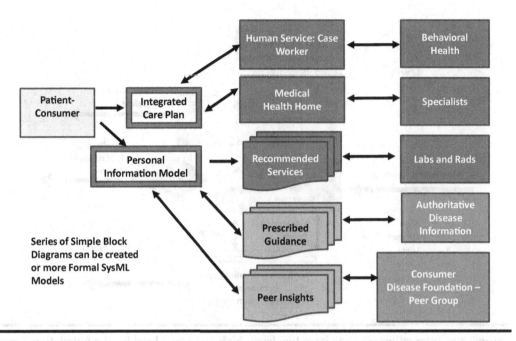

Figure 8.8   Patient–consumer pipes model for the integration care plan and the personal information model.

Series of Risk Models: Multiple Outcomes Possible

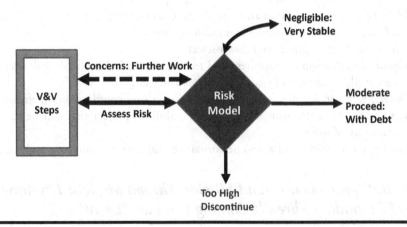

Figure 8.9   Each integration point will go through a risk assessment or multiple times as the risk is reduced and it is ready to be used.

Incremental Integration Steps with Adaptable Features

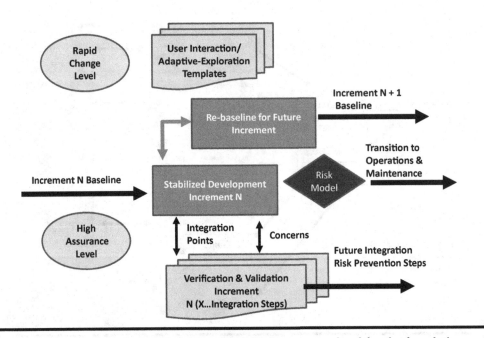

Figure 8.10 Integration plan can have two levels high assurance level for the foundation and a rapid change level for those changes that are frequent and introduce less risk.

We learn this experience when we are forced to upgrade to Windows 10 or move to a new browser or move to a new major release.

8.5.4 Key Partial Alignment Steps

- Prioritize patient–consumer topics and provider topics and their integration–alignment
- Four times a year have an Integration-Architect Sprint and their
  - Identify desired capabilities and look ahead one- to-three quarters
  - *Exploration*: identify resources and viable options
  - *Valuation*: Assess options and down-select
  - *Foundation*: develop management and technical foundation and down-select
  - *Create* Agile Integration Roadmap updates and share
  - *Development*: enable development via alliance partner coordination to create shared services and initiate an open service pilot capabilities project that can be shared with a community of users
  - *Operations*: monitor and assess performance and create an ongoing technical debt list

8.5.5 Definitions of End-to-End Mission Thread Models: Keystone and Secondary Threads Coming from an "Event"

The new model of healthcare processes and underlying information perspective must create a value-delivery network with the patients at one end and the providers at the other with a set of ongoing interactions. In the military and intelligence worlds, these systems are linked by mission threads. For healthcare, they are more likely "care and cure threads" with the related networks. But many of the other concepts from the workshop approach defined by the SEI SOS project can be leveraged. Other concepts of event processing and resource management and incremental commitment management can also be translated to a new "care and cure" collaborative, value-delivery concept of ways that healthcare can operate in the future. Using a community perspective (as shown in Figure 8.11) must be an ongoing process that watches and prepares to select the collaboration and competitive paths and the level of commitment for each:

- Conceptual and Logical Interoperability
- Integration Points
- Decision Points and the Ability to Manage Operational Changes to Support Continuous Integration
- Phased Incremental Interoperability Updates

Each quarter each of these items will be reviewed and progress will be tracked to foster increase both the integration and interoperability level. A scorecard can be used to track the progress.

Some of those commitments will be internal, but others will be a part of "cooperative agreements" either as part of an industry initiative, or as a specific agreement where "the best of the best" agree to work together with a clear goal in mind. Forming agreements (as shown in Figure 8.12) is very important, and healthcare will begin to establish relationships and partnerships, such as

Systems of Systems for Medicaid

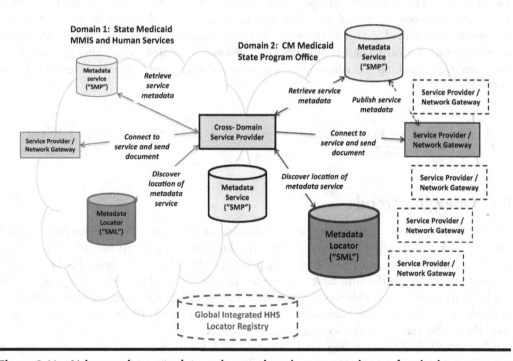

Figure 8.11 Using service meta data and cross-domain connected sets of registries to manage the dynamic environment between communities.

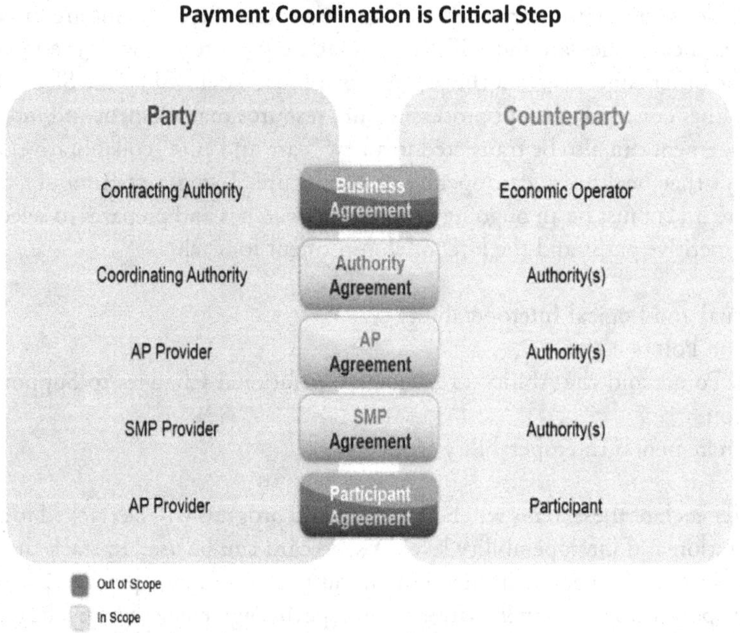

Payment Coordination is Critical Step

Figure 8.12 Getting agreements with all partners in the virtual network.

shown on the FHIR Argonaut API project, to be actively engaged to solve the interoperability issues. Organizations often send representatives to standards meetings but do not really make the investment required, and the buyers buckle to the leaders. Some alternative interoperability approaches such as clearing houses or joint non-profits may be needed. Approaches like these have been effective in banking and telecom, and are addressed with a more concrete recommendation in Chapter 9.

Shared Services for Integration and Interoperability: Open Services Shared Investment Project—Plan for 2017.

8.6 Emerging Trends

ONC and the many working groups that are producing the Interoperability 10-year plan, and the industry groups, such as the EHR Association, HL7, HIMSS, along with pressure from Congress, can bring healthcare IT vendors to the tipping point of collaboration and competition to define a coopetition strategy. At the same time, the Stevens Tech SERC, the SEI/CMU SOS projects, and the DoD are evolving many ideas on incremental commitment, portfolio management, and value networks; however, there has been little translation into healthcare. Healthcare can learn much from these other transformation experiences and practices.

The INCOSE SOS Workshop for Healthcare 2015 has created a set of possible mapping constructs that can be leveraged and extended. There are also value-delivery models—e3 and a proposed value modeling language in draft by the OMG. The SERC and INCOSE Challenge teams are researching new design and implementation tools and governance process for a collaborative governance process for SOS, but there is a need for new SOS value-delivery governance approaches and tools. We can no longer look at each project individually, but we must have an integrated whole where all the dependencies are clearly defined.

The US DoD has an ongoing series of collaborative information exchanges in an SOS with special attention leveraging the work of Barry Boehm, Jo Ann Lane, Suprannika Koomanojwong, and Richard Turner in The Incremental Commitment Spiral Model: Principle for Successful Systems and Software—2014 and the ongoing effort of CMU SEI.

These ideas are being refined but they will be new HHSs—which tend to use a very high risk legislative schedule and inflexible waterfall approach.

> Over the next years, an HHSs with SOS incremental commitment approach will be developed—January 2017.
>
> New tools like an Agile Blueprint will be developed—Spring of 2017.

8.7 Conclusion

The next few years are critical to providing an environment where meaningful changes can be planned, and where integration–interoperability–analytics can be a foundation for excellence across the entire nation, not just locally. The driving focus has to be the patient–consumers or a tangle of integration points will be created resulting in "hairball of integration points" that have occurred within large government and industry projects that did not have a focus. Remember the focus on getting the "man to the moon," our focus must be improving the patient–consumer experience and reducing the confusion with integrated services and information.

Quality care and the best information for curing disease must have the fundamentals of Wave 2 established in all corners, both for patients in the United States, and for export to the global healthcare marketplace.

It is time for organizations to step forward and create their own directions. Simplicity is key, but organizations have to get started as shown in Figure 8.13.

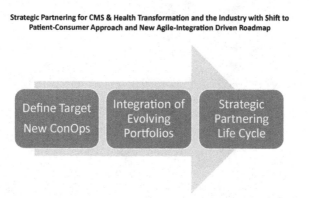

Figure 8.13   Take the first three steps forward.

8.8 The Practical Stuff

Each organization can sit and wait, or create its own strategic approach, establish its incremental commitments, and define its roadmap and evolutionary pathways:

- Use one of the many communication appliances as the end point manager to create a set of logical channels with topic rule-based routing and alerting of the types of messages
- Address one or two topics and logical channels each quarter and evolve the shared services
- Include failure controls and resiliency capabilities: stuff happens
- Drive the integration and interoperability with integration scenarios
- Get feedback from the users, and update the versions based on recommendations and the involvement of the communities

Chapter 9

Using Virtual Health Networks to Build a Resource-Event-Agent Healthcare Paradigm

Abstract

Protection in the healthcare environment means more than just security, privacy, and identity protection. It also requires safe, bi-directional communication among patients, family members, and advocates, and the set of providers who support a patient, and with whom the patient has consented to share information. This chapter describes a vision for a paradigm; it also describes the gaps in the end-to-end SOS that are used in addressing other complex problems, while also identifying gaps that are especially involved in engaging a patient in his or her own care, and changing behavior. This long-term research and standardization effort needs to start now in order to be ready for 2017–2020.

9.1 Introduction

This chapter also discusses some of the recently (2014) completed grants (SHARP grants), along with some older work that may now be more relevant. Further, we examine some "notional research-piloting," with a high-level design and a simulation approach that is used by DoD projects prior to large-scale investment. Organizations have taken initiatives such as the SERC lead by Stevens Tech, the interoperability funding announced in February 2015 by ONC, or the CMS CMMI grants program, to create a proof of concept of the Resource-Event-Agent (REA) approach with end-to-end value-delivery networks within healthcare.

To understand this new paradigm, it is essential to first understand the resources needed to address specific health events, including those events that will actually save money and prevent more expensive events. Over the last 20 years, an accounting approach that links REAs to a balance sheet has slowly evolved. This approach was originally defined by Professor Bill McCarthy from Michigan State University, but now needs to be extended and adopted more quickly and broadly.

Use a New Resource-Event-Agent (REA) Paradigm Tailored to Healthcare

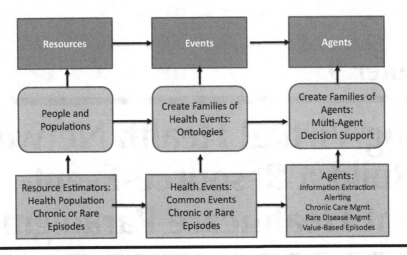

Figure 9.1   REAs model translated to healthcare.

Accountability and affordability have to be put into some context to illustrate how resources are used from the perspective of healthcare and the related events. The accounting approach is tailored to healthcare in Figure 9.1. This conceptual healthcare alignment to the REA approach can relate resource usage to health events. An approach such as this was never needed previously because healthcare was episode-driven and not driven by a customer's needs or the customer life-cycle needs. Even moving to value-based purchasing still focuses on the episode of care and not the person-centric approach of other industries. This shift in perspective allows both the patient and the set of providers who are providing their services to think about the value of the service from the patient perspective. This person-centric, accounting approach can also be used to consider one's own health, that is, wellness, from a life-cycle perspective and to better understand the resources consumed and needed. This approach can also be used to consider disease progression, events that can prevent and slowdown disease progression, or even prevent a disease from starting!

9.2 Challenges for Protecting System of Systems Overlay Networks with Service-Defined Networks

One of the key approaches to protect and separate information exchanges into topic-based service-defined networks can be grouping health events and consents into logical channels. In addition, their related attribute-based access control mechanism and security and privacy policies can be defined with a service-based software defined network. The software defined network from the open grid forum software defined network should be aligned with healthcare patient-to-provider communication and related to the NIST security guidelines. A trusted set of national value-delivery networks can be defined and built with the Open-HISE to have both basic capabilities and allow adaptations that meet local needs and extensions using a shared services governance process. This approach can leverage the experience of the Information Sharing Environment, including the NIEM and OMG standardization effort with the earlier DIRECT and CONNECT efforts along with FHIR efforts. Additional dynamic management and knowledge learning features needed by healthcare must be addressed, but, by building on previous complex systems projects, the risks are reduced and the underlying technology can be leveraged by other industries. This will allow healthcare to build upon the successful efforts and still address the dynamics of healthcare.

The healthcare IT transformation must include both patient and provider use cases and user-centered design approaches, but must incorporate threat, vulnerability, and error-driven use cases as well. It must also consider the new family of problem-related use cases, and include "threat models," privacy invasions, and other new healthcare security and privacy concerns based on mobility, transparency, and the many enabling technology threats identified by the SHARPS academic research. The new NIST Security directions, along with the ONC Security Working Group, are defining conditions such as those below:

- Man-in-the-middle
- Insider attacks
- Denial of services
- Identity theft
- Fraud
- Variety of consent rights viewpoints by patients
- Different healthcare privacy protection laws
- Need to share and need to protect conflicts
- Use of some of the traditional defenses in depth and policy-based security aspects

It will be essential to define an approach to bring the best practices in security, privacy, and resiliency engineering to the healthcare community, identify the weakest links in the connected healthcare networks, and require that those weaknesses be corrected in a timely manner.

9.3 Emerging Technology and Approaches

Healthcare IT needs to take some new approaches, and a summary of these needs must be presented to the ONC Policy Committee. Some of the topics that can be used as part of the next wave include the following:

- Policy machines
- Attribute-based access controls
- Supply chain risk management translated to health information networks
- Continuous compliance and monitoring
- Identity management
- Fraud prevention
- Exception handling and closing the gaps
- CERTs: Linked with risk sharing
- Insider threat management
- Resilience management
- Controlled data access Services
- Cloud data protections

- SHARPS research…(what has come of these projects)
  - Data segments for privacy
  - Attribute-based encryption
  - Mobile security
  - Context integrity

9.4 Integrating Security, Privacy, and Identity into the Process and Shared Services

A health and human services business service framework must contain an integrated security, privacy, and identity process life cycle that uses and extends a family of shared services.

Far too often, the security, privacy, and identity approaches became a focus late in the life cycle. This becomes a stumbling block to going operational, and is used as a political "gotcha" by those who want to maintain the status quo. Security and privacy design issues and activities must be integrated into each system of systems project. All incremental life cycles with four integrated releases per year must address the security, privacy, and identity concerns first. All the portfolios of integration-interoperable shared services representing government-sponsored contractors work need to be available as open sources with open services that leverage standards, or that can create changes that can be submitted to the standards development organizations. The development, integrator, and package vendors must agree to create shared services, or at least to provide public open services or open APIs. Vendors who agreed to align as "Integration–Interoperable Certified Product Vendors" will be preferred vendors for the government, and can have an advantage in state and commercial negotiations.

As each new release is planned, the solution architecture must go through a set of "discovery actions" and report the findings following these steps:

1. Create and update an end-to-end risk threat thread analysis and set of protection policies (see Section 9.6 for detail)
2. Define a series of protected anchor points and event logs
3. Build and create a diverse set of protection guards with integrated security reporting and alerting capabilities
4. Build a risk analysis and early vulnerability detection tracking system
5. Select and prioritize a set of repair, replace, and upgrade capabilities for each of the four annual releases
6. Define a security dashboard for each of the virtual health information networks of which your organization is a member
7. Certify integration–interoperability vendors, and provide them with a certification report and "logo" on being assessed as meeting the milestone
8. Provide a repository or open government-sponsored services, links to open solution services, and links to certified vendors

It will also be necessary to design new security features and an overall approach to build security and privacy into the complete life cycle. That new design will also require providing a common approach with the elements below:

- Develop new security
- Define privacy and identity shared services

- Create a set of local and sharable test cases for security threats and protection features
- Provide an integration and feedback process to resolve the integration and error handling process with a focus on key design aspects, such as resolving multiple identities that exist for patients and for providers. Provide a common payment interface for many systems that need to be managed in a "billfold" of health identities, and alternative payment approaches that may reveal more sensitive health information during payment integrity verification steps

9.5 Multi-Layered Protections Models with Protection-Policy Agents

Security policies need to be defined in a formal way that computers can understand, and disseminated to the users and managers. The NIST security policy guidance can be the basis for building a set of common protection policies for integration and interoperability, translating them into a reusable set of policies understandable to more healthcare leaders, IT leaders, and security specialist communities. (SAML, XACML, and other advanced concepts such as the NIST policy machine.)

9.5.1 Policy Alignment

General healthcare policies are difficult for patients to understand. In addition, neither patients nor providers have any patient consent protection policies related to their healthcare communities.

More than 7000 rare diseases affect over 30 million people (10% of the US population) and indirectly affect many more of their family members. It is important that patients and providers see the personal benefit in sharing data. The CF foundation is a good example of an early "care and cure" network that over the last 10 years has lengthened the life expectancy of adults with CF by more than 10 years. The CF approach can become the foundation of a "care and cure" value-delivery network. CF and other disease areas have built their own protection approaches. A common set of rare disease protection controls can be defined by a standards group. This set of disease-focused management protection policies (see Figure 9.2) can address the following issues:

- Managing sensitive data with attribute-based access control and attribute-based encryption
- Managing continuous consent for selected attribute areas that can be accessed
- Defining the related "care and cure" value networks and the topics/attributes that are information shared and events shared. Defining the policy and conditions in which the patient grants his or her participation based on rules related to attribute-based permissions. These attribute-based protections will support a set of sharing and consent negotiation policies with aligned agreements for a set of attributes and related events/entities
- Addressing both HIPAA and a range of state laws including notifications of any breaches can be addressed with shared services

9.5.2 Surrounding the Exchanges with Protection Agents

The policy machine agent can manage policies, and also ensure that the protections and consents are managed. Agent support software can manage exchanges from patients in a health event. For example, strict protections may be desirable unless a patient is in an emergency situation, such as having been helicoptered to a shock trauma facility where the patient may want to share all. Each end-to-end scenario must be evaluated according to HIPAA standards, and a process will need to identify "gaps" to be adjusted with new legislation and improved guidance (See Figure 9.3).

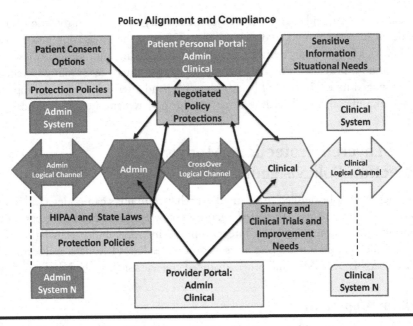

Figure 9.2 Architecture with policy integration and policy machines.

With the new paradigms of patient-centric healthcare and patients understanding the value of their electronic healthcare, attention to patient privacy and security will only increase. The patient is now a consumer and owner of his own information, and is an integral part of ensuring patient-protected information is shared, but shared securely, in timely manner, and electronically following their preferences.

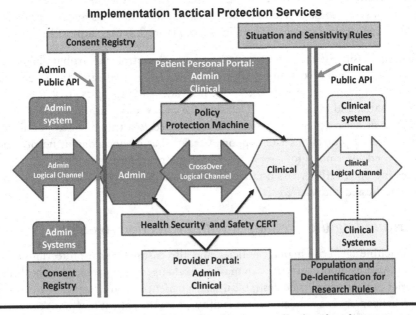

Figure 9.3 Protection agents that monitor and enforce organizational and cross-organizational agreements.

The overall approach must ensure not only that information flows, but also that payment authorization and insurance information flow, and that any information is shared both with the patient and providers, but also with the research community that is looking for a cure and looking for evidence of best practices that can be shared. Sharing of information and learning from that information should not be labor-intensive, but should occur automatically with the background as secondary uses of data. Not only outcomes and quality should be shared, but also the cost for the end-to-end and total care should be assessed and benchmarked across the regions. Cost benchmarking can add more to the affordability goal that is so important to transformation. With such flow and sharing, "price transparency" begins to become the norm, and not the exception.

One of the next key steps must involve moving from paper consent steps and rigid consent management to an automated dynamic consent process as shown in Figure 9.4.

A common agent model should be created to provide automated review for safety and other warnings that close the healthcare risk gaps. Alerts are very important, but can be a nuisance. Agents can be adapted and tailored to the persons: patient or provider preferences and the importance or risk that is identified. Previous systems did not provide the right balance of alert needs and preferences, and often resulted in alert fatigue, or just alert turnoff and living with the risks. Neither is acceptable. Your personal agent has to work with the agents from the labs, clinics, or providers that are part of your care teams. Today's generation of agents can work as a team, such as a group of multi-agent safety agents as shown in Figure 9.5. Multi-agent models must show how the agents can work together in teams. The model must illustrate a practical application based on previous team experiences, and show a way of integrating the fragmented healthcare IT system without requiring massive rewriting and replacing of systems. Agents can be the bridge that can integrate all ecosystem elements together: from patient-centric to provider paths of communication, and secondary information extraction to public health, quality and outcomes, and research with clinical trials, rare disease management practices, and other evidence-based analysis.

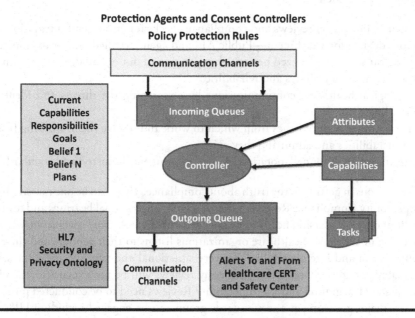

Figure 9.4   Moving from paper consent to agents that manage consent agreements.

Multi-Agent Safety Agents for Clinical Handoff and Constraint Management

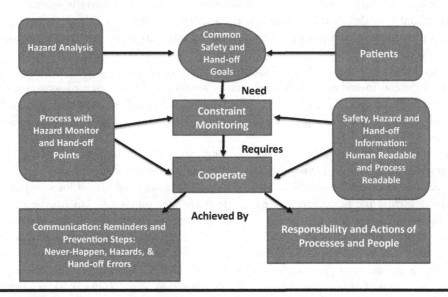

Figure 9.5   Multi-agents working together to meet the policy intent.

9.6 Test and Risk Assessment Driven Integration and Interoperability Compliance

Over the last few years, many innovations have been tested, but there have been only limited tests of integration and interoperability. New pilot projects need to address these integration and interoperability issues, such as:

- Create new protection reviews and compliance checks for end-to-end integration
- Approve devices for attachment—Public API and agent certified—prior to connection
- Define clear sets of authorized personnel: separation of duties and defining minimal access
- Define the types of facilities and reliabilities
- Create logical healthcare communications by researching the threats and identifying the weakest link
    - Recommend a set of issues from which to work and resolve them: working from known vulnerabilities and admitting they exist
- Create an approach for collaboration among government, industry, and standards groups

There are options in getting to the truth about compliance. There can be one massive Integration and Interoperability Compliance Review or even a set of Congressional hearings and testimony but it has been found that leadership needs to be engaged and a much more specific answer is needed. Today, everyone in the major healthcare organizations listens to their vendors and their solutions but the "integration and interoperability" are very situational and very specific. One set of questions is probably going to be too broad and many reviews will be too expensive. Therefore, a set of regional or state Integration and Interoperability Reviews need to be conducted probably semi-annually. The major government and standards group can be engaged including Hl&, HIMSS, and government organizations such as ONC and CMS. The Integration and Interoperability

Review can focus on product readiness and alignment and identify known risks and gaps that need to be addressed. Each review will include findings, answers by vendors on specific questions including commitments to make changes and when to make them, it will include walkthroughs and key end-to-end scenarios, and encourage the use of proof of concept demonstrations. The results will include findings, risks, and recommendations that can be documented and shared.

9.7 Creating a Common Approach for a Disease-Focused Management Network

To eradicate diseases like polio or ebola today, or some of the more than 7000 genetic-driven diseases in the future, more than a few medical researchers will be needed; however, it is essential that the crowd be organized and working together. An April 2014 Quality and Safety supplement describes the success of the CF movement lead by the CF Foundation, and recommends that their approach could become the benchmark for other movements. This chapter describes the generalization of their concepts into a reference model, process framework, shared services, and smart APIs, along with agents and ontology-based software that can become the overall approach needed. This technology solution will need leadership and participant advocates who can step forward to tailor and adapt the solutions to their specific communities.

9.7.1 Using Portals and Ontologies with Smart Registries

Establishing a collaborative environment requires the creation of a common ground of communication where the views and scientific terminology of experts and providers can meet the health literacy level of patients–family–advocates. Figure 9.6 shows how a series of linked ontologies can be described in human readable formats, as well as formats that the computer can use. These linked ontologies provide the basis for computers to search, extract, and link data from patients to data needed for clinical trials and outcome-evidence-based research that can be driven by the bi-directional patient–provider communication shown in Figure 9.6.

9.7.2 Establishing a Common Improvement Process and Information Sharing Process

Disease-focused management organizations, such as the CF Foundation, have shown great progress in improving the lives of children and adults with CF and their families, and have increased life expectancy over the last 12 years by more than 10 years from 32 years of age to 42 years. Can their success provide a roadmap that can be leveraged for other diseases and health conditions? One approach to improving healthcare IT communication may be to create a disease-focused management analysis framework that builds on the CF-improvement approach and others, as shown in Figure 9.7. This process and the automated libraries and reusable ontologies are an important focus in the author's research.

9.7.3 Creation of a Common Reference Model for Disease-Focused Improvement and Collaboration

Because there are more than 7000 rare diseases with 200,000 or more patients (with their families) involved, members of these small communities of advocates can and have become the drivers

Basic Reference Model for Health Registries

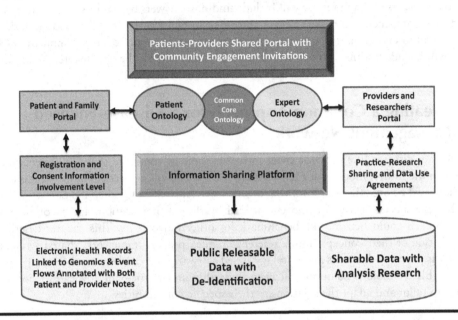

Figure 9.6 Bi-directional communication support with ontology supported portal and mapping between complex medical terminology and the health literacy level of the patient and family members.

Disease-Specific Focused Network & Analysis Framework

- Create a Strategic Roadmap and Collaborative Patients-Supporters-Providers & Researchers Network – along with Pharma & Government Researchers
- Define a Baseline and Goal-Oriented Quality and Outcome Measures
- Establish Value Delivery Networks with Value Payments and Bundled Payments

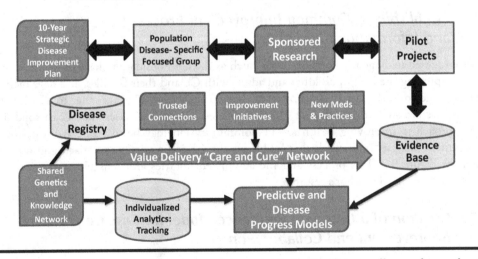

Figure 9.7 Generalizing the CF improvement approach to support any disease-focused management and improvement initiative.

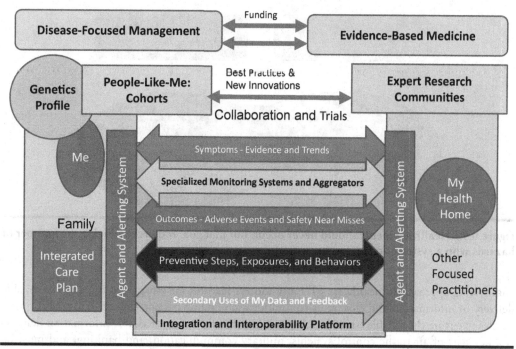

Figure 9.8 Common collaborative bi-directional reference model.

for change. Healthcare IT and networking can become key enablers of collaboration, but, if each organization is inventing its own model, there will be much waste and many missteps. A reference model such as the one below, built with shared services and smart APIs, can greatly facilitate the evolution of disease-focused management change as the industry has seen with the success of CF. Further research and prototypes in this area are a research focus of the author. The focus on communication improvement for the many types of rare diseases is shown in Figure 9.8.

9.7.4 Safer Networks with Handoff Controls and Hazard Alerts Built into Safe Process Models

In early aviation, manufacturing, railway, and military accidents, the improvement approach taken was one of fighting each accident, and what are called "never events," and driving to each root cause. A safer set of engineering practices is needed. Nancy Leveson at MIT has been working on a Safer World based on a new engineering approach (references), and the author of this book sees the need for a similar approach to healthcare IT. Further research and prototyping in this area are required.

9.7.5 Hazard Analysis for the Network Function and the Medical Practices

Healthcare IT must have a new systematic analysis of the hazard threats from: (1) failure events that should never happen or (2) omission of communication that must occur. A new safety system

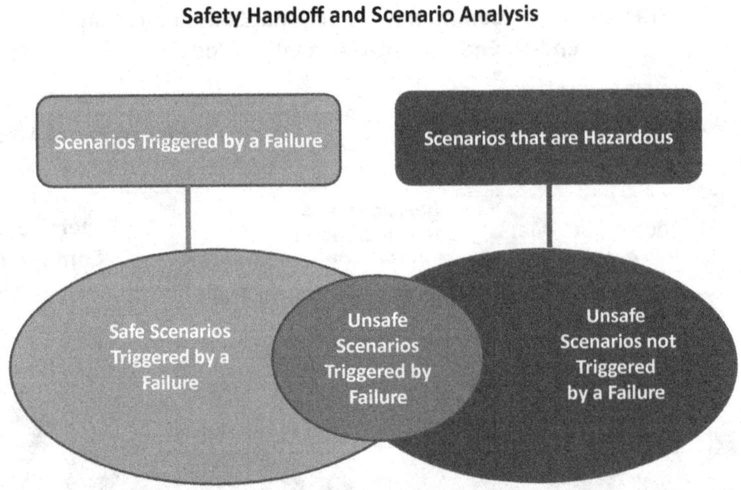

Safety Handoff and Scenario Analysis

Figure 9.9 **Health accidents should never occur, but that goal requires reducing the number of hazards with a systematic approach.**

engineering approach to healthcare IT must address features for error handling and the reliable delivery of information and closure of communication among patient–doctors–lab results–pharmacies to ensure the reliable communication of health information. Reliable information delivery is a key part of air traffic control systems, military communication, and banking, and must be brought into healthcare IT, as this information delivery must fit within the standards of groups such as the Joint Commission, the ONC Usability and Safety committee, or a number of different safety projects. This is another example where healthcare IT does not need to reinvent the process, but tailor it to healthcare.

New approaches (such as those in Figure 9.9) address areas such as

■ Creating a "never events" taxonomy
■ Describing the new safer world approach: STAMP-TPA

High-risk processes in all industries use "controlled processes" that can have monitoring, alerting, and advisory capabilities. If these capabilities are distributed across the fragmented healthcare IT environment, the entire system can be safer and more reliable. Although this process will take years, the types of safety improvements that have been used in other industries can be represented in a common way, such as in Figure 9.10.

9.7.6 Handoff Management and Agent Alerts

Handoffs have been studied extensively in other industries, like managing nuclear power, space networks, or air traffic control systems. Early healthcare systems, like intensive care systems and adding "paper checklists" to provide improved patient safety, can now be upgraded with new smart technology as shown in Figure 9.11.

Safety agents can have a common structure as shown in Figure 9.12, and much of the research that has been done over the last few years can be used to create a very new agent model such as this. A pilot project is needed in this area.

Keeping Consistent Identities and Direct Discovery of Identity Exchange Points

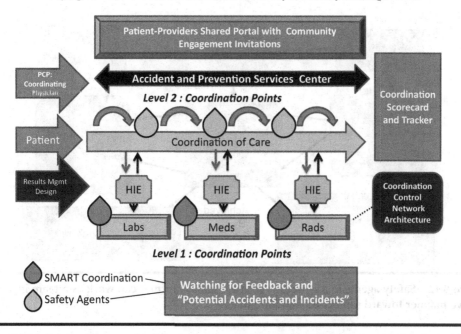

Figure 9.10 Key healthcare processes can now be "controlled" with automated safety tools.

Basic Reference Model for Health Registries:
Personalized with Agents and Support Tools for Patients and Providers

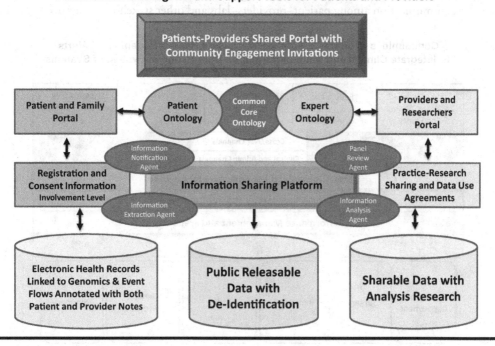

Figure 9.11 Safety agents can monitor handoffs, identify and prevent hazards, and support automated feedback and improvement.

Multi-Agent Safety Agents for Clinical Handoff and Constraint Management

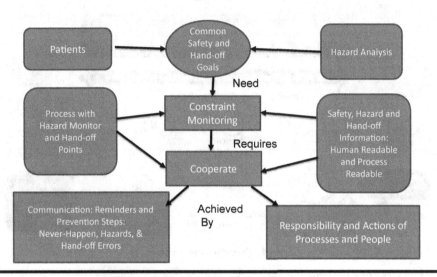

Figure 9.12 Safety agents in a structure with a common format can work as a team in a cooperative manner toward safety and handoff goals.

9.7.7 Creating a Safety and Protection Service Layer

One approach to agent-based safety protection creates a safety and protection service layer as shown in Figure 9.13, using intelligent software agents to monitor and ensure that the reliable and inclusive communication among patient–providers–labs and other stakeholders has occurred, and

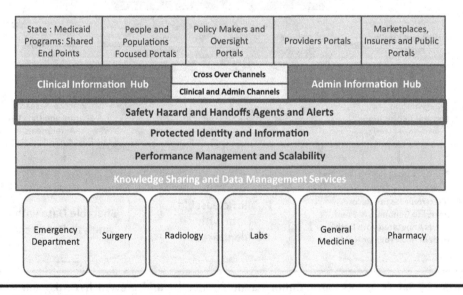

Figure 9.13 Safety-hazard management can be a layer of protection.

that the protection agents watch for any roadblocks or gaps in communications that may occur. This agent-based approach for inclusion in safety intention-based models can be used by government and industry to ensure that safety is managed and built into all parts of the safety-focused value health delivery networks.

9.8 Conclusion

Many ideas and next steps were generated as this book was being developed. The author has noted the need to accomplish the following tasks in the transitioning of healthcare IT:

1. Define health events and relate them to the Business Process Management Notation 2.02 events common elements, but include health events related to common health life events, and include linked medical ontologies with the use of the general medicine ontology.
2. Define a system of systems integration process, including approaches such as defining integration points, defining the strategic integration alignment process, defining and reaching agreements on integration behaviors and integration oversight, including integration reviews, readiness scorecards, and an assemblage of integration tests.
3. Create a pilot project with a set of linked medical ontologies, including creating common discovery and search features.
4. Create an integration and interoperability ontology and method to use as part of the administrative and governance process.
5. Create a basic health event agent that can be adapted, integrated, and extended into the many health pathways from patients to providers and all shared data sources.
6. Create safety agents and safety rules that can allow critical process to be under safety control policies.

Chapter 10

Introducing New Approaches to Meet the Challenges of Integration, Scale, and Event Coordination

---

Abstract

Health services, with event integration, interoperability, and a shift to a patient–consumer approach, face a number of additional challenges as the services try to scale and reach everyone, independent of zip code. At the same time, this dramatic change cannot require starting over. Starting over is too expensive and would take too long. Fortunately, there are other approaches that exist.

The alternatives must provide a migration path and a framework that follows a minimum set of standards. Healthcare standards have not addressed the large-scale SOS challenges, ways to track the responsibility and resources usage, and an approach to address the scale that is needed.

The ONC developed a standards advisory that completed its second version in December 2015. The problem is that it still relies on the same old hub-and-spoke approach for health information exchanges, and does not truly turn the paradigm from provider to facility interoperability or address the new cloud and mobile applications.

This chapter introduces three major shifts

- REA models that can link health events to the resources and responsibilities of the agents/peoples or organizations providing the services
- SOS approach to group the services and content into logical functions: alliances
- Intercloud health, human services and research alignment framework
- Connecting local health accountable communities to National Disease Foundation networks
- Leveraging the bridging agent concept for aligned information, services and protection

10.1 Leveraging Industry and SOS Experiences

Healthcare IT must address the many aspects of the security-identity management and access control protections that have been faced by the financial industry, government security, and intelligence programs. Fortunately, the experiences of those industries can be leveraged. A new HHS Intercloud approach, such as shown in Figure 10.1, can move interoperability and information sharing forward, and not be stuck using an older hub-and-spoke model that will require many states and regions to build their own systems versus sharing an Intercloud approach.

10.1.1 Intercloud Framework

Some of the key features of an Intercloud approach include the following:

- Define an Intercloud framework for HHSs with linked research
- Handle patient–consumer cloud with individual task and personal information in a cloud
- Use Clouds as migration and scaling strategy: handle dynamic workloads
- Clouds have many versions: Amazon, Google, Oracle, etc., but need to have a federation of clouds with commonality in addresses, names, identification, trust, presence, messaging, time domain, and resource semantics
- Applications can be integrated together and content shared from multiple clouds
- Intercloud Standards (P2302): Intercloud GW, Intercloud Root, and Exchange
- Intercloud Security Services: Service Level Agreements (SLA), Accounting and Auditing, Policy Management, and Exception Handling

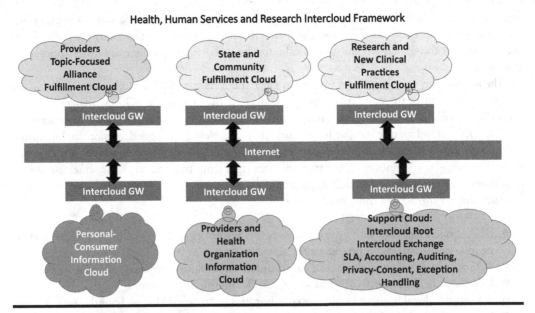

Figure 10.1 Intercloud-based open-health ISE can follow new industry standards.

The following standards (P2302-Standard for Intercloud Interoperability and Federation) should be used:

- Cloud to Cloud Interoperability
- Set of standard protocols managed by the GW and a support Cloud with directory, registration authority, trust authority, cloud management, and governance coordination
- Standards are evolving through an Intercloud Testbed development, and some health organizations, like NIH and some portions of CMS, have moved to the Cloud
- Interoperability Standards from ONC Standards Advisory do not address the Intercloud interoperability needs

Cloud Management Standards: Benefits

- Bridging innovation can tie the pieces together: Intercloud GWs, but not requiring the replacement of major capabilities but the insertion of bridging agents discussed in Section 10.4
- Quicker time to value
- Shorter deployment cycle with tools and testing built into the support Cloud
- Lower risk because integration and interoperability can follow a pattern
- Existing providers, states, neighborhoods can select their own Clouds, as long as they support the P2302 and define any extensions available
- The Intercloud framework can be a foundation for integration and foster innovation without starting over again

Over the last few years, security threats and vulnerabilities have appeared as headlines. Behind the scenes, many groups from government units (such as NIST, the Department of Homeland Security, Intelligence agencies, the DoD) to the private sector (including the financial industry, groups like the SEI, the Stevens Tech lead SERC, and INCOSE) have had to address these secure access issues with standards and education webinars, and adding lessons learned to the growing experience in dealing with very large complex systems. There are currently few healthcare case studies and examples from which to model secure access; and, until the government and health standards groups are open to leveraging their varied but related experience, much unnecessary reinventing of the wheel will occur. However, some crossover learning can and should occur; one of the purposes of this chapter, and of this book in general, is to foster that leveraging and tailoring of ideas and successes to healthcare IT transformation.

During the period from 2010 to 2013, ONC created a set of grant research projects—SHARPS and Beacon Communities; unfortunately, these projects are not currently funded. Follow-on grants with smaller consolidated funding and technology transfer initiatives should be considered. The results of the research grants and the results from other earlier adopters of innovative programs are being discussed at the extensive ONC working groups that are being convened. The year 2014 brought outstanding research findings (see References). ONC needs to factor more protections into its architecture and road mapping approach. A series of ONC FACA committees and working groups are addressing key issues, and the ideas here reflect the extension and integration of many of those from healthcare, industry, and complex government agencies.

If integrated and included in the overall roadmap, these concepts can offer a breakthrough approach in healthcare IT. To fill some of the key gaps, this chapter recommends: (1) creating a new healthcare Security and privacy profile for interconnected information networks and (2) compiling a summary of the standards and key emerging technologies that are needed for: (a) improved patient–provider information protection and (b) an aligned Healthcare Cybersecurity Framework.

It is essential to define another set of subdomains for healthcare and to create a universal core of

- Key concepts
- Core data elements
- A set of terminology for integration and interoperability (defined in an I & I ontology)

The INCOSE SOS and related SERC work have created an ontology that can become the starting point for a healthcare specific integration and interoperability ontology.

An integration and interoperability roadmap can be addressed state by state, but the common element is defining extensions to MITA that can reflect both state HHSs information and a common set of shared services. At the 2014 MESC, Jessica Kahn noted that more than 18 states were addressing interoperability and integration and the associated proposal for MITA extensions, and could be encouraged to create common open-shared services for interoperability that can be used by all states.

Interoperability is now a hot topic being addressed by ONC, by industry groups, and even by legislators in the twenty-first century Cures draft legislation. The key is to get a common set of definitions and common expectation of what interoperability means with real examples. This chapter also includes recommendations for the ONC Interoperability Workgroup. The workgroup is defining a set of capabilities as part of their shared services portfolio; the Security, Usability, and Safety Workgroup is also working on a similar set of shared services. This chapter and others in this book will be shared with those ONC workgroups.

It is recommended that each ONC workgroup create a related shared services portfolio, and that an initial basic set of capabilities be developed within the many related healthcare IT contracts, and shared with the government–contractor–industry community.

ONC can develop an integration series of fishbone diagrams and arrow diagrams as discussed in Chapter 8, but unfortunately, they think in terms of small scenarios and not end-to-end delivery of services to the patient. A set of shared services needs to be defined that supports the end-to-end delivery of services. A standards group like Health Service Specification Project could define a set of event process chains, and also define a set of shared services that would be needed. These portfolios of common shared services can become the keystone elements of government to industry integration and interoperability, and a government and community shared service governance process, as well as a set of responsibilities for the implementation and use defined. The government projects, such as Medicaid, could contribute to the initial shared services as part of their development, along with an open-shared services industry initiative. Joint proposals with federal–state–industry joining together can be achieved with clear responsibility and integration of the shared services collaboration project. Joint projects, such as the ISE for the intelligence community, can be a model for such projects. A special project office can be established and put into the legislation of the twenty-first century Cures law. This recommendation will be made.

WHAT WE CAN LEARN FROM THE USE OF INTERMEDIARIES IN TELECOM AND BANKING INFORMATION SHARING

Phil Cooke

Healthcare as a market segment is undergoing a significant shift from a distribution-oriented, service delivery model to a consumer-oriented delivery model. Patients will make choices based on convenience, quality, price, overall value, proven performance, etc. Such market shifts occurred in banking and telecommunications previously, with "lessons learned" applicable to healthcare.

In banking, the introduction of automated teller machines (ATMs), allowed for 24-h banking. Initially, banks had proprietary machines/networks. One bank's ATM could not connect to another bank's ATM—no interoperability. However, as consumers utilized ATMs more and more, a need/desire arose to have access to "their" money, regardless of where the ATM was located. Networks, such as Pulse and Cirrus were formed to provide broader access. These were intermediaries that allowed one bank's ATM to interface and interact with another bank's network for the convenience of the consumer. Eventually, ATMs became ubiquitous and interconnection/interoperability became the standard, and seamless, for customers. For a fee, no problem. EHRs and Health Information Exchanges (HIEs) will follow a similar evolution, though probably faster than with ATMs.

Telecom also evolved quickly to interoperability for the convenience of and value to the consumer. Specifically, the Federal Communications Commission (FCC) made a ruling that mobile operators had to allow their customers to change carriers without having to give up their mobile phone numbers. No longer did the carrier "own" the number, as has always been the case; the consumer owned the number until it was relinquished. The systems to manage telephone numbers for the carriers were not designed to be shared, especially with other carriers. The FCC allowed a Local Number Portability Council, with all national carriers as members, to oversee interoperability via a clearinghouse. The clearinghouse was an enterprise independent of any one carrier. The FCC and Communication Security Reliability and Interoperability Council (CSRIC) selected a firm to be the clearinghouse, based on responses to requests for proposals. The clearinghouse served the same purpose as interoperability. Just like consumers own their phone numbers, patients will "own" their health records—not physicians or clinics or labs or hospitals, as has always been the case in the past. Interoperability will evolve, or be directed via regulation, to ensure that consumers exercise their free market choices.

A detailed integration roadmap for the next 18 months can show that the government-sponsored roadmap can fit with similar roadmaps by an affiliated set of open consortia.

The result of the government and open consortia based portfolios will be a baseline for healthcare industry collaboration, and a phased roadmap of shared services can spur innovation. In addition, governance of government-sponsored and aligned open sources can have a consistent set of transparent reviews where SOS design aspects can be evaluated, and the areas needing improvement can be identified. This can include detailed community reviews, but also foster higher level goals, such as approaches to creating safer business processes and improved handoffs, and integrating adverse reporting into the process. The improvements can identify conditions that should "never happen," more dynamic reporting, and building in root cause analysis into all problem resolutions, so that improvement recommendations can be considered in this next wave of changes.

For many generally healthy people, healthcare is not at the top of their priority lists; they may address prevention and specific episodes of care, but they would not see much of a need for sharing medical records or other health information. However, there are also others who may have one or more rare genetic diseases; their treatment can result in chronic and ongoing actions that can cross the many boundaries of healthcare domains. These 30 million people and their networks of 10–20 family members and friends (who touch almost all Americans) find the "integrated focus" provided by interoperability compelling. Therefore, if common, logical channels of integration and interoperability can be defined, these "rare disease" communities can utilize the power of 7000 communities of 200,000–500,000 people enabled by secure access to linked health information. A common reference model for a "care and cure" network can be defined by HSSP and be included in the twenty-first century Cures legislation. The disease foundations can become the champions of the deployment process throughout the country.

Once basic integration and interoperability shared services and APIs are put into place, and a responsible organization is in charge to market and outreach, the market can take over. As has been discussed in regard to telecom and banking, clearinghouse functions needed to be established. Those clearinghouses, and similar ones for healthcare, can provide the power of the network; that power can be triggered by the government initiatives, but sustaining the clearinghouse functions will need to be with private health information exchanges. There do not need to be 50 exchanges; a set of regional exchanges with backup capabilities can provide the cost effectiveness and reliability needed. Governance can be supported, and a set of regular shared services and open APIs can be released as an open source capability. There are some key technology and implementation barriers that must be addressed, but with the mix of coopetition that is expected to be achieved and with the standards alignment exercises, a set of focused research grants can be used to fill in those gaps. This chapter shares the gaps noted by the author with specific approaches and research initiatives that must be refined over the next few years to fill in some of the key gaps, such as the use of attribute-based protections, safety agents.

This chapter also advocates and describes how not only patients, but also their families and friends, along with researchers, can become the market drivers, or the "community" for improving care, and also the drivers for research on safety and chronic care management.

There are many separate networks forming for specific diseases, specific cancer conditions, Medicaid high utilization patients, and regional networks. However, their compatibility, level of interoperability, and financial sustainability are in doubt unless an organization such as ONC can establish a master integration plan, a roadmap, and a governance approach such as that shown in Figure 10.2.

10.2 New Standards for a New Era: End-to-End Focus

Healthcare standards have gone through many phases, and have had intended and unintended consequences; but as we enter a new era, a new phase of standards activity and results is needed. One of the most important actions is that ONC is creating a Standards Advisory. It is currently limited to only the HL7, and does not take into account the many other standards that can be leveraged; however, that will be expanded in the future.

Figure 10.3 shows a brief history of the key standards perspectives and the outcomes that have been achieved. It has followed the "Goldilocks" approach: too loose, too tight and complex, and

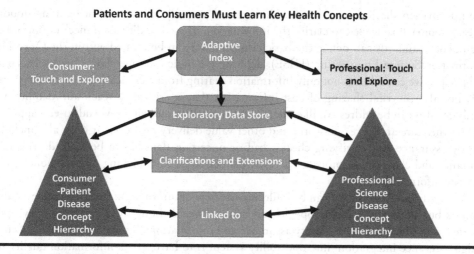

Figure 10.2   Open-health ISE roadmap and key elements.

now working to find the "just right" level; but only in the case of the simple set of HSSP has HL7 joined with other industries OMG to gain experience from other industry segments. A next generation of HSSP is needed to address more end-to-end services and to integrate other standards in healthcare such as workflow, rules, decision modeling, and others.

New HSSP activities should look at a set of end-to-end user scenarios, and define the information sharing services that are needed and the alignment of information across the boundaries.

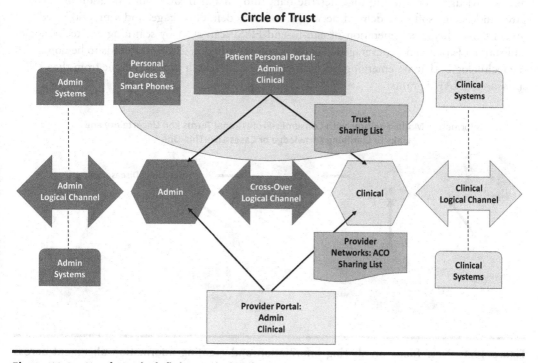

Figure 10.3   Key focus is defining a circle of trust.

The information sharing must not only be received properly, but also must be understood, and an easy approach is needed to clarify the information. These "quality assurance" or "information alignment" standards can define the basic elements that can be created within the Open Health Information System Engineering (HISE), defining the basic interoperability issues. This end-to-end perspective can address not only information sharing from a clinical interoperability perspective, but also the vital sharing of cost information that is critical to reach affordability. Other attributes also can be addressed, like safety, trust, usability, and with new end-to-end approaches, such as the "care and cure" networks and other value delivery networks. It must also include the quality assurance and clarifying checks; bad or uncertain data has to be flagged. This quality assurance and clarification process may even include some time picking up the phone to obtain accurate information.

A key attribute assessment can be built into the flow of information. It can be achieved during changes but as part of ongoing operational quality checks. Long lived and frequently updated systems need to have built in quality assurance and information alignment steps. Part of creating a high assurance integration–interoperability system is to have a data-information quality scorecard and built in flagging and improvement process. Early concepts of this process are shown in Figure 10.4.

Earlier generations of business process and workflow were not flexible enough and configurable with reference models; those issues have been resolved in other industries like supply chain management and the linking of the telecom and financial industry systems. The use of flexible-configurable reference models that use proven approaches, such as event process chain techniques, can be leveraged to connect the many healthcare patients and providers without having to "reinvent the wheel." Some changes may be needed. However, some research in Europe has already addressed a number of issues with the dynamics of processes, practices, new diseases, new knowledge, and linking together the data into virtual information. In addition, healthcare can leverage software defined networks, software defined storage, and semantic-based and linked data. This next generation of end-to-end HSSP can start by scanning the technologies and standards that can be leveraged. That was accomplished in 2008 and needs to be done with the technologies that are emerging, including ideas and research gaps that came from the ONC-sponsored SHARP grants.

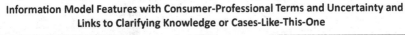

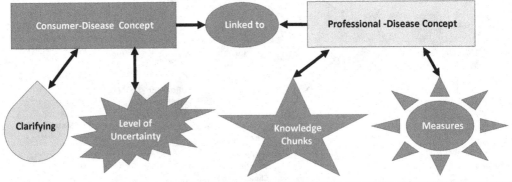

Figure 10.4 New focus on sharing information and creating information alignment across cloud boundaries.

10.3 Expanding Community Experience to Neighborhood, Accountable Health Communities, and Fostering Both Care and Cures

Today, patient–consumers feel confused and overwhelmed by healthcare complexity when confronted with an emergency or having to deal with a chronic or complex disease situation. It does not get any easier on the provider and community-caseworkers side. They must deal with many patients in a time-crunch and with more information but with little assistance from the software. Both patient–consumers and providers–consumers must be connected but it does not have to be a connection at the electronic health record level but rather at a high relationship level, and patient–consumers must understand and relate to services in their neighborhoods and fit in with accountable health communities and related value-driven health accountable care organizations. There are a number of issues that must be addressed—summarized in Figure 1.7 in Chapter 1.

Those high health utilizers need to become part of local and national communities where they are engaged and take responsibility for their health and wellness with the providers and community-caseworkers as guides. This community involvement is especially important to those suffering from the many not-so-rare diseases. They need to be members of peer communities that focus on both improving care and fostering new cures. We have called these Care and Cure Networks. It is great to have vision but where are we today? An evolutionary approach is shown in Figure 10.5.

10.3.1 Communities for Vets and Disease Foundations

For example, the Veterans Administration to foster its transformation has used the Jive software tool in early 2016.

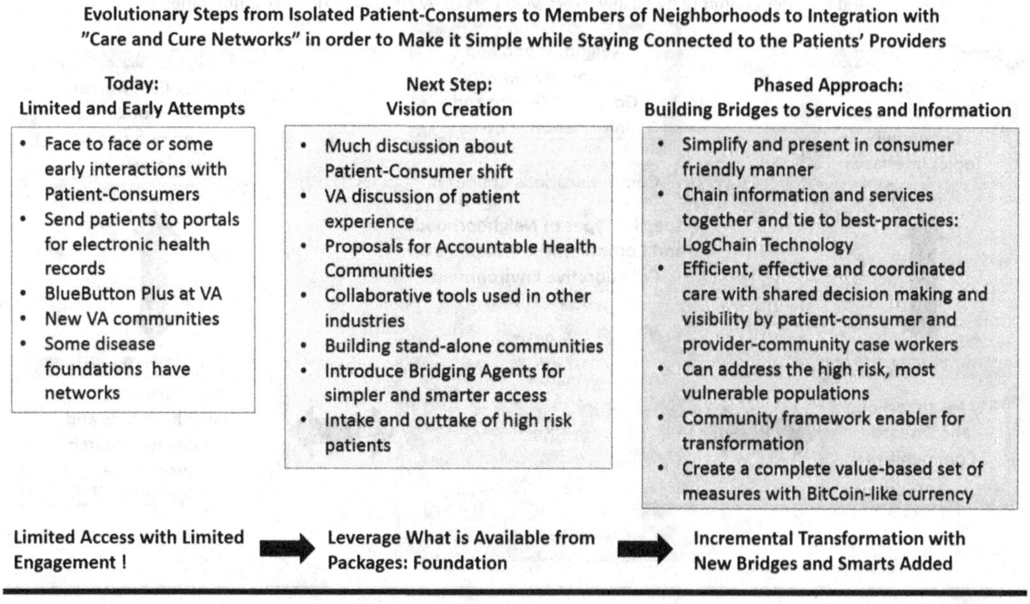

Evolutionary Steps from Isolated Patient-Consumers to Members of Neighborhoods to Integration with "Care and Cure Networks" in order to Make it Simple while Staying Connected to the Patients' Providers

Today: Limited and Early Attempts	Next Step: Vision Creation	Phased Approach: Building Bridges to Services and Information
• Face to face or some early interactions with Patient-Consumers • Send patients to portals for electronic health records • BlueButton Plus at VA • New VA communities • Some disease foundations have networks	• Much discussion about Patient-Consumer shift • VA discussion of patient experience • Proposals for Accountable Health Communities • Collaborative tools used in other industries • Building stand-alone communities • Introduce Bridging Agents for simpler and smarter access • Intake and outtake of high risk patients	• Simplify and present in consumer friendly manner • Chain information and services together and tie to best-practices: LogChain Technology • Efficient, effective and coordinated care with shared decision making and visibility by patient-consumer and provider-community case workers • Can address the high risk, most vulnerable populations • Community framework enabler for transformation • Create a complete value-based set of measures with BitCoin-like currency
Limited Access with Limited Engagement !	➡ Leverage What is Available from Packages: Foundation	➡ Incremental Transformation with New Bridges and Smarts Added

Figure 10.5 A phased approach is needed to link national disease driven initiatives to local neighborhood health communities.

The features include the following:

■ The Department of Veterans Affairs runs the largest integrated healthcare system in the world.
  – 340,000 staff; 1,100 hospitals and clinics; and 2,000 facilities spread across the country
  – Providing 90 million outpatient visits to nearly 9 million patients, and benefits to nearly 13.5 million total veterans
  – A roughly $170 billion operating budget in FY 2016
■ VA developed a collaborative platform to foster and disseminate best practices and innovations across geographic areas, facilities, and areas of expertise.
■ During 2016 VA has built and is rolling out VA Pulse, a collaborative platform that uses Jive to drive and support VA's transformation. In just two years, through customized platform design, pilot testing, and strategic outreach, VA Pulse:
  – Became VA's largest and fastest-growing collaborative community.
  – Grew to 60,000 users through viral adoptions and self-registration.
  – Supports more than 2,300 individual collaboration groups.
■ A similar approach can be done by the HHS Office of Reform or the many Centers for Medicare and Medicaid Innovation (CMMI). Keeping the many successes quiet only works for a while and now is the time to be proud of the many improvements that have occurred.

A general neighborhood and community framework can be created with an overall registry and set of common underlying shared services that can be used for both neighborhoods and for disease communities (what was called care and cure networks) and to assure that the common set of service and information services can be used anywhere, independent of zip code. A standard set of neighborhood and community set ups can be defined with common checklists and standard services and information models. The high level conceptual view is shown in Figure 10.6.

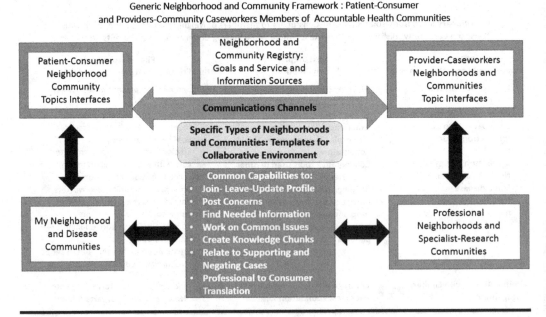

Figure 10.6 Generic neighborhood and communities structure with registry and common capabilities.

10.3.2 Lessons Learned

Continuous improvement and innovation takes an open environment where many good ideas can be shared. One of the reasons that the scientific community has been successful is that the best ideas are vetted and published. The successes in this early stage of healthcare transformation are being kept quiet so that it does not get killed by the politics of resistance. In 2017 and beyond those good stories must come out. A collaborative social environment can help break through the resistance to change and be supported by collaborative team technologies.

10.3.3 State Innovation Models, Medicaid Population Communities, and a Framework for Accountable Health Communities

These ideas for collaborative communities with local grassroots leadership are popping up in initiatives such as:

- Delaware Neighborhood concept and tie to Patient–Consumer Portal
- Medicaid shift to being patient–consumer oriented versus functional oriented
- Putting innovations within an Accountable Health Community approach

But each of these communities cannot afford to design their own overall framework where complexity and overload can be managed with "bridging agents." The overall approach will become part of the Healthcare LinkedIn Innovation Community.

This will take an evolutionary approach to link the National Disease Foundation efforts or even Cancer Moonshot 2020 to the local and personal trusted sources of healthcare, where the new care and new cure approaches are used, and where the trust has to occur to get the information sharing and the sharing of critical genomic data to occur. This is shown in Figure 10.7. The problem is that there is a limited "architecture" approach even among the most progressive organizations like cystic fibrosis or MS or cancer. They are run by a doctor researcher and the

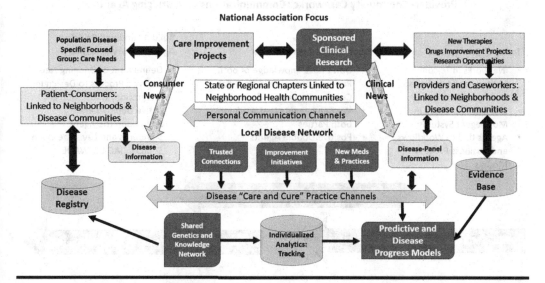

Figure 10.7 Generic neighborhood to disease foundation networks where care and cure improvements can go from isolated national research to local and rapid deployment projects.

focus is often only on the cure aspect and not the ability to live with the disease. Although a few organizations like CFF have initiatives in place, they alone cannot take upon an initiative that uses advanced health IT ideas. But they can if there are groups that can work together. The states also have the same problem. The key is to create a shared services environment and get states working with disease foundations

Define a Neighborhood-Community Framework: December 2016, evolving to this vision with a pilot project in 2017.

10.4 Creating Bridging Agents That Include Interoperability-As-Service: Have Knowledge of All Interfaces, Integration, and Information Needs

10.4.1 Bridging Agents Close the Information and Service Gaps and Provide the Underlying Complexity Management, Workload Overload, Protection and Safety Needed to Make Health and Human Services Work for All

Today patients and consumers are unhappy with the information they receive from their providers and community caseworkers. They cannot meaningfully use the information provided and the providers-community case workers are overloaded and stressed by their workloads. This has happened in other industries and intelligent software often called agents have been created and simplify and make the work more efficient and understandable for all.

The situation today can be shown in this high level infograph, Figure 10.8.

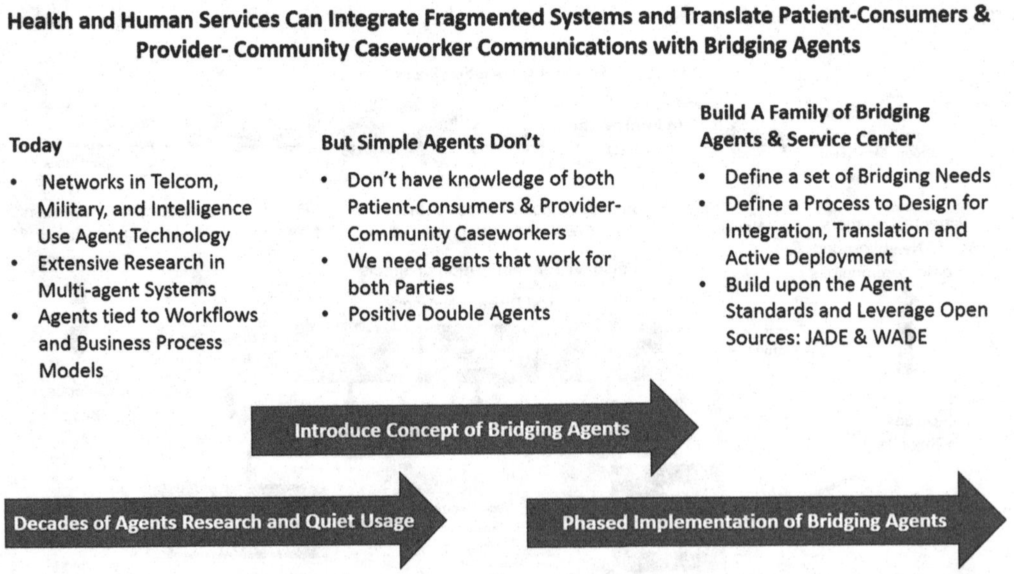

Health and Human Services Can Integrate Fragmented Systems and Translate Patient-Consumers & Provider- Community Caseworker Communications with Bridging Agents

Today
- Networks in Telcom, Military, and Intelligence Use Agent Technology
- Extensive Research in Multi-agent Systems
- Agents tied to Workflows and Business Process Models

But Simple Agents Don't
- Don't have knowledge of both Patient-Consumers & Provider-Community Caseworkers
- We need agents that work for both Parties
- Positive Double Agents

Build A Family of Bridging Agents & Service Center
- Define a set of Bridging Needs
- Define a Process to Design for Integration, Translation and Active Deployment
- Build upon the Agent Standards and Leverage Open Sources: JADE & WADE

Introduce Concept of Bridging Agents

Decades of Agents Research and Quiet Usage

Phased Implementation of Bridging Agents

Figure 10.8 Incremental game plan moving to an environment protected and supported by families of bridging agents.

Today, there are many uses of agents in telecom, in complex military and intelligence situations, and there is extensive research on multi-agent processes and open source approaches such as Java Agent Development (JADE) and its companion products such as Workflow Agent Development Environment (WADE) but these simple agents do not have the knowledge to link across the many silos that healthcare has created. Agents must understand both sides, both the patient–consumer and the provider–caseworkers, or other two-sided agents. These agents must represent the interests of both sides and make a simple bridge, not just for delivering messages but to assure understanding. These agents must close the semantic and syntactic and reduce the confusion and complexity. There is not one agent but a family of bridging agents that can work across the divides and support aggregation and analysis, hide the many sign ins, and reduce the workload from both the patient–consumers' and providers' points of view, along with the many other viewpoints and issues that can be addressed with a variety of bridging agents. Bridging agents will have open APIs.

10.4.2 Bridging Agent Common Framework and Range of Types

The bridging agents can have a common structure such as shown in Figure 10.9.

The two partners will share with the bridging agents knowledge about their needs, intents, and key usage factors such as background and knowledge of underlying concepts and language levels. For example, the patient–consumers could use a consumer-friendly medical vocabulary while the providers use a more detailed medical language that is aligned to consumer terminologies. But the key focus is on improving and simplifying communications in complex medical situations.

The set of user experiences and provider interactions must be shared and aligned. But there is an asymmetry of knowledge between the consumer and professional vocabularies along with the long history of the medical profession assuming that the patient–consumer does not care or really understand or is not anxious about the truth. Not only can patient–consumers handle information but they are demanding it. Intelligent agents can be the logical bridges between both patient–consumers and providers but also with all the special needs that will guarantee the

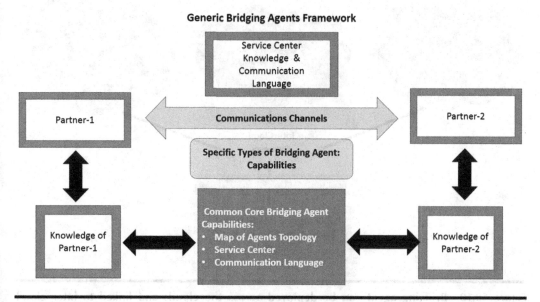

Figure 10.9   Bridging agent common framework and set of common shared capabilities.

protections, consents, and safety that is expected from health and human services. A family of bridging agents are defined that go beyond services to be smart enough to detect errors, gaps, and changes, with intelligence baked into each "agent" but each agent works as a team member with other agents through the shared service center. The newer intercloud gateways and allocating bridges to selected cloud entities are shown in Figure 10.10.

Providing a people-centric interaction provides a one-stop set of services and a set of agents that can aggregate information, provide integrated sets of services, protect your interests, and watch for any issues that maybe of high risk. The bridging agents can also provide the controls while using underlying "interoperability-as-a-service" (Int-a-a-S) such as those of the HL7 Fast Health Interoperability Reference model (FHIR) linked through information and service channels. The bridging agent will have a profile of the patient–consumer or the provider–caseworker and will have rules and processes it can handle as part of its bridging role. Bridges will be connected to logical channels between patients and their providers, their hospitals, and to partner clouds of neighborhoods and one or more disease communities of which they are members. The communities could be related to diseases/afflictions/interests of theirs or their family and friends. The agents can help the needs of people who want to take charge of their healthcare but want help in managing the complexity and reducing the confusion. While everyone may not care enough about their health or be able to access their EMRs, someone in their family or circle of friends or advocates does care and can make a difference. These advocates can be supported by the agents that have been given your consent and permission.

An important part of bridging agents that include an Int-a-a-S is the interfaces and links to partner clouds that are tailored to a health community of interest, for example, disease management/information—a person is a member of a community such as cystic fibrosis or MS or a community of cancer patients or a community made up of a regional accountable care organization.

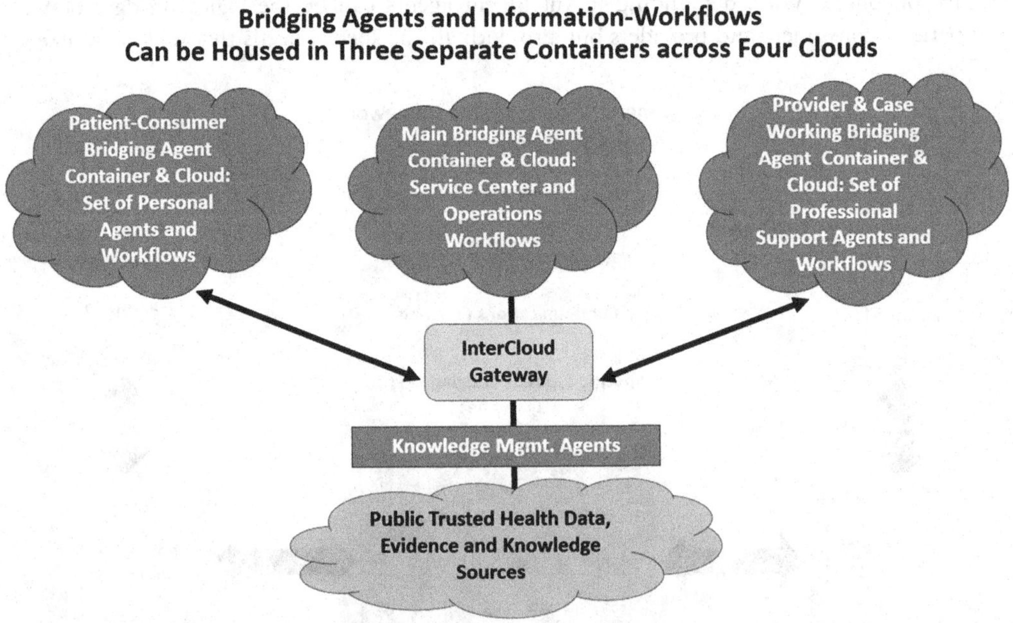

**Bridging Agents and Information-Workflows
Can be Housed in Three Separate Containers across Four Clouds**

Figure 10.10 Bridging agent can be deployed across the clouds and linked to inter cloud gateways.

One of the key elements addressed by bridging agents is their ability to change, adapt, and work with other agents as a family that today addresses many needs and can change with future modifications. These agents can be put on top of existing systems. The work on health information exchanges is not lost, but relocated to a set of partner clouds. This approach will be validated through a prototype or pilot initiative. These many types of bridging agents are shown in Figures 10.11 and 10.12.

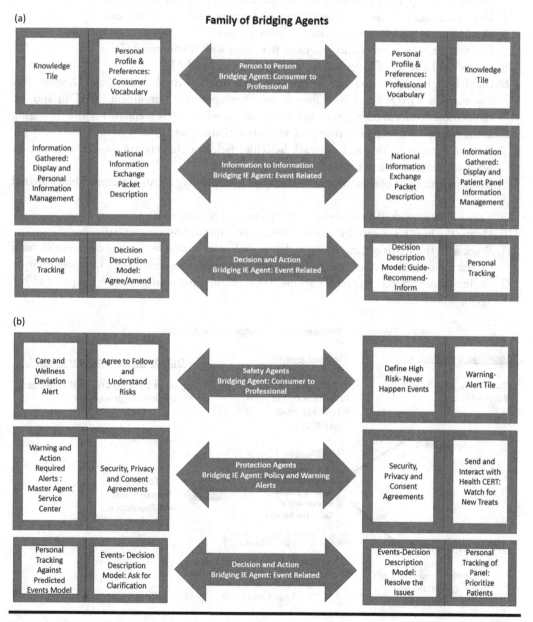

Figure 10.11 Bridging agents can support many needs from people to people to technical support.

10.4.3 *Incremental and Evolutionary Deployment*

While transformation will require a vision it also requires an incremental and evolutionary approach that closes the gaps following an iterative process.

An overall roadmap for installing the bridges for health events is shown in Figure 10.13.

The "bridging agent" pilot project will include defining the following steps and the layers shown in Figure 10.14.

1. Define a set of partner community interoperability concepts of operations
2. Define the business case and eventual target Interoperability Architecture
3. Document the people-centric system of systems approach
4. Define a set of interoperability use cases that align with Meaningful Use 3
5. Define the basic set of interoperability shared services and API
6. Build bridging agents on top of existing agent tools such as Java Agent Development Environment (JADE) and Workflow Agent Development Environment (WADE) and use the National Information Exchange Model along with FHIR standards and a "bridging agent profile" that adapts to your evolving interests and goals
7. Prepare demonstrations and outreach activities (select a challenging project where smart bridging technology can show its value)
8. Invite partners and communities to participate in a bridging agents "Interoperability Shared Service" pilot
9. Create a nationwide development, deployment, and scaling plan
10. Define the next few capability evolution steps on a quarter-by-quarter basis
11. Work with standards organizations to define a reference model for partner communities and for the basic set of services and providing inter-cloud partner community interoperability
12. Define future efforts: protection agents, safety agents, personal genomics agents, and the agents service center

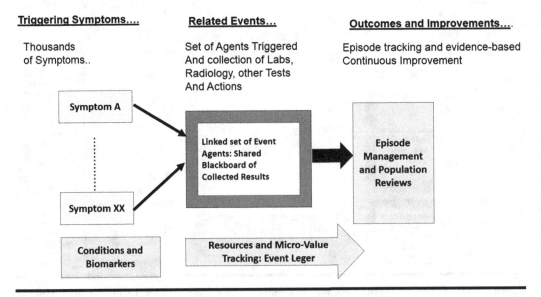

Figure 10.12   Health events can be key to moving to outcomes and improvements.

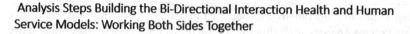

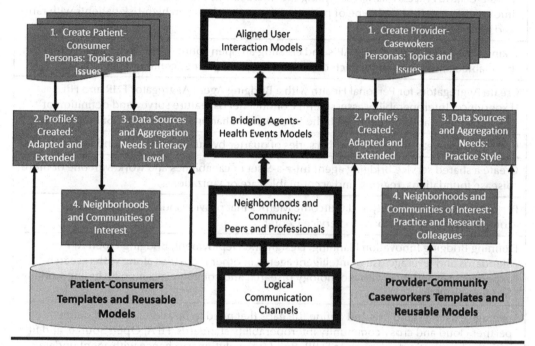

Figure 10.13 **A set of parallel tasks for defining the levels of bridges between patient–consumer and provider-community caseworkers at multiple levels.**

Some of the unique aspects of the logical "Int-a-a-S in the cloud" include where it begins with a people-centric approach, creating channels of communication to personal providers, facilities, disease foundation partners, and/or cohorts.

The consistent sharing of information is under a user's control. This includes always getting back the interactions, information, such as labs or radiology tests, and the actions and decisions made. The analysis begins with the people-patients and advocates centric interactions. It leverages both traditional health information exchanging services but puts them into a community cloud that can be tailored to individual partner communities. It makes the cloud technology securely accessible to everyone across the country. Bridging agents that include Int-a-a-S use cloud technologies and knowledge in the form of ontologies. The bridging agents follow logical communication pathways for information and decision making and creating an integrated care plan. It works by creating a personal-provider, tracking a set of services for progress, and alerting to hazards and safety conditions. But the key is that it integrates the system components from the people-centric view.

10.4.4 What Are the Many Benefits?

This approach offers great value both in the improved operations, by closing the gaps and also by reducing the ongoing cost of maintenance and support. The overall benefits are shown in the table below.

Define Bridging Agents Interoperability-as-a-Service (Int-a-a-S) Capabilities: Starting with a **People-Centric Process Analysis** analyzing the interactions, the decision making, and the information needs of each type of patient with a strong focus on high-risk patients with rare and chronic conditions.

Taking the Shared Services and APIs and creating an open source pool of capabilities that can be adapted and extended for each channel and type of partner community needs.

Create Aggregators for Personal Health with a Bridging Agent Aggregator EHR and HIE Experience: Interoperability assessment. Conduct needs feature survey and definition of key capabilities and alignment with the Information Sharing Environment (ISE) capabilities.

Conduct a one-year pilot project with a series of quarter-by-quarter decisions and focused tasks

Create a shared service bridging agent Int-a-a-S set of capabilities and work with one or more disease foundations, regions, and accountable care organizations.

Partner Community Quality and Outcome Metrics that provide individual and cohort comparison: send workloads to Service Center

Defining Bridging Innovation Planning, Design and Deployment, Bridging Open API Standards and leverage use of intelligent agents in other industries along with research experience: experience with technology research and commercialization including working with universities.

Leverage existing standards and define the gaps that need to be addressed and define partner cloud and cross-community interoperability standards. FIPA, Open Source, and fit with the health standards such as FHIR. Build for evolutionary change with agent update and error notifications.

Bridging agents will work with a logical set of channels that will define a network of networks website and collaborative agents that foster shared social networking behavior. The agents can reduce the confusion and complexity and can share experience with set of network learning agents. Learning can include how to form and promote partner communities and create a learning health system within a community.

Enterprise Data Management: Extensive experience with a process that uses semantic data patterns and master data management that is tailored to healthcare. Strong focus on Healthcare Reference Data and Terminology Mapping and alignment.

Agents also provide Protective Security, Privacy, Consent, Identity, and Breach Management: Define a range of protected shared services that tie to NIST-**attribute-based access controls** and the use of policy-based protection technologies that can be leveraged by healthcare organizations for a trusted value-driven network. Recommend extensions to ISE.5 Framework

Cloud Computing Assessment and Planning: Experience with virtual data centers and virtual desk top analysis and strategic planning. The agents can appear in a number of clouds and the agent topology and relationship is maintained in the Agent Master Service Center.

Agents providing services can be part of a subscription or by usage that can charge as part of a ICD "coordination code" or a fixed price can be part of an overall Partner Community Payment System for a pay for usage service with basic level, medium usage, and heavy usage levels.

The agent Master Service Center will deploy agents, update the agents with new versions, and track errors, volume, and performance limitations. The Master Service Center will watch the behavior of a set of bridging agents.

10.5 Conclusion

Many ideas and next steps were generated as this book was being developed. The author has noted the need to accomplish the following tasks in the transitioning of healthcare IT:

1. Define health events and relate them to the BPMN 2.02 events common elements, but include health events related to common health life events, and include linked medical ontologies with the use of the general medicine ontology
2. Define an SOS integration process, including approaches such as defining integration points, defining the strategic integration alignment process, defining and reaching agreements on integration behaviors and integration oversight, including integration reviews, readiness scorecards, and an assemblage of integration tests
3. Create a pilot project with a set of linked medical ontologies, including creating common discovery and search features
4. Create an integration and interoperability ontology and method to use as part of the administrative and governance process
5. Create a basic health event agent that can be adapted, integrated, and extended into the many health pathways from patients to providers and all shared data sources
6. Create safety agents and safety rules that can allow critical process to be under safety control policies

Chapter 11

Health Ecosystem Security–Privacy–Consent Architecture: Patient–Consumer Protection Agents, Association Privacy Impact and Notices with Association Security–Privacy Layered Architecture

Abstract

Some of the challenges of the 1st Wave of healthcare IT systems are related to their poor security features. The laws have created a patchwork, and healthcare has not leveraged the many years of experience from other industries. Major inhibitors to patient–consumer use of one website or an associated set of websites are the variety of privacy notices, the patient's–consumer's concern about how the data will be used and protected, and the confusing and complex presentation of all that complex information. Security, privacy, and consent policies invariably get lawyers involved who create complex protection documents. They may be necessary, but a new framework is needed that presents the information in a way that a normal patient–consumer and advocate can understand. Over the last 10 years, an annual Privacy and Usability conference has been organized, and the concepts have been maturing; but these concepts now need to be applied in patient–consumer health communities and associations. The Federal Enterprise Architecture (FEA) Security and Privacy Policies and a set of NIST complex guidelines have been integrated into a Health Ecosystem Security–Privacy–Consent Architecture that can be used in the other chapters of this book; this information should be presented to the Health and Human Service work groups and standards organizations to fit with the shift to patient and consumer focus.

11.1 Introduction

This chapter attempts to jumpstart the transformation of healthcare security with a foundation security architecture that has evolved from many years of industry experience. It takes the spotty patchwork of ideas and limited health-specific research, and puts them into a new Security Architecture. This Security Architecture includes the related elements of identity, consent, privacy, fraud and breach control, and continuous monitoring of, and learning from, new insider and outsider attack patterns. Recently, reports from Government Accountability Office (GAO) and industry have pointed out the security vulnerabilities of the healthcare system. Significant amounts of money flow through healthcare, and organized crime has joined the network with new forms of cyber-fraud. They are seemingly aided by the insider threats from the curious or malicious, especially those snooping through personal health records of celebrities and politicians. Organized crime has come to healthcare to steal identities and to bill for services never rendered. A new set of health security approaches are needed. This health security must be clearly explained as critical protection that the public welcomes; patient–consumer must also understand its importance as being more than that of the HIPAA form in the doctor's office.

A new architecture, life cycle approach and security monitoring, scorecards and alerts are needed, and must be fostered by federal agencies and supported with a new generation of HIPAA legislation. This chapter proposes such change and includes draft approaches that can be used to start government-industry initiatives.

The chapter defines a Healthcare Ecosystem Protection Architecture with a protection process and an industry-government supported Health Computer Emergency Readiness Team (CERT). The Health CERT will understand the threats and the personal health information and any patterns of medical fraud. The Health CERT can build upon the SEI CERT efforts and other efforts such as that in banking. The Health CERT must have the ability to share and learn about new vulnerabilities, often called zero-day events and to distribute workarounds and new protection patches, and to improve vulnerability assessments. Today, large healthcare organizations are trying to address security, privacy, identity, consent, and to keep the insiders and new digital organized crime out of patient-related databases. Healthcare can catch up by leveraging the extensive experience of homeland security, defense, banking, intelligence, and other global systems, and commit to creating a Healthcare Security Center of Excellence that can be part of the HHSs architecture.

11.2 Challenges

The benefits of HHSs interoperability also introduce many challenges. Many of the health privacy policies were developed before all the initial deployment of packages, and the issue with security is that it is only as strong as its weakest links. So currently the health portals present a series of notices that people do not understand. Complex policies are presented as notices that people could only understand if they were privacy experts, and even then, they would have to pay strict attention to each one for content and consistency.

There are two camps regarding health privacy policies: those who want to formalize them, and those who want to create simplified notices. It seems that both are necessary, with a clear mapping from the high-level concepts to the detailed. So it is necessary to create a framework that can handle both formal policies and simple notices.

The real challenge, however, is integration of privacy and security across boundaries. To achieve the patient–consumer focus, we must align and integrate a diverse set of privacy and security policies across the sites that are providing services to the patient–consumer. Policy alignment among alliances providing services would be welcome so that the privacy, security, and consent policies can be consistent for that patient–consumer population.

In other areas, a given community of interest or community of practices may have agreed to a common set of policies and procedures, and a common core process and architecture; these needed to be aligned. Yes, you might need to get the lawyers to come into the room—that will be great fun!

One of the big issues we face is that the early security, privacy, and consent are usually on paper. Even the most sophisticated clinical center, like NIH, uses paper forms, and those paper consents are focused on the limited focus on one clinical trial, and whether that patient's–consumer's data will be of value. Retrieving that paper is essential, creating a real barrier in this day and age.

All aspects of security, privacy, and consent must be dynamic and support the continuous growth of threats. A sound security approach is really essential for everything else discussed.

11.3 Leveraging the Research and Early Best Practices

■ *ONC and NSF Have Sponsored Research:* Security, privacy, and consent have had a small, unfunded community of researchers with a little money sent through the SHARP-S grants, and with follow up by NSF called Trustworthy Health and Wellness (THAW), with researchers from Dartmouth, Illinois, Johns Hopkins University, Michigan, and Vanderbilt). In addition, ONC has its security and privacy working group. Industry also has its working groups, but the limited expertise is not aligned. A common process and architecture with the challenges and threats could allow those innovations to be leveraged and brought into usage.

■ *Key Issues Like a Design Space for Effective Privacy Notices:* There is other interesting work being performed at the Privacy Lab at CMU whose recommendation is using effective privacy notices that patient–consumer can really understand.

■ *Attribute-Based Access Control and Use of Policy Management for a Community of Users:* NIST has also sponsored research and created new draft standards for new attribute-based access control and a policy machine along with threat information sharing practices. All of these standards are needed to achieve a patient–consumer world where policies have management and monitoring across traditional boundaries, and where alerts and exceptions can be sent to the Health CERT for study, recovery, and resolution.

Some of these early research results will be integrated into the process and architecture centric approach described in the rest of the chapter.

11.4 Solution Process and Architecture and Shared Services Framework

Security, privacy, consent, and exception handling policies, monitoring, and management have to be distributed across the large and currently fragmented health ecosystem. This parallel overlay ecosystem could be given many names; I have named it the Healthcare Ecosystem Protection Architecture (HEPA), and will describe many of the elements and how to leverage the fine research elements that exist.

HEPA and Security, Privacy, and Consent Shared Services

HEPA is divided into communities or alliances, or you can think of them as Clouds that follow the same security, privacy, and consent policies and support the same patient–consumer population and the related alliance of service and information sources. Between these Clouds, there are logical channels and security, privacy, and consent that are managed by the Intercloud gateway. Support functions and interfacing with the Health CERT occur within the Support Cloud.

It is essential to understand for whom you are providing this protection. The protection is for the patient–consumer, and of course for all of those organizations they have trusted with their personal information, and to deliver them services in an integrated fashion.

11.5 Creating a Patient–Consumer System Flow with Threats and Enforcement Points

Unfortunately, this author has not created an approach to avoid all the security, privacy, and consent analysis, but has found it much better to build in the analysis than to wait until the end, and have a team trying to independently certify that this is ready to go operational. Business analysts, systems analysts, systems engineering, and almost everyone else like to refer those problems to the "security guy." Other areas, like quality and safety, have tried to make it everyone's issue and have been successful. Homeland Security has pushed for building in security and making everyone alert. This culture of designing and evolving security, privacy, and consent into the life cycle is vital. As the patient–consumer end-to-end flow is analyzed, the security, privacy, and consent policies and protection capabilities must be built into the iterative process.

Patient–consumer focus security, privacy, and consent concerns around the system flow, and include the following processes and are related to architecture and shared services.

- Security–privacy–consent integrated impact assessment
- Roles of notices (security, privacy, and consent)
- Different notices for different audiences
- Relevant and actionable information
- Layered and contextualized notices
- Design space for notices
- Handling a range of access devices and supporting the disabled

The individual security protection for health networks needs to provide a shared set of protection mechanisms that understands health threats and addresses new threats (zero-day) with a collaborative protection scheme, and shares the mechanism by notifying the rest of the healthcare community. It monitors the overall health information at rest and when it is flowing and is not interrupted with man-in-the-middle type attacks where information can be funneled off as a covert data breach. The protection of communication of healthcare information between different systems without harm is critical to trusting the information and to assuring that fraud, data breaches, and insider snooping of personal health information does not grow. The good news is that messages now can flow somewhat securely, but the bad news is that those same types of attacks that have shown up in other industries now appear in healthcare fraud.

For example, one of the candidates for the 2016 U.S. Presidential election is hospitalized, and a curious advocate for one of the other candidates decides to try to find out the nature of the health issue. Unless the proper insider threat protections have been created, that information can quickly be leaked to a tabloid, and the candidate's campaign can be in jeopardy; such a leak is nearly undetectable. Almost all the attack patterns and threat scenarios can be translated from other industries to healthcare systems risk and attack patterns. These patterns must become protected, or the desired interoperability can become misused by organized fraud or snoopy insiders. For instance, a man-in-the-middle attack can be set for the transmission of a discharge summary from a corrupt consultant using an electronic patient record (EPR) system in an acute hospital to a primary care physician in her surgery using a local system. A stream of information can be achieved, resulting in fraud.

The key strengths of the HEPA and the methods used for implementing security shared services are that the protection models can be quickly produced and implemented following a technology vendor agnostic approach that can be translated into many implementation projects. The use of a common set of threat and attack driven scenarios can provide a common alerting and discussion focus for the collaborative industry protection work that is needed. The goals and policies for security, privacy, consent, and other health specific protection approaches can be driven in a one-off manner and an architecture first, build it in approach can be used.

One of the key elements of the HEPA is its focus on the trust from the patient–consumer perspective using a new vision for HIPAA and cyber security. This will require looking into a new personal health protection process and framework that will be used by the federal health architecture, and will become part of an overall approach that will use the components shown in Figure 11.1.

Health Trust Profiles link to partner circles of trust and a process that builds in security and uses an ensemble of smart protection agents.

The new security approach will have a level of trust and a set of new protections that uses a distributed set of protection agents that can be organized along all communication paths. The protection agents can be general or have a specific role, such as defending against organized fraud and insider threats. A family of protection agents can be key building blocks that are shared and open to wide use. At least the security exchanges have to be defined to support collaboration among the Health CERT and protection vendors.

Some of the key aspects of this new security approach will have to evolve with these building blocks:

■ Define a *Health Trust Profile* that is related to each type of user profile and the alignment of the protection policies proposed and protection points that will be guarded by protection agents along the end-to-end service and information scenarios. The key is to establish a new and consistent library of security, privacy, and consent policies and related protection agents that can be reused, adapted, and extended. These policies must be defined in terms that patient–consumer–provider can understand, and built on what a New 2nd Generation of HIPAA "should say" based on suggestions that have been proposed over the last few years; these are now recommended in new legislation that is in committees—such as the ONC Security Workgroup and Standards Groups—Summer 2016). The consumer friendly language can link and derive from formal languages such as SAML and XACML, but with a consumer friendly vocabulary and set of related icons (Figure 11.2).

Time frame: Propose a Health Trust Profile that can be used by non-security specialists and mapped to policy–protection agents—Spring of 2017.

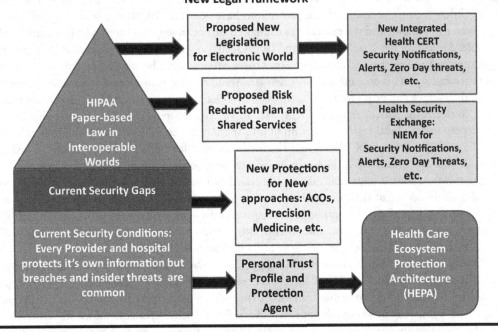

Figure 11.1 Moving from current disconnected security to an integrated security approach.

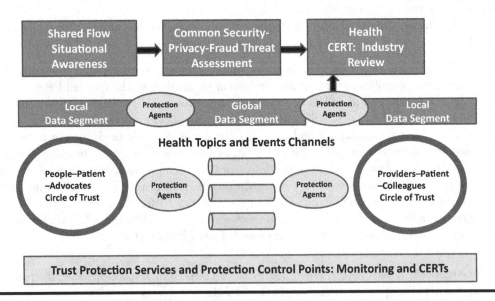

Figure 11.2 Integrating protection services and protection agents across the architecture.

- Define the network of Health Trust with ecosystem partners agreeing on protection policies with a formal language such as SAML: *Protection Network Chained Partner Agreements.* Key problems for any patient–consumer are the many user names and passwords that need to be created, and maintaining a managed set of favorites. As described earlier in Chapter 2, it is important to define the association of services and information related to a given population, such as those with disabilities, and to easily create an association agreement, especially involving security, privacy, and consent issues. A set of common templates can be established along with a diagramming technique for a Network Chain that cross partners and Interclouds (Figure 11.3).

Time frame: Define a diagramming technique that supports an end-to-end flow from patient–consumer through the set of services, information content, and includes policies and protection agents and a set of common templates for adaptation and extension—Summer 2017.

- *Health Cyber Security Framework:* Define a set of trust providers that handle security exchanges and alerts, and support the layered assurance features that, along with an Open Security Exchange API, interconnect the security support organizations in health care. This will be based on defining a Common Support Health Cyber Security Framework, which will be based on NIST Cyber Security framework (expected in 2016) (Figure 11.4).

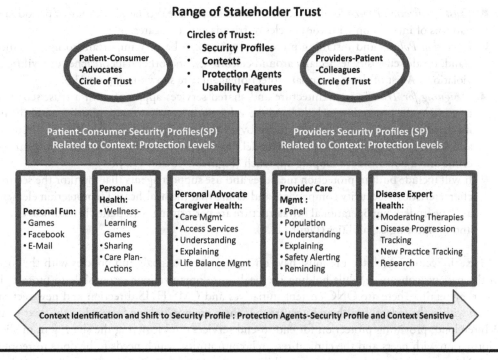

Figure 11.3   Creating a chain-link-of-trust from the patient–consumer to the provider and the provider's colleagues.

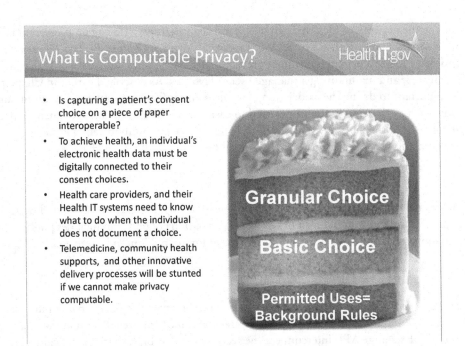

Figure 11.4 Simple concept of a layered cake of protection with available choices. But I like Chocolate Cake! But the concept is very good.

- *Trust Verification Process* for design, pre-connection, and real-time verification of periods and patterns of interaction with your circles of friends and advocates.
- *Protection Policies* and installing protection agents can be very important to fight medical fraud, insider curiosity (especially around celebrities), and other data breaches or civil rights violations. A list of those potential protection agents are shown in Figure 11.5.
- *Designing for Trust* is an architecture and shared services approach with a trust scorecard that tracks the protection included and the value of the continuous monitoring and learning mechanisms built in. This will be driven by a risks, attacks, and threats (RATS) discovery, and a design and deployment process model. It will protect against a new fraud of organized crime and a new insider snooping approach (Figures 11.6 and 11.7).
- It will include built in protection measures and use support agents that monitor the security characteristics of security components and assure that the healthcare IT protection elements and the underlying operational infrastructure are performing with periodic readiness checks and monitoring capabilities (Figure 11.8).

Health Security Architecture must have an agreed to set of goals and policies with the focus on the patient–consumer, while holding the healthcare organizations responsible to protect the data they retain. There are ONC current initiatives and CMS/HHS direction and new security profile within the federal health architecture, but these are not looking forward to the next phase of Intercloud, providing protection for end-to-end services, and fostering the sharing of medical information with peers and the clinical research community. Much needs to be done to reorient the ONC narrow view of health interoperability, and to use the system of systems and Intercloud security standards that are quickly evolving.

Policy-Based Protection Agents and Linked to Layer Assurance

Privacy Aspect	Consumer Presentation	Protection Mechanism	Exchange to Layer Services
Permitted Usage= Background Rules	Consumers and Providers are confused about who can use what data and when: Outreach Campaign Needed	Series of Basic Formal Policies and Certified Tests	Work with the Office of Civil Rights, ONC and CMS
Basic Choice	Opt-In (with Opt-out) but encourage Rare/Chronic Users to become part of "Care and Cure Networks"	Reduce the paper forms at each doctor visit: small form and IPAD entry: Personal Consent Files	Dynamic Consent Management with alerts when "your protected data used" – Notices of Usage- email
Granular Choices	By Channels: Topic-Events and Data Segments	Protection Agents assigned to both perform "rules-behavior checks" and create audit logs	The data tags will be used to route between security, safety and fraud protection agents and to send to appropriate assurance layer.
High Risk: Icing or Chocolate Chips	Certain aspects of a patients life: can be protected like they were personal "top-secret"	Protection Agents will use "Attribute-Based Access Control" to alert prior then permission.	These types of critical areas will need to go through a person at the security, safety, or fraud levels
New Threats	Update protections based on new Fraud and Scams and prevent and track Data Breaches	Providers and Consumers upon request can receive the alerts on any protection violations from their protection agents.	Create a shared Health CERT that can track both security issues but also act as the Safety and Counter Fraud Center will provide the trust violations and warning to providers and patients

Figure 11.5 ONC standards advisory and healthcare interoperability in general need to leverage the many security standards.

From Fragmented to Associated-Managed Group of Related Services and Content

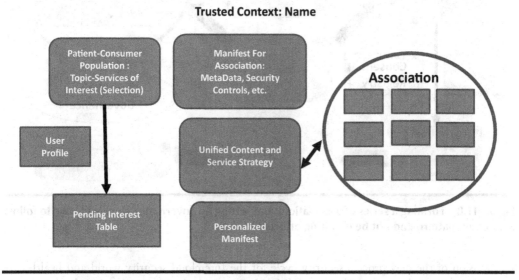

Figure 11.6 Dealing with all the security, privacy, and consent policies needs to address common combination of services and content from an association of sites and service providers that are supporting a set of services defined as the manifest.

Privacy-Consent-Assessment, Notice Design and Monitoring Elements

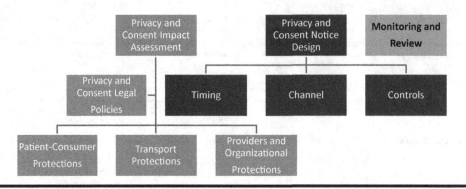

Figure 11.7 All those important, but often annoying, notices for security, privacy, and consent have to follow a common policy and design pattern so that both machine and people can understand.

Association will Synchronize and have Secure-Error Management: Flag Damaged or Poisoned Content and Issues

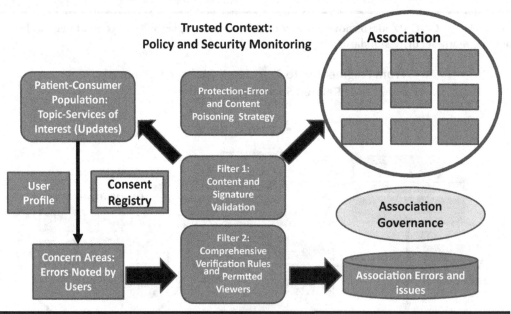

Figure 11.8 Forming a series of associations and setting up governance steps will have to follow a common pattern and not be daunting efforts.

A vision of the new process security cycle for the Intercloud security world and health care must involve open discussion of vulnerabilities that are addressed in an iterative phase each and every quarter. Security, privacy, consent, and other availability and resiliency issues are addressed in a continuous fashion shown in the cycle in Figure 11.9.

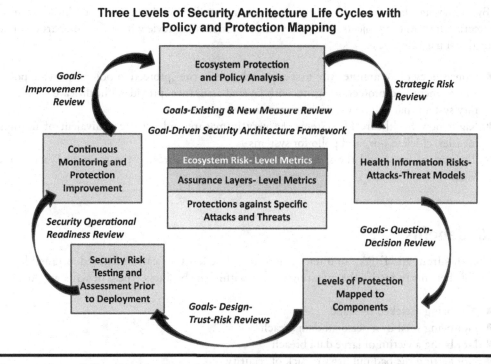

Three Levels of Security Architecture Life Cycles with Policy and Protection Mapping

Figure 11.9 Building the security architecture is not a one-step process, but an iterative process that needs to be updated each and every quarter with senior leadership selecting the improvements and understanding the risks.

Todays' Health Security Architecture: Vulnerable, Isolated, and Not Ready for Health Interoperability

■ Focuses around the enterprise and EHR and related systems
■ No end-to-end protection and not ready for better interoperability, accountable care, value-based purchasing, and mHealth-Telehealth
■ Needs to focus on the patient–caregiver–advocates and improve, not inhibit information sharing
■ Divides the problem into small communities, eventually allowing the individual to understand the policies or "terms of services"
■ Often hides behind HIPAA as a reason to not share—as opposed to using it for sharing—new legislation clarifying health privacy is needed
■ Risk to the fight the threats from the curious-insiders, the new organized crime that has been attracted to medical fraud, and even creating fake websites selling bogus health insurance
■ Needs to build from an end-to-end point of view with common protection points and shared threats and risk models. This will need improved security information sharing and Safe Harbor regulations
■ Learns from the fraud prevention in other industries such as banking
■ Defines a shared set of protection agents that can be easily integrated into a Software-Defined Network Protection Profile
■ Creates an overall vision and phased approach to reach these goals

By achieving these aims, the time and patience will have been taken to build security architecture into all the projects, and to have security assurance-review steps that are part of a new Protection-First Life Cycle:

- Consistency of an architecture first approach, where the "protection points" provide policy enforcement and protection agents with layered assurance, provides a healthcare IT immunity system that can be vaccinated against new threats
- Right now healthcare IT systems are very immature and get the equivalent of mumps, measles, chicken pox, and polio for systems
- The cost of fraud and the string of data breaches will threaten the move to Wave 2 and Wave 3

11.6 Benefits

The benefits from an HEPA can often be hard to define but they can be defined as tangible and intangible benefits to justify the investment costs within the business. These benefits would be

- Not being attacked by fraud
- Not being sued by a personal data breach
- Not being a victim of large data breach
- Not getting the bad publicity of lack of security

Profiling of standards and architecture

- Building a Reference Model

Time frame: Propose a Health Intercloud security, privacy, and consent reference model—Target 2018.

It will take about 2 years for the standards groups to create a complete reference model, but even longer unless some initial draft concepts are presented.

1. The Privacy–Consent Registry and alignment between patient–consumer and providers are shown in Figure 11.10.
2. Defining a standard data model and set of templates for defining circles of trust and relating to the levels of sharing (Figure 11.11).
3. Defining a set of context of usage from home or provider's office to mobile protected to mobile public locations, and the "exposure" that information can be shared from notices only to full health information.
4. Define an end-to-end reference model and the types and patterns of protection agents' installation (Figure 11.12).
5. Gather all the experience and ideas from the research community and put them together into a coherent recommendation. Unfortunately, all the research is not aligned, and the researchers and the practitioners have not exchanged ideas on a regular basis.

Privacy-Consent Registry for Patient-Consumer Groups, Transport and Provider and Health Organizations

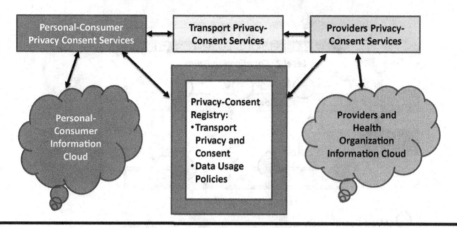

Figure 11.10 Protection and consent can be registered and protection during both storage and transport need to be built in.

Start with Trusted Protection Services

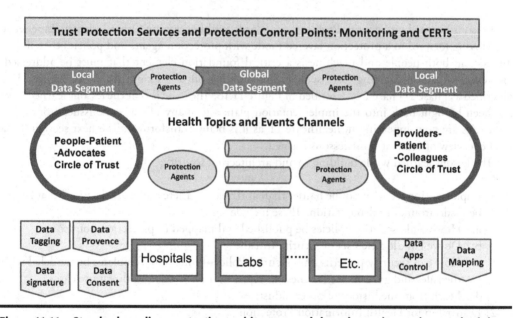

Figure 11.11 Standards–policy–protection architecture and shared security services methodology.

6. Develop an incremental security, privacy, and consent improvement plan that aligns with the layer cake, and is linked to the types of relationships that patient–consumer have as shown in the conceptual model in Figure 11.13.

7. A multi-level set of protections will be the result that will require the insiders or outsiders to break through a number of levels of protections. This is often called protection in depth and is shown in Figure 11.14.

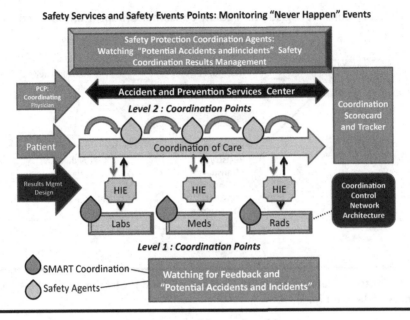

Figure 11.12 High-level protection points and layered architecture.

Lessons Learned on Security Profiling, Standards, and Leveraging Other Industry Experience

Moving forward to a protection layered mode with protection agents and policies that all can understand both people and machine is a critical foundation element that must be addressed. However, we are not starting from scratch, but building off of a long history. See Figure 11.15 described as Phase 1. Phase 2 is described in Figure 11.16. The issue is that the lessons learned have not been brought back into the implementation plan, and many of the same issues from other industries are now appearing in healthcare IT as it is being transformed. The next section has a brief overview of some of those lessons learned.

The lessons learned while building in and architecting security:

1. Implementing security can be harder than anticipated. There are many decisions that had to be made around implementation. These include
    a. How would security policies be published and mapped to protection points?
    b. Do we handle a rich set of security threats?
    c. How can security patterns and Security Policy–Protection Templates be modeled with the rules and governance for these to represent risk-attack and threat use cases.
    d. Learn from the history of other industries.
2. Leadership for Health Information Protection
    a. *Government Role:* As an industry security team lead by ONC–CMS–DHA (Defense Health Agency) and industry groups and hospital associations and public pressure. Wave 2 of Protected Health Information must make some key decisions as we progress, but any future developments of common content can take these lessons and incorporate them from the start.
    b. *Association Roles:* AMIA, AMA, etc.
3. Process and architecture for protected ecosystem driven, and split into domains as part of the strategy of building the full model as pieces of the jigsaw over a period of time.

Counter Fraud Services and Fraud Alert Patterns: Fraud and ID Theft Centers

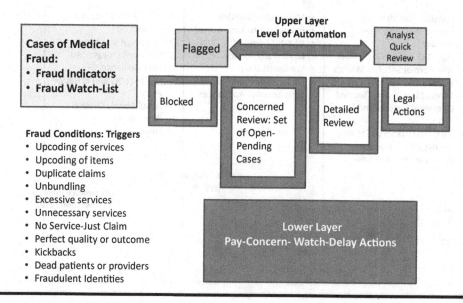

Figure 11.13   Basic relationships in security risks–attack patterns and threats: Keeping the RATS out!

Integrated Multi-Layered Health Assurance Services: Agents Monitor and Send Messages to Layered Assurance Level for Aggregation-Analysis-Alerting

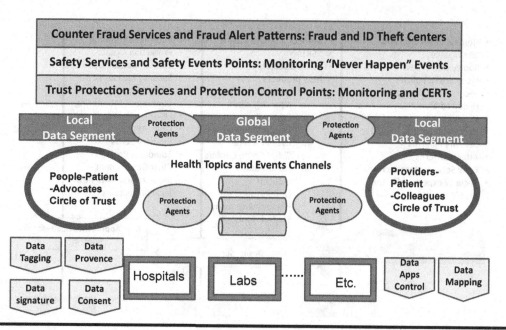

Figure 11.14   Layered protections built into the process.

Early Security Phase 1

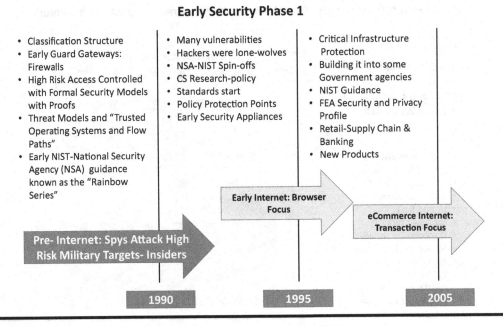

- Classification Structure
- Early Guard Gateways: Firewalls
- High Risk Access Controlled with Formal Security Models with Proofs
- Threat Models and "Trusted Operating Systems and Flow Paths"
- Early NIST-National Security Agency (NSA) guidance known as the "Rainbow Series"

- Many vulnerabilities
- Hackers were lone-wolves
- NSA-NIST Spin-offs
- CS Research-policy
- Standards start
- Policy Protection Points
- Early Security Appliances

- Critical Infrastructure Protection
- Building it into some Government agencies
- NIST Guidance
- FEA Security and Privacy Profile
- Retail-Supply Chain & Banking
- New Products

Pre- Internet: Spys Attack High Risk Military Targets- Insiders

Early Internet: Browser Focus

eCommerce Internet: Transaction Focus

1990   1995   2005

Figure 11.15   History of security with Internet protections: Phase 1.

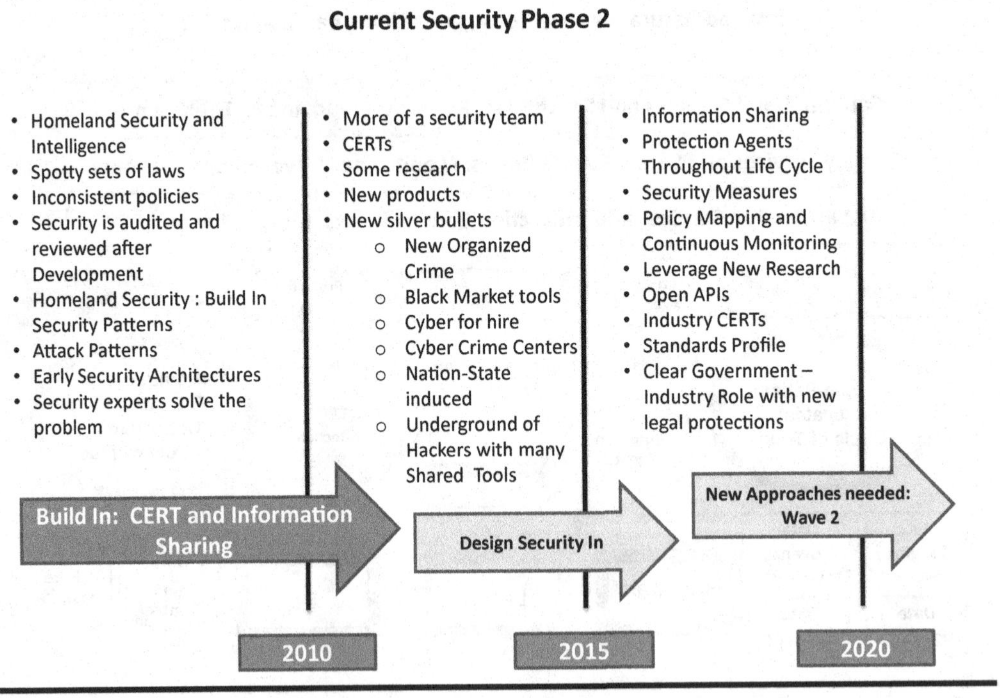

Current Security Phase 2

- Homeland Security and Intelligence
- Spotty sets of laws
- Inconsistent policies
- Security is audited and reviewed after Development
- Homeland Security : Build In Security Patterns
- Attack Patterns
- Early Security Architectures
- Security experts solve the problem

- More of a security team
- CERTs
- Some research
- New products
- New silver bullets
  o New Organized Crime
  o Black Market tools
  o Cyber for hire
  o Cyber Crime Centers
  o Nation-State induced
  o Underground of Hackers with many Shared Tools

- Information Sharing
- Protection Agents Throughout Life Cycle
- Security Measures
- Policy Mapping and Continuous Monitoring
- Leverage New Research
- Open APIs
- Industry CERTs
- Standards Profile
- Clear Government – Industry Role with new legal protections

Build In: CERT and Information Sharing

Design Security In

New Approaches needed: Wave 2

2010   2015   2020

Figure 11.16   History of security with Internet protections: Phase 2 and futures.

4. New laws and protections.
5. Governance is crucial to build consistency in cross product canonical models. This must be considered when planning what models to build next, and forms the basis for consistency within modeling and publishing of content.
6. Collaborative security approach within existing HIPAA myth "culture" and practices gains more traction. This has shown itself by not only providing content, but collaborating with developers so it fits into current practices and tooling.
7. Understand the requirements of consumers for their identity and protection and overcome the paper HIPAA era myths.

11.7 Where Do We Go from Here?

Security, privacy, and consent have to be owned by healthcare IT, and innovation; a simple, but customized, plan-do-check-act improvement cycle needs to be used in an incremental commitment cycle with a quarter-by-quarter assessment and planning cycle. This is shown as a continuous improvement cycle. One of the critical steps is to establish the Health CERT as shown in Figure 11.17.

Far too often, the issues are identified at "go-live." However, they are not integrated back into architecture, protection policy, and agent changes; and the risks and vulnerabilities remain until some disaster occurs when they must be handled in a crisis. One of the problems is the language of security, privacy, and consent has to be raised to an understandable policy level and the threats addressed with examples. It has to become real to the healthcare CIO, Chief Medical Information Officer, and the Boards. One method would be to create a strategic dashboard, such as shown in Figure 11.18. This must be visible and at the level that both senior management and security–privacy experts can understand.

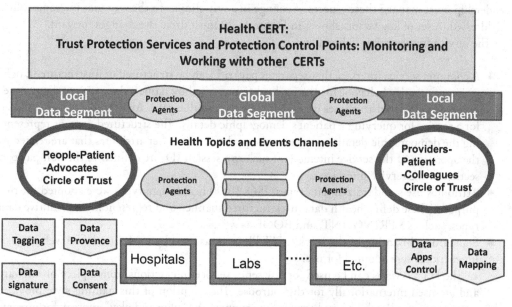

Implementation Model with Health CERT:

Health CERT:
Trust Protection Services and Protection Control Points: Monitoring and Working with other CERTs

Local Data Segment — Protection Agents — Global Data Segment — Protection Agents — Local Data Segment

Health Topics and Events Channels

People-Patient -Advocates Circle of Trust — Protection Agents — Protection Agents — Providers-Patient -Colleagues Circle of Trust

Data Tagging — Data Provence — Data signature — Data Consent

Hospitals — Labs — ...... — Etc.

Data Apps Control — Data Mapping

Figure 11.17 Implementation model with protection agents reporting issues to Health CERT.

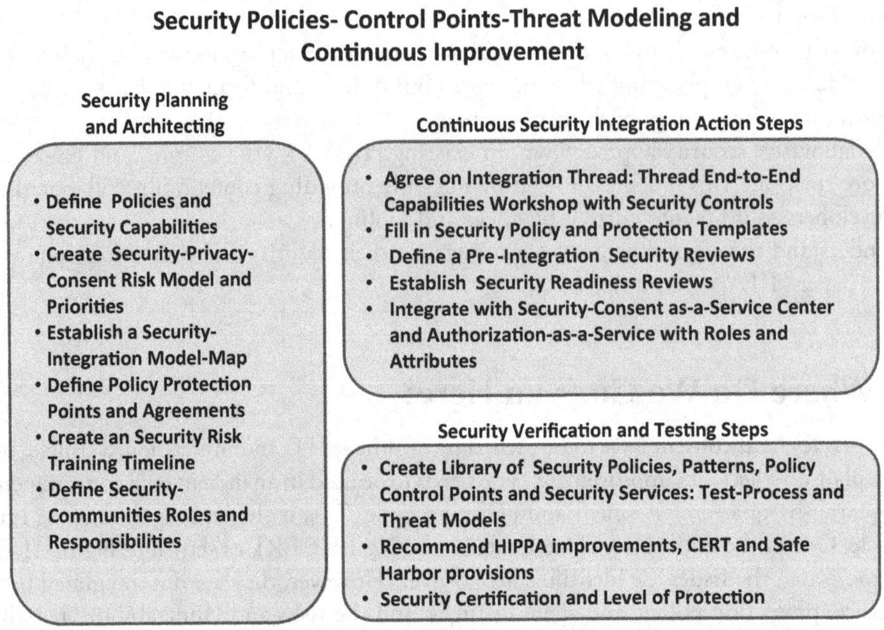

Security Policies- Control Points-Threat Modeling and Continuous Improvement

Security Planning and Architecting

- Define Policies and Security Capabilities
- Create Security-Privacy-Consent Risk Model and Priorities
- Establish a Security-Integration Model-Map
- Define Policy Protection Points and Agreements
- Create an Security Risk Training Timeline
- Define Security-Communities Roles and Responsibilities

Continuous Security Integration Action Steps

- Agree on Integration Thread: Thread End-to-End Capabilities Workshop with Security Controls
- Fill in Security Policy and Protection Templates
- Define a Pre-Integration Security Reviews
- Establish Security Readiness Reviews
- Integrate with Security-Consent as-a-Service Center and Authorization-as-a-Service with Roles and Attributes

Security Verification and Testing Steps

- Create Library of Security Policies, Patterns, Policy Control Points and Security Services: Test-Process and Threat Models
- Recommend HIPPA improvements, CERT and Safe Harbor provisions
- Security Certification and Level of Protection

Figure 11.18 Framework for collecting security policies and integrating and verifying policy controls: Policy dashboard.

Strengthening the security foundation will take some time, but progress can be made if it is not too visible, and if it can be understood by the medical and technical leadership, and not only by the security expert. A foundation tracking can be shown in a diagram as in Figure 11.19.

For healthcare transformation to really succeed, there must be tremendous trust in the system. Leadership must manage these aspects of change in a way similar to the way that interoperability is addressed. A set of key factors shown in Figure 11.20 must drive the changes forward.

The service framework is defined by

■ A common service interface that separates payload (can be structured or unstructured), definition of security behavior for the payload (represented by name-value pair), and any other non-payload related attributes (represented by name-value pair). An example of this could be for a service for querying a patient's demographic details. The structured content representing the demographic details returned is the payload. Any other attributes that are related to the operation of the service interaction, such as a session ID, are defined in the non-payload section of the service interface.

■ Attributes use standardized data types. ISO 21090 health data types were adopted for this purpose. These define health data in a structured manner, and represent more primitive data types, such as STRING, INT, and BOOL as well.

■ Standardized naming of the service. HTTP verbs as used by OMG to define web services interactions were adopted for use.

The HTTP verbs can be used for any set of service interactions from a piece of software and are used internationally for this purpose. The adoption of this naming style provides consistency, predictability, and structure to support the "plug and play" strategy for integration of products using web services within a standard API architecture.

Health Security Architecture: Common Foundation and Special Characteristics

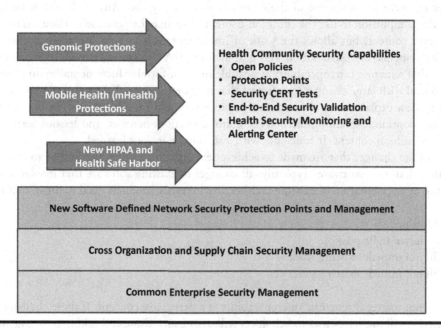

Figure 11.19   One aspect of security is constantly strengthening the foundation.

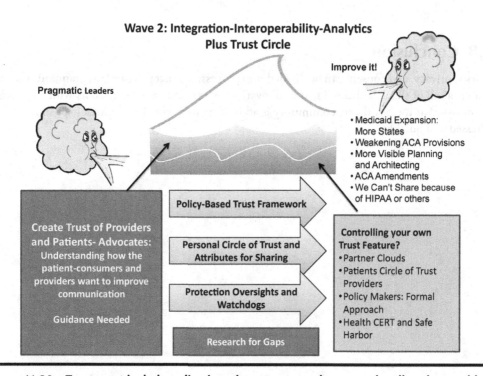

Figure 11.20   Trust must include policy-based trust, personal trust, and well-understood built in protections.

The use of this service framework is applicable to any technology implementation of service, and does not necessitate the use of the common content payload. Any payload can be utilized without the compulsion to use the common content. This may be perverse to the aims of achieving common content, but allows the work of implementation to be achieved incrementally. It fosters the principle of collaboration and granulizing HIA to demonstrate to stakeholders that implementing semantic interoperability is possible in a comfortable incremental manner, without having to deal with large changes to software that may be considered risky and disruptive.

This section explains how the common content was sold to an organization that had some barriers to adoption, explaining methods of communication, benefits, and lessons learned from selling the common content. It concludes with a section on lessons learned.

Most of the changes that are made to achieve semantic interoperability will be to legacy software rather than new software. Typically, all changes to existing software that involve a level of refactoring or augmentation of existing architecture in legacy products need to prove that they

- Add value
- Are shown to be possible
- Will not impede existing work
- Will not impede existing practices

It does not matter if semantic interoperability is a persuasive concept. If these challenges cannot be met, it will not happen as stakeholders will disengage. Those embarking on using any new standards or concepts need to have answers to these challenges to achieve success. This was no different for HIA common content.

11.8 Conclusion

Security, privacy, and consent can be divided into process, architecture, and use standards that can assure that all of this healthcare IT and innovation process can provide benefits with a managed level of risk that the healthcare community is addressing together. The research gaps must also be addressed and quickly.

Chapter 12

The Book as a Step on the Journey: Seeking and Receiving Advice

As you can see, this book is a recipe, a roadmap; but many of the ingredients and key spices need to be added. There is a large community of innovators who are seeking better healthcare IT solutions and looking for new innovation approaches.

There seems to be a second gust of wind coming from the bipartisan efforts at both the congressional and senate levels. These efforts do not get much attention; the headlines seem to focus on repealing Obamacare, as opposed to improving Obamacare (see the graphic in Figure 12.1).

In addition, the many states that have innovative grants or Medicaid Reform grants are really the incubators for innovation. Again, the good news has not traveled, but must be collected and made more public.

All the many state innovation programs, the Medicaid Reforms, and the many regional health improvements could follow a process similar to that in Figure 12.2. The key is to make the new healthcare delivery system a beneficial experience for the patients–consumers, and to make life easier for the many healthcare professionals and volunteers involved in the "mission of love and respect" that it deserves to be. This will require new strategy, business architecture, and alignment of the federal–state–regional–neighborhood and many personal processes. Healthcare IT transformation can make the best processes and best health and human services spread to every corner of the country and to all parts of world. Those pockets of excellence and improvement can be distributed far and wide.

As the Wave 2 transformation is incrementally and quietly moving forward, the "hype" about genetics, epigenetics, and "-omics" is quieting, and steady progress is being made as the secrets of our human understanding are being revealed. That systems medicine Wave 3 shown in Figure 12.5 is revealing itself each day at NIH and with other research groups, but in a more methodical way. The hope is still alive that the systems medicine process will arrive. It may just take a little longer, and require the continued faith and commitment to fund the research, to work closely with the disease foundations, and to use projects like the BRAIN projects, Encode Projects, BD2K, and the one million genomes to continue to unravel the mysteries of the complex creatures that we are.

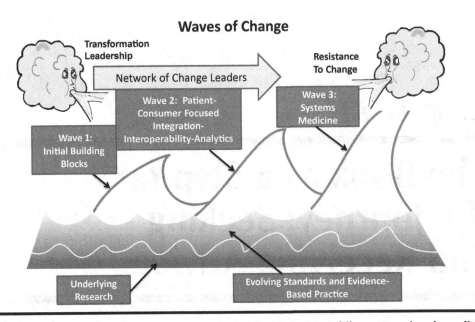

Figure 12.1 Second gust of change can come during 2016–2017 while overcoming the politics resisting practical and vital change.

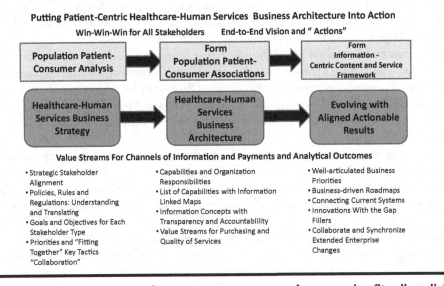

Figure 12.2 Following a common three-step process to move from one-size-fits-all medicine to population patient-centric medicine, Wave 2 can evolve.

"Cancer Moonshot 2020"—Is This the Game-Changer?

The real game-changer is the "Cancer Moonshot 2020" announced on January 12, 2016 in a press release and briefing in San Francisco, with an announcement by President Obama, that Vice President Joe Biden will act as the government lead and work through what is officially called the National Immunotherapy Coalition, LLC. The key element disclosed thus far is the collaboration among a vast number of government, academic, and community oncologists, and insurance companies, with the focus on a new combination approach to targeted cancers.

This alliance approach is a truly remarkable step forward. This approach pulls all of the associations together around a combination immunotherapy that will require a combination of tasks and a data-driven approach with the healthcare IT infrastructure that can become the basis not only for cancer progress, but also for progress in all areas. The key is the recognition that, like the moonshot, this cannot be accomplished with scientists toiling alone, but working together with the patients. The key elements include

■ Using the collaborative spirit to support the patients and to break down barriers
■ Using this new approach as an opportunity to make progress and to understand what has worked successfully on unique patients
■ Creating a broader clinical trial base where today only 1/50 are part of a clinical trial, but in the future, that could grow to 20/50 with more than 100,000 genomes collected
■ Acknowledging that the responsibility will involve everyone, but with a key start with the political leadership of Joe Biden

The key may be the understanding that has been achieved based on admitting the complexity of cancer, and acknowledging that, like any recovery program, the approach used in the past has had limited patient success. In the past, the patients–consumers hoped that cancer would be attacked with this kind of alliance approach; now it will finally be happening. The hope is that the "Cancer Moonshot 2020" will create that underlying infrastructure that everyone can use.

One of the key differences emphasized throughout the book is the move planned integration. Today, integration is an art form or magic that is done once by "someone" who is not clearly defined. The integration of small mobile apps probably gives the wrong impression that integration is easy. A new set of integration guides especially for a system of systems that connect health and human services and new approaches like bridging agents and associated methodologies are needed. The concepts are shown in Figure 12.3.

But again, integration has to be captured as a shared set of services that can be used by all. I have brought up the concept of Strategic Transformation and Reusable Technology (START) and almost got a project going. An open version is shown in Figure 12.4. Only by having shared services and bridges that many can build and an engineering approach to integration can we close the fragmented and disjointed health and human services systems.

The transformation technology can be a great help, and this author hopes to play a role and help to influence the necessary IT transformation. This transformation can lead to the systems medicine vision shown in Figure 12.5.

The book provides an interesting forum for seeking and finding advice. Normally, these types of change efforts require more one-on-one consulting or small group sessions. The problem is getting the ideas out in a timely fashion. In order to achieve this, some of the ideas have been developed at more of a conceptual level, and a more refined logical model is needed. But for completeness, these ideas are less mature or less well formed, and need to be refined with the help of others. That is a risk, but it is necessary in a rapidly changing field.

As I have told people about the book effort and sharing ideas, I got both encouragement and skepticism. It is a big effort (see acknowledgment for all those who helped), and must be kept up. My plan is to update selected chapters and to create blogs, but, most importantly, I will need to have a process to seek additional advice, and to adjust the advice to improve. An excellent article

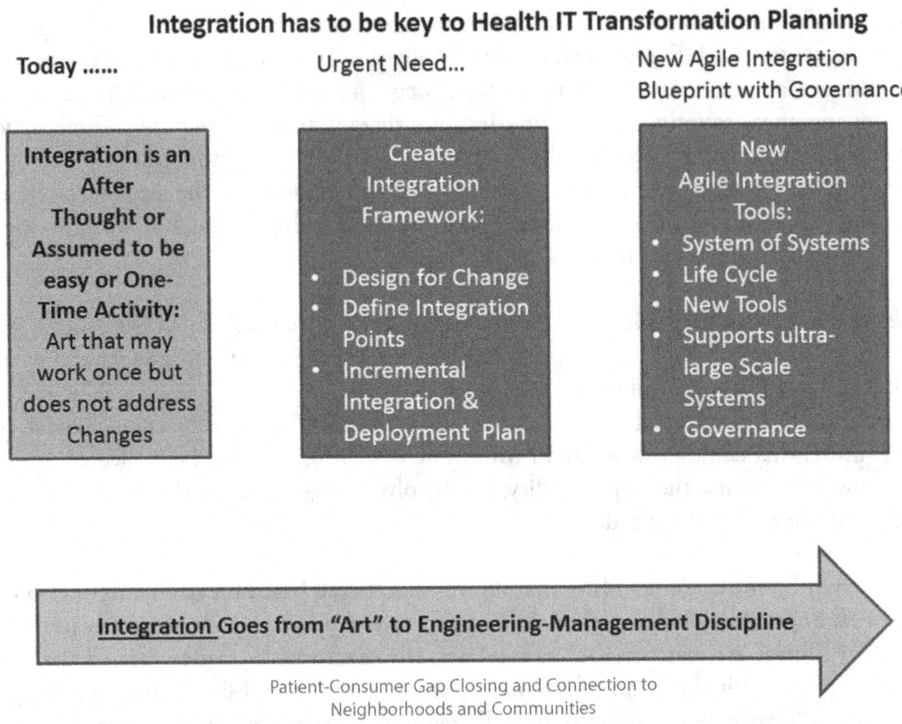

Integration has to be key to Health IT Transformation Planning
Today ......
Urgent Need...
New Agile Integration Blueprint with Governance
Integration is an After Thought or Assumed to be easy or One-Time Activity: Art that may work once but does not address Changes
Create Integration Framework:
• Design for Change
• Define Integration Points
• Incremental Integration & Deployment Plan
New Agile Integration Tools:
• System of Systems
• Life Cycle
• New Tools
• Supports ultra-large Scale Systems
• Governance
Integration Goes from "Art" to Engineering-Management Discipline
Patient-Consumer Gap Closing and Connection to Neighborhoods and Communities

Figure 12.3 Moving integration forward as key to health IT transformation planning.

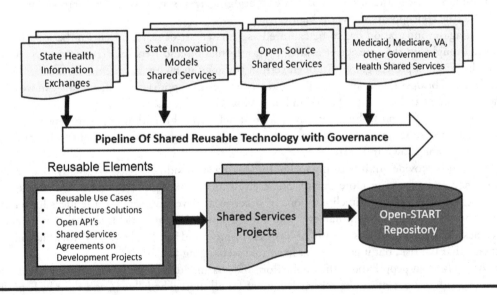

Open- Strategic Transformation and Reusable Technology (START): Transformation Needs Partners Working Together
State Health Information Exchanges
State Innovation Models Shared Services
Open Source Shared Services
Medicaid, Medicare, VA, other Government Health Shared Services
Pipeline Of Shared Reusable Technology with Governance
Reusable Elements
• Reusable Use Cases
• Architecture Solutions
• Open API's
• Shared Services
• Agreements on Development Projects
Shared Services Projects
Open-START Repository

Figure 12.4 Leveraging and sharing the many reusable elements between government and non-profit funded projects.

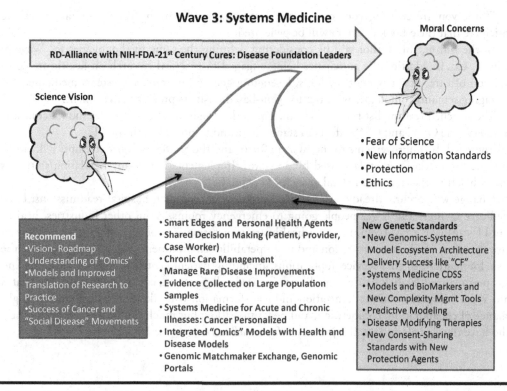

Wave 3: Systems Medicine

RD-Alliance with NIH-FDA-21ˢᵗ Century Cures: Disease Foundation Leaders

Science Vision

Moral Concerns

- Fear of Science
- New Information Standards
- Protection
- Ethics

Recommend
- Vision- Roadmap
- Understanding of "Omics"
- Models and Improved Translation of Research to Practice
- Success of Cancer and "Social Disease" Movements

- Smart Edges and Personal Health Agents
- Shared Decision Making (Patient, Provider, Case Worker)
- Chronic Care Management
- Manage Rare Disease Improvements
- Evidence Collected on Large Population Samples
- Systems Medicine for Acute and Chronic Illnesses: Cancer Personalized
- Integrated "Omics" Models with Health and Disease Models
- Genomic Matchmaker Exchange, Genomic Portals

New Genetic Standards
- New Genomics-Systems Model Ecosystem Architecture
- Delivery Success like "CF"
- Systems Medicine CDSS
- Models and BioMarkers and New Complexity Mgmt Tools
- Predictive Modeling
- Disease Modifying Therapies
- New Consent-Sharing Standards with New Protection Agents

Figure 12.5   Visionaries, new laws, and funding of NIH will drive the changes, but the fear of new sciences and the needs for genetic standards must be addressed.

from *Harvard Business Review* (Jan–Feb 2015) titled "The Art of Giving and Receiving Advice" by David A. Garvin and Joshua D. Margolis defines the guidelines for advising:

1. Finding the right fit
2. Developing a shared understanding
3. Crafting alternatives
4. Converging on a decision
5. Putting advice into action

As an implementation guide to action, these chapters are just a start. I hope the ideas and new approaches shared can help, but I recognize that all will need to be refined, and I welcome feedback.

The other hope I have is that there is a second gust of wind, and that a set of new bipartisan and industry lead activities will push progress in an even more accelerated manner as shown in Figure 12.1.

Maybe pragmatic politics will win out, and the early results of reduced hospital readmission and other improvements can be replicated wherever Americans live; hopefully, this can be shared with the global community.

Please provide feedback and *help* create a better Wave 2 approach.

We request feedback and will be posting additional refinements at www.bdc-healthit.com. Please send any feedback to john.dodd@bdc-healthit.com.

While you are creating your own Wave 2 roadmap and refining your many activities, we anticipate that the e-book or errata will be generated.

In the future, this author will be considering defining the same methodologies for Wave 3, Wave 4, etc. In addition, he anticipates being engaged in practical research on healthcare coordination of care, new payment methods, leveraging genetics to move to systems medicine, and leveraging semantic ontologies with ties to agent-based business process management.

The attached reading list may be helpful. The author suggests that the reader should continue to observe the ONC and CMS efforts to standardize and improve healthcare IT.

There will be improvements to the ACA in 2016, and the Supreme Court attempts will eliminate the use of the marketplace used by 36 states. Implementation of any legislation/statute is generally left to the state and federal agencies to regulate.

Change will occur. Already there is good progress on reducing hospital readmissions; large Medicare savings; and fewer people going to emergency rooms. As in other industries, healthcare IT can have a positive impact on healthcare transformation, but it will take some time to have the effect of a better integration and interoperability environment. Wave 2 will complete the basic foundation, so that service applications, including patient-centric mobile applications and new personalized medicine driven by disease-focused collaboration, can move forward; but that is into Wave 3. Incremental modernization and transformation will take time, effort, and the right balance of collaboration, competition, and new innovation; but much can be learned from others who have traveled along a similar journey. *May we all catch a great wave of progress!*

Appendix A: Wave 2

Chapter Notes and Footnotes

Preface

1. "Finding a Way Forward, Together" HHS Secretary Sylvia Mathews Burwell
New American Foundation, Washington, DC January 15, 2015.
   a. "I'm a believer in a nation that people who share common interests and common dreams ought to be able to find a common ground."
   b. "Working across the aisle and across the sector."
   c. "This is especially true in healthcare, where our system is on the threshold of positive and transformational change."
   d. "Promise of a new Innovation Economy."
   e. "I will be vigorous in making the case that this law is working, and that families, businesses, and taxpayers are better off as a result."
   f. "The people I've met are not concerned about the next headline: they're concerned about the next generation."
   g. Governors from 27 states plus DC—including those that disagree with elements of the Affordable Care Act—have reached the same conclusion: Expansion (of Medicaid) is good for the people and economies of their states.
   h. Indiana, Wyoming, Tennessee, and Utah are now considering Medicaid Expansion.
   i. "It is now within our common interest to build a healthcare delivery system that's better, smarter and healthier—a system that delivers better care, a system that spends health-care delivery dollars more wisely."
   j. A system that makes us healthy, rather than waiting to care for us when we get sick.
   k. A system where medical information—and medical bills—are easier to understand.
   l. A system that puts information in the hands of patients and their doctors and empowers them to make better choices.
   m. We are making progress: As a country, we have achieved a 17% in harms nationwide since 2010.
   n. What we won't do—can't do—is go it alone.
      I also hope that we can move beyond the back and forth of the Affordable Care Act and focus on the substance of access, affordability, and quality.
2. President announces February 5th New and Enhanced Initiatives to Support Older Americans.
3. Congressional Hearing for the twenty-first Century Cure and draft legislation.
4. Series of Office of National Coordinator for Healthcare IT Meetings over the last 10 years.

5. Paul Starr, *Ready and Reaction: The Peculiar American Struggle over HealthCare Reform*, revised edition, Yale University Press, 2010.
6. Leading the Transformation of the HealthCare Delivery—The Launch of NEJM Catalyst December 9, 2015.

Chapter 1: Executive Summary

1. Federal HIT Strategy: December 2014.
2. ONC 10-year Interoperability Plan: January 30, 2015.
3. 2015 Interoperability Standards Advisory: December 2014.
4. Robert A. Greene, MD, Sam Ho, MD, Ash Genaldy, PhD, A Person-Focused Model of Care for the Twenty-First Century: A System of Systems 17, No. 3, 2014. EMS Perspective, Population Health Management, Volume.
5. Some of the terminology is different than is often used within Defense and other disciplines.
6. Stephen J. Andrioles, *Ready Technology: Fast Tracking New Business Technology*, CRC Press, Taylor & Francis, 2015.
7. Edited by: Margaret Schulte, *Go-Live: Smart Strategies from Davies Award-Winning HER Implementation*, HIMSS, 2015.
8. State Innovation Grants, CMMI Grants, and Medicaid Reforms showing great progress— many of these "successes" are getting drowned out by the negative stories but they are the drivers for change and the call for patient–consumer focus by many organizations.
9. Further reading to see some of those studies from Commonwealth Fund, Brookings Institute, Rand Health, Roberts Wood Johnson Foundation, and the CMS Center for Medicare and Medicaid Innovation (CMMI) along with ONC.
   a. START: Strategic Transformation with Reusable Technology presentation that Tom Baden made at one of the conferences and portfolios of Interoperability Service
   b. Relate to "Communities of Health" Robert Woods Johnson Grants and white papers
   c. Health Disparities and relation to other human services disparities

Chapter 2: The Steps Needed to Plan and Design a Patient–Consumer-Driven Architecture for Wave 2

1. Patient–consumer meetings in the state of Delaware and numerous meeting with parents and family of people with high risk, rare diseases, and disabilities. Draft concepts have been presented at conferences like Stewards of Change and in discussion at healthcare conferences and meetings for over 18 months. Many of the ideas are also borrowed from approaches used for Title 1 Education programs.
2. Eric Topol, MD, *The Creative Destruction of Medicine: How the Digital Revolution Will Create Better Health Care*, Basic Books, 2012.
3. Maureen Bisognano and Charles Kenney, *Pursuing the Triple AIM: Seven Innovators Show the Way to Better Care, Better Health, and Lower Cost*, Jossey-Bass, 2012.
4. Clayton M. Christensen, Jerome H. Grossman, Jason Hwang, *The Innovator's Prescription: A Disruptive Solution to Health Care*, McGraw-Hill, 2009.
5. George C. Halvorson, *Health Care Will Not Reform Itself: A User's Guide to Refocusing and Reforming American Health Care*, CRC Press, 2009.

6. Michael E. Porter, Elizabeth Olmsted Teisberg, *Redefining Health Care: Creating Value-Based Competition on Results*, Harvard Business School Press, 2006.

7. Martin Cagan, *Inspired: How to Create Products Customer Care for?* SVPG Press, 2008.

8. Dean Schlinnger, Debra Keller, *Health Literate Patient: The Other Side of the Coin: Attributes of a Health Literate Healthcare Organization*, 2015.

9. Eric Jensen, *Engaging Students with Poverty in Mind: Practical Strategies for Raising Achievement*, ASCD, Alexandria, VA, August 2013. www.jensenlearning.com

10. Glyn Elwyn et al., *Shared Decision Making: A Model of Clinical Practice*, JGIM, May 23, 2012.

11. Qing T, Zeng, and Tony TSE, *Exploring and Developing a Consumer Health Vocabulary*, JAMIA, August 16, 2005.

12. Discussion Paper: Health Literacy: A Necessary Element for Achieving Health Equity, Robert A. Logan et al., National Academy of Medicine, 2015.

13. Michael Seedor et al., *Incorporating Expert Terminology and Disease Risk Factors into Consumer Health Vocabularies*, PAC Symp. BioComputing, 2013.

14. National Center for Human Factors in Healthcare, www.medicalhumanfactors.net

15. Abdul Wassy, Manos Athanassouth, Stratos Idreos, *Queriosity: Automated Data Exploration*, daslab web site, December 2015.

16. Startos Idreos et al., *Overview of Data Exploration Techniques*, ACM, 2015.

17. Alan Dix et al., *Personal Ontology Creation and Visualization for a Personal Interaction Management System*. CHI, 2008.

18. Coopetition: Series of Coopetition Maps for each of the Healthcare Ecosystem are being developed. The standards groups with their technical leaders are very important. But the company leadership and the company strategies have to move from the win–loss paradigm to a win–win with a clear goal of providing a foundational value-delivery network and the boards of directors must accept that coopetition can be best for not only the company but also the industry and their overall customers. There seem to be tipping points when an industry reaches the conclusion that there is a common ground that collaboration is necessary and there still can be more innovation and more competitive areas.

    One approach is to define a Network Analysis: Verna Allen's online book on Network Analysis and the techniques can both use to define the coopetition between the roles that fit with the value-delivery networks. http://www.valuenetworksandcollaboration.com/home.html

Chapter 3: Wave 2 Integration Using System of Systems Health and Human System Model Integration Process with Integration Maps and Risk Management

1. DOD Collaborative System of Systems Seminar Series which has gone on from 2014 to present time. This approach has many ideas that are being brought into health and human services to reduce the fragmentation. The activities started in 2008 with the Systems Engineering Guide for Systems of Systems, Version 1.0 August 2008 and the briefing series along with work by the Software Engineering Institute has expanded. There are monthly briefings that are open to the public System of Systems Engineering Collaborative Information Exchange. Briefings over the last few years included—18 in 2015, 15 in 2014, and 14 in 2013. Many of the ideas have been influenced by those briefings.

2. Jody Hofer Gittel, *High Performance Healthcare: Using the Power of Relationships to Achieve Quality, Efficiency, and Resilience*, McGraw-Hill, 2009.
3. Rajkumar, Conway, Tavenner, CMS—Engaging multiple payers in payment reform, *JAMA*, May 21, 2014.
4. Farzad Mostashari et al., Health reform and physician-led accountable care: A paradox of primary care physician leadership. *JAMA*, May 14, 2014.
5. Medicaid IT website at CMS.
6. Series of Medicaid Enterprise Service Conferences and National Association of Medicaid Director Conferences.
7. Systems Engineering Guide for Systems of Systems Version 1.0, DOD, August 2008.
8. TTCP Technical Report Tr-JSA/TP4-1-2014 Recommended Practices: Systems of Systems Confederation in Engineering Systems, August 2014.
9. Systems of System Engineering Collaborative Information Exchange (SOSCIE)—2015–18 Briefings, 2014–15 Briefings, 2013–14 Briefings.
10. International Council of Systems Engineering (INCOSE)—System of Systems Working Group.
11. Azad M. Madni and Michael Sieves, *System of Systems Integration: Key Considerations and Challenges*, USC, 2014.
12. Suter et al., *Ten Key Principles for Successful Health System Integration*, Health Quality, 2009.
13. Many of the ideas from the Justice-Intelligence Department Interoperability efforts can be translated to an approach for Healthcare and also tie it to human service needs.
    a. Communication Interoperability Guidebook—July 2013
    b. Interoperability Scorecard
    c. Information Sharing Environment
    d. Global Reference Architecture
    e. OMG, OASIS, and many other standards involved

Chapter 4: From Host-Centric to Patient–Consumer-Information-Centric Interoperability Enabling New Care Coordination and Analytics Building Blocks

1. Laura Kolkman and Bob Brown, *The Health Information Exchange Formation*.
2. Guide; *The Authoritative Guide for Planning and Forming an HIE in Your State, Region, or Community*, HIMSS, 2011.
3. Peter A. Ubel, MD, *Critical Decision: How You and Your Doctor Can Make the Right Medical Choices Together*, Harper Books, 2012.
4. ACF Human Services Interoperability Model—2009.
5. Information Sharing Environment and National Information Exchange Model.
6. HS2.0 Getting Started on the Road to Interoperability Stewards of Change, 2013.
7. Dahmann, J. and K. Baldwin. 2008. Understanding the current state of US defense systems of systems and the implications for systems engineering. *Proceedings of the IEEE Systems Conference*, April 7–10, in Montreal, Canada.
8. Department of Defense. 2008. *Systems Engineering Guide for System of Systems*, version 1.0.
9. Maier, M. 1998. Architecting principles for systems-of-systems. *Systems Engineering* 1, no. 4:267–284.

10. Valerdi, R. 2005. Constructive systems engineering cost model. PhD dissertation, University of Southern California.
11. Valerdi, R. and M. Wheaton. 2005. ANSI/EIA 632 as a standardized WBS for COSYSMO, AIAA-2005-7373, *Proceedings of the AIAA 5th Aviation, Technology, Integration, and Operations Conference*, Arlington, Virginia.
12. Wang, G., R. Valerdi, A. Ankrum, C. Millar, and G. Roedler. 2008. COSYSMO reuse extension, *Proceedings of the 18th Annual International Symposium of INCOSE*, The Netherlands.

Chapter 5: Using New Medicaid Reform with Next-Generation MITA for Patient–Consumer-Information-Centric Health and Human Services Interoperability Architecture and Shared Services in 2018–2020 Time Frame

1. Medicaid and Behavior Health Alignment: Medicaid and SAMSHA: 2007.
2. Meetings with States with Administration and Family and 10 States interested in Strategic Transformation and Reusable Technology, February 2010.
3. Medicaid Reform review of programs in New York, Arkansas, Tennessee, and other state initiatives and discussions with State Medicaid Directors.
4. Medicaid Enterprise System Conference 2014 presentations.
5. National Association of Medicaid Directors: 2014 Fall conference (identify key information).
6. Nicole Huberfeld and Jessica L. Roberts, "A Theory of Universality of Medicaid"—Fall 2014 white paper.
7. AMA calls for Medicaid Expansion Nov. 10, 2014.

Medicaid Expansion Options and Alternatives

Believing that all patients should have access to the care they need, the AMA is concerned about the high number of low-income adults who remain uninsured in states that have opted not to expand their Medicaid programs. A new AMA policy passed today encourages policymakers at all levels to focus their efforts on working together to identify realistic coverage options for adults currently in the coverage gap, even if states choose not to adopt the Medicaid expansion outlined in the Affordable Care Act. The policy encourages states that are not participating in Medicaid expansion programs to develop waivers that support expansion plans that best meet the needs and priorities of their low-income adult populations. Further, the AMA encourages the Centers for Medicare & Medicaid Services to approve waivers that are consistent with the goals and spirit of expanding insurance coverage. The policy also urges that states use a transparent process for evaluating the success of their efforts to expand access to care and to report the results annually on their Medicaid websites.

"The AMA is sensitive to state concerns about expanding Medicaid in a traditional manner, but we believe they must find ways to expand health insurance coverage to their uninsured populations, especially as coverage disparities continue to grow between expansion and non-expansion states," said AMA Immediate Past Board Chair, David O. Barbe, MD "We encourage states that would otherwise reject the opportunity to expand their Medicaid programs to develop expansion waivers that help increase coverage options for their low-income adult residents."

Chapter 6: Fostering Innovation and Integration, Alignment and Continuous Planning into Your Evolutionary Life Cycle

1. Robert D. Atkinson and Stephen J. Ezell, *Innovation Economics: The Race for Global Advantage,* Yale University Press, 2012
2. ITIF.org white papers www.itif.org
3. Agile Blueprints.
4. Michael E. Porter, Robert S. Kaplan, "How Should We Pay for Health Care? Working Paper 15-041, December 2, 2014.
    a. "Improving provider incentives and reimbursement must become a central component in healthcare reform."
    b. "We believe that reimbursement through bundled payments is the only approach that providers, payers, and suppliers in a healthy competition to increase patient value."
    c. "Value-based payment is a single payment for treating patient with a specific medical condition a full cycle of care. The payment includes care for common complications and morbidities, but not for treatments unrelated to the medical condition."
    d. Bundled payment: The Playbook
        i. Assemble the team.
        ii. Define the medical condition and the covered cycle of care.
        iii. Define and measure the outcomes that matter.
        iv. Set the risk stratification or risk adjustment approach.
        v. Estimate the provider costs over the cycle of care.
        vi. Pursue initial process improvement.
        vii. Commit to a guarantee, collaborate with upstream and downstream providers.
        viii. Negotiate a price.
        ix. Divide the bundled reimbursement amongst multiple providers.
        x. Report outcomes to the payers and public.
        xi. Leap of Faith-Medicare's New Physician Payment System by Johnathan Oberlander, and Miriam J. Laugesen, *NEJM,* September 24, 2015.

Chapter 7: Analytics Framework for Range of Health Services

1. Jason Burke, *Health Analytics: Gaining the Insights to Transform Health Care,* Wiley, 2013.
2. Joachim Roski, George W. Bo-Linn, and Timothy A. Andrews, Creating value in health care through big data: Opportunities and policy implications, *Health Affairs,* July 2014.
3. John Wenneberg, *Tracking Medicine: Researcher's Quest to Understand Health Care,* Oxford University Press, 2010.
4. Kenneth Brigham, MD, Michael ME, Johns, MD, *Predictive Health: How We Can Reinvent Medicine to Extend Our Best Years,* Basic Books, 2012.
5. Trevor L. Strome, *Health Analytics for Quality and Performance Improvement,* Wiley, 2013.
6. Yasar A. Ozcan, *Quantitative Methods in Health Care Management: Techniques and Applications,* second edition, Jossey-Bass, 2009.
7. Institute for Health Metrics and Evaluation: www. Healthdata.org
8. Health Compare open government data for benchmarking and tracking organizational improvement: www.healthdata.gov

9. Data for Health: Learning What Works Executive Summary: A Report from the Data for Health Advisory Committee, Robert Woods Johnson Foundation, April 2, 2015.
10. A Closer Look at Evidence-Based Performance Measurement: A Part of FasterCures Value and Coverage Issue Brief Series, 2015
11. M. K. Ross, Wei Wei, L. Ohno-Machado, *"Big Data" and Electronic Health Record*, IMIA Yearbook of Medical Informatics, 2014.
12. Javier Andreu-Perez, Carmen C. Y. Poon, Robert D. Merrifield, Stephen T.C. Wong, and Guang-Zhong Yang, Big data for health, *IEEE Journal of Biomedical and Health Informatics*, July 2015.

Chapter 8: Incremental Commitment Planning, Governance, and Tracking Value-Risk-Integration

1. Bridget C. Booske, Angela M. K. Rohanm, David A. Kindig, Patrick L. Remington, *Grading and Reporting Health and Health Disparities: Preventing Chronic Disease*, Vol. 7, No. 1, Jan 2010.
2. David A. Kindig, MD, PhD, *Purchasing Population—Paying for Results*, Michigan Press, 1997.
3. MBSE and System of Systems Healthcare Workshops, INCOSE and OMG, January 2015.
4. Barry Boehm, Jo AnnLane, Supannika Koolmawojwong, Richard Turner, *The Incremental Commitment Spiral Model: Principles for Successful Systems and Software,* Addison-Wesley Profession, 1st Edition, June 13, 2014.

Chapter 9: Using Virtual Health Networks to Build a Resource-Event-Agent Healthcare Paradigm

1. WS-DARWIN: A Decision-Support Tool for Web-Service Evolution; Marios Fokaefs and Eleni Stroulia, 2013 IEEE International Conference on Software Maintenance. There is extensive research on how system of systems can evolve and the key architecture features and governance aspects. Research and product support in this area is needed.
2. Clifton Leaf, *The Truth in Small Doses: Why We're Losing the War on Cancer and How to Win it.* Simon & Schuster, 2013. Cancer can be divided into a set of rarer cancer or cancer groups and be part of the care and cure approach. Cancer will be key focus in the Precision Medicine focus and the genetic components can be leveraged.
3. Prakash M. Nadkarni, *Metadata-driven Software Systems in BioMedicine: Adapting Systems That Can Adapt to Changing Knowledge.* Springer, 2011-Chapter 6—Medical Clinical Decision Support Systems: General Considerations has a great description of the needs for alerts, the problems with existing systems and some general key practices, but no solution. The type of solution recommended is based on the alerting experience for air traffic control, space satellite operations, manufacturing automation, and military command and control brought to integrated health care.
4. Standards gaps exist in the ONC 2015 Standards Advisory, and the HL7/FHIR initiative is a great improvement; many of the OMG, W3C, OASIS, and other standards are not leveraged and aligned with the vision of where healthcare needs to go. A next generation of end-to-process chain-based and other event research initiatives need to be integrated into an event reference model that can be dynamically adapted to changing healthcare needs and be a learning system. New standards like software defined networks, software storage networks, and new

Business Process Modeling Notation, Dynamic Case Management, Decision Modeling Notation, and other standards can be leveraged in healthcare transformation projects. Also the SEI/CMU System of Systems and Cybersecurity projects, along with not abandoning the SHARP grant projects and looking at similar projects in Europe, provide a foundation that can be leveraged and introduced into the standards and open source-shared services community. A core set of standards need to be defined and a set of open service-based shared services, such as the Argonaut Project, have to be created; it is also essential to build upon efforts like DIRECT and CONNECT, and to show that integration–interoperability-alerting-analytics is not a technical problem, but a market failure that can be addressed with new products or "plug and play" extension aligned with a common standards core.

5. The Wave 3 Systems Medicine and Value-Based Networking can be built upon the foundation of WAVE 2, and will take longer to research-pilot and deploy in the special value-delivery networks, like the proposed "care and cure networks" and accountable care models and other reference models with common capabilities, a defined adaptability and extension approach. A set of pilots with government, disease foundation, and industry teammates need to sponsor a set of early draft reference models and leverage the many fine research projects that have been waiting in the wings.

6. Nancy G. Leveso, *Safeware, Systems, Safety and Computers*, Addison-Wesley, 1995.

7. Nancy G. Leveson; *Engineering a Safer World*, MIT Press, 2012.

8. Workshops on Engineering a Safer World, 2012, 2014, MIT.

9. Nancy Leveson, A STPA Primer, Version 1, August 2013.

10. Massimiliamo de Leoni, Adaptive Process Management in Highly Dynamic and Persona Scenarios, PhD thesis 2009, Sapienza Universitit di Roma.

11. Dena Schulman-Green et al., Process of self-management of chronic illness, *Journal of Nursing*, Jun. 2012.

12. Series of Process-Oriented Information Systems in Healthcare (ProHealth).

13. Lucian Sacchi et al., Patient-tailored workflow patterns from clinical practice guideline, *MEDINFO*, 2013.

14. David Stevens and Bruce C. Marshall, A decade of healthcare improvement in cystic fibrosis: Lessons for other chronic diseases, *BMJ Quality Safety*, 2014, 23, i1–i3.

15. Peter J. Mogayzel, Jr., Jordan Duvitz, Laura C. Marrow, and Leslie A. Hazle, Improving chronic care delivery and outcome: The impact of the cystic fibrosis care center network, *BMJ Quality Safety*, 2014, 23, 13–18.

16. Jim Sinur, James Odell, and P. Fingar, *BPM the Next Wave,* September 3, 2013.

17. www.jamesodell.com

18. James Odell, Agent Technology—An Overview, paper, 2011.

19. James Odell, Ontology, paper, 2011.

20. James Odell, Agent UML-Too Radical or Not Radical Enough—Progress Report on AUMU, September 2004.

21. Adi Fux, Mor Peleg, Pnina Soffe, *How Can Personal Context Improve Adherence to Clinical Guidelines?* KR4HC/ProHealth Workshop, 2012.

22. Biemel et al. *Guiding Criteria for Building Valuable Ontology Exchange Situation Based Access Control (SITBAC) Ontology in the Light of these Criteria*, September 2011.

23. Gonzalez-Ferrer et al. *Data Integration for Clinical Decision Support Based on Open EHR Architypes and HL7 Virtual Medical Record*, 2011.

24. Mor Peleg, *Computer-Interpretable Clinical Guidelines: A Methodological Review*, 2013.

25. Mobiguide: www.mobiguide-project.eu

Chapter 10: Introducing New Approaches to Meet the Challenges of Integration, Scale, and Event Coordination

1. David A. Garvin and Joshua D. Margolis, The Art of Giving and Receiving Advice, January–February 2015. *Harvard Business Review* (HBR.ORG).
2. Page 61
   a. "But advice seekers and givers must clear significant hurdles, such as deeply ingrained tendency to prefer their own opinions, irrespective of their merit, and the fact that careful listening is hard and time-consuming work."
   b. "The whole interaction is a subtle and intricate art. On both sides, it requires emotional intelligence, self-awareness, restraint, diplomacy, and patience. The process can derail in many ways, and getting it wrong can have damaging consequences—misunderstanding and frustration, decision gridlock, subpar solutions, frayed relationships, and thwarted personal development—with substantial costs to individuals and their organizations."
3. Page 62
   a. "Advice seekers must identify their blind spots, recognize when and how to ask for guidance, draw useful insights from the right people, and overcome an inevitable defensiveness about their own views. Advisers, too, face a myriad of challenges as they try to interpret messy situations and provide guidance on seemingly intractable problems."
4. Standard for Intercloud Interoperability and Federation (SIIF)—P3202.
5. IEEE Intercloud Testbed: www.intercloudtestbed.org
6. Many research papers and progress reports on InterCloud Testbed.

This chapter primarily addresses a number of technology specific solution gaps that need to be filled, and although I have done extensive searching for solutions to fill these gaps, I have filled these in with my own ideas. These are some of the sources of the challenges and related sources.

Accountable Health Communities, a series of Winter and Spring 2016 presentations were developed by CMS CMMI (https://innovation.cms.govn/initiatives/ahcm)

■ Model Overview and Application Requirements: January 21, 2016
■ Accountable Health Communities Model: State Medicaid Agency Roles—February 10, 2016
■ Accountable Health Communities Model: Learning System and Implementation Planning Guide
■ Implementation Planning Guide

Delaware Center for Health Innovation

■ Healthy Neighborhoods Operating Model: September 10, 2015—work group consensus paper
■ Integration of Behavioral Health and Primary Care: January 11, 2016—work group consensus paper
■ Healthy Neighborhoods Rollout Approach: January 13, 2016

Bridging Agents

■ Provisional Patent: May 2016—author John C. Dodd
■ Limited use of agents in healthcare can be found

Chapter 11: Health Ecosystem Security–Privacy–Consent Architecture: Patient–Consumer Protection Agents, Association Privacy Impact and Notices with Association Security–Privacy Layered Architecture

1. SP-1800-1 Security Electronic Health Records in Mobile Devices.
2. NIST-1800-3 Sept 29, 2015 Drafted Attribute Based Access Control.
3. Fei Lu, Rahan Ramanath, Norman Sadeh, Noah A. Smith, *A Step Towards a Usable Privacy Policy: Automatic Alignment of Privacy Statements*, Coling 2014. www.usableprivacy.org
4. Ashwini Rao, Florian Schaub, Norman Sadeh, *What Do They Know about Me? Contents and Concerns of Online Behavioral Profile*, BioMedCOn 2014. Duri, St
5. Cristian Bravo-Lillo, Lorrie Cranor, Saranga Komanduri, Stuart Schechter, Manya Sleeper, Harder to ignore? Revisiting pop-up fatigue and approaches to prevent it, *Symposium on Usable Privacy and Security (SOUPS)*, 2014.
6. Enrico Cohera and Roger Clarke: eConsent: The design and implementation of consumer consent in an electronic environment, *JAMA*, Mar/April 2004.
7. Florian Schaub, Rebecca Balebako, Adam Durity, Lorrie Faith Cranor, A design space for effective privacy notices, *SOUPS*, 2015.
8. A Comparison of Attribute-based Access Control Standards and Data Services, December 2015, 800-175.
9. Common Platform Enumerator: Names from SWID Tag—NISTIR 8085—December 17, 2015.
10. Guide for the Creation of Interoperate System Identification (SWID) NISTIR-8060, December 17, 2015.
11. Policy Machine: Features, Architecture, and Specification, NISTIR 7987 Revision 1, October 2015.
12. Jesus Luna et al., Leveraging the potential of cloud security services level agreements through standards, *IEEE Cloud Computing*, May–June 2015.
13. Ramaswamy Chandramevli, Analysis of network segment techniques in cloud data centers, *International Conference and Cloud Computing and Application*, July 27–30, 2015.
14. V. Hu et al. Implementing and Managing Policy Rules in Attribute Based Access Control, IR 2015, August 13–15, 2015.
15. Mobile Device Security Cloud and Hybrid Builds-Approach, Architecture and Security Architecture, SP-1800-4, December 2015.
16. Secure Virtual Network, Configuration for Virtual Machine (VM) Protection, SP-800-125B, September 2015.
17. NISTIR-8062 (Draft) Privacy Risk Management for Federal Information Systems, May 2015.
18. Draft Guide to Cyber Threat Information Sharing, SP-800-150, October 28, 2014.
19. Draft Security Recommendation for Hypervisor Deployment, SP-800-125A, October 20, 2014.

Chapter 12: The Book as a Step on the Journey: Seeking and Receiving Advice

1. *Cancer Moon Shoot Web site*: www.cancermoonshoot2020.org

David A. Garvin and Joshua D. Margolis, The art of giving and receiving advice. *Harvard Business Review*, January–February 2015.

Appendix B: List of Acronyms, Definitions, and Key Organizations Mentioned

Administration for Children and Families (ACF)

Adverse event: An adverse event is any unfavorable and unintended sign, symptom, or disease associated with the use of a medical treatment or procedure that occurs during the course of a medical study or medical care set of activities. A serious adverse event includes any untoward medical occurrence that results in death, is life threatening, requires inpatient hospitalization, results in persistent or significant disability, or leads to a congenital anomaly or birth defect.

Regulations have been published by the Department of Health and Human Services (DHHS) regarding reporting of adverse events under 45 CFR 46 of the Code of Federal Regulations. This requires the principal investigator to follow written procedures and ensure prompt reporting to the IRB, institutional officials, and the department or agency head of any unanticipated problems involving risks to subjects.

Affordable Care Act (ACA): The Patient Protection and ACA is a landmark health bill signed into law by President Barack Obama in 2010. The law mandates universal healthcare coverage for all Americans, and requires massive shifts in the way healthcare is practiced in the United States. Among those changes, doctors will be reimbursed based on the quality of care that they provide, as opposed to receiving a set fee for the services they provide. The ACA mandates large shifts in the IT infrastructure of healthcare as well. The ACA has met fierce criticism and worked its way up to the Supreme Court, which ultimately upheld its constitutionality.

American Hospital Association (AHA): The AHA is the national organization that represents and serves all types of hospitals, healthcare networks, and their patients and communities. Close to 5000 hospitals, healthcare systems, networks, other providers of care, and 42,000 individual members come together to form the AHA. Founded in 1898, the AHA provides education for healthcare leaders and is a source of information on healthcare issues and trends.

American Medical Association (AMA): As the nation's healthcare system continues to evolve, the AMA is dedicated to ensuring sustainable physician practices that result in better health outcomes for patients. This work is captured in the AMA's 5-year strategic plan, which aims to ensure that enhancements to healthcare in the United States are physician-led, advance the physician–patient relationship, and ensure that healthcare costs can be prudently managed.

The AMA's plan emphasizes three core areas of focus:
- Improving health outcomes
- Accelerating change in medical education
- Professional satisfaction and practice sustainability (**http://www.ama-assn.org**).

American Medical Informatics Association (AMIA)

American Recovery and Reinvestment Act (ARRA): Congress passed the ARRA on February 17, 2009. President Obama signed the act into law 4 days later. A direct response to the economic crisis of 2008, the ARRA had three immediate goals: to create new jobs and save existing ones, to spur economic activity and invest in long-term growth, and to foster more accountability and transparency in government spending.

The law directed about $150 billion in new funds to the healthcare industry. It included $87 million for Medicaid, $24.7 billion to subsidize private health insurance for people who lose or have lost their jobs, $19.2 billion for health IT, and $10 billion for the NIH. The act also provided $650 million to support prevention and wellness activities targeting obesity, smoking, and other risk factors for chronic disease, as well as $500 million for health professions training programs, including $300 million to revitalize the National Health Service Corps (NHSC).

Application Programming Interface (API): A set of routines, protocols, and tools for building software applications. An API expresses a software component in terms of its operations, inputs, outputs, and underlying types. An API defines functionalities that are independent of their respective implementations, which allows definitions and implementations to vary without compromising each other. A good API makes it easier to develop a program by providing all the building blocks. A programmer then puts the blocks together.

In addition to accessing databases or computer hardware, such as hard disk drives or video cards, an API can ease the work of programming GUI components. For example, an API can facilitate integration of new features into existing applications (a so-called "plug-in API"). An API can also assist otherwise distinct applications with sharing data, which can help to integrate and enhance the functionalities of the applications.

Web APIs: When used in the context of web development, an API is typically defined as a set of Hypertext Transfer Protocol (HTTP) request messages, along with a definition of the structure of response messages, which is usually in an Extensible Markup Language (XML) or JavaScript Object Notation (JSON) format. While "web API" historically has been virtually synonymous for web service, the recent trend (so-called Web 2.0) has been moving away from Simple Object Access Protocol (SOAP)-based web services and SOA toward more direct REST (Representational State Transfer) style web resources and resource-oriented architecture. Part of this trend is related to the Semantic Web movement toward RDF, a concept to promote web-based ontology engineering technologies. Web APIs allow the combination of multiple APIs into new applications known as The Association for Molecular Pathology (AMP) was founded in 1995 to provide structure and leadership to what was, at the time, the newly emerging field of molecular diagnostics. Through the efforts of its Board of Directors, Committees, Working Groups, and members, AMP has established itself as the primary resource for expertise, education, and collaboration on what is now one of the fastest growing fields in science. AMP members influence policy and regulation on the national and international levels; ultimately serving to advance innovation in the field and protect patient access to high quality, appropriate testing mashups.

Association for Molecular Pathology (AMP): Organization whose 2000+ members include individuals from academic and community medical centers, government, and industry; including, basic and translational scientists, pathologist and doctoral scientist laboratory directors, medical technologists, and trainees. AMP members span the globe with members in more than 45 countries and a growing number of AMP International Affiliate Organizations. The number of AMP members is growing rapidly; they are united by the goal of advancing the science and implementation of molecular pathology (**http://www. amp.org/about/index.cfm**).

American Society for Quality (ASQ): The Healthcare Division of the ASQ encourages research, innovation, and the formation of learning partnerships to advance knowledge of healthcare quality. Members include providers of healthcare and services, supporters of the providers, and others allied to the field. The Division disseminates information relating to applications, research, innovations in quality theory and practice in healthcare. The ASQC Health Divisions mission is to contribute to the continuous improvement of the quality of healthcare by establishing and sustaining a vigorous education and training program (**http://asqhcd.org/**).

BEACON Communities: Beacon Communities are funded through the US Department of Health and Human Services' Beacon Community Cooperative Agreement Program. The program provides funding to 17 selected communities through the United States that have made progress in developing secure, private, and accurate systems of EHR adoption and HIE . The Beacon program supports communities to build and strengthen their health IT infrastructure and exchange capabilities to improve care coordination, increase quality, and slow the growth of healthcare spending. The 17 communities focus on specific and measurable improvement goals in three areas for health systems: quality, cost-efficiency, and population health to demonstrate the ability of health IT to transform local healthcare systems.

Business Intelligence (BI)

BIPARTISAN Policy Center (BPC): Founded in 2007 by former Senate Majority Leaders Howard Baker, Tom Daschle, Bob Dole, and George Mitchell, the BPC is a non-profit organization that drives principled solutions through rigorous analysis, reasoned negotiation, and respectful dialog. With projects in multiple issue areas, BPC combines politically balanced policymaking with strong, proactive advocacy, and outreach.

Healthcare issues are at the forefront of the national debate. BPC is committed to developing bipartisan policy recommendations that will improve healthcare quality, lower costs, and enhance healthcare coverage and delivery. The project focuses on coverage and access to care, delivery system reform and cost containment, and long-term care (**http:// bipartisanpolicy.org/**) (**www.bpc.org**).

Blue Button Initiative: President Obama announced, on August 2, 2010, the "Blue Button" capability, which allows Veterans to download their personal health information from their My HealtheVet account. The Department of Veterans Affairs developed the Blue Button in collaboration with the CMS and the DOD, along with the Markle Foundation's Engagement Workgroup. Blue Button became operational at the end of August 2010, and the initiative was made available nationally in October 2010. My HealtheVet allows veterans to self-enter their personal health indicators, such as blood pressure, weight, and heart rate; emergency contact information; test results; family health history; military health history; and other health-related information. Users who receive VA healthcare services can also refill their prescriptions and view appointments, allergies, and laboratory results online.

Business Process Management Notation (BPMN)

Brookings Institute: Engelberg Center: The Brookings Institution is committed to developing innovative policy solutions to our nation's most pressing challenges. The rising costs and poor quality of healthcare in the United States continue to rank among the nation's most imminent domestic policy challenges. While much of the healthcare debate focuses on strategies to expand health insurance coverage, it is also essential to improve the healthcare delivery system, and provide patients and their families with the high quality, affordable healthcare services they need.

Established in 2007, the Engelberg Center for Health Care Reform at Brookings is dedicated to providing practical solutions to achieve high quality, innovative, affordable healthcare. To achieve its mission, the Center conducts research, develops policy recommendations, and provides technical expertise to test and evaluate innovative healthcare solutions. The Center's activities fall within the *Health Care Innovation and Value Initiative*, and align with our key focus areas listed below:

– Finance and payment reforms that promote the adoption of value-based payment models, including ACOs, bundled payments, performance-based incentives, and shared savings.

– Delivery system reforms that encourage the widespread adoption of practical, evidence-based strategies that improve population health and reduce healthcare costs.

– Accountable care delivery throughout the United States and abroad that supports improvements in population health and patient experience, and leads to reduction in costs and savings for healthcare providers, payers, and patients.

– Biomedical innovation that supports the development and improvement of biologics, medical devices, post-marketing surveillance, and regulatory requirements.

– Public health strategies and policies that seek to prevent chronic disease and illness, address social determinants of health, and improve the overall health of communities nationwide (**http://www.brookings.edu/about/centers/health/about-us**).

Bundled Payments: The reimbursement of healthcare providers, such as hospitals and physicians, on the basis of expected costs for clinically defined episodes of care. A bundled payment is also known as an episode-based payment, case rate, package pricing, and episode-of-care payment. Bundled payments have been described as the middle ground between fee-for-service reimbursement and capitation. They have been proposed in the healthcare reform debate as a strategy for reducing healthcare costs, especially during the Obama administration. The advantages of bundled payments include discouraging unnecessary care and encouraging coordination across providers.

Carnegie Mellon University (CMU)

Center for Clinical Standards and Quality (CCSQ): in CMS

Center for Medicare and Medicaid Innovation (CMMI)

Centers for Disease Control (CDC)

Centers for Medicare & Medicaid Services (CMS): Federal agency within the United States DHHS that administers the Medicare program and works in partnership with state governments to administer Medicaid, the State Children's Health Insurance Program (SCHIP), and health insurance portability standards.

Cyber Emergency Response Team (CERT)

Children's Health Insurance Program (CHIP)

CHIME: The College of Healthcare Information Management Executives is an executive organization dedicated to serving chief information officers and other senior healthcare IT leaders. With more than 1400 CIO members and over 100 healthcare IT vendors and professional services firms, CHIME provides a highly interactive, trusted environment enabling senior professional and industry leaders to collaborate; exchange best practices; address professional development needs; and advocate the effective use of information management to improve the health and healthcare in the communities they serve.

Clinical and Laboratory Standards Institute (CLSI): A not-for-profit membership organization that brings together the global laboratory community for a common cause: fostering excellence in laboratory medicine by facilitating a unique process of developing clinical laboratory testing standards based on input from and consensus among industry, government, and healthcare professionals. For over 40 years, members, volunteers, and customers have made Clinical and Laboratory Standards Institute (CLSI) a respected, transformative leader in the development and implementation of clinical laboratory testing standards. Through unified efforts, the organization continues to set and uphold the standards that drive quality test results, enhance patient care delivery, and improve the public's health around the world (**http://clsi.org/**).

Clinical Decision Support Consortium (CDS): Members of the CDS Consortium are intimately involved in creating and providing CDS tools and services in EHRs that can be used in both academic settings and community-based physician practices. These investigators share a common interest in and goal of enhancing the widespread adoption of CDS tools and services to improve the delivery of healthcare both domestically and worldwide. The goal of the CDS Consortium is to assess, define, demonstrate, and evaluate best practices for knowledge management and clinical decision support in healthcare IT at scale— across multiple ambulatory care settings and EHR technology platforms (**http://www. cdsconsortium.org/**).

Clinical Decision Support Systems (CDSSs): CDSSs form a significant part of the field of clinical knowledge management technologies through their capacity to support the clinical process and use of knowledge, from diagnosis and investigation through treatment and long-term

Computerized Physician Order Entry (CPOE): The process of capturing a physician's instructions for a patient's care electronically to improve the efficiency of care delivery.

Cost-Effectiveness Analysis (CEA): CEA is a form of economic analysis that compares the relative costs and outcomes (effects) of two or more courses of action. CEA is distinct from cost–benefit analysis, which assigns a monetary value to the measure of effect. CEA is often used in the field of health services, where it may be inappropriate to monetize health effect. Typically the CEA is expressed in terms of a ratio where the denominator is a gain in health from a measure (years of life, premature births averted, and sight-years gained) and the numerator is the cost associated with the health gain. The most commonly used outcome measure is quality-adjusted life years. Cost-utility analysis is similar to CEA. Cost-effectiveness analyses are often visualized on a cost-effectiveness plane consisting of four-quadrants. Outcomes plotted in Quadrant I are more effective and more expensive, those in Quadrant II are more effective and less expensive, those in Quadrant III are less effective and less expensive, and those in Quadrant IV are less effective and more expensive.

CROSSTALK: Periodical that publishes many SOS and software engineering articles from a Defense and Large Scale systems perspective that can be related to the new Healthcare SOS needs. (**http://www.crosstalkonline.org/**).

Cystic Fibrosis (CF)

Department of Health and Human Services (DHHS): The US government's principal agency for protecting the health of all Americans and providing essential human services, especially for those who are least able to help themselves.

DeVOPS

DIRECT and CONNECT are two of the projects sponsored by the Office of National Coordinator of Health IT.

Decision Management Notation (DMN): Object Management Group standard for decision definition and execution in declarative manner.

Department of Defense (DOD)

Ecosystem: A community of living organisms (plants, animals, and microbes) in conjunction with the non-living components of their environment (things like air, water, and mineral soil), interacting as a system. These biotic and abiotic components are regarded as linked together through nutrient cycles and energy flows.

Emergency Department Information Systems (EDIS): EHR systems designed specifically to manage data and workflow in support of Emergency Department patient care and operations. A 2010 KLAS report highlights a trend toward enterprise EDIS that offer superior integration with existing EHR systems rather than stand alone, best-of-breed solutions. EDIS will play a key role in any hospital's ability to meet Meaningful Use Stage 1 Criteria.

Electronic Health Record (EHR): A digital collection of patient health information compiled at one or more meetings in any care delivery setting. A patient's record typically includes patient demographics, progress notes, problems, medications, vital signs, past medical history, immunizations, laboratory data, and radiology reports. The term EHR is often used to refer to the software platform that manages patient records maintained by a hospital or medical practice.

Electronic Health Record Association (EHRA)

Electronic Medical Record Adoption Model (EMRAM): An eight-step process that allows healthcare organizations to analyze their level of EMRA, chart their accomplishments and track their progress against other healthcare organizations across the country. Each of the stages is measured by cumulative capabilities and all capabilities within each stage must be reached before moving to the next stage. All lower-level stages must be completed before a higher level will be considered completed. There is also an ambulatory, A-EMRAM, specific to outpatient services (**himssanalytics.org**).

Enterprise Architecture (EA)

Enterprise Data Council (EDC)

E-Prescribing: The ability to electronically send an accurate, error-free, and understandable prescription directly to a pharmacy. Included in the Medicare Modernization Act of 2003, it represents an important means to improve the quality of patient care. The July 2006 IOM report on the role of e-prescribing in reducing medication errors expanded its popularity, which helped spread awareness of its benefits. The adoption of standards to facilitate e-prescribing is one of the key action items in the plan to expedite the adoption on EMRs. The benefits of e-prescribing are many and include reducing illegibility; providing warning and alert systems, which reduce medication errors; and offering access to patients' medical history. E-prescribing also reduces or eliminates phone calls and call-backs to pharmacies, eliminates faxes to pharmacies, and streamlines the refill process.

Federal Advisory Committee Act (FACA)

Food and Drug Administration Safety and Innovation Act (FDASIA): Signed into law on July 9, 2012, expands the FDA's authorities and strengthens the agency's ability to safeguard and advance public health by

- *Giving the authority to collect user fees* from industry to fund reviews of innovator drugs, medical devices, generic drugs, and biosimilar biological products.
- *Promoting innovation* to speed patient access to safe and effective products.
- *Increasing stakeholder involvement* in FDA processes.
- *Enhancing the safety of the drug supply chain.*

To help the public keep track of the agency's progress on these and other provisions, the agency has established a *3-year implementation plan*, which is planned to be updated on a monthly basis.

Fast Healthcare Interoperability Resources (FHIR): FHIR, pronounced "Fire" defines a set of "Resources" that represent granular clinical concepts. The resources can be managed in isolation, or aggregated into complex documents. Technically, FHIR is designed for the web; the resources are based on simple XML or JSON structures, with an http-based RESTful protocol where each resource has predictable URL. Where possible, open internet standards are used for data representation (**http://wiki.hl7.org/index.php?title=FHIR**).

General Services Administration (GSA)

Government Accountability Office (GAO)

Health Information Exchange (HIE)

Healthcare Services Specification Program (HSSP): An open, global community focused on improving health interoperability within and across organizations through the use of SOA and standard services. The intention is to reduce implementation complexity, promote effective integration, foster marketplace support, and drive down implementation costs and barriers impacting healthcare solutions (**www.hssp.wikispaces.com**).

Healthcare Associated Infections (HAIs): Infections caused by a wide variety of common and unusual bacteria, fungi, and viruses during the course of receiving medical care. Many medical advances are said to come with a risk of HAI. These infections related to medical care can be devastating and possibly deadly. As the ability to prevent HAIs grows, the infections are becoming increasingly unacceptable. Recent successes in HAI elimination have been encouraging, and reductions have been demonstrated for other HAIs as well. However, they have been proven to be a significant cause of morbidity and mortality. At any given time, one in 20 hospital patients have an HAI. Hospital-acquired HAIs alone are responsible for $28 to $33 billion in preventable healthcare expenditures every year.

Healthcare Information and Management Systems Society (HIMSS): A cause-based, global, not-for-profit enterprise producing health IT through leadership, education, events, market research, and media services around the world. The organization leads efforts to optimize health engagements and care outcomes using IT. Founded in 1961, HIMSS encompasses more than 52,000 individuals, of whom more than two-thirds work in health-care provider, governmental, and not-for-profit organizations across the globe, plus over 600 corporations and 250 not-for-profit partner organizations, that share this cause. HIMSS, headquartered in Chicago, serves the global health IT community with additional offices in the United States, Europe, and Asia, and includes communities such as Clinical and BI and related work groups (**http://www.himss.org**).

Health IT for Economic and Clinical Health (HITECH) Act: Enacted as part of the American Recovery and Reinvestment Act of 2009, was signed into law in February 2009. It promotes the adoption and meaningful use of health IT. Subtitle D of the HITECH Act addresses the privacy and security concerns associated with the electronic transmission of health information, partly through several provisions that strengthen the civil and criminal enforcement of the HIPAA rules. The act stipulates that, as of 2011, healthcare providers will be offered financial incentives for demonstrating meaningful use of EHRs. Incentives will be offered until 2015. After that point, penalties may be charged for failing to demonstrate such use. The act also established grants for training centers for the personnel required to support a health IT infrastructure.

HHS: US Department of Health and Human Services

HIMSS Innovation Center: Opened as part of the Global Center for Health Innovation in Cleveland, Ohio, on October 8, 2013. The Innovation Center is a demonstration, exhibition and education facility which allows industry experts to come together to solve clinical challenges around continuity of care, referral processes, public health, and more. Healthcare leaders will be able to participate in partially or fully automated technical demonstrations, testing events and exhibitions, showcase their system capabilities and collaborate with industry experts, as well as access ongoing services, exhibitions, educational programming, and consumer-oriented applications (**himssinnovationcenter.org**).

HIPAA 5010: An upgrade made to the existing form of HIPAA, as opposed to a significant change in the way HIPAA-defined benchmarks have been set for processing transactions in the industry. The HIPAA, which was signed into law in 1996, required Medicare and all other health insurance payers to comply with the EDI standards established by the Secretary of Health and Human Services and the Accredited Standards Committee for electronic healthcare transactions.

The updated version of the healthcare transactions standard, HIPAA 5010, replaced version 4010A1, the previous set of standards, on January 1, 2012. The newer standard enables improved data and provides the foundation for ICD-10 medical coding standard. It will also impact some aspects of HIPAA regulations in a more significant manner. These include health information processing aspects, such as claims and encounters; issues related to enrollment in healthcare stimulus plans; issues related to authorization, request, referral and response; and the issuing of payment/remittance advices.

Health Information Exchange (HIE): The transmission of healthcare-related data among facilities, health information organizations and government agencies, according to national standards for interoperability, security, and confidentiality. It is an important part of the health IT infrastructure under development in the United States, and the associated National Health Information.

HISE: Health Information System Engineering a work group formed by the National Council of System Engineers (NCOSE)

Healthcare Services Specification Project (HSSP)

Health Level 7 International (HL7)

ICD-10: *The International Classification of Diseases*, 10th Revision, *Clinical Modification* (ICD-10-CM)—A revision of the ICD-9-CM system which physicians and other providers currently use to code all diagnoses, symptoms, and procedures recorded in hospitals and physician practices. The ICD-10-CM revision has more than 68,000 diagnostic codes, compared to the 13,000 found in ICD-9-CM. The revision also includes twice as many categories, and is more specific in identifying treatment. For example, ICD-10 provides codes to distinguish between a left or right leg; ICD-9 does not. DHHS had intended to require implementation by October 1, 2014. However, on April 1, 2014, President Obama signed into law H.R. 3402 which prevents DHHS from establishing ICD-10 as the standard code set before October 1, 2015.

Information Exchange Package Documentation (IEPD): A key part of the National Information Exchange Model that is part of the information sharing environment used by the federal and state governments.

Information Technology (IT)

Interoperability Defined: A healthcare systems ability to connect with other systems. Basic interoperability is the sharing of data. Advanced interoperability includes the uniform presentation of healthcare data, uniform user controls, and uniform protection of patient confidentiality.

Integrated Delivery Network (IDN): A network of facilities and providers that work together to offer a continuum of care to a specific geographic area or market. The concept was developed in the 1980s, and has since evolved to address common concerns, such as capitation, excess capacity, decreased margins, and complaints from patients regarding access. IDNs include many types of associations across the continuum of care. For example, one network could include a short- and long-term hospital, Hospital Management Plans (HMP), Physician Health Organization (PHO), home health agency and hospice services. Multi-hospital systems and mergers may be considered limited IDNs, since different entities are joining together to provide care. Some members of a network provide identical or complementary services to patients. Such associations, in which members of a network provide a similar level of care, can be called horizontal integration.

Integrating Healthcare Enterprise (IHE): IHE is a global initiative that creates framework for passing vital health information, whether from application to application or system to system, seamlessly. The initiative brings together healthcare IT stakeholders to implement standards for communicating patient information efficiently throughout and among healthcare enterprises by developing a framework for interoperability. Rather than create new standards, IHE drives the adoption of standards to address specific clinical needs. Today, IHE is multi-domain with integration profiles for radiology, cardiology, laboratory, and IT infrastructure, which enable interoperability both within and across multiple enterprises. Profiles also specify how standards are to be used to address clinical needs, eliminating ambiguities while reducing configuration and interfacing costs, and ensuring a higher level of practical interoperability (**http://www.ihe.net/**).

IHE Domains: IHE is organized by *clinical and operational domains*. In each domain users with clinical and operational experience identify integration and information sharing priorities, and vendors of relevant information systems develop consensus, standards-based solutions to address them.

Each domain includes a technical committee, whose primary task is developing and documenting the solutions (known as integration profiles), and a planning committee, whose primary tasks are long-term scope planning and organizing deployment activities (such as testing events and educational programs). Each domain develops and maintains its own set of Technical Framework documents. Coordination among domains is the responsibility of the Domain Coordination Committee, comprising representatives from each of the domain planning and technical committees.

The active IHE domains are listed below:
- Anatomic pathology
- Cardiology
- Dental
- Eye care
- IT infrastructure
- Laboratory
- Patient care coordination
- Patient care devices
- Pharmacy
- Quality, research, and public health
- Radiation oncology
  - Radiology mammography
  - Nuclear medicine

Institute for Healthcare Improvement (IHI)

Institute of Medicine (IOM)

International Council on Systems Engineering (INCOSE): A not-for-profit membership organization founded to develop and disseminate the interdisciplinary principles and practices that enable the realization of successful systems.

Mission

Share, promote, and advance the best of systems engineering from across the globe for the benefit of humanity and the planet.

Vision

The world's authority on Systems Engineering.

Goals
- To provide a focal point for dissemination of systems engineering knowledge.
- To promote international collaboration in systems engineering practice, education, and research.
- To assure the establishment of competitive, scalable professional standards in the practice of systems engineering.
- To improve the professional status of all persons engaged in the practice of systems engineering.
- To encourage governmental and industrial support for research and educational programs that will improve the systems engineering process and its practice (**http://incose.org/about/index.aspx**).

INCOSE SOS Workgroup: The purpose of the working group is to advance and promote the application of Systems Engineering to SOS, often referred to as SOS Engineering (SOSE). SOS and SOSE are topics that interest a significant number of INCOSE members globally, both individuals and organizations. Therefore, we believe that a WG forum to share understanding of SOS and SOSE issues, good practice and background, and contribute to maturing the understanding of the available body of knowledge in this area will provide a valuable service to the wider INCOSE community (**http://www.incose.org/practice/techactivities/wg/details.aspx?id=sos**).

International Society of Nutrigenetics/Nutrigenomics (ISNN): ISNN established in 2005, under the Presidency of Artemis P. Simopoulos, MD (USA). It is the purpose of the Society to increase the understanding of the role of genetic variation and individual dietary response, and the role of nutrients in gene expression generally. This purpose is pursued through research and education of professionals and the general public. The Society provides an open access journal (**http://www.nutritionandgenetics.org/**).

Institute of Healthcare Systems (IHS): Brandeis University: Home to many innovations in healthcare research and policy, and is dedicated to providing rigorous technical solutions to policymakers and other stakeholders who are striving to improve quality, efficiency, and value. The institute respects the complexity of healthcare, the corresponding need for rigorous and robust approaches to meaningful and stable reform, and the vital strength of empirical illumination and validation (**http://sihp.brandeis.edu/ihs/index.html**).

Institute of Systems Biology (ISB): A non-profit biomedical research organization based in Seattle, Washington. It was founded in 2000 by systems biologist Leroy Hood, immunologist Alan Aderem, and protein chemist Ruedi Aebersold. ISB was established on the belief that the conventional models for exploring and funding breakthrough science have not caught up with the real potential of what is possible today. ISB serves as the ultimate environment where scientific collaboration stretches across disciplines, where its researchers have the intellectual freedom to challenge the status quo, and where grand visions for breakthroughs in human health inspire a collective drive to achieve the seemingly impossible. The Institute's core values ensure that it always keeps its focus on the big ideas that eventually will have the biggest impact on human health. Since 2000, ISB has grown to about 200 staffers, which includes 9 faculty members and laboratory groups (**https://www.systemsbiology.org/**).

JASON is a series of research studies coordinated by Mitre and has recently looked at the Electronic Health Record interoperability and integration issues and created a report that triggered as similar ONC work group.

Key Performance Indicator (KPI)

Massachusetts Institute of Technology (MIT)

Maryland Chesapeake Regional Information System for Our Patients (MD CRISP)

Meaningful Use: Set of criteria for the use of EHR systems to improve patient care by healthcare providers. The initial meaningful use criteria involved the installation of an EHR system in a Medicare or Medicaid provider office, and the use in some way, such as with electronic prescriptions. This is called Meaningful Use 1 and goes through 2016, while Meaningful Use 2 can begin as early as 2015 and will go until 2019, with more focus on interoperability and work across hospitals and provider networks. Meaningful Use 3 will show coordination of care and will support a set of new value-delivery networks. The concept of meaningful use was developed by the NQF; their ideas included improved population health, coordination of care, improved safety, and patient engagement. The HITECH Act established incentives for adopting Meaningful Use criteria beginning in 2012, with the possibility of penalties for failure to achieve the standards by 2015. In August 2012, CMS released the final rules for Meaningful Use Stage 2.

Medicaid Enterprise Systems Conference (MESC)

Medicaid IT Architecture (MITA)

Medicaid Management Information System (MMIS)

Medicaid Statistical Information System (MSIS)

Medical Device Manufacturer's Association (MDMA): MDMA was created in 1992 by a group of medical-device company executives who believed that the innovative and entrepreneurial sector of the industry needed a strong and independent voice in the nation's capital.

Since its inception, MDMA can claim credit for a number of policy achievements, from the defeat of legislative proposals to foist "user fees" upon the industry in 1993 and 1994, to the development and passage of the landmark FDA Modernization Act of 1997. Today, MDMA is the leading voice representing the interests of innovative and entrepreneurial medical technology companies. We provide educational and advocacy assistance to more than 270 members. MDMA members all share a common goal: to provide patients and clinicians with timely access to safe and effective medical technologies that improve the quality of life.

Mobile Health or mHealth: The delivery of healthcare using portable or wireless devices. It includes telehealth which ranges from simple monitoring of patients to telemedicine, which is the delivery of clinical services at a distance.

Most Wired Hospitals: An award given annually by Hospitals & Health Networks (H&HN) magazine to the top 100 hospitals in the country making the most progress in the adoption of health IT. Hospitals elect to participate in a survey, and winners are chosen as a result of the survey data. Winners receive recognition in the July H&HN cover story, as well as the use of a Most Wired Winner logo for promotional activities and a Most Wired award plaque.

A new analytic structure has been implemented to stratify hospitals based on progress in adoption, implementation, and use of IT in four areas. The structure is said to produce more meaningful benchmarks, and participating organizations will be identified as Foundational, Core, Advanced, Expert, or Leader in each of four focus areas for the use of IT. The focus areas include infrastructure, business and administrative management, clinical quality and safety, and care continuum (**http://www.hhnmostwired.com/**).

National Association of Accountable Care Organizations (NAACOS): Incorporated in Washington DC and is supported through membership fees, business partner fees, conferences, and with in-kind contributions of its members. ACOs offer enormous opportunity for patients and providers to work together to increase quality of care, lower costs, and improve the health of the community. The Patient Protection and Affordable Care Act of 2010 (ACA) opened up new opportunities for Medicare and Medicaid beneficiaries to take advantage of are in an ACO and gave ACOs new opportunities to serve this important population. ACOs from around the country have come together to form NAACOS with the following mission:

- Foster growth of ACO models of care.
- Participate with Federal Agencies in development and implementation of public policy.
- Provide industry-wide uniformity on quality and performance measures.
- Educate members in clinical and operational best practices.
- Collectively engage the vendor community.
- Educate the public about the value of accountable care (**https://www.naacos.com/**).

National Association of Medicaid Directors (NAMD)
National Association of State Chief Information Officers (NASCIO)
National Health IT Week: Celebrated its eighth year in existence in 2013, the same year that the US Senate passed a Resolution declaring National Health IT Week. Each year in September, hundreds of organizations come together to raise awareness regarding the health IT community and help people move forward in and understand the stages of meaningful use. Participants of National Health IT Week believe that healthcare reform is not possible without system-wide adoption of health IT, which improves the quality of healthcare delivery, increases patient safety, decreases medical errors, and strengthens the interaction between patients and healthcare providers (**healthitweek.org**).

Nationwide Health Information Network (NHIN): The NHIN is a set of standards, services, and policies that enable secure HIE over the Internet. The network provides a foundation for the exchange of health information across diverse entities, within communities and across the country, helping to achieve the goals of the HITECH Act. It is comprised of a diverse set of Federal agencies and non-federal organizations that have come together to securely exchange electronic health information. NHIN is considered a critical part of the national health IT agenda and enables health information to follow the consumer, be available for clinical decision making, and support appropriate use of healthcare information beyond direct patient care to improve population health.

National Strategy for Trusted Identities in Cyberspace (NSTIC): Helping individuals and organizations utilize secure, efficient, easy-to-use, and interoperable identity credentials to access online services in a manner that promotes confidence, privacy, choice, and innovation (**http://www.nist.gov/nstic/index.html**).

National Center for Advancing Translational Sciences (NCATS): at NIH
National Health Service (NHS): Britain
National Information Exchange Model (NIEM)
National Institutes of Health (NIH)
National Institutes of Standards and Technology (NIST)
National Library of Medicine (NLM)
National Medicaid EDI HIPAA Workgroup (NMEH)
New York SHINE: Center that provides mental health and substance abuse services for HIV+ adults
North Carolina State University (NCSU)
Advancing Open Standards for the Information Society (OASIS)
Object Management Group (OMG)
Office of Management and Budget (OMB)
Office of the National Coordinator for Healthcare IT (ONC): The principal Federal entity charged with coordination of nationwide efforts to implement and use the most advanced health IT and the electronic exchange of health information. The position of National Coordinator was created in 2004, through an Executive Order, and legislatively mandated in the HITECH Act.

Open CDS (http://www.opencds.org/)
OpenClinical—created to
  - Promote decision support, clinical workflow, and other knowledge management technologies in patient care and clinical research.
  - Disseminate methods and tools for building healthcare knowledge applications that comply with the highest quality, safety, and ethical standards.
  - Build a community of individuals, organizations, and commercial companies who believe in the value of knowledge management, and who wish to contribute to the definition and adoption of open technical standards for medical applications (**http://www.openclinical.org/dss.htmlare**).

    An open-source Multi-disciplinary Design Analysis and Optimization (OpenMDAO) framework, written in Python. It can be used to develop an integrated analysis and design environment for the user's engineering challenges.

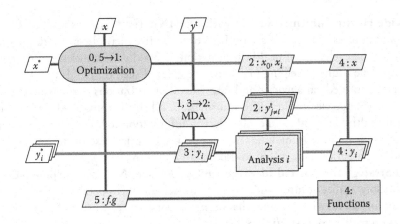

In layman's terms: OpenMDAO is a piece of software that links other pieces of software together. It allows the user to combine analysis tools (or design codes) from multiple disciplines, at multiple levels of fidelity, and to manage the interaction between them. OpenMDAO is specifically designed to manage the dataflow (the actual data) and the workflow (what code is run when) in conjunction with optimization algorithms and other advanced solution techniques. OpenMDAO also has extensive optimization capabilities built into the software (**http://openmdao.org/**).

Open Multi-Processing (OpenMP): An API that supports multi-platform shared memory multi-processing programming in C, C++, and Fortran, on most processor architectures and operating systems, including Solaris, AIX, HP-UX, Linux, Mac OS X, and Windows platforms. It consists of a set of compiler directives, library routines, and environment variables that influence run-time behavior. OpenMP is managed by the non-profit technology consortium *OpenMP Architecture Review Board* (or *OpenMP ARB*), jointly defined by a group of major computer hardware and software vendors, including AMD, IBM, Intel, Cray, HP, Fujitsu, Nvidia, NEC, Red Hat, Texas Instruments, Oracle Corporation, and more. It uses a portable, scalable model that gives programmers a simple and flexible interface for developing parallel applications for platforms ranging from the standard desktop computer to the supercomputer.

An application built with the hybrid model of parallel programming can run on a computer cluster using both OpenMP and Message Passing Interface, or more transparently through the use of OpenMP extensions for non-shared memory systems (**http://openmp.org/wp/**).

Open Service Interface Definitions (OSIDs): A service-based architecture to promote software interoperability. The OSIDs are a suite of interface contract specifications that describe the integration points among services and system components. The OSIDs are an architectural tool used to create choice among a variety of different and independently developed applications and systems. The OSIDs are a project management tool used to thin-slice a development project (**http://osid.org/**).

The P4 Medicine Institute (P4Mi): Driving innovative approaches to disease prevention and maintenance of health and wellness by applying systems biology to medicine and care delivery. P4Mi is recruiting clinical centers, research institutions, and industrial partners to collaborate in a network of integrated demonstration projects to accelerate the emergence of a P4 healthcare system that delivers more effective clinical care at lower cost. The P4Mi's mission is to bring P4 Medicine—Predictive, Preventive, Personalized, and Participatory—to patients and society (**http://p4mi.org/**).

Path to 21st Century Cures: Congressional gathering of many ideas starting in May 2014.

House Energy and Commerce Committee Chairman Fred Upton (R-MI) today announced the launch of 21st Century Cures, a new initiative that aims to accelerate the pace of cures and medical breakthroughs in the United States. Chairman Upton, along with committee member Rep. Diana DeGette (D CO), explain in a new video that over the next several months, members will take a comprehensive look at the full arc of this process—from discovery to development to delivery—to determine what steps we can take to ensure we are taking full advantage of the advances this country has made in science and technology and use these resources to keep America as the innovation capital of the world.

In the twenty-first century, healthcare innovation is happening at lightning speed. From the mapping of the human genome to the rise of personalized medicines that are linked to advances in molecular medicine, we have seen constant breakthroughs that are changing the face of disease treatment, management, and cures. Health research is moving quickly, but the federal drug and device approval apparatus is in many ways the relic of another era. We have dedicated scientists and bold leaders at agencies like the NIH and the FDA, but when our laws don't keep pace with innovation, we all lose.

If we want to save more lives and keep this country the leader in medical innovation, we have to make sure there's not a major gap between the science of cures and the way we regulate these therapies.

That is why, for the first time ever, we in Congress are going to take a comprehensive look at what steps we can take to accelerate the pace of cures in America. We are looking at the full arc of this process—from the *discovery* of clues in basic science, to streamlining the drug and device *development* process, to unleashing the power of digital medicine and social media at the treatment *delivery* phase.

We know we don't have all the answers. That's why we're asking questions first. We are listening. We want to know how to close the gaps between advances in scientific knowledge about cures and the regulatory policies created to save more lives. See more at: http://energycommerce.house.gov/cures#sthash.ANd38vdk.dpuf (**http://energycommerce. house.gov/cures**).

Patient-Centered Medical Home (PCMH): The Agency for Healthcare Research and Quality recognizes that revitalizing the Nation's primary care system is foundational to achieving high quality, accessible, efficient healthcare for all Americans. The primary care medical home, also referred to as the PCMH, advanced primary care, and the healthcare home, is a promising model for transforming the organization and delivery of primary care. This web site provides policymakers and researchers with access to evidence-based resources about the medical home and its potential to transform primary care and improve the quality, safety, efficiency, and effectiveness of US healthcare (**http://pcmh. ahrq.gov/**).

Patient-Centered Outcomes Research Institute: A non-profit, non-governmental organization located in Washington, DC. Congress authorized the establishment of PCORI in the Patient Protection and ACA of 2010. The organization's mandate is to improve the quality and relevance of evidence available to help patients, caregivers, clinicians, employers, insurers, and policy makers make informed health decisions. Specifically, it funds comparative clinical effectiveness research, or CER, as well as support work that will improve the methods used to conduct such studies. The goal of its work is to determine which of the many healthcare options available to patients and those who care for them work best in particular circumstances. This is accomplished by taking a particular approach to CER called <u>PCOR</u>, research that addresses the questions and concerns most relevant to patients, and it involves patients, caregivers, clinicians, and other healthcare stakeholders, along with researchers, throughout the process. This approach is reflected in the organization's vision:

Patients and the public have information they can use to make decisions that reflect their desired health outcomes.

And *our mission*:

2010

MARCH
- Congress passes Patient Protection and Affordable Care Act, authorizing establishment of Patient-Centered Outcomes Research Institute (PCORI)

SEPTEMBER
- US Government Accountability Office (GAO) appoints PCORI Board of Governors ⓛ

2011

JANUARY

Major PCORI Milestones

PCORI helps people make informed healthcare decisions, and improves healthcare delivery and outcomes, by producing and promoting high-integrity, evidence-based information that comes from research guided by patients, caregivers, and the broader healthcare community.

In pursuing its mission and seeking to achieve its vision, it is building on the work of others. It is not the first organization to fund CER to improve outcomes in conditions that affect large numbers of people or pose a substantial burden on society. Nor is it the first funder to pay attention to the views of patients and other healthcare stakeholders in its work. But it is the largest single research funder that has CER as its main focus, and incorporates patients and other stakeholders throughout the process more consistently and intensively than others have before. They call this "research done differently" **Posted: October 6, 2014 (http://www.pcori.org/).**

Pharmacy Choice: An online pharmacy community and application service provider/professional services company serving the pharmaceutical industry. Our pharmacy community web portal provides pharmacists, pharmacy technicians, pharmacy job seekers, students, and others with the most comprehensive suite of web-based tools and information available, including pharmacy career services, RX drug information and continuing education for pharmacists.

Industry-Specific Information for the Pharmacy Community

Our core philosophy is to make your life easier: Our pharmacy community offers easy and instant access to everything today's pharmaceutical professional needs to succeed.

Our network of websites and affiliate companies put thousands of pharmacy-related resources at your fingertips. For an even more comprehensive selection of RX industry info, check out the other sites in the pharmacy choice network.

RxCareerCenter: The largest pharma-specific job board on the Internet, RxCareerCenter provides pharmacy job candidates with a secure and confidential system for finding RX career opportunities. Employers are provided with a complete backend management system for loading their open jobs and tracking resumes.

RxSchool: This educational hub is where the pharmacy community—including pharmaceutical organizations, educators and students—come together in a web-based distance-learning environment. RxSchool offers everything from continuing education for pharmacists to pharmacy technician certification training courses (**http://www.pharmacychoice.com/**).

Features
The National Association of Boards of Pharmacy is the only professional association that represents the state boards of pharmacy in all 50 United States, the District of Columbia, Guam, Puerto Rico, the Virgin Islands, New Zealand, nine Canadian Provinces, and four Australian states.
Pharmacy Compounding Accreditation Board is a web site dedicated for pharmacists and compounding pharmacies. They have information on accreditation, and PCAB® Information & News

Policy and Legislation: Practically every major rule and regulation that guides the development and use of healthcare IT is the result of highly specific government policy, especially since the 2009 passage of the HITECH Act. This policy can range from Federal mandates, such as those setting up to the meaningful use incentive program, requirements related to the switchover to ICD-10 coding, or state and regional regulations with regard to HIE. DHHS, CMS, and ONC are the key federal agencies related to health IT development.

Predictive Model Markup Language (PMML)
Primary Care Provider (PCP)
Privacy and Security: Refers to the confidentiality of a medical systems' data with special concern for patients' records. Regulations concerning the protection of patients' medical records are issued by DHHS in the HIPAA Rules. The US Congress established the framework for HIPAA in the Health Insurance Portability and Accountability Act, which was signed into law by President Clinton in 1996. The HITECH Act signed into law by President Obama in 2009 extended HIPAA to business partners of healthcare providers and required disclosure of HIPAA violations. Violations of HIPAA rules are subject to monetary penalties; fines have reached over $4 million. Definitions gathered from Healthcare IT News December 6, 2014 (**http://www.healthcareitnews.com/news**).

Quality and Safety: Quality and safety are paramount concerns in healthcare settings. Within the scope of IT, everything from efficacy of EHRs to the proper coding of diagnoses and prescription of medication falls under the remit of quality and safety. One of the key selling points of EHRs is that they improve patient safety, but as healthcare IT becomes more and more integrated into the medical world, it is crucial to be vigilant about systems' clinical quality measures.

Resource Description Framework (RDF)
Representational State Transfer (REST)
The Service-Aware Interoperability Framework (SAIF): Goal is to create and manage easy-to-use, traceable, consistent, and coherent interoperability specifications (ISs) regardless of the message, document, or service interoperability-paradigm. The SAIF focus is on managing and specifying artifacts that explicitly express the characteristics of software components that affect interoperability. SAIF's approach is to organize and manage architectural complexity with a set of constructs, best practices, processes, procedures, and categorizations. SAIF's scope is the interoperability space between system components. Specifically, SAIF manages the interworking among distributed systems that may involve information exchanges or service interactions and state changes; SAIF is not EA. SAIF combines four subframeworks, that together form a basis for defining comparable interoperability specifications (Information and Behavioral Frameworks), and formalizing governance and conformity assessment methods (Governance and Enterprise Conformance and Compliance Frameworks) critical to defining and using interoperability specifications.

- The *Information Framework (IF)* defines information models that specify the static semantics of interactions. This includes patterns for structured and unstructured data, documents, messages and services, metadata, quality measures and transformations. The IF scope includes the needs of direct clinical care, supportive, and information infrastructure areas. The models, terminologies, vocabularies, and value sets specify the static semantics for expressing concepts, relationships (including cardinalities), constraints, rules, and operations needed to specify data, data type bindings, vocabulary, and value set bindings.

- The *Behavioral Framework (BF)* defines constructs that specify dynamic semantics of interactions in an interoperability specification. The BF focus is the accountability required to achieve working interoperability. Accountability is a description of "who does what when." Accountability manifests itself as implicit or explicit contracts at the enterprise, business, capability, service, and at the interface implementation levels. BF accountability is described by the relationships among various stakeholders and system components, applications, and their system roles. These relationships involve information exchanges and state changes within use case scenarios.

- The *Governance Framework (GF)* purpose is to relate decisions and policies, to the IF and BF, managed within the ECCF. The GF scope includes core decision and configuration management processes concerning conformance, escalation, communication, vitality, and precepts. The GF defines expectations, grants power, verifies performance, and manages configuration baselines. Governance consists of either a separate process or parts of management or leadership processes. Sometimes a governing board or council is set up to administer these processes and systems.

- The *Enterprise Conformance and Compliance Framework (ECCF)* goal is to ensure working interoperability (WI) among various healthcare organizations; WI is also known as compatibility among healthcare systems. The ECCF purpose is to manage the relationship between architectural artifacts and implementations of those artifacts. The objective of a fully qualified ECCF is to be a clear, complete, concise, correct, consistent, and traceable interoperability specification, which is easy to use. The ECCF is an assessment framework, which supports configuration management baselines and risk assessments throughout a business-capability lifecycle. The ECCF is used to specify information exchange interoperability and conformance statements for documents, messages, and services. The ECCF contains definitions of terms, such as conformance, compliance, consistency, and traceability. An ECCF provides a template, called a specification stack (SS) that allows you to specify business objects, components, capabilities, applications, and systems organized as a matrix of Reference Model Open Distributed Processing viewpoints and Model Driven Architecture layers.

Jointly, the IF and BF allow the specification of business objects, components, capabilities, applications, systems and their respective roles, responsibilities, and information exchanges. The HL7 implementation of the IF and BF draws on storyboards, Domain Analysis Models, *Detailed Clinical Models* and templates, Reference Information Model, vocabulary concepts, HL7 core principles plus message, document and service models.

SAIF provides external stakeholders with a clear picture of exactly what is required to use and interoperate with an organization's software components. A given component's specification is SAIF-compliant if it species "just enough" to enable the desired interoperability for the component as determined by how the capability is being used in its deployment context, such as within a lab, or within a wider enterprise community of partners (**http://wiki.hl7. org/index.php?title=SAIF_main_page**).

Software Engineering Institute (SEI)
Substance Abuse and Mental Health Services Administration (SAMSHA)
Systems Engineering Research Center (SERC): A University-Affiliated Research Center of the US DOD, leverages the research and expertise of faculty, staff, and student researchers from more than 20 collaborating universities throughout the United States. SERC is unprecedented in the depth and breadth of its reach, leadership, and citizenship in Systems Engineering. Led by *Stevens Institute of Technology* and principal collaborator, the *University of Southern California*, the SERC has more engaged more than 400 researchers since its founding in 2008—a community of broad experience, deep knowledge, and diverse interests. SERC researchers have worked across many domains and industries, including finance, telecommunications, computing, transportation, in addition to defense, enabling them to bring broad perspectives to their research.

- **Enterprises and SOS**—We lack the foundational SE principles, methods, processes, and tools to enable the DOD to architect, design, analyze, monitor and evolve complex enterprises, and SOS to provide the DOD with an overwhelming competitive advantage over its current and future adversaries.
- **Trusted Systems**—We need to achieve much higher levels of system trust by applying the systems approach to achieving system assurance and trust for the increasingly complex, dynamic, cyber-physical-human net-centric systems, and SOS of the future.
- **Systems Engineering and Management Transformation**—We lack the systems engineering and management methods, processes, tools and practices to enable rapid, concurrent, flexible, scalable definition and analysis of the increasingly complex, dynamic, multi-stakeholder, cyber-physical-human DOD systems, and SOS of the future (**http://www.sercuarc.org/**).

Shared Services: The provision of a service by one part of an organization or group where that service had previously been found in more than one part of the organization or group. Thus the funding and resourcing of the service is shared, and the providing department effectively becomes an internal service provider. The key here is the idea of "sharing" within an organization or group. This sharing needs to fundamentally include shared accountability of results by the unit from where the work is migrated to the provider. The provider on the other hand needs to ensure that the agreed results are delivered based on defined measures (KPIs, cost, quality, etc.) (**https://cio.gov/wp-content/uploads/downloads/2013/04/CIOC-Federal-Shared-Services-Implementation-Guide.pdf**).

Software Engineering Institute/Carnegie Mellon University (SEI-CMU)—Focus on SOS and Capability Maturity Management Initiative: Through SEI work in practices for SOS, we deliver approaches, techniques, and technologies for the *interoperation* of independently evolving SOS, including

– Determining the feasibility of and building a plan for legacy system migration to a SOA environment.
– Evaluating technologies intended to support systems interoperability (**http://www.sei.cmu.edu/**).

Stage 7 Hospital Directory: According to HIMSS Analytics, Stage 7 hospitals are considered to be completely paperless. In 2005, HIMSS launched the EMR Adoption Model to track adoption of EMR applications within hospitals and health systems. The EMRAM scores hospitals in the HIMSS Analytics Database on their progress in completing eight stages, with the goal of reaching Stage 7—the pinnacle of an environment where paper charts are no longer used to deliver patient care.

Stage 7 healthcare organizations support the sharing and use of patient data that ultimately improves process performance, quality of care, and patient safety. Clinical information can be readily shared via standard electronic transactions, with all entities within HIE networks. This stage allows the healthcare organization to support the true sharing and use of health and wellness information by consumers and providers alike. Also at this stage, organizations use data warehousing and mining techniques to capture and analyze care data for performance improvement and advancing clinical decision support protocols.

Strategic Transformation and Reusable Technology (START)—An Initiative to Foster the Use of Shared Services across the Many State Funded Improvement Initiatives—The Author Recommends That This be Encouraged

Strategic Health IT Advanced Research Program (SHARP)—ONC Sponsored Research Initiatives

Area One: Security and Health IT (**www.sharps.org**).
Area Two: Patient-Centered Cognitive Support: Collaboration and Usability.
Area Three: Health Care Applications and Network Design.
Area Four: Secondary Use and EHR Information (**www.sharpc.org**).

System of Systems (SOS)

Task User Reference Framework (TURF)

Universal Core (UCORE)

Usability for Healthcare IT Systems: Guideline such as those at (**http://guidelines.usability.gov/**).

Medical Human Factor Engineering (**http://nchfeh.org/bio.html**).

Usability Body of Knowledge and Focus on Areas Such as Cognitive Task Analysis: The Usability Body of Knowledge is dedicated to creating a living reference that represents the collective knowledge of the usability profession. Such a collection of knowledge for the usability profession will necessarily be broad and inclusive in scope, because our profession is inherently multi-disciplinary and draws on a wide range of other practices.

The Usability Bok is derived from published literature, conference proceedings, and the experiences of practitioners accumulated over many years. It is a guide to existing resources, and will evolve as the practice of usability evolves.

Explore the content that is available, and then consider volunteering to add more content! (**http://www.usabilitybok.org/cognitive-task-analysis**).

World Wide Web Consortium (W3C)
Extensible Business Reporting Language (XBRL)
Extensible Markup Language (XML)

Appendix C: Definitions for SOS

Terminology	Defense SOS Concepts	Adapted for Healthcare
A System	A collection of elements that together produce some results that cannot be elements operating individually	
Ecosystem	Actors, intangible knowledge elements that are focused on shared challenge	Healthcare can have ecosystems focused on pharmaceutical, research, behavioral health, and each of the 7000 rare diseases may be mini-ecosystem
SOS	Designation the case where constituent elements of a system are collaborating that exhibit two prospects: 1. Operation independence (each constituent operates to achieve a useful independent of it's participation in the SOS) 2. Managerial independence (each constituent system is managed and included at least in part, to achieve its own goals rather than SOS goals)	

Terminology	*Defense SOS Concepts*	*Adapted for Healthcare*
Directed SOS	Built to manage and fulfill a specific purpose. It is controlled managed during long-term operations to continue to fulfill those purposes and any new areas the system owners may wish to address	
Acknowledged SOS	A designated manager but independent system components that maintain their ownership but changes are based on collaboration between SOS and the system	
Collaborative SOS	Voluntarily collaborative to fulfill the agreed upon central purpose	
Virtual SOS	Lacks a central management and a centrally agreed upon purpose. Large-scale behavior emerges	

Systems Engineering Guide to Systems of Systems: OUSD 2008.

Terminology	*Defense SOS Concepts*	*Adapted for Healthcare*
Open Architecture	Interfaces and capabilities are clearly defined and use global or local standards	Systems have at least a basic set of open interfaces and basic capabilities: Extension permitted
Interoperability	Ability of two or more subsystems to exchange information and utilize that information	Ability of two or more SOS to exchange information and utilize that information as a logical channel about a patient or disease improvement and research collaboration
Open Standards	Standards that are widely used, consensus based, published, and maintained by recognized industry standards organizations	Same: OMH/HI7 and the many other pieces need a semantic bridging capability and ability to translate the "terminology to the Level of Health Literacy of Most Patients"

Terminology	Defense SOS Concepts	Adapted for Healthcare
Level of System Interoperability 1 Understanding Patterns for System of Systems Integration, Rick Kazman, Claus Nielsen, Klaus Schmed, December 2013, Technical Note CMU/SEI-20.3-TR-017	Information exchange (data level) Basic behavior interaction (service level), complex behavior interaction (logic/business process level), and user interface sharing (UI level)	Many of the interaction patterns can be tailored to dynamics of healthcare
Level of System Interoperability 2- Morris 2004	Level 0—Isolated Level 1—Connected Level 2—Functional Level 3—Domain-shared data Separate applications Level 4—Enterprise-interactive manipulation shared data and application	Levels 3 and 4 are elements that are needed for the dynamic nature of healthcare
Level of Systems Interoperability: Dodd-2014	Private-identified uses connection: 1 Information sharing Pub-Sub: 2 Event-filter agent-based logical channels: 3 Primary paths and second paths with semantic translation: 4 Shared data views and crowd feedback and knowledge exchange: 5	Each of these levels can have "elements" that are added to a basic foundation with incremental semantic improvement. Supporting the dynamics of cases and learning healthcare systems will require new smart agents and ontologies

Terminology	Defense SOS Concepts	Adapted for Healthcare
Reusability	Ability of an artifact to provide the same capability in multiple contexts	Same plus use of shared services and standard set of application program interfaces
Extensibility	Ability to add new capabilities to system components or to add components and subsystems to system	New capabilities can be composed together and design for change aspects can be used to adapt and extend such as business rules, process models, table changes, variants picked from choices, etc.

(Continued)

Terminology	Defense SOS Concepts	Adapted for Healthcare
Maintainability	The ease with which a maintenance of a functional unit can be performed in accordance with a prescribed requirements. Downtime is permitted but backup systems and minimal capabilities are required	Changes can be made with limited downtime and only with individual elements of the SOS logical channel being down at a time. Near 100% uptime during changes. Designed for change for individual case or based on evidence and "professional" decision making with "auditable notes"

Terminology	Defense SOS Concepts	Adapted for Healthcare
Mission Thread	A sequence of end-to-end activities and events beginning with an opportunity to detect a threat or element that might have to be attacked and ending with commander's assessment of damage after an attack	Life course of health events along a logical channel supporting a type of episode of care or disease improvement research or the linked set of coordination activities
Military Platform	Military talks about vehicles, ships, aircraft, even the soldier is platform	The patient may be a platform or the capabilities of the electronic health record or the data that must be shared with public health, quality measures, or payment management
Open or Industry Platform	Industry platform (Cusumano)—such as iPhone, Windows, Web, and many open platforms that networks can build around such as those for banking or insurance	Leverage the experience from these other industries and determine the balance point between standards and foster innovation by addition of new features
Keystone Healthcare Open Platforms of System of Systems: Dodd 2014	What are the common building blocks that can be used to break the monolithic healthcare problem into a patient–provider bi-directional set of pathways	Series of shared services elements and application programming interface and use of new agents and ontologies

Appendix D: Personas and Population Analysis Reaching to "Stories from the Ground"

The many high-level diagrams have to be linked to real people with their needs and common shared experience and unique difference this appendix will be used as part of an ongoing patient-centric to population health analysis needs process. It is primarily shared for use by those that want to take one of the key steps understanding the patient–consumers and the population you and others are going to serve. Some pieces like Delaware Secretary of Health Rita Landgraf naturally think about the people, she meets and presents their stories to the Delaware Health Center Innovation meetings. But most of need as we are implementing those system need to step back and think about who that end-user is going to be and to actually try to share the concepts, the pilot system and learn from their feedback. These persona's have to become the drivers to patient–consumer centric and population focused implementation.

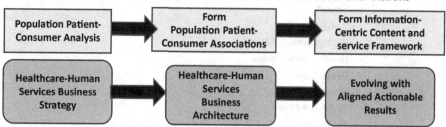

Putting Patient-Centric Healthcare-Human Services   Business Architecture Into Action

Win-Win-Win for All Stakeholders   End-to-End Vision and "Actions"

| Population Patient-Consumer Analysis | → | Form Population Patient-Consumer Associations | → | Form Information-Centric Content and service Framework |

| Healthcare-Human Services Business Strategy | → | Healthcare-Human Services Business Architecture | → | Evolving with Aligned Actionable Results |

Value Streams For Channels of Information and Payments and Analytical Outcomes

- Strategic Stakeholder Alignment
- Policies, Rules and Regulations: Understanding and Translating
- Goals and Objectives for Each Stakeholder Type
- Priorities and "Fitting Together" Key Tactics "Collaboration"

- Capabilities and Organization Responsibilities
- List of Capabilities with Information Linked Maps
- Information Concepts with Transparency and Accountable
- Value Streams for Purchasing and Quality of Services

- Well-articulated Business Priorities
- Business-driven Roadmaps
- Connecting Current Systems
- Innovations With the Gap Fillers
- Collaborate and Synchronize Extended Enterprise Changes

Gather Stories from the Ground and Understand Needs

Create a Series of Patient-Consumer Persona's

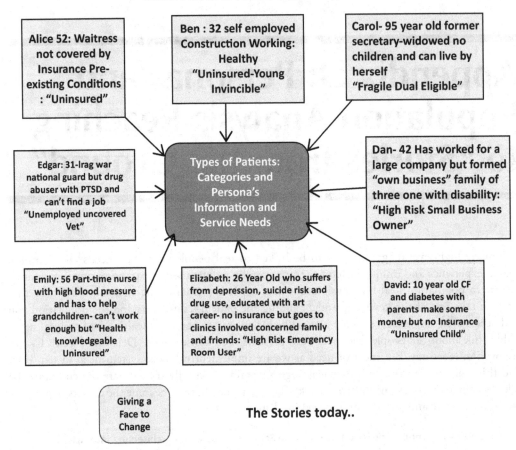

The Stories today..

- **Ben**-32 self employed Construction Working: Healthy **"Uninsured-Young Invincible"**
  - Works
  - Health Insurance Access
  - Health Provider Access
  - Health Literacy
  - Health Proactive
  - Health Conditions
  - Health Risks
  - Health Special or Rare Condition
  - Patient–Like me or Disease Management Focused Involvement
  - Family and Friends in Help

Giving a Face to Change

The Stories today..

- Emily: 56 Part-time nurse with high blood pressure and has to help grandchildren- can't work enough but knows she needs coverage.

- "Health knowledgeable Uninsured"

  - Health Insurance Access
  - Health Provider Access
  - Health Literacy
  - Health Proactive
  - Health Conditions
  - Health Risks
  - Health Special or Rare Condition
  - Patient–Like me or Disease Management Focused Involvement
  - Family and Friends in Help

Giving a Face to Change

The Stories today..

- Elizabeth: 26 Year Old who suffers from depression, suicide risk and drug use, educated with art career- no insurance but goes to clinics involved concerned family and friends:

- "High Risk Emergency Room User"

  - Health Insurance Access
  - Health Provider Access
  - Health Literacy
  - Health Proactive
  - Health Conditions
  - Health Risks
  - Health Special or Rare Condition
  - Patient–Like me or Disease Management Focused Involvement
  - Family and Friends in Help

Giving a
Face to
Change

The Stories today..

- Edgar: 31-Iraq war national guard but drug abuser with PTSD and can't find a job
- "Unemployed uncovered Vet"
  - Health Insurance Access
  - Health Provider Access
  - Health Literacy
  - Health Proactive
  - Health Conditions
  - Health Risks
  - Health Special or Rare Condition
  - Patient—Like me or Disease Management Focused Involvement
  - Family and Friends in Help

Giving a
Face to
Change

The Stories today..

- Emily: 56 Part-time nurse with high blood pressure and has to help grandchildren- can't work enough but knows she needs coverage.
- "Health knowledgeable Uninsured"
  - Health Insurance Access
  - Health Provider Access
  - Health Literacy
  - Health Proactive
  - Health Conditions
  - Health Risks
  - Health Special or Rare Condition
  - Patient—Like me or Disease Management Focused Involvement
  - Family and Friends in Help

Stories from the Ground

- A couple from Harrington had to pay the penalty for going uninsured last year and visited a Marketplace Guide to enroll for 2015. They qualified for a monthly premium tax credit and their premium is less than $100 a month. The woman said she felt fortunate and blessed to have coverage this year.

- A Wilmington woman reported a decrease in income and was able to reduce her monthly premium from $100 to $43, allowing her to select a dental plan as well.

- After Marketplace Guide helped a Bridgeville man create an email address and set up his Marketplace account, he qualified for a tax credit of $547, which reduced his monthly premium to about $114.

Index

Printed in the United States
by Baker & Taylor Publisher Services